MATCH • B

CW00393647

PREMIER FOOTBALL REVIEW

1993

Edited by David Kennedy

Published by Sports Projects Ltd

ACKNOWLEDGEMENTS

Premier Football Review 1993
First published in Great Britain in July 1993
by Sports Projects Limited

© 1993 Sports Projects Limited
188 Lightwoods Hill, Smethwick, Warley,
West Midlands B67 5EH.

ISBN 0-946866-11-2

Printed and bound in Great Britain
by Butler & Tanner Limited

Editor: David Kennedy

Cover Design: Bernard Gallagher

Design and layout: Phil Lees,
Nadine Goldingay, Trevor Hartley

Key to symbols

❏	Player booked
■	Player sent off
† ‡	Player substituted
‡75 †70	Time of substitution
61p	Figure in goals column indicates time of goal. The letter 'p' indicates a goal scored from a penalty kick.

Welcome to the brave new world

THE FIRST season of the FA Premier League will live forever in the memory.

Manchester United pipped Aston Villa for the inaugural championship, and Crystal Palace, Nottingham Forest and Middlesbrough lost their place in the sun after a tense and thrilling survival battle.

It was the making of history... and now that history has been set down on paper by David Kennedy in this indispensable review of the 1992-93 season.

Match by match, goal by goal, this is chapter one of the Premier League Story, and the first in a series designed to record every statistic of football's brave new world.

FA PREMIER LEAGUE • CONTENTS

FA PREMIER LEAGUE • CONTENTS

Date	Saturday 15 August 1992
Venue	Highbury Stadium, 3.00pm

ARSENAL (2) 2
NORWICH CITY (0) 4

Attendance	24,030
Referee	Allan GUNN
Linesmen	A. Black, D.C. Richards

ARSENAL
Red & White Shirts, White shorts | Goals

1	David SEAMAN	
2	Lee DIXON	
3	Nigel WINTERBURN	
4	David HILLIER	
5	Steve BOULD	28
6	Tony ADAMS	
7	John JENSEN	
8	Alan SMITH	
9	Kevin CAMPBELL	39
10	Paul MERSON ‡	
11	Anders LIMPAR	
	Substitutes	
12	Colin PATES	
14	Ian WRIGHT ‡73	
Gk	Alan MILLER	

NORWICH CITY
Yellow Shirts, Green shorts | Goals

1	Bryan GUNN	
2	Ian CULVERHOUSE	
3	Mark BOWEN	
4	Ian BUTTERWORTH	
5	John POLSTON	
6	Gary MEGSON ‡	
7	Ruel FOX	82
8	Rob NEWMAN	
9	Chris SUTTON †	
10	Jeremy GOSS ❑	
11	David PHILLIPS	72
	Substitutes	
12	Mark ROBINS †58	69, 84
14	Ian CROOK ‡ 87	
Gk	Mark WALTON	

Date	Saturday 15 August 1992
Venue	Stamford Bridge, 3.00pm

CHELSEA (0) 1
OLDHAM ATHLETIC (0) 1

Attendance	20,699
Referee	Jim BORRETT
Linesmen	W.M. Jordan, P. Rejer

CHELSEA
Blue shirts, Blue shorts | Goals

1	Dave BEASANT	
2	Steve CLARKE	
3	Gareth HALL	
4	Vinnie JONES	
5	Paul ELLIOTT	
6	Mal DONAGHY	
7	Graham STUART	
8	Robert FLECK	
9	Mick HARFORD ❑	84
10	Andy TOWNSEND	
11	Damien MATTHEW †	
	Substitutes	
12	Eddie NEWTON †76	
14	Joe ALLON	
Gk	Kevin HITCHCOCK	

OLDHAM ATHLETIC
White & Red shirts, White shorts | Goals

1	Jon HALLWORTH	
2	Steve REDMOND	
3	Andy BARLOW	
4	Nick HENRY ❑	86
5	Richard JOBSON	
6	Ian MARSHALL	
7	Gunnar HALLE	
8	Roger PALMER ‡	
9	Graeme SHARP	
10	Mike MILLIGAN	
11	Paul BERNARD	
	Substitutes	
12	Craig FLEMING	
14	Neil TOLSON ‡68	
Gk	John KEELEY	

Date	Saturday 15 August 1992
Venue	Highfield Road, 3.00pm

COVENTRY CITY (1) 2
MIDDLESBROUGH (0) 1

Attendance	12,681
Referee	Howard KING
Linesmen	U.D. Rennie, P.R. Richards

COVENTRY CITY
Sky Blue shirts, Sky Blue shorts — Goals

1	Steve OGRIZOVIC	
2	Terry FLEMING	
3	Kenny SANSOM	
4	Stewart ROBSON	
5	Andy PEARCE	
6	Peter ATHERTON	
7	Michael GYNN	
8	Lee HURST ‡	
9	Robert ROSARIO	
10	John WILLIAMS	9
11	David SMITH †	51
	Substitutes	
12	Sean FLYNN †70	
14	Phil BABB ‡75	
Gk	Jonathan GOULD	

MIDDLESBROUGH
Red shirts, White shorts — Goals

1	Stephen PEARS	
2	Chris MORRIS	
3	Jimmy PHILLIPS	
4	Alan KERNAGHAN	
5	Derek WHYTE	
6	Andy PEAKE	
7	Tommy WRIGHT	
8	Robbie MUSTOE †	
9	Paul WILKINSON	63
10	John HENDRIE	
11	Willie FALCONER	
	Substitutes	
12	Bernie SLAVEN †54	
14	Jon GITTENS	
Gk	Ian IRONSIDE	

Date	Saturday 15 August 1992
Venue	Selhurst Park, 3.00pm

CRYSTAL PALACE (1) 3
BLACKBURN ROVERS (1) 3

Attendance	17,086
Referee	Roger MILFORD
Linesmen	D.C. Madgwick, G.P. Barber

CRYSTAL PALACE
Red and Blue striped shirts, Red shorts — Goals

1	Nigel MARTYN	
2	John HUMPHREY	
3	Richard SHAW	
4	Gareth SOUTHGATE	63
5	Eric YOUNG	
6	Andy THORN	
7	Eddie McGOLDRICK	
8	Geoff THOMAS	
9	Mark BRIGHT	37
10	John SALAKO †	
11	Chris COLEMAN ‡	
	Substitutes	
12	Simon RODGER †73	
14	Simon OSBORN ‡81	90
Gk	Paul HEALD	

BLACKBURN ROVERS
White & Blue shirts, White shorts — Goals

1	Bobby MIMMS	
2	David MAY	
3	Alan WRIGHT ‡	
4	Tim SHERWOOD	
5	Colin HENDRY	
6	Kevin MORAN	
7	Stuart RIPLEY	42
8	Mark ATKINS	
9	Alan SHEARER	66, 81
10	Mike NEWELL	
11	Tony DOBSON	
	Substitutes	
12	Roy WEGERLE	
14	Chris PRICE ‡28	
Gk	Matt DICKINS	

Date   Saturday 15 August 1992
Venue   Goodison Park, 3.00 pm

EVERTON (1) 1
SHEFFIELD WEDNESDAY (1) 1

Attendance   27,687
Referee   Kelvin MORTON
Linesmen   J.B. Robinson, P.M. Roberts

EVERTON
Blue shirts, White Shorts   Goals

1	Neville SOUTHALL	
2	Matthew JACKSON	
3	Andy HINCHCLIFFE	
4	John EBBRELL	
5	Dave WATSON	
6	Gary ABLETT	
7	Mark WARD	
8	Peter BEARDSLEY	
9	Paul RIDEOUT	
10	Barry HORNE †	44
11	Peter BEAGRIE	
	Substitutes	
12	Robert WARZYCHA †69	
14	Mo JOHNSTON	
Gk	Jason KEARTON	

SHEFFIELD WEDNESDAY
Yellow & Black Shirts, Black shorts   Goals

1	Chris WOODS	
2	Roland NILSSON	
3	Phil KING	
4	Carlton PALMER	
5	Nigel PEARSON	15
6	Paul WARHURST	
7	Chris WADDLE ‡	
8	Graham HYDE	
9	David HIRST †	
10	Paul WILLIAMS	
11	Nigel WORTHINGTON	
	Substitutes	
12	Gordon WATSON †81	
14	Chris BART-WILLIAMS ‡38	
Gk	Kevin PRESSMAN	

Date   Saturday 15 August 1992
Venue   Portman Road, 3.00 pm

IPSWICH TOWN (1) 1
ASTON VILLA (0) 1

Attendance   16,818
Referee   Alf BUKSH
Linesmen   M.D. Dearing, J.A. Elwin

IPSWICH
Blue & White shirts, White shorts   Goals

1	Craig FORREST	
2	Phil WHELAN	
3	Neil THOMPSON	
4	Mick STOCKWELL †	
5	John WARK	
6	Andy LINIGHAN	
7	Geraint WILLIAMS	
8	Paul GODDARD	
9	Gavin JOHNSON ❏	31
10	Jason DOZZELL ‡	
11	Chris KIWOMYA	
	Substitutes	
12	Simon MILTON †89	
14	Eddie YOUDS ‡69	
Gk	Jason WINTERS	

ASTON VILLA
Claret & Blue shirts, Blue shorts   Goals

1	Nigel SPINK	
2	Earl BARRETT	
3	Steve STAUNTON	
4	Shaun TEALE ❏	
5	Paul McGRATH	
6	Kevin RICHARDSON †	
7	Tony DALEY	
8	Garry PARKER	
9	Ray HOUGHTON	
10	Dalian ATKINSON	84
11	Stephen FROGGATT	
	Substitutes	
12	Cyrille REGIS †54	
14	Ugo EHIOGU	
Gk	Les SEALEY	

Date	Saturday 15 August 1992
Venue	Elland Road, 3.00 pm

LEEDS UNITED (1) 2
WIMBLEDON (0) 1

Attendance	25,795
Referee	Gerald ASHBY
Linesmen	T. Lynch, W. Nattrass

ARSENAL
White Shirts, White Shorts   Goals

1	John LUKIC	
2	Jon NEWSOME ‡	
3	Tony DORIGO	
4	David BATTY †	
5	Chris FAIRCLOUGH	
6	Chris WHYTE	
7	Eric CANTONA ❑	
8	Rod WALLACE	
9	Lee CHAPMAN	14, 86
10	Gary McALLISTER	
11	Gary SPEED	
	Substitutes	
12	Steve HODGE †45	
14	Gordon STRACHAN ‡80	
Gk	Mervyn DAY	

WIMBLEDON
Blue shirts, Blue shorts   Goals

1	Hans SEGERS	
2	Roger JOSEPH	
3	Gary ELKINS	
4	Warren BARTON	76
5	John SCALES ‡	
6	Scott FITZGERALD	
7	Paul MILLER	
8	Robbie EARLE	
9	Dean HOLDSWORTH ❑	
10	Lawrie SANCHEZ	
11	Andy CLARKE †	
	Substitutes	
12	Gerald DOBBS †70 ❑	
14	Dean BLACKWELL ‡48	
Gk	Neil SULLIVAN	

Date	Saturday 15 August 1992
Venue	Bramall Lane, 3.00pm

SHEFFIELD UNITED (1) 2
MANCHESTER UNITED (0) 1

Attendance	28,070
Referee	Brian HILL
Linesmen	R. Pearson, B.L. Polkey

SHEFFIELD UNITED
Red & White striped shirts, White shorts   Goals

1	Simon TRACEY	
2	Kevin GAGE	
3	David BARNES	
4	John GANNON ❑ ‡	
5	Paul BEESLEY	
6	Alan McLEARY	
7	Carl BRADSHAW	
8	Michael LAKE ❑	
9	Alan CORK	
10	Brian DEANE	5, 50p
11	Glyn HODGES †	
	Substitutes	
12	Ian BRYSON †68	
14	Charlie HARTFIELD ‡86	
Gk	Alan KELLY	

MANCHESTER UNITED
Blue Shirts, Blue shorts   Goals

1	Peter SCHMEICHEL	
2	Denis IRWIN	
3	Clayton BLACKMORE ❑	
4	Steve BRUCE	
5	Darren FERGUSON	
6	Gary PALLISTER	
7	Andrei KANCHELSKIS ‡	
8	Paul INCE †	
9	Brian McCLAIR	
10	Mark HUGHES	61
11	Ryan GIGGS	
	Substitutes	
12	Mike PHELAN †7	
14	Dion DUBLIN ‡68	
Gk	Gary WALSH	

Date	Saturday 15 August 1992
Venue	The Dell, 3.00 pm

SOUTHAMPTON (0) 0
TOTTENHAM HOTSPUR (0) 0

Attendance	19,654
Referee	Vic CALLOW
Linesmen	C. Jones, M.R. Sims

SOUTHAMPTON
Red & White striped shirts, Black shorts   Goals

1	Tim FLOWERS	
2	Jason DODD	
3	Micky ADAMS ❑	
4	Terry HURLOCK	
5	Richard HALL ❑	
6	Steve WOOD	
7	Matthew LE TISSIER	
8	Glenn COCKERILL	
9	Kerry DIXON	
10	David SPEEDIE	
11	Francis BENALI	
	Substitutes	
12	Iain DOWIE	
14	Jeff KENNA	
Gk	Ian ANDREWS	

TOTTENHAM HOTSPUR
Light Blue shirts, Light Blue shorts   Goals

1	Ian WALKER	
2	Terry FENWICK	
3	Justin EDINBURGH	
4	David HOWELLS	
5	Jason CUNDY	
6	Neil RUDDOCK ❑	
7	Andy TURNER ‡	
8	Gordon DURIE	
9	Vinny SAMWAYS ❑	
10	Darren ANDERTON	
11	Paul ALLEN	
	Substitutes	
12	Dean AUSTIN	
14	Andy GRAY ‡75	
Gk	Erik THORSTVEDT	

Date	Sunday 16 August 1992
Venue	City Ground, 4.00pm

NOTTINGHAM FOREST (1) 1
LIVERPOOL (0) 0

Attendance	20,038
Referee	Mike REED
Linesmen	B. Lowe, P.J. Robinson

NOTTINGHAM FOREST
Red shirts, White shorts   Goals

1	Mark CROSSLEY	
2	Brian LAWS	
3	Stuart PEARCE	
4	Terry WILSON	
5	Steve CHETTLE	
6	Roy KEANE ❑	
7	Gary CROSBY †	
8	Scot GEMMILL	
9	Nigel CLOUGH	
10	Teddy SHERINGHAM	29
11	Ian WOAN	
	Substitutes	
12	Kingsley BLACK †84	
14	Gary BANNISTER	
Gk	Andy MARRIOTT	

LIVERPOOL
Green shirts, Green shorts   Goals

1	David JAMES	
2	Nicky TANNER	
3	David BURROWS ❑	
4	Steve NICOL	
5	Ronnie WHELAN	
6	Mark WRIGHT	
7	Dean SAUNDERS	
8	Paul STEWART	
9	Ian RUSH ❑ †	
10	Mark WALTERS ‡	
11	Michael THOMAS	
	Substitutes	
12	Steve McMANAMAN †45	
14	Ronnie ROSENTHAL ‡76	
Gk	Mike HOOPER	

Date	Monday 17 August 1992
Venue	Maine Road, 7.45pm

MANCHESTER CITY (1) 1
QPR (0) 1

Attendance	24,471
Referee	Martin BODENHAM
Linesmen	T.A. Atkinson, P.J. Robinson

MANCHESTER CITY
Light Blue shirts, White shorts · Goals

1	Tony COTON	
2	Andy HILL	
3	Ian BRIGHTWELL	
4	Fitzroy SIMPSON ❏	
5	Keith CURLE	
6	Michel VONK	
7	David WHITE	37
8	Paul LAKE †	
9	Niall QUINN	
10	Rick HOLDEN	
11	Steve McMAHON	
	Substitutes	
12	Mike SHERON †76	
14	Garry FLITCROFT	
Gk	Martyn MARGETSON	

QPR
Red & Black hooped shirts, Black shorts · Goals

1	Jan STEJSKAL	
2	David BARDSLEY	
3	Clive WILSON	
4	Ray WILKINS	
5	Darren PEACOCK ❏	
6	Alan McDONALD	
7	Andy IMPEY	
8	Ian HOLLOWAY	
9	Les FERDINAND	
10	Dennis BAILEY †	
11	Andy SINTON	47
	Substitutes	
12	Garry THOMPSON †90	
14	Danny MADDIX	
Gk	Tony ROBERTS	

Date	Tuesday 18 August 1992
Venue	Ewood Park, 7.45pm

BLACKBURN ROVERS (0) 1
ARSENAL (0) 0

Attendance	16,454
Referee	Joe WORRALL
Linesmen	T. Heilbron, K.M. Lynch

BLACKBURN ROVERS
Blue & White shirts, White shorts · Goals

1	Bobby MIMMS	
2	David MAY ❏	
3	Tony DOBSON	
4	Tim SHERWOOD ❏	
5	Colin HENDRY	
6	Kevin MORAN	
7	Stuart RIPLEY	
8	Mark ATKINS	
9	Alan SHEARER	84
10	Mike NEWELL	
11	Jason WILCOX	
	Substitutes	
12	Chris PRICE	
14	Roy WEGERLE	
Gk	Matt DICKINS	

ARSENAL
Yellow shirts, Blue shorts · Goals

1	David SEAMAN	
2	Lee DIXON	
3	Nigel WINTERBURN	
4	David HILLIER	
5	Steve BOULD	
6	Tony ADAMS	
7	John JENSEN †	
8	Alan SMITH	
9	Kevin CAMPBELL	
10	Jimmy CARTER	
11	Anders LIMPAR ‡	
	Substitutes	
12	Colin PATES †77	
14	Perry GROVES ‡84	
Gk	Jim WILL	

Date	Tuesday 18 August 1992
Venue	Selhurst Park, 8.00pm

WIMBLEDON (0) 0
IPSWICH TOWN (1) 1

Attendance	4,954
Referee	Robbie HART
Linesmen	M.K. Bullivant, W.J. Norbury

WIMBLEDON
Blue shirts, Blue shorts   Goals

1	Hans SEGERS	
2	Roger JOSEPH ‡	
3	Gary ELKINS	
4	Warren BARTON	
5	Dean BLACKWELL	
6	Scott FITZGERALD	
7	Paul MILLER	
8	Robbie EARLE	
9	Dean HOLDSWORTH	
10	Lawrie SANCHEZ	
11	Greg BERRY †	

Substitutes

12	Andy CLARKE †65	
14	Gerald DOBBS ‡65	
Gk	Neil SULLIVAN	

IPSWICH TOWN
White shirts, White shorts   Goals

1	Craig FORREST	
2	Phil WHELAN	
3	Neil THOMPSON	
4	Mick STOCKWELL	
5	John WARK	
6	David LINIGHAN	
7	Geraint WILLIAMS	
8	Paul GODDARD	
9	Gavin JOHNSON	37
10	Jason DOZZELL	
11	Chris KIWOMYA †	

Substitutes

12	Simon MILTON †71	
14	Eddie YOUDS	
Gk	Jason WINTERS	

Date	Wednesday 19 August 1992
Venue	Villa Park, 7.45pm

ASTON VILLA (0) 1
LEEDS UNITED (0) 1

Attendance	29,151
Referee	Keith HACKETT
Linesmen	M.E. Alexander, D.C. Madgwick

ASTON VILLA
Claret & Blue shirts, White shorts   Goals

1	Nigel SPINK	
2	Earl BARRETT	
3	Steve STAUNTON	
4	Shaun TEALE	
5	Paul McGRATH	
6	Kevin RICHARDSON	
7	Tony DALEY	
8	Garry PARKER	
9	Ray HOUGHTON	
10	Dalian ATKINSON	77
11	Dwight YORKE †	

Substitutes

12	Cyrille REGIS †29	
14	Ugo EHIOGU	
Gk	Les SEALEY	

LEEDS UNITED
White Shirts. White Shorts   Goals

1	John LUKIC	
2	Jon NEWSOME	
3	Tony DORIGO	
4	David BATTY †	
5	Chris FAIRCLOUGH	
6	Chris WHYTE	
7	Eric CANTONA ‡	
8	Rod WALLACE	
9	Lee CHAPMAN	
10	Gary McALLISTER	
11	Gary SPEED	84

Substitutes

12	Steve HODGE †45	
14	Gordon STRACHAN ‡79	
Gk	Mervyn DAY	

Date	Wednesday 19 August 1992
Venue	Anfield, 7.30pm

LIVERPOOL (1) 2
SHEFFIELD UNITED (1) 1

Attendance	33,107
Referee	David ELLERAY
Linesmen	M.A. Cooper, P.R. Richards

LIVERPOOL
Red Shirts, Red Shorts — Goals

1	David JAMES	
2	Rob JONES	
3	David BURROWS	
4	Steve NICOL	
5	Ronnie WHELAN	
6	Mark WRIGHT	
7	Dean SAUNDERS †	
8	Paul STEWART	65
9	Steve McMANAMAN	
10	Mark WALTERS	43
11	Michael THOMAS	
	Substitutes	
12	Ronnie ROSENTHAL †80	
14	Nicky TANNER	
Gk	Bruce GROBBELAAR	

SHEFFIELD UNITED
Yellow shirts, White shorts — Goals

1	Simon TRACEY	
2	Kevin GAGE	
3	David BARNES	
4	John GANNON ‡	
5	Paul BEESLEY	
6	Alan McLEARY	
7	Carl BRADSHAW †	
8	Michael LAKE	
9	Ian BRYSON	
10	Brian DEANE	35
11	Glyn HODGES	
	Substitutes	
12	Alan CORK †66	
14	Charlie HARTFIELD ‡75	
Gk	Alan KELLY	

Date	Wednesday 19 August 1992
Venue	Old Trafford, 8.00pm

MANCHESTER UNITED (0) 0
EVERTON (1) 3

Attendance	31,901
Referee	Keren BARRATT
Linesmen	J.B. Robinson, E.J. Walsh

MANCHESTER UNITED
Red shirts, White Shorts — Goals

1	Peter SCHMEICHEL	
2	Denis IRWIN	
3	Clayton BLACKMORE	
4	Steve BRUCE	
5	Darren FERGUSON ❑	
6	Gary PALLISTER	
7	Andrei KANCHELSKIS	
8	Paul INCE ‡	
9	Brian McCLAIR	
10	Mark HUGHES	
11	Ryan GIGGS †	
	Substitutes	
12	Dion DUBLIN †81	
14	Mike PHELAN ‡45	
Gk	Gary WALSH	

EVERTON
Blue shirts, Blue shorts — Goals

1	Neville SOUTHALL	
2	Alan HARPER	
3	Andy HINCHCLIFFE	
4	John EBBRELL	
5	Dave WATSON	
6	Gary ABLETT	
7	Robert WARZYCHA ‡	80
8	Peter BEARDSLEY	45
9	Paul RIDEOUT †	
10	Barry HORNE	
11	Mark WARD	
	Substitutes	
12	Peter BEAGRIE †71	
14	Mo JOHNSTON ‡81	90
Gk	Jason KEARTON	

| Date | Wednesday 19 August 1992 |
| Venue | Ayresome Park, 7.45pm |

MIDDLESBROUGH (2) 2
MANCHESTER CITY (0) 0

Attendance	15,369
Referee	Steve LODGE
Linesmen	D.E. Binsley, A.J. Hill

MIDDLESBROUGH
Red shirts, White shorts   Goals

1	Ian IRONSIDE	
2	Chris MORRIS	
3	Jimmy PHILLIPS	
4	Alan KERNAGHAN	
5	Derek WHYTE	
6	Andy PEAKE	
7	Bernie SLAVEN	15, 17
8	Willie FALCONER	
9	Paul WILKINSON	
10	Tommy WRIGHT ‡	
11	John HENDRIE	
	Substitutes	
12	Jamie POLLOCK	
14	Robbie MUSTOE ‡82	
Gk	Ben ROBERTS	

MANCHESTER CITY
Light Blue shirts, Light Blue shorts   Goals

1	Tony COTON	
2	Andy HILL	
3	Ian BRIGHTWELL	
4	Fitzroy SIMPSON	
5	Keith CURLE	
6	Michel VONK	
7	David WHITE ❑	
8	Paul LAKE †	
9	Niall QUINN ■	
10	Rick HOLDEN	
11	Steve McMAHON	
	Substitutes	
12	Mike SHERON †8	
14	Peter REID	
Gk	Martyn MARGETSON	

| Date | Wednesday 19 August 1992 |
| Venue | Carrow Road, 7.45pm |

NORWICH CITY (0) 2
CHELSEA (1) 1

Attendance	15,164
Referee	Gerald ASHBY
Linesmen	E.B. Crompton, B.L. Polkey

NORWICH CITY
Yellow shirts, Green shorts   Goals

1	Bryan GUNN	
2	Ian CULVERHOUSE	
3	Mark BOWEN	
4	Ian BUTTERWORTH	
5	John POLSTON †	
6	Gary MEGSON	
7	Ruel FOX	
8	Rob NEWMAN	
9	Mark ROBINS	59
10	Jeremy GOSS	
11	David PHILLIPS	57
	Substitutes	
12	Chris SUTTON †42	
14	Ian CROOK	
Gk	Mark WALTON	

WIMBLEDON
Blue shirts, Blue shorts   Goals

1	Dave BEASANT	
2	Steve CLARKE	
3	Gareth HALL	
4	Vinnie JONES ❑	
5	Paul ELLIOTT	
6	Mal DONAGHY	
7	Graham STUART ❑	15
8	Joe ALLON ‡	
9	Mick HARFORD	
10	Andy TOWNSEND	
11	Damien MATTHEW †	
	Substitutes	
12	Eddie NEWTON †70	
14	John SPENCER ‡75	
Gk	Kevin HITCHCOCK	

Date	Wednesday 19 August 1992
Venue	Boundary Park, 7.30pm

OLDHAM ATHLETIC (1) 1
CRYSTAL PALACE (0) 1

Attendance	11,063
Referee	Mike PECK
Linesmen	A. Streets, M. Warden

OLDHAM ATHLETIC
Blue shirts, Blue shorts   Goals

1	Jon HALLWORTH	
2	Steve REDMOND	
3	Andy BARLOW ❑	
4	Nick HENRY	
5	Richard JOBSON	
6	Ian MARSHALL	
7	Gunnar HALLE	
8	Roger PALMER	
9	Graeme SHARP	16
10	Mike MILLIGAN	
11	Paul BERNARD	
	Substitutes	
12	Craig FLEMING	
14	Neil TOLSON	
Gk	John KEELEY	

CRYSTAL PALACE
Red & Blue striped shirts, Red shorts   Goals

1	Nigel MARTYN	
2	John HUMPHREY	
3	Richard SHAW	
4	Gareth SOUTHGATE	
5	Eric YOUNG ❑	
6	Andy THORN	
7	Chris COLEMAN	
8	Geoff THOMAS	
9	Lee SINNOTT	
10	John SALAKO ‡	
11	Eddie McGOLDRICK	50
	Substitutes	
12	Simon OSBORN	
14	Dean GORDON ‡25	
Gk	Paul HEALD	

Date	Wednesday 19 August 1992
Venue	Loftus Road, 7.45pm

QPR (0) 3
SOUTHAMPTON (1) 1

Attendance	10,925
Referee	Ray BIGGER
Linesmen	M.R. Sims, P.A. Josper

QPR
Blue & White hooped shirts, White shorts   Goals

1	Tony ROBERTS	
2	David BARDSLEY	70
3	Clive WILSON	
4	Ray WILKINS	
5	Darren PEACOCK	
6	Alan McDONALD ❑	
7	Andy IMPEY	
8	Ian HOLLOWAY	
9	Les FERDINAND ❑	58, 86
10	Dennis BAILEY †	
11	Andy SINTON	
	Substitutes	
12	Garry THOMPSON †89	
14	Danny MADDIX	
Gk	Peter CALDWELL	

SOUTHAMPTON
Red & White striped shirts, Black shorts   Goals

1	Tim FLOWERS	
2	Jason DODD ‡	
3	Micky ADAMS ■	
4	Terry HURLOCK	
5	Kevin MOORE ❑	
6	Steve WOOD	
7	Matthew LE TISSIER	31
8	Glenn COCKERILL ❑	
9	Kerry DIXON	
10	David SPEEDIE †	
11	Francis BENALI ❑	
	Substitutes	
12	Iain DOWIE †65	
14	Jeff KENNA ‡23	
Gk	Ian ANDREWS	

Date	Wednesday 19 August 1992
Venue	Hillsborough, 7.45pm

SHEFFIELD WEDNESDAY (1) 2
NOTTINGHAM FOREST (0) 0

Attendance	29,623
Referee	Philip DON
Linesmen	E. Lomas, T. Lynch

SHEFFIELD WEDNESDAY
Blue & White striped shirts, Black shorts   Goals

1	Chris WOODS	
2	Roland NILSSON	
3	Phil KING ‡	
4	Carlton PALMER ❑	
5	Nigel PEARSON	
6	Paul WARHURST	
7	Danny WILSON	
8	Chris BART-WILLIAMS	
9	David HIRST	16, 78
10	Paul WILLIAMS	
11	Nigel WORTHINGTON	
	Substitutes	
12	Trevor FRANCIS	
14	John HARKES ‡77	
Gk	Kevin PRESSMAN	

NOTTINGHAM FOREST
Red shirts, White shorts   Goals

1	Mark CROSSLEY	
2	Brian LAWS ❑	
3	Stuart PEARCE	
4	Terry WILSON	
5	Steve CHETTLE	
6	Roy KEANE	
7	Gary CROSBY	
8	Scot GEMMILL	
9	Nigel CLOUGH	
10	Teddy SHERINGHAM	
11	Ian WOAN ❑	
	Substitutes	
12	Kingsley BLACK	
14	Gary BANNISTER	
Gk	Andy MARRIOTT	

Date	Wednesday 19 August 1992
Venue	White Hart Lane, 7.45pm

TOTTENHAM HOTSPUR (0) 0
COVENTRY CITY (2) 2

Attendance	24,388
Referee	Dermot GALLAGHER
Linesmen	J.A. Elwin, S.W. Dunn

TOTTENHAM HOTSPUR
White shirts, Navy Blue shorts   Goals

1	Ian WALKER ‡	
2	Terry FENWICK	
3	Justin EDINBURGH	
4	David HOWELLS	
5	Jason CUNDY †	
6	Neil RUDDOCK	
7	Andy TURNER	
8	Gordon DURIE ❑	
9	Vinny SAMWAYS	
10	Darren ANDERTON	
11	Paul ALLEN	
	Substitutes	
12	John HENDRY	
14	Andy GRAY †4	
Gk	Erik THORSTVEDT ‡45	

COVENTRY CITY
Sky Blue shirts, Sky Blue shorts   Goals

1	Steve OGRIZOVIC	
2	Terry FLEMING	
3	Kenny SANSOM	
4	Stewart ROBSON	
5	Andy PEARCE ❑	
6	Peter ATHERTON	
7	Michael GYNN	
8	Lee HURST	
9	Robert ROSARIO ❑	
10	John WILLIAMS †	4, 29
11	David SMITH	
	Substitutes	
12	Peter NDLOVU †70	
14	Lloyd McGRATH	
Gk	Jonathan GOULD	

Date	Saturday 22 August 1992
Venue	Villa Park, 3.00pm

ASTON VILLA (0) 1
SOUTHAMPTON (0) 1

Attendance	17,894
Referee	Kelvin MORTON
Linesmen	P.M. Roberts, J.B. Robinson

ASTON VILLA
Claret & Blue shirts, White Shorts — Goals

		Goals
1	Nigel SPINK	
2	Earl BARRETT	
3	Steve STAUNTON	
4	Shaun TEALE	
5	Paul McGRATH	
6	Kevin RICHARDSON	
7	Ray HOUGHTON	
8	Garry PARKER	
9	Dwight YORKE †	
10	Dalian ATKINSON	64
11	Stephen FROGGATT ‡	
Substitutes		
12	Frank McAVENNIE †37	
14	Ugo EHIOGU ‡77	
Gk	Les SEALEY	

SOUTHAMPTON
Red & White stripes, Black shorts — Goals

		Goals
1	Tim FLOWERS	
2	Jeff KENNA	
3	Micky ADAMS	79
4	Terry HURLOCK	
5	Richard HALL	
6	Kevin MOORE ❏	
7	Matthew LE TISSIER †	
8	Glenn COCKERILL	
9	Kerry DIXON	
10	David SPEEDIE	
11	Francis BENALI	
Substitutes		
12	Iain DOWIE †37 ❏	
14	Tommy WIDDRINGTON	
Gk	Ian ANDREWS	

Date	Saturday 22 August 1992
Venue	Ewood Park, 3.00pm

BLACKBURN ROVERS (0) 1
MANCHESTER CITY (0) 0

Attendance	19,433
Referee	Robbie HART
Linesmen	R.H. Andrews, J. McGrath

BLACKBURN ROVERS
Blue & White shirts, White Shorts — Goals

		Goals
1	Bobby MIMMS	
2	David MAY	
3	Alan WRIGHT †	
4	Tim SHERWOOD	
5	Colin HENDRY	
6	Kevin MORAN	
7	Stuart RIPLEY	
8	Mark ATKINS	
9	Alan SHEARER	
10	Mike NEWELL	69
11	Tony DOBSON	
Substitutes		
12	Chris PRICE †71	
14	Roy WEGERLE	
Gk	Matt DICKINS	

MANCHESTER CITY
Purple shirts, Purple shorts — Goals

		Goals
1	Tony COTON	
2	Andy HILL	
3	Ian BRIGHTWELL	
4	Fitzroy SIMPSON	
5	Keith CURLE	
6	Michel VONK	
7	David WHITE	
8	Mike SHERON	
9	Niall QUINN	
10	Rick HOLDEN	
11	Steve McMAHON	
Substitutes		
12	Garry FLITCROFT	
14	Peter REID	
Gk	Martyn MARGETSON	

Date	Saturday 22 August 1992
Venue	Old Trafford, 3.00pm

MANCHESTER UNITED (0) 1
IPSWICH TOWN (0) 1

Attendance	31,704
Referee	Gerald ASHBY
Linesmen	T.J. Stevens, A. Streets

MANCHESTER UNITED
Red shirts, White shorts · Goals

1	Peter SCHMEICHEL	
2	Denis IRWIN	57
3	Clayton BLACKMORE ‡	
4	Steve BRUCE	
5	Darren FERGUSON	
6	Gary PALLISTER	
7	Andrei KANCHELSKIS †	
8	Mike PHELAN	
9	Brian McCLAIR	
10	Mark HUGHES	
11	Ryan GIGGS	
	Substitutes	
12	Dion DUBLIN †87	
14	Neil WEBB ‡65	
Gk	Gary WALSH	

IPSWICH TOWN
Blue & White shirts, Blue shorts · Goals

1	Craig FORREST	
2	Phil WHELAN ❏ †	
3	Neil THOMPSON	
4	Mick STOCKWELL	
5	John WARK ❏	
6	David LINIGHAN	
7	Geraint WILLIAMS	
8	Paul GODDARD	
9	Gavin JOHNSON	
10	Jason DOZZELL ‡	
11	Chris KIWOMYA	56
	Substitutes	
12	Simon MILTON †83	
14	Eddie YOUDS ‡73	
Gk	Clive BAKER	

Date	Saturday 22 August 1992
Venue	Ayresome Park, 3.00pm

MIDDLESBROUGH (2) 4
LEEDS UNITED (0) 1

Attendance	18,649
Referee	David ALLISON
Linesmen	N.S. Barry, T. Heilbron

MIDDLESBROUGH
Red shirts. White shorts · Goals

1	Ian IRONSIDE	
2	Chris MORRIS	
3	Jimmy PHILLIPS	
4	Alan KERNAGHAN	
5	Chris WHYTE	
6	Andy PEAKE	
7	Bernie SLAVEN †	
8	Willie FALCONER	
9	Paul WILKINSON ‡	7, 8
10	Tommy WRIGHT	47
11	John HENDRIE	59
	Substitutes	
12	Jamie POLLOCK †77	
14	Robbie MUSTOE ‡45	
Gk	Brian HORNE ?	

LEEDS UNITED
White shirts, White shorts · Goals

1	John LUKIC	
2	Jon NEWSOME ‡	
3	Tony DORIGO	
4	David BATTY ❏ †	
5	Chris FAIRCLOUGH	
6	Chris WHYTE	
7	Eric CANTONA	68
8	Rod WALLACE	
9	Lee CHAPMAN	
10	Gary McALLISTER	
11	Gary SPEED ❏	
	Substitutes	
12	Steve HODGE †76	
14	Gordon STRACHAN ‡45	
Gk	Mervyn DAY	

Date	Saturday 22 August 1992
Venue	Carrow Road, 3.00pm

NORWICH CITY (0) 1
EVERTON (0) 1

Attendance	14,150
Referee	John KEY
Linesmen	W.J. Norbury, M. Stobbart

NORWICH CITY
Yellow shirts, Green shorts — Goals

1	Bryan GUNN	
2	Ian CULVERHOUSE	
3	Mark BOWEN	
4	Ian BUTTERWORTH	
5	Chris SUTTON	
6	Gary MEGSON ‡	
7	Ruel FOX	67
8	Rob NEWMAN †	
9	Mark ROBINS	
10	Jeremy GOSS	
11	David PHILLIPS	
	Substitutes	
12	Ian CROOK †67	
14	Lee POWER ‡86	
Gk	Mark WALTON	

EVERTON
Blue shirts, White shorts — Goals

1	Neville SOUTHALL	
2	Alan HARPER	
3	Andy HINCHCLIFFE	
4	John EBBRELL ‡	
5	Dave WATSON	
6	Gary ABLETT	
7	Robert WARZYCHA †	
8	Peter BEARDSLEY	55
9	Paul RIDEOUT	
10	Barry HORNE	
11	Mark WARD	
	Substitutes	
12	Peter BEAGRIE †78	
14	Mo JOHNSTON ‡86	
Gk	Jason KEARTON	

Date	Saturday 22 August 1992
Venue	Boundary Park, 3.00pm

OLDHAM ATHLETIC (3) 5
NOTTINGHAM FOREST (0) 3

Attendance	11,632
Referee	Ron GROVES
Linesmen	T.A. Atkinson, D.S. Oliver

OLDHAM ATHLETIC
Blue shirts, Blue shorts — Goals

1	Jon HALLWORTH	
2	Steve REDMOND ❏	
3	Neil POINTON	
4	Nick HENRY	43
5	Richard JOBSON	
6	Ian MARSHALL	
7	Gunnar HALLE	46
8	Paul BERNARD	59
9	Graeme SHARP	38
10	Mike MILLIGAN	
11	Neil ADAMS †	31
	Substitutes	
12	Roger PALMER †75	
14	Craig FLEMING	
Gk	John KEELEY	

NOTTINGHAM FOREST
Red shirts, White shorts — Goals

1	Mark CROSSLEY	
2	Brian LAWS	
3	Stuart PEARCE	66p
4	Terry WILSON †	
5	Steve CHETTLE	
6	Roy KEANE	
7	Gary CROSBY	
8	Scot GEMMILL	
9	Nigel CLOUGH	
10	Teddy SHERINGHAM ‡	
11	Ian WOAN	
	Substitutes	
12	Kingsley BLACK †45	
14	Gary BANNISTER ‡64	86, 88
Gk	Andy MARRIOTT	

Date Saturday 22nd August 1992
Venue Loftus Road, 3.00pm

QPR (2) 3
SHEFFIELD UNITED (1) 2

Attendance 10,932
Referee Peter FOAKES
Linesmen A. Schneider, B. Wigginton

QPR Blue & White hooped shirts, White shorts		Goals
1	Jan STEJSKAL	
2	David BARDSLEY	
3	Clive WILSON	
4	Ray WILKINS	
5	Alan McDONALD	
6	Darren PEACOCK ❑ .	
7	Simon BARKER	14
8	Ian HOLLOWAY †	
9	Les FERDINAND	3
10	Dennis BAILEY	84
11	Andy SINTON	
	Substitutes	
12	Garry THOMPSON †28	
14	Danny MADDIX	
Gk	Tony ROBERTS	

SHEFFIELD UNITED Yellow shirts, Black shorts		Goals
1	Simon TRACEY	
2	Kevin GAGE ❑	
3	David BARNES †	
4	John GANNON	
5	Paul BEESLEY ❑	
6	Alan McCLEARY ‡	
7	Ian BRYSON	
8	Michael LAKE ❑	
9	Alan CORK	4
10	Brian DEANE	63
11	Glyn HODGES ❑	
	Substitutes	
12	Adrian LITTLEJOHN †88	
14	Charlie HARTFIELD ‡48	
Gk	Alan KELLY	

Date Saturday 22nd August 1992
Venue Hillsborough, 3.00pm

SHEFFIELD WEDNESDAY (2) 3
CHELSEA (0) 3

Attendance 26,338
Referee Roger DILKES
Linesmen B.L. Polkey, K.M. Lynch

SHEFFIELD WEDNESDAY Blue & White stripes, Black shorts		Goals
1	Chris WOODS	
2	Roger NILSSON	
3	Phil KING †	
4	Carlton PALMER	
5	Nigel PEARSON	
6	Paul WARHURST	
7	John HARKES ‡	
8	Chris BART-WILLIAMS	
9	David HIRST	27, 37p
10	Paul WILLIAMS	
11	Nigel WORTHINGTON	
	Substitutes	
12	Trevor FRANCIS †69	
14	Danny WILSON ‡77	81
Gk	Marlon BERESFORD	

CHELSEA Yellow shirts, Yellow shorts		Goals
1	Dave BEASANT	
2	Steve CLARKE	
3	Gareth HALL	
4	Vinnie JONES	49
5	Paul ELLIOTT	
6	Mal DONAGHY	
7	Graham STUART	57
8	Robert FLECK	
9	Mick HARFORD ‡	
10	Andy TOWNSEND	
11	Eddie NEWTON	64
	Substitutes	
12	Damien MATTHEW	
14	Joe ALLON ‡77	
Gk	Kevin HITCHCOCK	

Date	Saturday 22 August 1992
Venue	White Hart Lane, 3.00pm

TOTTENHAM HOTSPUR (1) 2
CRYSTAL PALACE (1) 2

Attendance	25,237
Referee	Philip DON
Linesmen	J.A. Elwin, D.C. Richards

TOTTENHAM HOTSPUR
White shirts, Navy Blue shorts   Goals

1	Erik THORSTVEDT	
2	Terry FENWICK †	
3	Justin EDINBURGH	
4	Steve SEDGLEY	88
5	David TUTTLE	
6	Neil RUDDOCK ❑ ■	
7	John HENDRY ‡	
8	Gordon DURIE	16
9	Vinny SAMWAYS ❑	
10	Darren ANDERTON	
11	Paul ALLEN ❑	
	Substitutes	
12	Dean AUSTIN †63	
14	Andy GRAY ‡63	
Gk	Chris DAY	

CRYSTAL PALACE
Blue & Red striped shirts, Red shorts   Goals

1	Nigel MARTYN	
2	John HUMPHREY	
3	Richard SHAW	
4	Gareth SOUTHGATE	
5	Eric YOUNG	80
6	Andy THORN ❑ ■	
7	Chris COLEMAN	
8	Geoff THOMAS ❑	
9	Lee SINNOTT	
10	Dean GORDON	
11	Eddie McGOLDRICK	21
	Substitutes	
12	Simon OSBORN	
14	Andy BARNES	
Gk	Paul HEALD	

Date	Saturday 22 August 1992
Venue	Selhurst Park, 3.00pm

WIMBLEDON (0) 1
COVENTRY CITY (1) 2

Attendance	3,759
Referee	Jim BORRETT
Linesmen	W.M. Jordan, P. Rejer

WIMBLEDON
Blue shirts, Blue shorts   Goals

1	Hans SEGERS	
2	Roger JOSEPH	
3	Gary ELKINS	
4	Warren BARTON	
5	Dean BLACKWELL	
6	Scott FITZGERALD ‡	
7	Gerald DOBBS †	
8	Robbie EARLE	
9	Dean HOLDSWORTH	73
10	Lawrie SANCHEZ	
11	Steve ANTHROBUS	
	Substitutes	
12	Paul MILLER †83	
14	Andy CLARKE ‡45	
Gk	Neil SULLIVAN	

COVENTRY CITY
Red shirts, White shorts   Goals

1	Steve OGRIZOVIC	
2	Terry FLEMING	
3	Kenny SANSOM	
4	Stewart ROBSON	
5	Andy PEARCE	
6	Peter ATHERTON	
7	Michael GYNN ‡	13
8	Lee HURST	
9	Robert ROSARIO	46
10	John WILLIAMS †	
11	David SMITH	
	Substitutes	
12	Peter NDLOVU †73	
14	Lloyd McGRATH ‡75	
Gk	Jonathan GOULD	

Date	Sunday 23 August 1992
Venue	Anfield, 4.00pm

LIVERPOOL (0) 0
ARSENAL (0) 2

Attendance	34,961
Referee	Ken REDFERN
Linesmen	B. Lowe, U.D. Rennie

LIVERPOOL
Red shirts, Red shorts   Goals

1	David JAMES	
2	Rob JONES †	
3	David BURROWS	
4	Jan MOLBY	
5	Ronnie WHELAN ❑	
6	Mark WRIGHT	
7	Dean SAUNDERS	
8	Nicky TANNER	
9	Steve McMANAMAN	
10	Mark WALTERS	
11	Michael THOMAS ‡	
	Substitutes	
12	Ronnie ROSENTHAL †74	
14	Mike MARSH ‡48	
Gk	Bruce GROBBELAAR	

ARSENAL
Yellow shirts, Blue shorts   Goals

1	David SEAMAN	
2	Lee DIXON ❑	
3	Nigel WINTERBURN	
4	David HILLIER	
5	Colin PATES	
6	Tony ADAMS ❑	
7	John JENSEN ❑	
8	Ian WRIGHT	80
9	Kevin CAMPBELL	
10	Ray PARLOUR ❑	
11	Anders LIMPAR ‡	53
	Substitutes	
12	David O'LEARY	
14	Paul MERSON ‡64	
Gk	Alan MILLER	

Date	Monday 24 August 1992
Venue	The Dell, 3.00pm

SOUTHAMPTON (0) 0
MANCHESTER UNITED (0) 1

Attendance	15,623
Referee	Ray LEWIS
Linesmen	M.J. Holohan, I.M.D. Mitchell

SOUTHAMPTON
Red & White striped shirts, Black shorts   Goals

1	Tim FLOWERS ❑	
2	Jeff KENNA	
3	Micky ADAMS	
4	Terry HURLOCK	
5	Kenneth MONKOU	
6	Kevin MOORE	
7	David SPEEDIE	
8	Glenn COCKERILL	
9	Kerry DIXON	
10	Iain DOWIE †	
11	Francis BENALI	
	Substitutes	
12	David LEE †55	
14	Richard HALL	
Gk	Ian ANDREWS	

MANCHESTER UNITED
Blue shirts, Blue shorts   Goals

1	Peter SCHMEICHEL	
2	Mike PHELAN	
3	Denis IRWIN	
4	Steve BRUCE	
5	Darren FERGUSON	
6	Gary PALLISTER	
7	Dion DUBLIN	89
8	Paul INCE	
9	Brian McCLAIR	
10	Mark HUGHES	
11	Ryan GIGGS	
	Substitutes	
12	Andrei KANCHELSKIS	
14	Danny WALLACE	
Gk	Gary WALSH	

Date	Tuesday 25 August 1992
Venue	Selhurst Park, 8.00pm

CRYSTAL PALACE (1) 1
SHEFFIELD WEDNESDAY (0) 1

Attendance	14,005
Referee	John MARTIN
Linesmen	G. Pearson, M. Stobbart

CRYSTAL PALACE
Red & Blue stripes, Red shorts   Goals

1	Nigel MARTYN	
2	John HUMPHREY	
3	Richard SHAW	
4	Gareth SOUTHGATE	
5	Eric YOUNG	41
6	Andy THORN	
7	Chris COLEMAN	
8	Geoff THOMAS	
9	Mark BRIGHT	
10	Dean GORDON	
11	Eddie McGOLDRICK	
	Substitutes	
12	Simon OSBORN	
14	Lee SINNOTT	
Gk	Paul HEALD	

SHEFFIELD WEDNESDAY
Yellow & Black shirts, Black shorts   Goals

1	Chris WOODS	
2	Paul WARHURST	
3	Phil KING	
4	Carlton PALMER ‡	
5	Nigel PEARSON	
6	Peter SHIRTLIFF	
7	Danny WILSON	
8	Graham HYDE ❏	
9	David HIRST	
10	Paul WILLIAMS	66
11	Nigel WORTHINGTON	
	Substitutes	
12	Trevor FRANCIS	
14	Chris BART-WILLIAMS ‡64	
Gk	Marlon BERESFORD	

Date	Tuesday 25 August 1992
Venue	Goodison Park, 7.30pm

EVERTON (0) 1
ASTON VILLA (0) 0

Attendance	22,372
Referee	Martin BODENHAM
Linesmen	T.A. Atkinson, M.A. Riley

EVERTON
Blue shirts, White shorts   Goals

1	Neville SOUTHALL	
2	Alan HARPER	
3	Andy HINCHCLIFFE	
4	John EBBRELL	
5	Dave WATSON	
6	Gary ABLETT	
7	Mark WARD	
8	Peter BEARDSLEY	
9	Paul RIDEOUT †	
10	Barry HORNE	
11	Mo JOHNSTON	88
	Substitutes	
12	Peter BEAGRIE †48	
14	Matthew JACKSON	
Gk	Jason KEARTON	

ASTON VILLA
Claret & Blue shirts, Light Blue shorts   Goals

1	Nigel SPINK	
2	Earl BARRETT	
3	Steve STAUNTON	
4	Shaun TEALE	
5	Paul McGRATH	
6	Kevin RICHARDSON	
7	Tony DALEY	
8	Garry PARKER †	
9	Ray HOUGHTON	
10	Dalian ATKINSON	
11	Stephen FROGGATT	
	Substitutes	
12	Cyrille REGIS †89	
14	Ugo EHIOGU	
Gk	Les SEALEY	

Date	Tuesday 25 August 1992
Venue	Portman Road, 7.45pm

IPSWICH TOWN (0) 2
LIVERPOOL (1) 2

Attendance	20,109
Referee	Bob HAMER
Linesmen	A. Schneider, G. Butland

IPSWICH TOWN
Blue & White shirts, White shorts   Goals

1	Craig FORREST	
2	Phil WHELAN	
3	Neil THOMPSON	
4	Mick STOCKWELL	
5	John WARK	
6	David LINIGHAN	
7	Geraint WILLIAMS	
8	Paul GODDARD †	
9	Gavin JOHNSON	
10	Jason DOZZELL	56
11	Chris KIWOMYA	90
	Substitutes	
12	Simon MILTON †73 ❑	
14	Eddie YOUDS	
Gk	Clive BAKER	

LIVERPOOL
Red shirts, Red shorts   Goals

1	David JAMES ❑	
2	Rob JONES	
3	David BURROWS	
4	Steve HARKNESS	
5	Ronnie WHELAN	
6	Mark WRIGHT ❑	
7	Dean SAUNDERS †	
8	Paul STEWART	
9	Ian RUSH	
10	Jan MOLBY	70p
11	Mark WALTERS	39
	Substitutes	
12	Steve McMANAMAN †77	
14	Mike MARSH	
Gk	Bruce GROBBELAAR	

Date	Tuesday 25 August 1992
Venue	Elland Road, 7.45pm

LEEDS UNITED (3) 5
TOTTENHAM HOTSPUR (0) 0

Attendance	28,218
Referee	Mike REED
Linesmen	E. Lomas, B. Lowe

LEEDS UNITED
White shirts, White shorts   Goals

1	John LUKIC	
2	Jon NEWSOME	
3	Tony DORIGO	
4	David BATTY	
5	Chris FAIRCLOUGH	
6	Chris WHYTE	
7	Eric CANTONA	26, 31, 46
8	Rod WALLACE	19
9	Lee CHAPMAN	66
10	Gary McALLISTER	
11	Gary SPEED	
	Substitutes	
12	Steve HODGE	
14	Gordon STRACHAN	
Gk	Mervyn DAY	

TOTTENHAM HOTSPUR
Yellow shirts, Yellow shorts   Goals

1	Erik THORSTVEDT	
2	Dean AUSTIN	
3	Justin EDINBURGH	
4	David HOWELLS	
5	Jason CUNDY	
6	Neil RUDDOCK	
7	Steve SEDGLEY	
8	Gordon DURIE	
9	Vinny SAMWAYS	
10	Darren ANDERTON	
11	Paul ALLEN	
	Substitutes	
12	David TUTTLE	
14	John HENDRY	
Gk	Chris DAY	

Date	Tuesday 25 August 1992
Venue	Bramall Lane, 7.45pm

SHEFFIELD UNITED (0) 2
WIMBLEDON (1) 2

Attendance	15,463
Referee	Keren BARRETT
Linesmen	P.J. Robinson, J. Leech

SHEFFIELD UNITED
Red & White striped shirts, White shorts

		Goals
1	Simon TRACEY	
2	Kevin GAGE	
3	Tom COWAN	
4	Charlie HARTFIELD	
5	Brian GAYLE	
6	Paul BEESLEY	48
7	Ian BRYSON ‡	
8	Michael LAKE	
9	Alan CORK	
10	Brian DEANE	
11	Glyn HODGES	67
	Substitutes	
12	Adrian LITTLEJOHN	
14	Carl BRADSHAW ‡80	
Gk	Alan KELLY	

WIMBLEDON
Blue shirts, Blue shorts

		Goals
1	Hans SEGERS	
2	Paul MILLER	
3	Brian McALLISTER	
4	Warren BARTON	34
5	Dean BLACKWELL	
6	Scott FITZGERALD	
7	Gerald DOBBS †	
8	Robbie EARLE	
9	Dean HOLDSWORTH ‡	74
10	Lawrie SANCHEZ	
11	Steve ANTHROBUS	
	Substitutes	
12	Andy CLARKE †68	
14	Gary ELKINS ‡82	
Gk	Neil SULLIVAN	

Date	Wednesday 26 August 1992
Venue	Highbury, 7.45pm

ARSENAL (2) 2
OLDHAM ATHLETIC (0) 0

Attendance	20,796
Referee	Roger MILFORD
Linesmen	D.C. Madgwick, D. Orr

ARSENAL
Red & White shirts, White shorts

		Goals
1	David SEAMAN	
2	Lee DIXON	
3	Nigel WINTERBURN	25
4	David HILLIER	
5	Steve BOULD ❏	
6	Tony ADAMS	
7	Ray PARLOUR	
8	Ian WRIGHT ‡	31
9	Kevin CAMPBELL	
10	Paul MERSON †	
11	Steve MORROW	
	Substitutes	
12	Colin PATES †78	
14	Alan SMITH ‡80	
Gk	Alan MILLER	

OLDHAM ATHLETIC
Blue shirts, Blue shorts

		Goals
1	Jon HALLWORTH	
2	Steve REDMOND ❏	
3	Neil POINTON ❏	
4	Nick HENRY ‡	
5	Richard JOBSON	
6	Ian MARSHALL	
7	Gunnar HALLE	
8	Paul BERNARD	
9	Graeme SHARP	
10	Mike MILLIGAN	
11	Neil ADAMS	
	Substitutes	
12	Roger PALMER	
14	Ian OLNEY ‡61	
Gk	John KEELEY	

Date	Wednesday 26 August 1992
Venue	Stamford Bridge, 7.30pm

CHELSEA (0) 0
BLACKBURN ROVERS (0) 0

Attendance	19,575
Referee	Ray BIGGER
Linesmen	M.R. Sims, P.A. Josper

CHELSEA
Blue shirts, Blue shorts   Goals

1	Dave BEASANT	
2	Steve CLARKE	
3	Gareth HALL	
4	Vinnie JONES	
5	Paul ELLIOTT ❑	
6	Mal DONAGHY	
7	Graham STUART	
8	Robert FLECK	
9	Mick HARFORD	
10	Andy TOWNSEND	
11	Dennis WISE	
	Substitutes	
12	Joe ALLON	
14	Eddie NEWTON	
Gk	Nick COLGAN	

BLACKBURN ROVERS
Red & Black striped shirts, Black shorts   Goals

1	Bobby MIMMS	
2	David MAY ❑	
3	Tony DOBSON	
4	Tim SHERWOOD	
5	Colin HENDRY	
6	Kevin MORAN	
7	Stuart RIPLEY	
8	Mark ATKINS	
9	Alan SHEARER	
10	Mike NEWELL	
11	Jason WILCOX	
	Substitutes	
12	Gordon COWANS	
14	Roy WEGERLE	
Gk	Matt DICKINS	

Date	Wednesday 26 August 1992
Venue	Highfield Road, 7.45pm

COVENTRY CITY (0) 0
QPR (1) 1

Attendance	13,563
Referee	Stephen LODGE
Linesmen	P. Rejer, B. Wiggington

COVENTRY CITY
Sky Blue shirts, Sky Blue shorts   Goals

1	Steve OGRIZOVIC	
2	Terry FLEMING	
3	Kenny SANSOM	
4	Stewart ROBSON	
5	Andy PEARCE	
6	Peter ATHERTON	
7	Michael GYNN	
8	Lee HURST ‡	
9	Robert ROSARIO	
10	John WILLIAMS †	
11	David SMITH	
	Substitutes	
12	Peter NDLOVU †45	
14	Lloyd McGRATH ‡64	
Gk	Jonathan GOULD	

QPR
Red & Black hooped shirts, Black shorts   Goals

1	Jan STEJSKAL	
2	David BARDSLEY	
3	Clive WILSON	
4	Ray WILKINS	
5	Darren PEACOCK	
6	Alan McDONALD	
7	Andy IMPEY	45
8	Simon BARKER	
9	Les FERDINAND †	
10	Dennis BAILEY	
11	Andy SINTON	
	Substitutes	
12	Gary PENRICE †56	
14	Danny MADDIX	
Gk	Tony ROBERTS	

Date	Wednesday 26 August 1992		*Date*	Saturday 29 August 1992
Venue	Maine Road, 7.45pm		*Venue*	Highbury Stadium, 3.00pm

MANCHESTER CITY (1) 3
NORWICH CITY (0) 1

Attendance	23,182
Referee	David ELLERAY
Linesmen	M.A. Cooper, M. Warren

ARSENAL (2) 2
SHEFFIELD WEDNESDAY (1) 1

Attendance	23,389
Referee	Paul DURKIN
Linesmen	M.J. Holohan, M.R. Sims

MANCHESTER CITY
Light Blue shirts, White shorts   Goals

1	Tony COTON ❑	
2	Ian BRIGHTWELL	
3	Terry PHELAN	
4	Fitzroy SIMPSON	
5	Keith CURLE	
6	Michel VONK	
7	David WHITE	45, 80
8	Mike SHERON	
9	Niall QUINN	
10	Rick HOLDEN	
11	Steve McMAHON	90
	Substitutes	
12	Garry FLITCROFT	
14	Peter REID	
Gk	Martyn MARGETSON	

ARSENAL
Red & White shirts, White shorts   Goals

1	David SEAMAN	
2	Lee DIXON ❑	
3	Nigel WINTERBURN	
4	David HILLIER	
5	Steve BOULD ❑	
6	Tony ADAMS	
7	John JENSEN	
8	Ian WRIGHT ❑	
9	Kevin CAMPBELL	
10	Paul MERSON ❑ ‡	27
11	Ray PARLOUR	8
	Substitutes	
12	Colin PATES	
14	Alan SMITH ‡83	
Gk	Alan MILLER	

NORWICH CITY
Yellow shirts, Green shorts   Goals

1	Bryan GUNN ❑	
2	Ian CULVERHOUSE	
3	Mark BOWEN	
4	Ian BUTTERWORTH	
5	Chris SUTTON	
6	Gary MEGSON	58
7	Ruel FOX †	
8	Jeremy GOSS	
9	Mark ROBINS ‡	
10	Ian CROOK	
11	David PHILLIPS	
	Substitutes	
12	Rob NEWMAN †56	
14	Colin WOODTHORPE ‡81	
Gk	Mark WALTON	

SHEFFIELD WEDNESDAY
Blue & White striped shirts, Black shorts   Goals

1	Chris WOODS	
2	Roland NILSSON	
3	Paul WARHURST	
4	Graham HYDE ❑	
5	Nigel PEARSON	
6	Peter SHIRTLIFF	
7	Danny WILSON †	
8	Chris BART-WILLIAMS	
9	David HIRST ❑ ‡	33
10	Paul WILLIAMS	
11	Nigel WORTHINGTON	
	Substitutes	
12	John HARKES †65	
14	Nigel JEMSON ‡73	
Gk	Kevin PRESSMAN	

Date	Saturday 29 August 1992
Venue	Stamford Bridge, 3.00pm

CHELSEA (0) 1
QPR (0) 0

Attendance	22,910
Referee	Alf BUKSH
Linesmen	D. Orr, D.C. Richards

CHELSEA
Blue shirts, Blue shorts   Goals

1	Dave BEASANT	
2	Steve CLARKE	
3	Gareth HALL	
4	Vinnie JONES	
5	Paul ELLIOTT	
6	Mal DONAGHY	
7	Graham STUART	
8	Robert FLECK	
9	Mick HARFORD	59
10	Andy TOWNSEND	
11	Dennis WISE ❑	
	Substitutes	
12	David LEE	
14	Eddie NEWTON	
Gk	Nick COLGAN	

QPR
Black & Red hooped shirts, Black shorts   Goals

1	Jan STEJSKAL	
2	David BARDSLEY ❑	
3	Clive WILSON	
4	Ray WILKINS	
5	Darren PEACOCK	
6	Alan McDONALD ❑	
7	Andy IMPEY	
8	Simon BARKER	
9	Les FERDINAND	
10	Dennis BAILEY †	
11	Andy SINTON	
	Substitutes	
12	Gary PENRICE †64	
14	Danny MADDIX	
Gk	Tony ROBERTS	

Date	Saturday 29 August 1992
Venue	Highfield Road, 3.00pm

COVENTRY CITY (0) 0
BLACKBURN ROVERS (0) 2

Attendance	14,541
Referee	Ray LEWIS
Linesmen	G.R. Hamblin, T.J. Stevens

COVENTRY CITY
Sky Blue shirts, Sky Blue shorts   Goals

1	Steve OGRIZOVIC	
2	Terry FLEMING	
3	Kenny SANSOM	
4	Sean FLYNN †	
5	Andy PEARCE ❑	
6	Brian BORROWS	
7	Paul McGRATH	
8	Lee HURST	
9	Robert ROSARIO	
10	Kevin GALLACHER	
11	David SMITH ‡	
	Substitutes	
12	John WILLIAMS †66	
14	Phil BABB ‡77	
Gk	Jonathan GOULD	

BLACKBURN ROVERS
Red & Black shirts, Black shorts   Goals

1	Bobby MIMMS	
2	David MAY	
3	Tony DOBSON	
4	Tim SHERWOOD	
5	Colin HENDRY	
6	Kevin MORAN ❑	
7	Stuart RIPLEY	
8	Mark ATKINS	79
9	Alan SHEARER ❑ †	69p
10	Mike NEWELL	
11	Alan WRIGHT	
	Substitutes	
12	Gordon COWANS	
14	Roy WEGERLE †83	
Gk	Matt DICKINS	

Date	Saturday 29 August 1992
Venue	Selhurst Park, 3.00pm

CRYSTAL PALACE (1) 1
NORWICH CITY (1) 2

Attendance	12,033
Referee	David ALLISON
Linesmen	G. Butland, M. Stobbart

CRYSTAL PALACE
Red & Blue striped shirts, Red shorts   Goals

1	Nigel MARTYN	
2	John HUMPHREY †	
3	Lee SINNOTT	
4	Gareth SOUTHGATE	
5	Eric YOUNG	
6	Andy THORN	
7	Chris COLEMAN ‡	
8	Geoff THOMAS	
9	Mark BRIGHT	
10	Dean GORDON	
11	Eddie McGOLDRICK	20
	Substitutes	
12	Simon OSBORN †79	
14	John SALAKO ‡62	
Gk	Paul HEALD	

NORWICH CITY
Yellow shirts, Green shorts   Goals

1	Bryan GUNN	
2	Ian CULVERHOUSE	
3	Mark BOWEN	
4	Ian BUTTERWORTH	
5	Chris SUTTON	
6	Gary MEGSON	
7	Ian CROOK	
8	Rob NEWMAN	
9	Lee POWER	16
10	Jeremy GOSS ‡	
11	David PHILLIPS	74
	Substitutes	
12	Colin WOODTHORPE	
14	Daryl SUTCH ‡68	
Gk	Mark WALTON	

Date	Saturday 29 August 1992
Venue	Goodison Park, 3.00pm

EVERTON (0) 0
WIMBLEDON (0) 0

Attendance	18,118
Referee	Howard KING
Linesmen	I.A. Madge, P.R. Richards

EVERTON
Blue shirts, White shorts   Goals

1	Neville SOUTHALL	
2	Alan HARPER	
3	Andy HINCHCLIFFE	
4	John EBBRELL	
5	Dave WATSON ❑	
6	Gary ABLETT	
7	Robert WARZYCHA	
8	Peter BEARDSLEY	
9	Paul RIDEOUT ‡	
10	Barry HORNE	
11	Mark WARD †	
	Substitutes	
12	Peter BEAGRIE †46	
14	Mo JOHNSTON ‡63	
Gk	Jason KEARTON	

WIMBLEDON
White shirts, Black shorts   Goals

1	Hans SEGERS	
2	Paul MILLER	
3	Brian McALLISTER ❑	
4	Warren BARTON	
5	Dean BLACKWELL	
6	Scott FITZGERALD	
7	Gerald DOBBS ‡	
8	Robbie EARLE ❑	
9	Dean HOLDSWORTH	
10	Lawrie SANCHEZ	
11	Steve ANTHROBUS ❑	
	Substitutes	
12	Roger JOSEPH	
14	Andy CLARKE ‡70	
Gk	Neil SULLIVAN	

Date Saturday 29 August 1992
Venue Elland Road, 3.00pm

LEEDS UNITED (1) 2
LIVERPOOL (1) 2

Attendance 29,597
Referee Roger DILKES
Linesmen W.J. Nattrass, R. Pearson

LEEDS UNITED
White shirts, White shorts   Goals

1	John LUKIC	
2	Jon NEWSOME	
3	Tony DORIGO	
4	David BATTY †	
5	Chris FAIRCLOUGH ‡	
6	Chris WHYTE	
7	Eric CANTONA ❏	
8	Rod WALLACE	
9	Lee CHAPMAN	87
10	Gary McALLISTER	7
11	Gary SPEED	
	Substitutes	
12	Steve HODGE †77	
14	Gordon STRACHAN ‡77	
Gk	Mervyn DAY	

LIVERPOOL
Red shirts, Red shorts   Goals

1	David JAMES	
2	Rob JONES	
3	David BURROWS	
4	Steve HARKNESS	
5	Ronnie WHELAN	44
6	Mark WRIGHT	
7	Dean SAUNDERS †	
8	Paul STEWART ‡	
9	Ian RUSH	
10	Jan MOLBY	70p
11	Jamie REDKNAPP	
	Substitutes	
12	Mark WALTERS †66	
14	Mike MARSH ‡71	
Gk	Mike HOOPER	

Date Saturday 29 August 1992
Venue Maine Road, 3.00pm

MANCHESTER CITY (3) 3
OLDHAM ATHLETIC (3) 3

Attendance 27,255
Referee Dermot GALLAGHER
Linesmen A. Black, B.L. Polkey

MANCHESTER CITY
Light Blue shirts, White shorts   Goals

1	Tony COTON	
2	Ian BRIGHTWELL	
3	Terry PHELAN	
4	Fitzroy SIMPSON	
5	Keith CURLE ❏	
6	Michel VONK	8
7	David WHITE	23
8	Mike SHERON ‡	
9	Niall QUINN	4
10	Rick HOLDEN	
11	Steve McMAHON †	
	Substitutes	
12	Peter REID †45	
14	Garry FLITCROFT ‡80	
Gk	Martyn MARGETSON	

OLDHAM ATHLETIC
Red & White shirts, White shorts   Goals

1	Jon HALLWORTH	
2	Steve REDMOND	
3	Neil POINTON	
4	Paul BERNARD	
5	Richard JOBSON	11
6	Ian MARSHALL ❏	
7	Gunnar HALLE	38
8	Ian OLNEY	
9	Graeme SHARP	
10	Mike MILLIGAN	29
11	Neil ADAMS	
	Substitutes	
12	Roger PALMER	
14	Craig FLEMING	
Gk	Ian GRAY	

Date	Saturday 29 August 1992
Venue	City Ground, 3.00pm

NOTTINGHAM FOREST (0) 0
MANCHESTER UNITED (1) 2

Attendance	19,694
Referee	Ken REDFERN
Linesmen	D.T. Colwell, K.M. Lynch

NOTTINGHAM FOREST
Red shirts, White shorts · Goals

1	Mark CROSSLEY	
2	Brian LAWS	
3	Stuart PEARCE	
4	Terry WILSON	
5	Steve CHETTLE	
6	Roy KEANE	
7	Gary CROSBY	
8	Scot GEMMILL	
9	Nigel CLOUGH	
10	Gary BANNISTER	
11	Ian WOAN	
	Substitutes	
12	Thorvaldur ORLYGSSON	
14	Kingsley BLACK	
Gk	Andy MARRIOTT	

MANCHESTER UNITED
Blue Shirts, Blue shorts · Goals

1	Peter SCHMEICHEL	
2	Mike PHELAN ‡	
3	Denis IRWIN	
4	Steve BRUCE ❏	
5	Darren FERGUSON	
6	Gary PALLISTER	
7	Dion DUBLIN ❏	
8	Paul INCE	
9	Brian McCLAIR	
10	Mark HUGHES †	17
11	Ryan GIGGS	50
	Substitutes	
12	Andrei KANCHELSKIS †86	
14	Clayton BLACKMORE ‡44	
Gk	Gary WALSH	

Date	Saturday 29 August 1992
Venue	Bramall Lane, 3.00pm

SHEFFIELD UNITED (0) 0
ASTON VILLA (1) 2

Attendance	18,773
Referee	Roger MILFORD
Linesmen	E. Lomas, T. Lynch

SHEFFIELD UNITED
Red & White striped shirts, White shorts · Goals

1	Simon TRACEY	
2	Kevin GAGE	
3	Tom COWAN	
4	John GANNON	
5	Brian GAYLE ❏	
6	Paul BEESLEY	
7	Mitch WARD	
8	Michael LAKE ‡	
9	Alan CORK †	
10	Brian DEANE	
11	Glyn HODGES	
	Substitutes	
12	Carl BRADSHAW †57	
14	Adrian LITTLEJOHN ‡45	
Gk	Alan KELLY	

ASTON VILLA
Claret & Blue Shirts, White shorts · Goals

1	Nigel SPINK	
2	Earl BARRETT	
3	Steve STAUNTON	
4	Shaun TEALE	
5	Paul McGRATH	
6	Kevin RICHARDSON	
7	Ray HOUGHTON	
8	Garry PARKER	2, 86
9	Cyrille REGIS ‡	
10	Dalian ATKINSON	
11	Stephen FROGGATT	
	Substitutes	
12	Frank McAVENNIE	
14	Ugo EHIOGU ‡72	
Gk	Les SEALEY	

Date	Saturday 29 August 1992
Venue	The Dell, 3.00pm

SOUTHAMPTON (0) 2
MIDDLESBROUGH (0) 1

Attendance	13,003
Referee	Rodger GIFFORD
Linesmen	M.D. Dearing, B.A. Wiggington

SOUTHAMPTON
Red & White striped shirts, Black shorts   Goals

1	Tim FLOWERS	
2	Jason DODD ❑	
3	Micky ADAMS	
4	Terry HURLOCK	
5	Kenneth MONKOU	
6	Kevin MOORE	
7	Matthew LE TISSIER	80
8	Neil MADDISON	
9	Kerry DIXON	
10	David SPEEDIE	
11	Perry GROVES ‡	
	Substitutes	
12	Jeff KENNA	
14	Nicky BANGER ‡73	83
Gk	Ian ANDREWS	

MIDDLESBROUGH
Blue Shirts, Blue shorts   Goals

1	Ian IRONSIDE	
2	Chris MORRIS	
3	Jimmy PHILLIPS	
4	Alan KERNAGHAN	
5	Derek WHYTE	
6	Andy PEAKE	
7	Bernie SLAVEN	
8	Willie FALCONER	
9	Paul WILKINSON	75
10	Tommy WRIGHT	
11	Robbie MUSTOE	
	Substitutes	
12	Jon GITTENS	
14	Gary PARKINSON	
Gk	Brian HORNE	

Date	Sunday 30 August 1992
Venue	Portman Road, 4.00pm

IPSWICH TOWN (1) 1
TOTTENHAM HOTSPUR (1) 1

Attendance	20,100
Referee	Keith HACKETT
Linesmen	W.M. Jordan, D.C. Madgwick

IPSWICH TOWN
Blue & White shirts, White shorts   Goals

1	Craig FORREST	
2	Phil WHELAN ❑	
3	Neil THOMPSON	
4	Mick STOCKWELL	
5	John WARK	45
6	David LINIGHAN ❑	
7	Geraint WILLIAMS	
8	Paul GODDARD †	
9	Gavin JOHNSON	
10	Jason DOZZELL	
11	Chris KIWOMYA	
	Substitutes	
12	Simon MILTON †82	
14	Eddie YOUDS	
Gk	Jason WINTERS	

TOTTENHAM HOTSPUR
Yellow Shirts, Yellow shorts   Goals

1	Ian WALKER	
2	Dean AUSTIN	
3	Justin EDINBURGH	
4	Steve SEDGLEY	
5	Jason CUNDY	29
6	Neil RUDDOCK	
7	Darren ANDERTON	
8	Gordon DURIE	
9	Vinny SAMWAYS	
10	Teddy SHERINGHAM	
11	Paul ALLEN ‡	
	Substitutes	
12	Terry FENWICK	
14	Andy GRAY ‡79	
Gk	Erik THORSTVEDT	

Date   Monday 31 August 1992
Venue   Carrow Road, 7.45pm

NORWICH CITY (1) 3
NOTTINGHAM FOREST (1) 1

Attendance   14,104
Referee   Brian HILL
Linesmen   M.K. Bullivant, P.A. Josper

NORWICH CITY
Yellow shirts, Green shorts   Goals

1	Bryan GUNN	
2	Ian CULVERHOUSE	
3	Mark BOWEN	
4	Ian BUTTERWORTH	
5	Chris SUTTON	
6	Gary MEGSON	
7	Ian CROOK	2
8	Rob NEWMAN	
9	Lee POWER	76
10	Jeremy GOSS	
11	David PHILLIPS	89

Substitutes

12	Mark ROBINS
14	Daryl SUTCH
Gk	Mark WALTON

NOTTINGHAM FOREST
Red shirts, White shorts   Goals

1	Mark CROSSLEY	
2	Brian LAWS	
3	Stuart PEARCE	
4	Terry WILSON	
5	Steve CHETTLE	
6	Roy KEANE	
7	Thorvaldur ORLYGSSON	
8	Scot GEMMILL	
9	Nigel CLOUGH	31
10	Gary BANNISTER	
11	Kingsley BLACK	

Substitutes

12	Gary CROSBY
14	Carl TILER
Gk	Andy MARRIOTT

LEAGUE TABLE

Up to and including 31.08.92

		P	W	D	L	F	A	Pts
1	Norwich City	6	4	1	1	13	9	13
2	Blackburn Rovers	5	3	2	0	7	3	11
3	Queen's Park Rangers	5	3	1	1	8	5	10
4	Everton	5	2	3	0	6	2	9
5	Arsenal	5	3	0	2	8	6	9
6	Coventry City	5	3	0	2	6	5	9
7	Leeds United	5	2	2	1	11	8	8
8	Ipswich Town	5	1	4	0	6	5	7
9	Manchester United	5	2	1	2	5	6	7
10	Middlesbrough	4	2	0	2	8	5	6
11	Sheffield Wednesday	5	1	3	1	8	7	6
12	Aston Villa	5	1	3	1	5	4	6
13	Oldham Athletic	5	1	3	1	10	10	6
14	Chelsea	5	1	3	1	6	6	6
15	Manchester City	5	1	2	2	7	8	5
16	Liverpool	5	1	2	2	6	8	5
17	Southampton	5	1	2	2	4	6	5
18	Crystal Palace	5	0	4	1	8	9	4
19	Sheffield United	5	1	1	3	7	10	4
20	Nottingham Forest	5	1	0	4	5	12	3
21	Tottenham Hotspur	5	0	3	2	3	10	3
22	Wimbledon	5	0	2	3	4	7	2

LEADING SCORERS

David HIRST	Sheffield Wednesday	5
Eric CANTONA	Leeds United	4
Lee CHAPMAN	Leeds United	4
Brian DEANE	Sheffield United	4
David PHILLIPS	Norwich City	4
Alan SHEARER	Blackburn Rovers	4
David WHITE	Manchester City	4
Paul WILKINSON	Middlesbrough	4

LEAGUE GOALSCORING FIGURES

Running Totals

Date	Games	Goals	Average	Games	Goals	Average
15.08.92	9	27	3.00	9	27	3.00
16.08.92	1	1	1.00	10	28	2.80
17.08.92	1	2	2.00	11	30	2.73
18.08.92	2	7	1.00	13	32	2.46
19.08.92	9	23	2.55	22	55	2.50
22.08.92	10	38	3.80	32	93	2.91
23.08.92	1	2	2.00	33	95	2.88
24.08.92	1	1	1.00	34	96	2.82
25.08.92	5	16	3.20	39	112	2.87
26.08.92	4	7	1.75	43	119	2.77
29.08.92	10	26	2.60	53	145	2.74
30.08.92	1	2	2.00	54	147	2.72
31.08.92	1	4	4.00	55	151	2.75

Date Tuesday 1 September 1992
Venue Anfield, 7.30pm

LIVERPOOL (0) 1
SOUTHAMPTON (0) 1

Attendance 30,024
Referee Robbie HART
Linesmen J. McGrath, E.J. Walsh

LIVERPOOL
Red shirts, Red shorts   Goals

1	David JAMES	
2	Rob JONES	
3	David BURROWS	
4	Steve HARKNESS	
5	Ronnie WHELAN	
6	Mark WRIGHT	60
7	Steve McMANAMAN	
8	Jamie REDKNAPP †	
9	Ian RUSH	
10	Jan MOLBY	
11	Mark WALTERS	
	Substitutes	
12	Michael THOMAS †64	
14	Mike MARSH	
Gk	Mike HOOPER	

SOUTHAMPTON
Blue shirts, White shorts   Goals

1	Tim FLOWERS	
2	Jason DODD	
3	Micky ADAMS	
4	Terry HURLOCK	
5	Kenneth MONKOU	
6	Kevin MOORE	
7	Matthew LE TISSIER	
8	Neil MADDISON	
9	Kerry DIXON	51
10	David SPEEDIE	
11	Francis BENALI	
	Substitutes	
12	Jeff KENNA	
14	Nicky BANGER	
Gk	Ian ANDREWS	-

Date Tuesday 1 September 1992
Venue Ayresome Park, 7.30pm

MIDDLESBROUGH (0) 2
IPSWICH TOWN (1) 2

Attendance 14,255
Referee Bob NIXON
Linesmen D.S. Oliver, K.M. Lynch

MIDDLESBROUGH
Red shirts, White shorts   Goals

1	Ian IRONSIDE †	
2	Gary PARKINSON	
3	Jimmy PHILLIPS	
4	Alan KERNAGHAN	54
5	Derek WHYTE	
6	Andy PEAKE	
7	Bernie SLAVEN	
8	Willie FALCONER	
9	Paul WILKINSON	82
10	Tommy WRIGHT	
11	Robbie MUSTOE	
	Substitutes	
12	Jon GITTENS	
14	Graham KAVANAGH	
Gk	Brian HORNE †55	

IPSWICH TOWN
White shirts, Blue shorts   Goals

1	Craig FORREST	
2	Phil WHELAN	
3	Neil THOMPSON	
4	Mick STOCKWELL	
5	John WARK	26
6	David LINIGHAN ❑	
7	Geraint WILLIAMS	
8	Paul GODDARD	59
9	Gavin JOHNSON	
10	Jason DOZZELL	
11	Eddie YOUDS ❑	
	Substitutes	
12	Simon MILTON	
14	Glenn PENNYFATHER	
Gk	Clive BAKER	

Date	Tuesday 1 September 1992
Venue	Boundary Park, 7.30pm

OLDHAM ATHLETIC (0) 2
LEEDS UNITED (0) 2

Attendance	13,848
Referee	Keren BARRETT
Linesmen	R.H. Andrews, J. Leech

OLDHAM ATHLETIC
Blue shirts, Blue shorts   Goals

1	Jon HALLWORTH	
2	Steve REDMOND	
3	Neil POINTON ❏	
4	Paul BERNARD	
5	Richard JOBSON	
6	Ian MARSHALL	
7	Gunnar HALLE †	
8	Ian OLNEY	85, 90
9	Graeme SHARP	
10	Mike MILLIGAN	
11	Neil ADAMS	
	Substitutes	
12	Roger PALMER †76	
14	Craig FLEMING	
Gk	Ian GRAY	

LEEDS UNITED
White shirts, White shorts   Goals

1	John LUKIC	
2	Jon NEWSOME	
3	Tony DORIGO	
4	David BATTY ❏	
5	Chris FAIRCLOUGH	
6	Chris WHYTE	
7	Eric CANTONA †	53, 76
8	Rod WALLACE	
9	Lee CHAPMAN	
10	Gary McALLISTER	
11	Gary SPEED	
	Substitutes	
12	Steve HODGE †89	
14	Gordon STRACHAN	
Gk	Mervyn DAY	

Date	Tuesday 1 September 1992
Venue	Selhurst Park, 8.00pm

WIMBLEDON (0) 0
MANCHESTER CITY (0) 1

Attendance	4,714
Referee	Mike REED
Linesmen	M.G. Wright, W.J. Norbury

WIMBLEDON
Blue shirts, Blue shorts   Goals

1	Hans SEGERS	
2	Steve ANTHROBUS	
3	Brian McALLISTER	
4	Warren BARTON	
5	Dean BLACKWELL	
6	Scott FITZGERALD	
7	Paul MILLER ‡	
8	Robbie EARLE	
9	John FASHANU	
10	Lawrie SANCHEZ ❏	
11	Dean HOLDSWORTH	
	Substitutes	
12	Roger JOSEPH	
14	Andy CLARKE ‡67	
Gk	Neil SULLIVAN ˙	

MANCHESTER CITY
White shirts, White shorts   Goals

1	Tony COTON	
2	Ian BRIGHTWELL	
3	Terry PHELAN	
4	Peter REID ‡	
5	Keith CURLE	
6	Michel VONK ❏	
7	David WHITE	49
8	Garry FLITCROFT	
9	Niall QUINN	
10	Fitzroy SIMPSON	
11	Rick HOLDEN	
	Substitutes	
12	Mike SHERON	
14	Steve McMAHON ‡80	
Gk	Martyn MARGETSON	

Date	Wednesday 2 September 1992
Venue	Villa Park, 7.45pm

ASTON VILLA (1) 1
CHELSEA (2) 3

Attendance	19,125
Referee	Peter FOAKES
Linesmen	S.W. Dunn, A. Streets

ASTON VILLA
Claret & Blue shirts, White shorts   Goals

		Goals
1	Nigel SPINK	
2	Earl BARRETT ❑	
3	Steve STAUNTON ❑	
4	Shaun TEALE	
5	Paul McGRATH	
6	Kevin RICHARDSON	30
7	Ray HOUGHTON	
8	Garry PARKER	
9	Cyrille REGIS †	
10	Dalian ATKINSON	
11	Stephen FROGGATT	
	Substitutes	
12	Frank McAVENNIE †70	
14	Ugo EHIOGU	
Gk	Les SEALEY	

CHELSEA
Blue shirts, Blue shorts   Goals

		Goals
1	Dave BEASANT	
2	Steve CLARKE †	
3	Gareth HALL	
4	Vinnie JONES	
5	Paul ELLIOTT	
6	Mal DONAGHY	
7	Eddie NEWTON	42
8	Robert FLECK	40
9	Mick HARFORD	
10	Andy TOWNSEND	
11	Dennis WISE	57
	Substitutes	
12	David LEE †45	
14	Joe ALLON	
Gk	Nicky COLGAN	

Date	Wednesday 2 September 1992
Venue	Old Trafford, 8.00pm

MANCHESTER UNITED (0) 1
CRYSTAL PALACE (0) 0

Attendance	29,736
Referee	Vic CALLOW
Linesmen	A. Black, P. Newall

MANCHESTER UNITED
Red shirts, White shorts   Goals

		Goals
1	Peter SCHMEICHEL	
2	Clayton BLACKMORE	
3	Denis IRWIN	
4	Steve BRUCE	
5	Darren FERGUSON	
6	Gary PALLISTER	
7	Dion DUBLIN †	
8	Paul INCE	
9	Brian McCLAIR	
10	Mark HUGHES	88
11	Ryan GIGGS	
	Substitutes	
12	Andrei KANCHELSKIS †44	
14	Lee MARTIN	
Gk	Gary WALSH	

CRYSTAL PALACE
Yellow shirts, Light Blue shorts   Goals

		Goals
1	Nigel MARTYN	
2	Simon OSBORN	
3	Lee SINNOTT	
4	Gareth SOUTHGATE	
5	Eric YOUNG ❑	
6	Andy THORN	
7	Chris ARMSTRONG	
8	Geoff THOMAS ❑	
9	Mark BRIGHT	
10	John SALAKO †	
11	Eddie McGOLDRICK	
	Substitutes	
12	John HUMPHREY †87	
14	Chris COLEMAN	
Gk	Paul HEALD	

Date   Wednesday 2 September 1992
Venue   Loftus Road, 7,45pm

QPR (0) 0
ARSENAL (0) 0

Attendance 20,868
Referee   Ron GROVES
Linesmen   M. Stobbart, C. Jones

QPR
Blue & White hooped shirts, White shorts   Goals

1	Tony ROBERTS	
2	David BARDSLEY	
3	Clive WILSON	
4	Ray WILKINS ❑	
5	Darren PEACOCK	
6	Alan McDONALD	
7	Andy IMPEY	
8	Simon BARKER	
9	Les FERDINAND ❑	
10	Dennis BAILEY †	
11	Andy SINTON ❑	
	Substitutes	
12	Gary PENRICE †74	
14	Danny MADDIX	
Gk	Peter CALDWELL	

ARSENAL
Red & White shirts, White shorts   Goals

1	David SEAMAN	
2	Lee DIXON ❑	
3	Nigel WINTERBURN ❑	
4	David HILLIER ❑ †	
5	Steve BOULD	
6	Tony ADAMS	
7	John JENSEN	
8	Ian WRIGHT	
9	Kevin CAMPBELL	
10	Paul MERSON ‡	
11	Ray PARLOUR	
	Substitutes	
12	Colin PATES †78	
14	Alan SMITH ‡78	
Gk	Alan MILLER	

Date   Wednesday 2 September 1992
Venue   Hillsborough, 7.45pm

SHEFFIELD WEDNESDAY (0) 1
COVENTRY CITY (1) 2

Attendance 22,874
Referee   Rodger GIFFORD
Linesmen   N.S. Barry, T. Heilbron

SHEFFIELD WEDNESDAY
Blue & White stripes, Black shorts   Goals

1	Chris WOODS	
2	Roland NILSSON	
3	Paul WARHURST ❑ †	
4	Carlton PALMER	
5	Nigel PEARSON	
6	Peter SHIRTLIFF	
7	Nigel JEMSON ‡	
8	Chris BART-WILLIAMS	62
9	Chris WADDLE	
10	Paul WILLIAMS	
11	Nigel WORTHINGTON	
	Substitutes	
12	Danny WILSON †86	
14	Trevor FRANCIS ‡54	
Gk	Kevin PRESSMAN	

COVENTRY CITY
Red shirts, White shorts   Goals

1	Steve OGRIZOVIC	
2	Terry FLEMING †	
3	Kenny SANSOM	
4	Stewart ROBSON	
5	Andy PEARCE ❑	
6	Peter NDLOVU	42
7	Lloyd McGRATH	
8	Lee HURST ❑ ‡	49
9	Robert ROSARIO	
10	Kevin GALLACHER	
11	John WILLIAMS ❑	
	Substitutes	
12	Brian BORROWS †71	
14	Phil BABB ‡63	
Gk	Jonathan GOULD	

Date	Wednesday 2 September 1992
Venue	White Hart Lane, 7.45pm

TOTTENHAM HOTSPUR (1) 2
SHEFFIELD UNITED (0) 0

Attendance	21,322
Referee	Ian MITCHELL (sub G.PEARSON 72)
Linesmen	I.M.D. Mitchell, G.T. Pearson

TOTTENHAM HOTSPUR
White shirts, Navy Blue shorts   Goals

1	Ian WALKER	
2	Dean AUSTIN	
3	Pat VAN DEN HAUWE	
4	Steve SEDGLEY	
5	Jason CUNDY	
6	Neil RUDDOCK ❑	
7	Darren ANDERTON †	
8	Gordon DURIE	46
9	Vinny SAMWAYS ‡	
10	Teddy SHERINGHAM	43
11	Paul ALLEN	
	Substitutes	
12	Andy TURNER †79	
14	Andy GRAY ‡79	
Gk	Erik THORSTVEDT	

SHEFFIELD UNITED
Yellow shirts, White shorts   Goals

1	Simon TRACEY ❑ ■	
2	Kevin GAGE	
3	Tom COWAN	
4	John GANNON	
5	Brian GAYLE	
6	Paul BEESLEY	
7	Ian BRYSON †	
8	Paul ROGERS	
9	Adrian LITTLEJOHN	
10	Brian DEANE	
11	Glyn HODGES ‡ ❑	
	Substitutes	
12	Alan CORK †64	
14	Charlie HARTFIELD	
Gk	Alan KELLY ‡83	

Date	Saturday 5 September 1992
Venue	Villa Park, 3.00pm

ASTON VILLA (2) 3
CRYSTAL PALACE (0) 0

Attendance	17,120
Referee	Ken REDFERN
Linesmen	D.T. Colwell, J. McGrath

ASTON VILLA
Claret & Blue shirts, White shorts   Goals

1	Nigel SPINK	
2	Earl BARRETT	
3	Steve STAUNTON	42
4	Shaun TEALE	
5	Paul McGRATH	
6	Kevin RICHARDSON	
7	Ray HOUGHTON	
8	Garry PARKER	
9	Dwight YORKE †	18
10	Dalian ATKINSON	
11	Stephen FROGGATT	72
	Substitutes	
12	Frank McAVENNIE †79	
14	Ugo EHIOGU	
Gk	Les SEALEY	

CRYSTAL PALACE
Yellow shirts, Light Blue shorts   Goals

1	Nigel MARTYN	
2	John HUMPHREY †	
3	Lee SINNOTT	
4	Gareth SOUTHGATE	
5	Eric YOUNG	
6	Simon OSBORN ‡	
7	Chris ARMSTRONG	
8	Geoff THOMAS	
9	Mark BRIGHT	
10	John SALAKO	
11	Eddie McGOLDRICK	
	Substitutes	
12	Chris COLEMAN †58	
14	Stuart MASSEY ‡58	
Gk	Paul HEALD	

Date	Saturday 5 September 1992
Venue	Ewood Park, 3.00pm

BLACKBURN ROVERS (1) 4
NOTTINGHAM FOREST (1) 1

Attendance	16,180
Referee	Bob NIXON
Linesmen	J. Leech, P. Newall

BLACKBURN ROVERS
Blue & White shirts, White shorts   Goals

1	Bobby MIMMS	
2	David MAY	
3	Tony DOBSON †	
4	Tim SHERWOOD	
5	Colin HENDRY	
6	Kevin MORAN	
7	Stuart RIPLEY	
8	Mark ATKINS	52
9	Alan SHEARER	3, 59p
10	Mike NEWELL	
11	Alan WRIGHT	
	Substitutes	
12	Gordon COWANS	
14	Roy WEGERLE †81	
Gk	Matt DICKINS	

NOTTINGHAM FOREST
Red shirts, White shorts   Goals

1	Mark CROSSLEY	62og
2	Brian LAWS	
3	Stuart PEARCE ❑	
4	Carl TILER ❑	
5	Steve CHETTLE	
6	Roy KEANE	
7	Thorvaldur ORLYGSSON	
8	Scot GEMMILL	
9	Nigel CLOUGH	
10	Gary BANNISTER	15
11	Gary CROSBY	
	Substitutes	
12	Lee GLOVER	
14	Steve STONE	
Gk	Andy MARRIOTT	

Date	Saturday 5 September 1992
Venue	Anfield, 3.00pm

LIVERPOOL (1) 2
CHELSEA (0) 1

Attendance	34,199
Referee	John KEY
Linesmen	R.H. Andrews, T.A. Atkinson

LIVERPOOL
Red shirts, Red shorts   Goals

1	David JAMES	
2	Rob JONES	
3	David BURROWS	
4	Steve HARKNESS	
5	Ronnie WHELAN	
6	Mark WRIGHT	
7	Dean SAUNDERS	27
8	Jamie REDKNAPP	89
9	Ian RUSH	
10	Jan MOLBY	
11	Steve McMANAMAN †	
	Substitutes	
12	Mark WALTERS †73	
14	Mike MARSH	
Gk	Bruce GROBBELAAR	

CHELSEA
Blue shirts, Blue shorts   Goals

1	Dave BEASANT ❑	
2	David LEE	
3	Gareth HALL	
4	Vinnie JONES	
5	Paul ELLIOTT †	
6	Mal DONAGHY	
7	Eddie NEWTON	
8	Robert FLECK	
9	Mick HARFORD	72
10	Andy TOWNSEND	
11	Dennis WISE ❑	
	Substitutes	
12	Ian PEARCE †12 ❑	
14	Joe ALLON	
Gk	Nicky COLGAN	

Date	Saturday 5 September 1992
Venue	Ayresome Park, 3.00pm

MIDDLESBROUGH (1) 2
SHEFFIELD UNITED (0) 0

Attendance	15,179
Referee	Alf BUKSH
Linesmen	W. Nattrass, P. Pearson

MIDDLESBROUGH
Red shirts, White shorts   Goals

1	Brian HORNE	
2	Chris MORRIS ❑	
3	Jimmy PHILLIPS	
4	Alan KERNAGHAN	
5	Chris WHYTE	
6	Andy PEAKE	
7	Bernie SLAVEN	
8	Willie FALCONER	35
9	Paul WILKINSON ❑	
10	Tommy WRIGHT	83
11	Robbie MUSTOE	
	Substitutes	
12	Gary PARKINSON	
14	Jamie POLLOCK	
Gk	Andy COLLETT	

SHEFFIELD UNITED
Yellow shirts, Black shorts   Goals

1	Simon TRACEY	
2	Kevin GAGE	
3	David BARNES ❑	
4	John GANNON ‡	
5	Brian GAYLE	
6	Paul BEESLEY ❑	
7	Carl BRADSHAW	
8	Paul ROGERS	
9	Alan CORK †	
10	Brian DEANE	
11	Glyn HODGES	
	Substitutes	
12	Ian BRYSON †52	
14	Charlie HARTFIELD ‡82	
Gk	Alan KELLY	

Date	Saturday 5 September 1992
Venue	Carrow Road, 3.00pm

NORWICH CITY (0) 1
SOUTHAMPTON (0) 0

Attendance	12,452
Referee	Keith HACKETT
Linesmen	D.C. Madgwick, G. Butland

NORWICH CITY
Yellow shirts, Green shorts   Goals

1	Bryan GUNN	
2	Ian CULVERHOUSE	
3	Mark BOWEN	
4	Ian BUTTERWORTH †	
5	Chris SUTTON	
6	Gary MEGSON	
7	Ian CROOK	
8	Rob NEWMAN	
9	Lee POWER	
10	Jeremy GOSS	
11	David PHILLIPS	
	Substitutes	
12	Mark ROBINS †32	87
14	Daryl SUTCH	
Gk	Mark WALTON	

SOUTHAMPTON
Red & White striped shirts, Black shorts   Goals

1	Tim FLOWERS	
2	Jason DODD	
3	Francis BENALI	
4	Terry HURLOCK	
5	Kenneth MONKOU	
6	Kevin MOORE	
7	Matthew LE TISSIER	
8	Neil MADDISON	
9	Iain DOWIE	
10	David SPEEDIE ❑	
11	Perry GROVES	
	Substitutes	
12	Jeff KENNA	
14	Nicky BANGER	
Gk	Ian ANDREWS	

Date	Saturday 5 September 1992
Venue	Boundary Park, 3.00pm

OLDHAM ATHLETIC (0) 0
COVENTRY CITY (0) 1

Attendance	11,254
Referee	David ALLISON
Linesmen	J. Hilditch, S.W. Dunn

OLDHAM ATHLETIC
Blue shirts, Blue shorts   Goals

1	Jon HALLWORTH	
2	Steve REDMOND	
3	Neil POINTON	
4	Nick HENRY ‡	
5	Richard JOBSON	
6	Ian MARSHALL	
7	Gunnar HALLE †	
8	Ian OLNEY	
9	Graeme SHARP	
10	Mike MILLIGAN	
11	Paul BERNARD	
	Substitutes	
12	Roger PALMER †86	
14	Neil ADAMS ‡62	
Gk	Ian GRAY	

COVENTRY CITY
Red shirts, White shorts   Goals

1	Steve OGRIZOVIC	
2	Brian BORROWS	
3	Kenny SANSOM	
4	Stewart ROBSON	
5	Andy PEARCE	
6	Peter NDLOVU	
7	Lloyd McGRATH	
8	Lee HURST	
9	Robert ROSARIO ❑ †	
10	Kevin GALLACHER ‡	55
11	John WILLIAMS	
	Substitutes	
12	Phil BABB †57	
14	Terry FLEMING ‡82	
Gk	Jonathan GOULD	

Date	Saturday 5 September 1992
Venue	Loftus Road, 3.00pm

QPR (0) 0
IPSWICH TOWN (0) 0

Attendance	12,806
Referee	Dermot GALLAGHER
Linesmen	D.C. Richards, A. Black

QPR
Blue & White hooped shirts, White shorts   Goals

1	Jan STEJSKAL	
2	David BARDSLEY	
3	Clive WILSON	
4	Ray WILKINS	
5	Darren PEACOCK ❑	
6	Alan McDONALD	
7	Andy IMPEY	
8	Simon BARKER	
9	Les FERDINAND	
10	Dennis BAILEY †	
11	Andy SINTON	
	Substitutes	
12	Gary PENRICE †60	
14	Ian HOLLOWAY	
Gk	Tony ROBERTS	

IPSWICH TOWN
Black & Red striped shirts, Black shorts   Goals

1	Craig FORREST	
2	Phil WHELAN ❑	
3	Neil THOMPSON	
4	Mick STOCKWELL	
5	John WARK	
6	David LINIGHAN	
7	Geraint WILLIAMS	
8	Paul GODDARD ‡	
9	Gavin JOHNSON	
10	Jason DOZZELL	
11	Eddie YOUDS †	
	Substitutes	
12	Frank YALLOP †77	
14	Glenn PENNYFATHER ‡90	
Gk	Clive BAKER	

Date	Saturday 5 September 1992
Venue	Hillsborough, 3.00pm

SHEFFIELD WEDNESDAY (0) 0
MANCHESTER CITY (1) 3

Attendance	27,169
Referee	Ray BIGGER
Linesmen	D.S. Oliver, T. Lynch

SHEFFIELD WEDNESDAY
Blue & white striped shirts, Black shorts   Goals

1	Chris WOODS ❑	
2	Roland NILSSON ‡	
3	Danny WILSON †	
4	Carlton PALMER ❑	
5	Nigel PEARSON	
6	Paul WARHURST	
7	Gordon WATSON	
8	Chris BART-WILLIAMS	
9	Chris WADDLE	
10	Paul WILLIAMS	
11	Nigel WORTHINGTON	
	Substitutes	
12	Trevor FRANCIS †66	
14	John HARKES ‡41	
Gk	Kevin PRESSMAN	

MANCHESTER CITY
White shirts, White shorts   Goals

1	Tony COTON	
2	Ian BRIGHTWELL	
3	Terry PHELAN	
4	Peter REID †	
5	Keith CURLE	
6	Michel VONK ❑	75
7	David WHITE	20, 55
8	Garry FLITCROFT	
9	Mike SHERON	
10	Fitzroy SIMPSON	
11	Rick HOLDEN ❑	
	Substitutes	
12	Steve McMAHON †76	
14	Adie MIKE	
Gk	Martyn MARGETSON	

Date	Saturday 5 September 1992
Venue	White Hart Lane, 3.00pm

TOTTENHAM HOTSPUR (0) 2
EVERTON (1) 1

Attendance	26,303
Referee	Robbie HART
Linesmen	R.E. Budden, W.J. Norbury

TOTTENHAM HOTSPUR
White shirts, Navy Blue shorts   Goals

1	Ian WALKER	
2	Dean AUSTIN	
3	Pat VAN DEN HAUWE	
4	Andy GRAY ❑	
5	Jason CUNDY	
6	David TUTTLE	
7	Darren ANDERTON †	
8	Gordon DURIE	
9	Vinny SAMWAYS	
10	Teddy SHERINGHAM	
11	Paul ALLEN	79
	Substitutes	
12	Andy TURNER †54	90
14	Justin EDINBURGH	
Gk	Erik THORSTVEDT	

EVERTON
Blue shirts, White shorts   Goals

1	Neville SOUTHALL	
2	Alan HARPER	
3	Andy HINCHCLIFFE	
4	John EBBRELL	
5	Dave WATSON	
6	Gary ABLETT	
7	Robert WARZYCHA ‡	
8	Peter BEARDSLEY	42
9	Mo JOHNSTON †	
10	Barry HORNE ❑	
11	Mark WARD	
	Substitutes	
12	Stuart BARLOW ‡57	
14	Peter BEAGRIE ‡78	
Gk	Jason KEARTON	

Date	Saturday 5 September 1992
Venue	Selhurst Park, 3.00pm

WIMBLEDON (1) 3
ARSENAL (1) 2

Attendance	12,906
Referee	Keith BURGE
Linesmen	M.K. Bullivant, R.J. Harris

WIMBLEDON
Blue shirts, Blue shorts   Goals

1	Hans SEGERS	
2	Terry GIBSON	
3	Brian McALLISTER ‡	
4	Warren BARTON	
5	Dean BLACKWELL	
6	Scott FITZGERALD	
7	Dean HOLDSWORTH	
8	Robbie EARLE	86
9	John FASHANU	80
10	Lawrie SANCHEZ ❏	39
11	Andy CLARKE †	
	Substitutes	
12	Steve ANTHROBUS †90	
14	Neal ARDLEY ‡67	
Gk	Neil SULLIVAN	·

ARSENAL
Red & White shirts, White shorts   Goals

1	David SEAMAN	
2	Lee DIXON	
3	Nigel WINTERBURN	
4	Colin PATES	
5	Steve BOULD	
6	Tony ADAMS ‡	
7	John JENSEN †	
8	Ian WRIGHT	34, 82
9	Kevin CAMPBELL	
10	Paul MERSON	
11	Ray PARLOUR ❏	
	Substitutes	
12	David O'LEARY †48	
14	Alan SMITH ‡79	
Gk	Alan MILLER	

Date	Sunday 6 September 1992
Venue	Old Trafford, 4.00pm

MANCHESTER UNITED (2) 2
LEEDS UNITED (0) 0

Attendance	31,296
Referee	Philip DON
Linesmen	T.A. Atkinson, U.D. Rennie

MANCHESTER UNITED
Red shirts, White shorts   Goals

1	Peter SCHMEICHEL	
2	Clayton BLACKMORE	
3	Denis IRWIN	
4	Steve BRUCE	44
5	Darren FERGUSON	
6	Gary PALLISTER	
7	Andrei KANCHELSKIS	28
8	Paul INCE	
9	Brian McCLAIR	
10	Mark HUGHES	
11	Ryan GIGGS	
	Substitutes	
12	Lee MARTIN	
14	Danny WALLACE	
Gk	Gary WALSH	

LEEDS UNITED
White shirts, White shorts   Goals

1	John LUKIC	
2	Jon NEWSOME ❏ ‡	
3	Tony DORIGO	
4	David BATTY	
5	Chris FAIRCLOUGH ❏	
6	Chris WHYTE	
7	Eric CANTONA	
8	Rod WALLACE †	
9	Lee CHAPMAN	
10	Gary McALLISTER	
11	Gary SPEED	
	Substitutes	
12	Gordon STRACHAN †16	
14	Steve HODGE ‡68	
Gk	Mervyn DAY	

Date	Saturday 12 September 1992
Venue	Highbury Stadium, 3.00pm

ARSENAL (0) 0
BLACKBURN ROVERS (0) 1

Attendance	28,643
Referee	Mike REED
Linesmen	M.G. Wright, R.E. Budden

ARSENAL
Red & White shirts, White shorts   Goals

1	David SEAMAN	
2	Lee DIXON	
3	Nigel WINTERBURN	
4	Ian SELLEY ❑	
5	Steve BOULD	
6	Tony ADAMS ❑	
7	John JENSEN ❑ †	
8	Ian WRIGHT ❑	
9	Alan SMITH	
10	Paul MERSON	
11	Ray PARLOUR ‡	
	Substitutes	
12	Steve MORROW †85	
14	Kevin CAMPBELL ‡77	
Gk	Alan MILLER	

BLACKBURN ROVERS
Yellow shirts, Yellow shorts   Goals

1	Bobby MIMMS	
2	David MAY	
3	Tony DOBSON ❑	
4	Tim SHERWOOD	
5	Colin HENDRY	
6	Kevin MORAN	
7	Stuart RIPLEY †	
8	Mark ATKINS	
9	Alan SHEARER	
10	Mike NEWELL	71
11	Alan WRIGHT	
	Substitutes	
12	Chris PRICE †84	
14	Roy WEGERLE	
Gk	Matt DICKINS	

Date	Saturday 12 September 1992
Venue	Stamford Bridge, 3.00pm

CHELSEA (2) 2
NORWICH CITY (0) 3

Attendance	16,880
Referee	Keren BARRATT
Linesmen	G.T. Pearson, M. Stobbart

CHELSEA
Blue shirts, Blue shorts   Goals

1	Dave BEASANT	
2	Gareth HALL	
3	Anthony BARNESS	
4	Andy TOWNSEND †	29
5	David LEE	
6	Mal DONAGHY	
7	Eddie NEWTON	
8	Robert FLECK	
9	Mick HARFORD	2
10	Nigel SPACKMAN	
11	Dennis WISE	
	Substitutes	
12	Graham STUART †74	
14	John SPENCER	
Gk	Nicky COLGAN	

NORWICH CITY
Yellow shirts, Green shorts   Goals

1	Bryan GUNN	
2	Ian CULVERHOUSE	
3	Mark BOWEN	
4	John POLSTON	
5	Chris SUTTON	
6	Gary MEGSON	
7	Ian CROOK †	
8	Rob NEWMAN	
9	Mark ROBINS	46, 74
10	Jeremy GOSS	
11	David PHILLIPS	79
	Substitutes	
12	Daryl SUTCH †76	
14	Colin WOODTHORPE	
Gk	Mark WALTON	

Date	Saturday 12 September 1992
Venue	Selhurst Park, 3.00pm

CRYSTAL PALACE (0) 2
OLDHAM ATHLETIC (1) 2

Attendance	11,224
Referee	Brian HILL
Linesmen	G.P. Barber, K.J. Hawkes

CRYSTAL PALACE
Red & Blue striped shirts, Red shorts   Goals

1	Nigel MARTYN	
2	John HUMPHREY	
3	Lee SINNOTT	
4	Gareth SOUTHGATE	
5	Eric YOUNG	
6	Simon OSBORN	
7	Paul WILLIAMS	
8	Geoff THOMAS †	
9	Chris ARMSTRONG ❑	64, 66
10	John SALAKO	
11	Eddie McGOLDRICK	
	Substitutes	
12	Chris COLEMAN †45	
14	George NDAH	
Gk	Paul HEALD	

OLDHAM ATHLETIC
Blue shirts, Blue shorts   Goals

1	Jon HALLWORTH	
2	Steve REDMOND	
3	Neil POINTON	
4	Nick HENRY †	
5	Richard JOBSON	
6	Ian MARSHALL	
7	Gunnar HALLE	
8	Ian OLNEY	19
9	Graeme SHARP	78
10	Mike MILLIGAN	
11	Paul BERNARD	
	Substitutes	
12	Neil ADAMS †46	
14	Craig FLEMING	
Gk	John KEELEY	

Date	Saturday 12 September 1992
Venue	Goodison Park, 3.00pm

EVERTON (0) 0
MANCHESTER UNITED (1) 2

Attendance	30,002
Referee	Mike PECK
Linesmen	R.H. Andrews, A. Streets

EVERTON
Blue shirts, White shorts   Goals

1	Neville SOUTHALL	
2	Alan HARPER	
3	Andy HINCHCLIFFE	
4	John EBBRELL †	
5	Dave WATSON	
6	Gary ABLETT	
7	Robert WARZYCHA	
8	Peter BEARDSLEY	
9	Mo JOHNSTON	
10	Barry HORNE	
11	Mark WARD	
	Substitutes	
12	Peter BEAGRIE †70	
14	Matthew JACKSON	
Gk	Jason KEARTON	

MANCHESTER UNITED
Red shirts, White shorts   Goals

1	Peter SCHMEICHEL	
2	Denis IRWIN	
3	Clayton BLACKMORE	
4	Steve BRUCE	76p
5	Darren FERGUSON	
6	Gary PALLISTER	
7	Andrei KANCHELSKIS	
8	Paul INCE	
9	Brian McCLAIR	29
10	Mark HUGHES	
11	Ryan GIGGS	
	Substitutes	
12	Lee MARTIN	
14	Danny WALLACE	
Gk	Gary WALSH	

Date	Saturday 12 September 1992
Venue	Portman Road, 3.00pm

IPSWICH TOWN (1) 2
WIMBLEDON (1) 1

Attendance	13,333
Referee	Steve LODGE
Linesmen	M.D. Dearing, J.A. Elwin

IPSWICH TOWN
Blue & White shirts, White shorts   Goals

1	Craig FORREST	
2	Phil WHELAN	
3	Neil THOMPSON	
4	Mick STOCKWELL	14, 48
5	John WARK	
6	David LINIGHAN	
7	Geraint WILLIAMS	
8	Glenn PENNYFATHER	
9	Gavin JOHNSON	
10	Jason DOZZELL	
11	Frank YALLOP ❑	
	Substitutes	
12	Adam TANNER	
14	Neil GREGORY	
Gk	Clive BAKER	

WIMBLEDON
White shirts, Black shorts   Goals

1	Hans SEGERS	
2	Warren BARTON	
3	Roger JOSEPH †	
4	Vinnie JONES	
5	Dean BLACKWELL	
6	John SCALES	
7	Terry GIBSON ‡	
8	Robbie EARLE	
9	John FASHANU	
10	Dean HOLDSWORTH	27
11	Andy CLARKE	
	Substitutes	
12	Paul MILLER †76	
14	Scott FITZGERALD ‡83	
Gk	Neil SULLIVAN	

Date	Saturday 12 September 1992
Venue	Maine Road, 3.00pm

MANCHESTER CITY (0) 0
MIDDLESBROUGH (1) 1

Attendance	25,244
Referee	Ray LEWIS
Linesmen	P.D. Harding, S.W. Dunn

MANCHESTER CITY
Light Blue shirts, White shorts   Goals

1	Tony COTON	
2	Ian BRIGHTWELL	
3	Terry PHELAN	
4	Peter REID	
5	Keith CURLE	
6	Michel VONK ❑ ‡	
7	David WHITE	
8	Garry FLITCROFT	42og
9	Mike SHERON	
10	Fitzroy SIMPSON ❑	
11	Rick HOLDEN	
	Substitutes	
12	Andy HILL	
14	Adie MIKE ‡67	
Gk	Martyn MARGETSON	

MIDDLESBROUGH
White shirts, Black shorts   Goals

1	Brian HORNE	
2	Chris MORRIS ❑	
3	Jimmy PHILLIPS	
4	Alan KERNAGHAN	
5	Chris WHYTE ❑	
6	Andy PEAKE ❑	
7	Robbie MUSTOE	
8	Willie FALCONER	
9	Paul WILKINSON	
10	Tommy WRIGHT	
11	John HENDRIE	
	Substitutes	
12	Bernie SLAVEN	
14	Jon GITTENS	
Gk	Ian IRONSIDE	

Date	Saturday 12 September 1992
Venue	City Ground, 3.00pm

NOTTINGHAM FOREST (0) 1
SHEFFIELD WEDNESDAY (1) 2

Attendance	19,420
Referee	Gerald ASHBY
Linesmen	P.J. Robinson, G.R. Hamblin

NOTTINGHAM FOREST
Red shirts, White shorts   Goals

1	Mark CROSSLEY	
2	Brian LAWS	
3	Stuart PEARCE	
4	Steve CHETTLE	
5	Carl TILER	
6	Roy KEANE ‡	
7	Gary CROSBY	
8	Scot GEMMILL	
9	Nigel CLOUGH	
10	Gary BANNISTER	87
11	Kingsley BLACK	
	Substitutes	
	Lee GLOVER	
	Ray McKINNON ‡45	
Gk	Andy MARRIOTT	

SHEFFIELD WEDNESDAY
Blue & White striped shirts, Black shorts   Goals

1	Chris WOODS	
2	John HARKES	
3	Viv ANDERSON	
4	Carlton PALMER	
5	Peter SHIRTLIFF	
6	Paul WARHURST ‡	39
7	Graham HYDE	57
8	Chris WADDLE †	
9	Mark BRIGHT	
10	Chris BART-WILLIAMS	
11	Nigel WORTHINGTON	
	Substitutes	
	Danny WILSON †69	
	Gordon WATSON ‡86	
Gk	Kevin PRESSMAN	

Date	Saturday 12 September 1992
Venue	Bramall Lane, 3.00pm

SHEFFIELD UNITED (1) 1
LIVERPOOL (0) 0

Attendance	20,632
Referee	John MARTIN
Linesmen	N.S. Barry, T. Heilbron

SHEFFIELD UNITED
Red & White striped shirts, White shorts   Goals

1	Simon TRACEY	
2	Kevin GAGE ❏	
3	Tom COWAN	
4	John GANNON ‡	
5	Brian GAYLE	
6	Paul BEESLEY	
7	Carl BRADSHAW	
8	Paul ROGERS	
9	Adrian LITTLEJOHN	4
10	Brian DEANE ❏	
11	Dane WHITEHOUSE †	
	Substitutes	
	Ian BRYSON †71	
	Alan CORK ‡85	
Gk	Alan KELLY	

LIVERPOOL
Green shirts, Green shorts   Goals

1	David JAMES	
2	Steve HARKNESS	
3	David BURROWS ❏	
4	Steve NICOL	
5	Ronnie WHELAN †	
6	Mark WRIGHT	
7	Ronnie ROSENTHAL	
8	Paul STEWART	
9	Ian RUSH ❏	
10	Jamie REDKNAPP ‡	
11	Mark WALTERS ❏	
	Substitutes	
	Jan MOLBY †59	
	Mike MARSH ‡76	
Gk	Bruce GROBBELAAR	

Date   Saturday 12 September 1992
Venue   The Dell, 3.00pm

SOUTHAMPTON (1) 1
QPR (0) 2

Attendance 14,125
Referee   Allan GUNN
Linesmen   D.C. Richards, P.A. Josper

SOUTHAMPTON
Red & White striped shirts, Black shorts   Goals

1	Tim FLOWERS	
2	Jason DODD	
3	Francis BENALI	
4	Terry HURLOCK	
5	Kenneth MONKOU	
6	Kevin MOORE	
7	Matthew LE TISSIER	11
8	Neil MADDISON ‡	
9	Iain DOWIE ❏	
10	David SPEEDIE	
11	Perry GROVES	
	Substitutes	
12	Jeff KENNA	
14	Nicky BANGER ‡65	
Gk	Ian ANDREWS	

QPR
Blue & White striped shirts, White shorts   Goals

1	Jan STEJSKAL	
2	Justin CHANNING ‡	56
3	Clive WILSON	
4	Ray WILKINS	
5	Darren PEACOCK	
6	Alan McDONALD	
7	Andy IMPEY	
8	Simon BARKER ❏	
9	Les FERDINAND	
10	Gary PENRICE ❏	
11	Andy SINTON	53
	Substitutes	
12	Ian HOLLOWAY	
14	Danny MADDIX ‡89	
Gk	Tony ROBERTS	

Date   Sunday 13 September 1992
Venue   Elland Road, 4.00pm

LEEDS UNITED (0) 1
ASTON VILLA (1) 1

Attendance 27,815
Referee   Joe WORRALL
Linesmen   D.E. Binsley, G.T. Grandidge

LEEDS UNITED
White shirts, White shorts   Goals

1	John LUKIC	
2	Jon NEWSOME †	
3	Scott SELLARS	
4	David BATTY	
5	Chris FAIRCLOUGH	
6	Chris WHYTE	
7	Eric CANTONA	
8	Gordon STRACHAN	
9	Lee CHAPMAN	
10	Gary McALLISTER	
11	Gary SPEED	
	Substitutes	
12	Steve HODGE †68	85
14	David ROCASTLE	
Gk	Mervyn DAY	

ASTON VILLA
Claret & Blue shirts, White shorts   Goals

1	Nigel SPINK	
2	Earl BARRETT	
3	Steve STAUNTON	
4	Shaun TEALE	
5	Paul McGRATH	
6	Kevin RICHARDSON	
7	Ray HOUGHTON	
8	Garry PARKER	19
9	Dean SAUNDERS	
10	Dalian ATKINSON	
11	Stephen FROGGATT	
	Substitutes	
12	Dwight YORKE	
14	Ugo EHIOGU	
Gk	Les SEALEY	

Date	Monday 14 September 1992
Venue	Highfield Road, 7.45pm

COVENTRY CITY (0) 1
TOTTENHAM HOTSPUR (0) 0

Attendance	15,348
Referee	Martin BODENHAM
Linesmen	R.J. Harris, M.A. Riley

COVENTRY CITY
Sky Blue shirts, Sky Blue shorts   Goals

1	Steve OGRIZOVIC	
2	Brian BORROWS	
3	Kenny SANSOM	
4	Peter ATHERTON ❏	
5	Andy PEARCE	
6	Peter NDLOVU	
7	Lloyd McGRATH	
8	Lee HURST	
9	Robert ROSARIO	
10	Kevin GALLACHER	
11	John WILLIAMS ❏	61
	Substitutes	
12	Phil BABB	
14	Terry FLEMING	
Gk	Jonathan GOULD	

TOTTENHAM HOTSPUR
Yellow shirts, Yellow shorts   Goals

1	Ian WALKER	
2	Dean AUSTIN	
3	Pat VAN DEN HAUWE	
4	Andy GRAY	
5	Jason CUNDY	
6	Neil RUDDOCK	
7	Darren ANDERTON †	
8	Gordon DURIE	
9	Vinny SAMWAYS ‡	
10	Teddy SHERINGHAM	
11	Paul ALLEN	
	Substitutes	
12	Andy TURNER †63	
14	Steve SEDGLEY ‡71	
Gk	Erik THORSTVEDT	

Date	Tuesday 15 September 1992
Venue	Ewood Park, 7.30pm

BLACKBURN ROVERS (1) 2
EVERTON (2) 3

Attendance	19,563
Referee	David ALLISON
Linesmen	M. Fletcher, E.B. Crompton

BLACKBURN ROVERS
Blue & White shirts, White shorts   Goals

1	Bobby MIMMS	
2	David MAY	
3	Tony DOBSON †	
4	Tim SHERWOOD ‡	
5	Colin HENDRY ❏	
6	Kevin MORAN	
7	Stuart RIPLEY	
8	Mark ATKINS ❏	
9	Alan SHEARER	12p, 74
10	Mike NEWELL	
11	Alan WRIGHT	
	Substitutes	
12	Jason WILCOX †57	
14	Roy WEGERLE ‡71	
Gk	Matt DICKINS	

EVERTON
Salmon Pink & Blue stripes, Blue shorts   Goals

1	Neville SOUTHALL	
2	Alan HARPER	
3	Andy HINCHCLIFFE	
4	Barry HORNE	
5	Dave WATSON	
6	Gary ABLETT	
7	Mark WARD †	
8	Peter BEARDSLEY	
9	Paul RIDEOUT ‡	
10	Tony COTTEE	22, 81
11	John EBBRELL	39
	Substitutes	
12	Robert WARZYCHA †10	
14	Matthew JACKSON ‡46	
Gk	Jason KEARTON	

Date	Saturday 19 September 1992
Venue	Villa Park, 3.00pm

ASTON VILLA (1) 4
LIVERPOOL (1) 2

Attendance	37,863
Referee	Philip DON
Linesmen	E.J. Walsh, B.L. Polkey

ASTON VILLA
Claret & Blue shirts, White shorts   Goals

1	Nigel SPINK	
2	Earl BARRETT	
3	Steve STAUNTON	
4	Shaun TEALE	
5	Paul McGRATH	
6	Kevin RICHARDSON	
7	Ray HOUGHTON ❑	
8	Garry PARKER	78
9	Dean SAUNDERS	44,66
10	Dalian ATKINSON ❑	54
11	Stephen FROGGATT	
	Substitutes	
12	Dwight YORKE	
14	Dariusz KUBICKI	
Gk	Les SEALEY	

LIVERPOOL
Green shirts, Green shorts   Goals

1	David JAMES	
2	Torben PIECHNIK ❑	
3	David BURROWS	
4	Steve NICOL	
5	Jamie REDKNAPP	
6	Mark WRIGHT	
7	Ronnie ROSENTHAL	84
8	Mike MARSH	
9	Don HUTCHISON	
10	Jan MOLBY	
11	Mark WALTERS	43
	Substitutes	
12	Nick TANNER	
14	Steve HARKNESS	
Gk	Bruce GROBBELAAR	

Date	Saturday 19 September 1992
Venue	Goodison Park, 3.00pm

EVERTON (0) 0
CRYSTAL PALACE (2) 2

Attendance	18,080
Referee	Dermot GALLAGHER
Linesmen	U.D. Rennie, M.A. Cooper

EVERTON
Blue shirts, White shorts   Goals

1	Neville SOUTHALL	
2	Alan HARPER	
3	Andy HINCHCLIFFE	
4	John EBBRELL	
5	Dave WATSON	
6	Gary ABLETT	
7	Peter BEAGRIE	
8	Peter BEARDSLEY ‡	
9	Paul RIDEOUT †	
10	Tony COTTEE	
11	Barry HORNE	
	Substitutes	
12	Mo JOHNSTON †46	
14	Matthew JACKSON ‡58	
Gk	Jason KEARTON	

CRYSTAL PALACE
Red & Blue striped shirts, Red shorts   Goals

1	Nigel MARTYN	
2	John HUMPHREY	
3	Lee SINNOTT	
4	Gareth SOUTHGATE	
5	Eric YOUNG	
6	Simon OSBORN	
7	Paul WILLIAMS	
8	Chris COLEMAN	
9	Chris ARMSTRONG	8, 17
10	John SALAKO	
11	Eddie McGOLDRICK	
	Substitutes	
12	Darren PATTERSON	
14	Stan COLLYMORE	
Gk	Paul HEALD	

Date	Saturday 19 September 1992
Venue	Carrow Road, 3.00pm

NORWICH CITY (1) 1
SHEFFIELD WEDNESDAY (0) 0

Attendance	14,367
Referee	Bob NIXON
Linesmen	A. Schneider, M.G. Wright

NORWICH CITY
Yellow shirts, Green shorts · Goals

1	Bryan GUNN	
2	Ian CULVERHOUSE	
3	Mark BOWEN	
4	Ian BUTTERWORTH	
5	Chris SUTTON	
6	Gary MEGSON	
7	Ian CROOK	
8	Rob NEWMAN	44
9	Mark ROBINS	
10	Jeremy GOSS	
11	David PHILLIPS	
	Substitutes	
12	Daryl SUTCH	
14	Darren BECKFORD	
Gk	Mark WALTON	

SHEFFIELD WEDNESDAY
Blue & White striped shirts, Black shorts · Goals

1	Chris WOODS	
2	John HARKES	
3	Nigel WORTHINGTON	
4	Carlton PALMER	
5	Peter SHIRTLIFF	
6	Viv ANDERSON	
7	Danny WILSON	
8	Chris WADDLE	
9	Mark BRIGHT	
10	Chris BART-WILLIAMS	
11	Trevor FRANCIS †	
	Substitutes	
12	Nigel JEMSON †51 ‡	
14	Nigel PEARSON ‡79	
Gk	Kevin PRESSMAN	

Date	Saturday 19 September 1992
Venue	Boundary Park, 3.00pm

OLDHAM ATHLETIC (1) 4
IPSWICH TOWN (0) 2

Attendance	11,150
Referee	John KEY
Linesmen	P.R. Richards, P. Newall

OLDHAM ATHLETIC
Blue shirts, Blue shorts · Goals

1	Jon HALLWORTH	
2	Steve REDMOND	
3	Neil POINTON	
4	Nick HENRY	82
5	Richard JOBSON	
6	Ian MARSHALL	32
7	Gunnar HALLE	56
8	Ian OLNEY	
9	Graeme SHARP	53
10	Mike MILLIGAN	
11	Paul BERNARD	
	Substitutes	
12	Roger PALMER	
14	Neil ADAMS	
Gk	John KEELEY	

IPSWICH TOWN
Whitee shirts, White shorts · Goals

1	Craig FORREST	
2	Phil WHELAN	
3	Neil THOMPSON	88
4	Mick STOCKWELL	
5	John WARK	75
6	David LINIGHAN	
7	Eddie YOUDS	
8	Glenn PENNYFATHER	
9	Gavin JOHNSON	
10	Jason DOZZELL	
11	Chris KIWOMYA	
	Substitutes	
12	Frank YALLOP	
14	David GREGORY	
Gk	Clive BAKER	

Date	Saturday 19 September 1992
Venue	Loftus Road, 3.00pm

QPR (0) 3
MIDDLESBROUGH (1) 3

Attendance	12,272
Referee	Jim BORRETT
Linesmen	P. Rejer, W.M. Jordan

QPR
Blue & White hooped shirts, White shorts   Goals

1	Jan STEJSKAL	
2	Justin CHANNING	
3	Clive WILSON †	
4	Ray WILKINS	
5	Darren PEACOCK	
6	Alan McDONALD ‡	
7	Andy IMPEY	
8	Simon BARKER	
9	Les FERDINAND	57
10	Gary PENRICE	73
11	Andy SINTON	90p
	Substitutes	
12	Ian HOLLOWAY †17 ❏	
14	Danny MADDIX ‡31	
Gk	Tony ROBERTS	

MIDDLESBROUGH
Red shirts, Black shorts   Goals

1	Brian HORNE	
2	Chris MORRIS	
3	Jimmy PHILLIPS	
4	Alan KERNAGHAN	37
5	Chris WHYTE	
6	Jamie POLLOCK †	
7	John HENDRIE ❏	
8	Willie FALCONER	86
9	Paul WILKINSON	
10	Tommy WRIGHT	58
11	Robbie MUSTOE	
	Substitutes	
12	Bernie SLAVEN †35	
14	Jon GITTENS	
Gk	Ian IRONSIDE	

Date	Saturday 19 September 1992
Venue	Bramall Lane, 3.00pm

SHEFFIELD UNITED (1) 1
ARSENAL (0) 1

Attendance	19,105
Referee	Roger DILKES
Linesmen	D.S. Oliver, R.H. Andrews

SHEFFIELD UNITED
Red & White stripes, White shorts   Goals

1	Alan KELLY	
2	Kevin GAGE	
3	Tom COWAN	
4	John GANNON	
5	Brian GAYLE	
6	Paul BEESLEY ❏	
7	Carl BRADSHAW	
8	Paul ROGERS	
9	Adrian LITTLEJOHN	
10	Brian DEANE	
11	Dane WHITEHOUSE	48
	Substitutes	
12	Alan CORK	
14	Glyn HODGES	
Gk	Phil KITE	

ARSENAL
Yellow shirts, Blue shorts   Goals

1	David SEAMAN	
2	Lee DIXON	
3	Nigel WINTERBURN	
4	Ray PARLOUR	
5	Steve BOULD	
6	Tony ADAMS	
7	John JENSEN	
8	Ian WRIGHT	85
9	Alan SMITH	
10	Paul MERSON †	
11	Anders LIMPAR ‡	
	Substitutes	
12	Andy LINIGHAN †71	
14	Mark FLATTS ‡71	
Gk	Alan MILLER	

Date	Saturday 19 September 1992
Venue	The Dell, 3.00pm

SOUTHAMPTON (1) 1
LEEDS UNITED (0) 1

Attendance	16,229
Referee	Alf BUKSH
Linesmen	G.P. Barber, K.J. Hawkes

SOUTHAMPTON
Red & White striped shirts, Black shorts   Goals

1	Tim FLOWERS	
2	Jason DODD	
3	Francis BENALI	
4	Terry HURLOCK	
5	Richard HALL ‡	
6	Kevin MOORE	
7	Matthew LE TISSIER	
8	Nicky BANGER	
9	Kerry DIXON	
10	David SPEEDIE	
11	Perry GROVES †	43
	Substitutes	
12	Neil MADDISON †73	
14	Jeff KENNA ‡22	
Gk	Ian ANDREWS	

LEEDS UNITED
Blue shirts, Blue shorts   Goals

1	John LUKIC	
2	David WETHERALL †	
3	Tony DORIGO	
4	David BATTY	
5	Chris FAIRCLOUGH	
6	Chris WHYTE ❑	
7	Gordon STRACHAN	
8	Steve HODGE ‡	
9	Lee CHAPMAN	
10	Gary McALLISTER	
11	Gary SPEED	83
	Substitutes	
12	Carl SHUTT †79	
14	Scott SELLARS ‡58	
Gk	Mervyn DAY	

Date	Saturday 19 September 1992
Venue	White Hart Lane, 3.00pm

TOTTENHAM HOTSPUR (0) 1
MANCHESTER UNITED (1) 1

Attendance	33,296
Referee	Ron GROVES
Linesmen	M.K. Bullivant, P.A. Josper

TOTTENHAM HOTSPUR
White shirts, Navy Blue shorts   Goals

1	Ian WALKER	
2	Dean AUSTIN ‡	
3	Pat VAN DEN HAUWE	
4	Andy GRAY †	
5	Jason CUNDY	
6	Neil RUDDOCK	
7	Steve SEDGLEY	
8	Gordon DURIE ❑	52
9	Andy TURNER	
10	Teddy SHERINGHAM	
11	Paul ALLEN	
	Substitutes	
12	John HENDRY †62	
14	David TUTTLE ‡45	
Gk	Erik THORSTVEDT	

MANCHESTER UNITED
Red shirts, White shorts   Goals

1	Peter SCHMEICHEL	
2	Denis IRWIN	
3	Clayton BLACKMORE	
4	Steve BRUCE ❑	
5	Darren FERGUSON	
6	Gary PALLISTER	
7	Andrei KANCHELSKIS ‡	
8	Paul INCE	
9	Brian McCLAIR	
10	Mark HUGHES	
11	Ryan GIGGS	45
	Substitutes	
12	Lee MARTIN	
14	Danny WALLACE ‡74	
Gk	Gary WALSH	

Date	Saturday 19 September 1992
Venue	Selhurst Park, 3.00pm

WIMBLEDON (1) 1
BLACKBURN ROVERS (1) 1

Attendance	6,117
Referee	Martin BODENHAM
Linesmen	M.D. Dearing, G.T. Pearson

WIMBLEDON
Blue shirts, Blue shorts   Goals

1	Hans SEGERS	
2	Warren BARTON	
3	Gary ELKINS	
4	Vinnie JONES ❑ ■	
5	John SCALES	
6	Dean BLACKWELL †	
7	Neal ARDLEY	24
8	Robbie EARLE ❑	
9	John FASHANU	
10	Dean HOLDSWORTH	
11	Andy CLARKE	
	Substitutes	
12	Scott FITZGERALD †69	
14	Paul MILLER	
Gk	Neil SULLIVAN	

BLACKBURN ROVERS
Red & Black striped shirts, Black shorts   Goals

1	Bobby MIMMS	
2	David MAY	
3	Tony DOBSON ■	
4	Tim SHERWOOD ❑	
5	Colin HENDRY	
6	Kevin MORAN ❑	
7	Stuart RIPLEY †	
8	Mark ATKINS	
9	Alan SHEARER	32
10	Mike NEWELL ■	
11	Alan WRIGHT	
	Substitutes	
12	Keith HILL †45	
14	Roy WEGERLE	
Gk	Matt DICKINS	

Date	Sunday 20 September 1992
Venue	Maine Road, 4.00pm

MANCHESTER CITY (0) 0
CHELSEA (1) 1

Attendance	22,420
Referee	Keith HACKETT
Linesmen	J. Hilditch, T.J. Stevens

MANCHESTER CITY
Light Blue shirts, White shorts   Goals

1	Tony COTON	
2	Ian BRIGHTWELL	
3	Terry PHELAN	
4	Peter REID ‡	
5	Keith CURLE	
6	Andy HILL	
7	David WHITE	
8	Garry FLITCROFT	
9	Mike SHERON	
10	Fitzroy SIMPSON ❑	
11	Rick HOLDEN	
	Substitutes	
12	David BRIGHTWELL	
14	Adie MIKE ‡71	
Gk	Martyn MARGETSON	

CHELSEA
Blue shirts, Blue shorts   Goals

1	Kevin HITCHCOCK	
2	Gareth HALL ❑ †	
3	Frank SINCLAIR	
4	Andy TOWNSEND	
5	David LEE	
6	Mal DONAGHY	
7	Eddie NEWTON	
8	Robert FLECK ‡	
9	Mick HARFORD	40
10	Nigel SPACKMAN	
11	Dennis WISE	
	Substitutes	
12	Graham STUART †83	
14	John SPENCER ‡71	
Gk	Alec CHAMBERLAIN	

Date	Monday 21 September 1992
Venue	City Ground, 7.30pm

NOTTINGHAM FOREST (0) 1
COVENTRY CITY (1) 1

Attendance	17,553
Referee	Kelvin MORTON
Linesmen	N.S. Barry, P.M. Roberts

NOTTINGHAM FOREST
Red shirts, White shorts — Goals

1	Mark CROSSLEY	
2	Brian LAWS ❑	
3	Stuart PEARCE	
4	Ray McKINNON	
5	Carl TILER	
6	Roy KEANE	
7	Gary CROSBY	
8	Scot GEMMILL	
9	Nigel CLOUGH	69
10	Gary BANNISTER	
11	Thorvaldur ORLYGSSON ❑	
	Substitutes	
12	Lee GLOVER	
14	Kingsley BLACK	
Gk	Andy MARRIOTT	

COVENTRY CITY
Sky Blue shirts, Sky Blue shorts — Goals

1	Steve OGRIZOVIC	
2	Brian BORROWS	
3	Kenny SANSOM	
4	Peter ATHERTON	
5	Andy PEARCE	
6	Peter NDLOVU	
7	Lloyd McGRATH ❑	
8	Lee HURST	
9	Robert ROSARIO	45
10	Kevin GALLACHER	
11	John WILLIAMS	
	Substitutes	
12	Phil BABB	
14	Terry FLEMING	
Gk	Jonathan GOULD	

Date	Saturday 26 September 1992
Venue	Ewood Park, 3.00pm

BLACKBURN ROVERS (1) 2
OLDHAM ATHLETIC (0) 0

Attendance	18,383
Referee	Vic CALLOW
Linesmen	E. Lomas, U.D. Rennie

BLACKBURN ROVERS
Blue & White shirts, White shorts — Goals

1	Bobby MIMMS	
2	David MAY	
3	Alan WRIGHT	
4	Tim SHERWOOD †	
5	Colin HENDRY ❑	
6	Kevin MORAN	
7	Stuart RIPLEY	61
8	Mark ATKINS	
9	Alan SHEARER	30
10	Mike NEWELL	
11	Gordon COWANS	
	Substitutes	
12	Nicky MARKER †83	
14	Roy WEGERLE	
Gk	Matt DICKINS	

OLDHAM ATHLETIC
Green shirts, Green shorts — Goals

1	Jon HALLWORTH	
2	Steve REDMOND	
3	Neil POINTON	
4	Gunnar HALLE	
5	Richard JOBSON ❑	
6	Ian MARSHALL ❑	
7	Neil ADAMS	
8	Ian OLNEY	
9	Graeme SHARP	
10	Mike MILLIGAN	
11	Paul BERNARD	
	Substitutes	
12	Craig FLEMING	
14	Willie DONACHIE	
Gk	John KEELEY	

Date   Saturday 26 September 1992
Venue   Stamford Bridge, 3.00pm

CHELSEA (0) 0
NOTTINGHAM FOREST (0) 0

Attendance   19,760
Referee   Joe WORRALL
Linesmen   C. Jones, I.M.D. Mitchell

CHELSEA
Blue shirts, Blue shorts   Goals

1	Kevin HITCHCOCK	
2	Gareth HALL †	
3	Frank SINCLAIR	
4	Andy TOWNSEND	
5	David LEE	
6	Mal DONAGHY	
7	Eddie NEWTON	
8	Robert FLECK ‡	
9	Mick HARFORD	
10	Nigel SPACKMAN	
11	Dennis WISE	
	Substitutes	
12	Graham STUART †65	
14	John SPENCER ‡69	
Gk	Alec CHAMBERLAIN	

NOTTINGHAM FOREST
Red shirts, White shorts   Goals

1	Mark CROSSLEY	
2	Brian LAWS	
3	Stuart PEARCE	
4	Ray McKINNON	
5	Carl TILER	
6	Roy KEANE	
7	Gary CROSBY	
8	Scot GEMMILL	
9	Nigel CLOUGH	
10	Gary BANNISTER	
11	Thorvaldur ORLYGSSON	
	Substitutes	
12	Steve CHETTLE	
14	Lee GLOVER	
Gk	Andy MARRIOTT	

Date   Saturday 26 September 1992
Venue   Highfield Road, 3.00pm

COVENTRY CITY (1) 1
NORWICH CITY (1) 1

Attendance   16,436
Referee   Alf BUKSH
Linesmen   J. Leech, P. Newall

COVENTRY CITY
Sky Blue shirts, Sky Blue shorts   Goals

1	Steve OGRIZOVIC	
2	Brian BORROWS	
3	Kenny SANSOM ‡	
4	Peter ATHERTON	
5	Andy PEARCE	
6	Peter NDLOVU	37
7	Lloyd McGRATH	
8	Lee HURST	
9	Robert ROSARIO	
10	Kevin GALLACHER	
11	John WILLIAMS	
	Substitutes	
12	Terry FLEMING	
14	Phil BABB ‡78	
Gk	Jonathan GOULD	

NORWICH CITY
Yellow shirts, Green shorts   Goals

1	Bryan GUNN	
2	Ian CULVERHOUSE	
3	Mark BOWEN	
4	John POLSTON ❑	
5	Chris SUTTON ❑	
6	Daryl SUTCH	
7	Ian CROOK	13
8	Rob NEWMAN	
9	Mark ROBINS	
10	Jeremy GOSS	
11	David PHILLIPS	
	Substitutes	
12	Colin WOODTHORPE	
14	Darren BECKFORD	
Gk	Mark WALTON	

Date	Saturday 26 September 1992
Venue	Stamford Bridge, 3.00pm

CRYSTAL PALACE (0) 1
SOUTHAMPTON (1) 2

Attendance	13,829
Referee	Jim BORRETT
Linesmen	W.M. Jordan, P. Rejer

CRYSTAL PALACE
Red & Blue striped shirts, Red shorts   Goals

1	Nigel MARTYN	
2	John HUMPHREY ‡	
3	Lee SINNOTT	
4	Gareth SOUTHGATE	
5	Eric YOUNG ❏	54
6	Simon OSBORN	
7	Paul WILLIAMS	
8	Chris COLEMAN	
9	Chris ARMSTRONG	
10	John SALAKO	
11	Eddie McGOLDRICK	
	Substitutes	
12	Darren PATTERSON	
14	Stan COLLYMORE ‡82	
Gk	Paul HEALD	

SOUTHAMPTON
Yellow shirts, White shorts   Goals

1	Tim FLOWERS	
2	Jason DODD	
3	Francis BENALI ❏	
4	Tommy WIDDRINGTON ❏ †	
5	Kenneth MONKOU	
6	Kevin MOORE	
7	Matthew LE TISSIER	
8	Perry GROVES ❏	
9	Iain DOWIE ❏	44, 88
10	David SPEEDIE	
11	Micky ADAMS	
	Substitutes	
12	Neil MADDISON †78	
14	Nicky BANGER	
Gk	Ian ANDREWS	

Date	Saturday 26 September 1992
Venue	Portman Road, 3.00pm

IPSWICH TOWN (0) 0
SHEFFIELD UNITED (0) 0

Attendance	16,353
Referee	Ron GROVES
Linesmen	W.J. Norbury, A. Schneider

IPSWICH TOWN
Blue & White shirts, White shorts   Goals

1	Craig FORREST ■	
2	Phil WHELAN	
3	Neil THOMPSON	
4	Mick STOCKWELL	
5	John WARK	
6	David LINIGHAN	
7	Eddie YOUDS †	
8	Geraint WILLIAMS ❏	
9	Gavin JOHNSON	
10	Jason DOZZELL	
11	Chris KIWOMYA ❏	
	Substitutes	
12	Paul GODDARD	
14	Glenn PENNYFATHER	
Gk	Clive BAKER †3	

SHEFFIELD UNITED
Yellow shirts, Red shorts   Goals

1	Alan KELLY	
2	Kevin GAGE	
3	Tom COWAN	
4	John GANNON	
5	Brian GAYLE ❏	
6	Paul BEESLEY	
7	Carl BRADSHAW ❏ †	
8	Paul ROGERS ❏	
9	Adrian LITTLEJOHN ❏	
10	Brian DEANE	
11	Dane WHITEHOUSE ‡	
	Substitutes	
12	Charlie HARTFIELD †89	
14	Alan CORK ‡69	
Gk	Phil KITE	

Date	Saturday 26 September 1992
Venue	Elland Road, 3.00pm

LEEDS UNITED (0) 2
EVERTON (0) 0

Attendance	27,915
Referee	Ken REDFERN
Linesmen	P.D. Harding, D.S. Oliver

LEEDS UNITED
White shirts, White shorts   Goals

1	John LUKIC	
2	Scott SELLARS †	
3	Tony DORIGO	
4	David BATTY	
5	Chris FAIRCLOUGH	
6	Chris WHYTE	
7	Gordon STRACHAN	
8	Eric CANTONA	
9	Lee CHAPMAN	63
10	Gary McALLISTER	61p
11	Gary SPEED	
	Substitutes	
12	Carl SHUTT †87	
14	Jon NEWSOME	
Gk	Mervyn DAY	

EVERTON
Blue shirts, Blue shorts   Goals

1	Neville SOUTHALL	
2	Alan HARPER	
3	Andy HINCHCLIFFE	
4	John EBBRELL	
5	Dave WATSON	
6	Gary ABLETT	
7	Robert WARZYCHA †	
8	Barry HORNE	
9	David UNSWORTH ‡	
10	Tony COTTEE	
11	PREKI	
	Substitutes	
12	Mo JOHNSTON †39	
14	Peter BEAGRIE ‡78	
Gk	Jason KEARTON	

Date	Saturday 26 September 1992
Venue	Anfield, 3.00pm

LIVERPOOL (2) 2
WIMBLEDON (2) 3

Attendance	29,574
Referee	Roger MILFORD
Linesmen	T.A. Atkinson, G.R. Hamblin

LIVERPOOL
Red shirts, Red shorts   Goals

1	Bruce GROBBELAAR	
2	Mike MARSH	
3	David BURROWS	
4	Torben PIECHNIK	
5	Jamie REDKNAPP	
6	Mark WRIGHT ❑	
7	Ronnie ROSENTHAL	
8	Steve McMANAMAN	39
9	Don HUTCHISON	
10	Jan MOLBY	35p
11	Mark WALTERS †	
	Substitutes	
12	Istvan KOZMA †83	
14	Nick TANNER	
Gk	David JAMES	

WIMBLEDON
Blue shirts, Blue shorts   Goals

1	Hans SEGERS	
2	Warren BARTON	
3	Justin SKINNER	
4	Vinnie JONES	
5	John SCALES ❑	
6	Scott FITZGERALD	
7	Neal ARDLEY ‡	
8	Robbie EARLE	27, 76
9	John FASHANU	12
10	Dean HOLDSWORTH †	
11	Andy CLARKE ❑	
	Substitutes	
12	Lawrie SANCHEZ †49 ❑	
14	Paul MILLER ‡75	
Gk	Neil SULLIVAN	

Date	Saturday 26 September 1992
Venue	Old Trafford, 3.00pm

MANCHESTER UNITED (0) 0
QPR (0) 0

Attendance	33,287
Referee	David ALLISON
Linesmen	M. Alexander, B. Lowe

MANCHESTER UNITED
Red shirts, White shorts   Goals

1	Peter SCHMEICHEL
2	Denis IRWIN
3	Clayton BLACKMORE
4	Steve BRUCE
5	Darren FERGUSON
6	Gary PALLISTER
7	Andrei KANCHELSKIS ‡
8	Paul INCE ❏
9	Brian McCLAIR
10	Mark HUGHES
11	Ryan GIGGS
	Substitutes
12	Lee MARTIN
14	Danny WALLACE ‡77
Gk	Gary WALSH

QPR
Blue & White hooped shirts, Blue shorts   Goals

1	Jan STEJSKAL
2	David BARDSLEY
3	Rufus BREVETT
4	Ray WILKINS
5	Darren PEACOCK
6	Danny MADDIX
7	Andy IMPEY
8	Ian HOLLOWAY
9	Les FERDINAND †
10	Gary PENRICE
11	Andy SINTON
	Substitutes
12	Simon BARKER †53
14	Justin CHANNING
Gk	Tony ROBERTS

Date	Saturday 26 September 1992
Venue	Ayresome Park, 3.00pm

MIDDLESBROUGH (0) 2
ASTON VILLA (1) 3

Attendance	20,905
Referee	David ELLERAY
Linesmen	J.B. Robinson, A. Butler

MIDDLESBROUGH
Red shirts, White shorts   Goals

1	Ian IRONSIDE	
2	Chris MORRIS ❏	
3	Jimmy PHILLIPS	
4	Alan KERNAGHAN ❏	
5	Derek WHYTE	
6	Andy PEAKE	
7	Bernie SLAVEN	62
8	Robbie MUSTOE	
9	Paul WILKINSON	
10	Jamie POLLOCK	
11	Tommy WRIGHT	
	Substitutes	
12	Mark PROCTOR	
14	Jon GITTENS	
Gk	Andy COLLETT	

ASTON VILLA
White shirts, Black shorts   Goals

1	Nigel SPINK	
2	Earl BARRETT	
3	Steve STAUNTON	
4	Shaun TEALE	
5	Paul McGRATH	86og
6	Kevin RICHARDSON	
7	Ray HOUGHTON	
8	Garry PARKER ‡	
9	Dean SAUNDERS	22, 74
10	Dalian ATKINSON	71
11	Stephen FROGGATT †	
	Substitutes	
12	Dwight YORKE †70	
14	Mark BLAKE ‡88	
Gk	Les SEALEY	

Date	Sunday 27 September 1992
Venue	Hillsborough, 4.00pm

SHEFFIELD WEDNESDAY (2) 2
TOTTENHAM HOTSPUR (0) 0

Attendance	24,895
Referee	Mike PECK
Linesmen	G.T. Grandidge, M. Warren

SHEFFIELD WEDNESDAY
Blue & White striped shirts, Black shorts   Goals

1	Chris WOODS	
2	John HARKES	
3	Nigel WORTHINGTON	
4	Carlton PALMER	
5	Peter SHIRTLIFF ❏	
6	Viv ANDERSON	32
7	Roland NILSSON ‡	
8	Chris WADDLE	
9	Mark BRIGHT	6
10	Chris BART-WILLIAMS	
11	Gordon WATSON	
	Substitutes	
12	Nigel JEMSON	
14	Danny WILSON ‡76	
Gk	Kevin PRESSMAN	

TOTTENHAM HOTSPUR
Yellow shorts, Yellow shirts   Goals

1	Ian WALKER	
2	Dean AUSTIN ‡	
3	Pat VAN DEN HAUWE	
4	Andy TURNER †	
5	Jason CUNDY	
6	David TUTTLE	
7	Steve SEDGLEY ❏	
8	Nick BARMBY	
9	Darren ANDERTON	
10	Teddy SHERINGHAM	
11	Paul ALLEN	
	Substitutes	
12	Kevin WATSON †67	
14	Justin EDINBURGH ‡67	
Gk	Erik THORSTVEDT	

Date	Monday 28 September 1992
Venue	Highbury Stadium, 7.45pm

ARSENAL (1) 1
MANCHESTER CITY (0) 0

Attendance	21,504
Referee	John MARTIN
Linesmen	B. Wiggington, M.G. Wright

ARSENAL
Red & White shirts, White shorts   Goals

1	David SEAMAN	
2	Lee DIXON	
3	Nigel WINTERBURN	
4	David HILLIER	
5	Steve BOULD	
6	Tony ADAMS	
7	John JENSEN	
8	Ian WRIGHT	19
9	Alan SMITH ‡	
10	Paul MERSON	
11	Kevin CAMPBELL	
	Substitutes	
12	Colin PATES	
14	Anders LIMPAR ‡75 ❏	
Gk	Alan MILLER	

MANCHESTER CITY
Light Blue shirts, Light Blue shorts   Goals

1	Tony COTON	
2	Ian BRIGHTWELL	
3	Terry PHELAN	
4	Peter REID	
5	Keith CURLE	
6	Andy HILL	
7	David WHITE	
8	Garry FLITCROFT ❏	
9	Niall QUINN	
10	Fitzroy SIMPSON	
11	Rick HOLDEN †	
	Substitutes	
12	Steve McMAHON †62	
14	David BRIGHTWELL	
Gk	Martyn MARGETSON	

LEAGUE TABLE

Up to and including 28.09.92

		P	W	D	L	F	A	Pts
1	Norwich City	10	7	2	1	19	12	23
2	Blackburn Rovers	10	6	3	1	17	8	21
3	Coventry City	10	6	2	2	12	8	20
4	Manchester United	10	5	3	2	11	7	18
5	Queen's Park Rangers	10	4	5	1	13	9	17
6	Aston Villa	10	4	4	2	17	12	16
7	Middlesbrough	9	4	2	3	18	13	14
8	Leeds United	10	3	5	2	17	14	14
9	Arsenal	10	4	2	4	12	11	14
10	Chelsea	10	3	4	3	13	12	13
11	Ipswich Town	10	2	7	1	12	12	13
12	Sheffield Wednesday	10	3	3	4	13	14	12
13	Everton	10	3	3	4	10	12	12
14	Manchester City	10	3	2	5	11	11	11
15	Oldham Athletic	10	2	5	3	18	19	11
16	Southampton	10	2	4	4	9	12	10
17	Tottenham Hotspur	10	2	4	4	8	15	10
18	Wimbledon	10	2	3	5	12	15	9
19	Liverpool	10	2	3	5	13	18	9
20	Sheffield United	10	2	3	5	9	15	9
21	Crystal Palace	10	1	5	4	13	17	8
22	Nottingham Forest	9	1	2	6	8	19	5

LEADING SCORERS

Alan SHEARER	Blackburn Rovers	10
David WHITE	Manchester City	7
Eric CANTONA	Leeds United	6
Mark ROBINS	Norwich City	6
Ian WRIGHT	Arsenal	6

LEAGUE GOALSCORING FIGURES

Running Totals

Date	Games	Goals	Average	Games	Goals	Average
01.09.92	4	11	2.75	59	162	2.75
02.09.92	5	10	2.00	64	172	2.69
05.09.92	10	26	2.60	74	198	2.68
06.09.92	1	2	2.00	75	200	2.67
12.09.92	9	23	2.56	84	223	2.65
13.09.92	1	2	2.00	85	225	2.65
14.09.92	1	1	1.00	86	226	2.63
15.09.92	1	5	5.00	87	231	2.66
19.09.92	9	29	3.22	96	260	2.71
20.09.92	1	1	1.00	97	261	2.69
21.09.92	1	2	2.00	98	263	2.68
26.09.92	9	19	2.11	107	282	2.63
27.09.92	1	2	2.00	108	284	2.63
28.09.92	1	1	1.00	109	285	2.61

Date	Saturday 3 October 1992
Venue	Highbury Stadium, 3.00pm

ARSENAL (1) 2
CHELSEA (0) 1

Attendance	27,780
Referee	Kelvin MORTON
Linesmen	I.A. Madge, G.T. Pearson

ARSENAL
Red & White shirts, White shorts

Goals

1	David SEAMAN	
2	Lee DIXON	
3	Nigel WINTERBURN	
4	David HILLIER	
5	Steve BOULD	
6	Tony ADAMS	
7	John JENSEN	
8	Ian WRIGHT	85
9	Alan SMITH	
10	Paul MERSON ‡	10
11	Kevin CAMPBELL	
	Substitutes	
12	Colin PATES	
14	Anders LIMPAR ‡84	
Gk	Alan MILLER	

CHELSEA
Blue shirts, Blue shorts

Goals

1	Kevin HITCHCOCK	
2	Gareth HALL ❑	
3	Frank SINCLAIR	
4	Andy TOWNSEND	
5	David LEE ❑	
6	Mal DONAGHY †	
7	Eddie NEWTON	
8	Robert FLECK	
9	Mick HARFORD ❑	
10	Nigel SPACKMAN	
11	Dennis WISE ❑	79
	Substitutes	
12	Graham STUART †19	
14	John SPENCER	
Gk	Alec CHAMBERLAIN	

Date	Saturday 3 October 1992
Venue	Ewood Park, 3.00pm

BLACKBURN ROVERS (4) 7
NORWICH CITY (1) 1

Attendance 16,312
Referee Roger DILKES
Linesmen J. McGrath, M. Warren

BLACKBURN ROVERS
Blue & White shirts, White shorts   Goals

1	Bobby MIMMS	
2	Richard BROWN	
3	Alan WRIGHT	
4	Tim SHERWOOD	27
5	Colin HENDRY	
6	Kevin MORAN †	
7	Stuart RIPLEY ‡	70
8	Mark ATKINS	
9	Alan SHEARER ❑	43,76
10	Roy WEGERLE	8, 32
11	Gordon COWANS	63
	Substitutes	
12	Nicky MARKER †79	
14	Jason WILCOX ‡79	
Gk	Darren COLLIER	

NORWICH CITY
Yellow shirts, Green shorts   Goals

1	Bryan GUNN	
2	Ian CULVERHOUSE	
3	Mark BOWEN	
4	Ian BUTTERWORTH	
5	Chris SUTTON ❑	
6	Daryl SUTCH	
7	Ian CROOK	
8	Rob NEWMAN	39
9	Mark ROBINS	
10	Jeremy GOSS	
11	David PHILLIPS ‡	
	Substitutes	
12	John POLSTON	
14	Lee POWER ‡63	
Gk	Mark WALTON	

Date	Saturday 3 October 1992
Venue	Highfield Road, 3.00pm

COVENTRY CITY (2) 2
CRYSTAL PALACE (2) 2

Attendance 11,808
Referee Gerald ASHBY
Linesmen R.H. Andrews, U.D. Rennie

COVENTRY CITY
Sky Blue shirts, Sky Blue shorts   Goals

1	Steve OGRIZOVIC	
2	Brian BORROWS	
3	Kenny SANSOM	
4	Peter ATHERTON	
5	Andy PEARCE	7
6	Peter NDLOVU	
7	Lloyd McGRATH	
8	Lee HURST	
9	Robert ROSARIO ❑ †	
10	Kevin GALLACHER	18
11	John WILLIAMS	
	Substitutes	
12	Terry FLEMING †89	
14	Phil BABB	
Gk	Jonathan GOULD	

CRYSTAL PALACE
Red & Blue striped shirts, Red shorts   Goals

1	Nigel MARTYN	
2	Richard SHAW	
3	Lee SINNOTT ❑	
4	Gareth SOUTHGATE	
5	Eric YOUNG	
6	Simon OSBORN	
7	Paul WILLIAMS	
8	Chris COLEMAN	8
9	Chris ARMSTRONG	
10	John SALAKO	
11	Eddie McGOLDRICK ❑	38
	Substitutes	
12	Geoff THOMAS	
14	Stan COLLYMORE	
Gk	Paul HEALD	

Date	Saturday 3 October 1992
Venue	Portman Road, 3.00pm

IPSWICH TOWN (3) 4
LEEDS UNITED (0) 2

Attendance	21,200
Referee	David ELLERAY
Linesmen	M.K. Bullivant, J.A. Elwin

IPSWICH TOWN
Blue & White shirts, White shorts   Goals

1	Craig FORREST	
2	Phil WHELAN	
3	Neil THOMPSON	
4	Mick STOCKWELL	
5	John WARK	36, 44p
6	David LINIGHAN	
7	Geraint WILLIAMS	
8	Paul GODDARD	
9	Gavin JOHNSON	
10	Jason DOZZELL	70
11	Chris KIWOMYA	25
	Substitutes	
12	Eddie YOUDS	
14	Glenn PENNYFATHER	
Gk	Clive BAKER	

LEEDS UNITED
Yellow shirts, Yellow shorts   Goals

1	John LUKIC	
2	Scott SELLARS †	
3	Tony DORIGO	
4	David BATTY ❑	
5	Chris FAIRCLOUGH	
6	Chris WHYTE	
7	Gordon STRACHAN	
8	Eric CANTONA	
9	Lee CHAPMAN	55
10	Gary McALLISTER	
11	Gary SPEED	64
	Substitutes	
12	David ROCASTLE †71	
14	Jon NEWSOME	
Gk	Mervyn DAY	

Date	Saturday 3 October 1992
Venue	Anfield, 3.00pm

LIVERPOOL (0) 1
SHEFFIELD WEDNESDAY (0) 0

Attendance	35,785
Referee	Martin BODENHAM
Linesmen	M.A. Riley, M. Fletcher

LIVERPOOL
Red shirts, Red shorts   Goals

1	Bruce GROBBELAAR	
2	Mike MARSH	
3	David BURROWS	
4	Steve NICOL	
5	Torben PIECHNIK	
6	Don HUTCHISON	80
7	Steve McMANAMAN	
8	Paul STEWART ❑ †	
9	Ian RUSH	
10	Jamie REDKNAPP	
11	Mark WALTERS	
	Substitutes	
12	Ronnie ROSSENTHAL †51	
14	Nick TANNER	
Gk	David JAMES	

SHEFFIELD WEDNESDAY
Blue & White shirts, Black shorts   Goals

1	Chris WOODS	
2	John HARKES	
3	Nigel WORTHINGTON	
4	Carlton PALMER ❑	
5	Peter SHIRTLIFF	
6	Viv ANDERSON	
7	Roland NILSSON	
8	Chris WADDLE	
9	Mark BRIGHT	
10	Chris BART-WILLIAMS ‡	
11	Paul WARHURST ❑ †	
	Substitutes	
12	Graham HYDE †74	
14	Gordon WATSON ‡88	
Gk	Kevin PRESSMAN	

Date	Saturday 3 October 1992
Venue	Maine Road, 3.00pm

MANCHESTER CITY (1) 2
NOTTINGHAM FOREST (0) 2

Attendance	22,571
Referee	Roger MILFORD
Linesmen	P. Rejer, S.W. Dunn

MANCHESTER CITY
Light Blue shirts, White shorts   Goals

1	Tony COTON	
2	Ian BRIGHTWELL	
3	Terry PHELAN	
4	Steve McMAHON †	
5	Keith CURLE ❑	
6	Andy HILL	
7	David WHITE	
8	Mike SHERON	
9	Niall QUINN	
10	Fitzroy SIMPSON ❑	64
11	Rick HOLDEN	17
	Substitutes	
12	Peter REID †54	
14	Adie MIKE	
Gk	Martyn MARGETSON	

NOTTINGHAM FOREST
Red shirts, Red shorts   Goals

1	Mark CROSSLEY	
2	Brian LAWS ❑	
3	Stuart PEARCE	83
4	Ray McKINNON	56
5	Carl TILER	
6	Roy KEANE	
7	Gary CROSBY	
8	Scot GEMMILL	
9	Nigel CLOUGH	
10	Gary BANNISTER	
11	Thorvaldur ORLYGSSON	
	Substitutes	
12	Steve CHETTLE	
14	Lee GLOVER	
Gk	Andy MARRIOTT	

Date	Saturday 3 October 1992
Venue	Ayresome Park, 3.00pm

MIDDLESBROUGH (0) 1
MANCHESTER UNITED (1) 1

Attendance	24,172
Referee	Mike REED
Linesmen	B. Lowe, R. Pearson

MIDDLESBROUGH
Red shirts, White shorts   Goals

1	Ian IRONSIDE	
2	Chris MORRIS	
3	Jimmy PHILLIPS	
4	Jon GITTENS	
5	Derek WHYTE	
6	Andy PEAKE	
7	Bernie SLAVEN	59
8	Robbie MUSTOE	
9	Paul WILKINSON	
10	Tommy WRIGHT	
11	Jamie POLLOCK ‡	
	Substitutes	
12	Mark PROCTOR	
14	John HENDRIE ‡53 ❑	
Gk	Stephen PEARS	

● *Alan KERNAGHAN injured warming-up before game.*

MANCHESTER UNITED
Blue shirts, Blue shorts   Goals

1	Peter SCHMEICHEL	
2	Denis IRWIN	
3	Mike PHELAN ❑ ‡	
4	Steve BRUCE	43p
5	Darren FERGUSON	
6	Gary PALLISTER ❑	
7	Clayton BLACKMORE	
8	Paul INCE ❑	
9	Brian McCLAIR	
10	Mark HUGHES †	
11	Ryan GIGGS ❑	
	Substitutes	
12	Bryan ROBSON †70	
14	Andrei KANCHELSKIS ‡82	
Gk	Gary WALSH	

Date	Saturday 3 October 1992
Venue	Loftus Road, 3.00pm

QPR (0) 4
TOTTENHAM HOTSPUR (1) 1

Attendance	19,845
Referee	Joe WORRALL
Linesmen	C. Jones, I.M.D. Mitchell

QPR
Blue & White hooped shirts, White shorts — Goals

1	Jan STEJSKAL		
2	David BARDSLEY		
3	Clive WILSON		
4	Ray WILKINS	59	
5	Darren PEACOCK		
6	Alan McDONALD		
7	Andy IMPEY		
8	Ian HOLLOWAY	52	
9	Dennis BAILEY		
10	Gary PENRICE	67, 79	
11	Andy SINTON		
	Substitutes		
12	Garry THOMPSON		
14	Danny MADDIX		
Gk	Tony ROBERTS		

TOTTENHAM HOTSPUR
Yellow shirts, Yellow shorts — Goals

1	Ian WALKER		
2	Justin EDINBURGH †		
3	Pat VAN DEN HAUWE		
4	Vinny SAMWAYS ❑		
5	Jason CUNDY ❑		
6	Neil RUDDOCK		
7	Steve SEDGLEY ‡		
8	Nick BARMBY		
9	Darren ANDERTON		
10	Teddy SHERINGHAM	28	
11	Paul ALLEN		
	Substitutes		
12	Terry FENWICK †24		
14	Andy TURNER ‡71		
Gk	Kevin DEARDEN		

Date	Saturday 3 October 1992
Venue	Bramall Lane, 3.00pm

SHEFFIELD UNITED (2) 2
SOUTHAMPTON (0) 0

Attendance	15,842
Referee	Ken REDFERN
Linesmen	J. Leech, B.L. Polkey

SHEFFIELD UNITED
Red & White striped shirts — Goals

1	Alan KELLY		
2	Kevin GAGE		
3	Tom COWAN		
4	John GANNON		
5	Brian GAYLE		
6	Paul BEESLEY		
7	Carl BRADSHAW		
8	Paul ROGERS		
9	Adrian LITTLEJOHN	26	
10	Brian DEANE		
11	Dane WHITEHOUSE ‡	4	
	Substitutes		
12	Alan CORK		
14	Mitch WARD ‡75		
Gk	Danny WAINWRIGHT		

SOUTHAMPTON
Blue shirts, Blue shorts — Goals

1	Tim FLOWERS		
2	Jason DODD		
3	Francis BENALI		
4	David SPEEDIE		
5	Kenneth MONKOU †		
6	Kevin MOORE		
7	Matthew LE TISSIER		
8	Glenn COCKERILL		
9	Iain DOWIE		
10	Perry GROVES		
11	Micky ADAMS		
	Substitutes		
12	Nicky BANGER †64		
14	Neil MADDISON		
Gk	Ian ANDREWS		

Date	Saturday 3 October 1992
Venue	Selhurst Park, 3.00pm

WIMBLEDON (1) 2
ASTON VILLA (2) 3

Attendance	6,849
Referee	Steve LODGE
Linesmen	G. Butland, B.A. Wigginton

WIMBLEDON
Blue shirts, Blue shorts   Goals

1	Hans SEGERS	
2	Warren BARTON ❑	
3	Gary ELKINS	
4	Paul MILLER	34
5	John SCALES	
6	Scott FITZGERALD	
7	Neal ARDLEY	
8	Robbie EARLE ❑	
9	John FASHANU †	
10	Lawrie SANCHEZ	
11	Andy CLARKE	90
	Substitutes	
12	Aiden NEWHOUSE †23	
14	Roger JOSEPH	
Gk	Neil SULLIVAN	

ASTON VILLA
Claret & Blue shirts, White shorts   Goals

1	Nigel SPINK	
2	Earl BARRETT ❑	
3	Steve STAUNTON	
4	Shaun TEALE	
5	Paul McGRATH	
6	Kevin RICHARDSON	
7	Ray HOUGHTON	
8	Garry PARKER	
9	Dean SAUNDERS	5, 29
10	Dalian ATKINSON	77
11	Stephen FROGGATT †	
	Substitutes	
12	Dwight YORKE †45	
14	Bryan SMALL	
Gk	Mark BOSNICH	

Date	Sunday 4 October 1992
Venue	Boundary Park, 4.00pm

OLDHAM ATHLETIC (1) 1
EVERTON (0) 0

Attendance	13,013
Referee	Philip DON
Linesmen	T. Heilbron, P.J. Robinson

OLDHAM ATHLETIC
Blue shirts, Blue shorts   Goals

1	Jon HALLWORTH	
2	Steve REDMOND	
3	Neil POINTON	
4	Nick HENRY	
5	Richard JOBSON	8
6	Ian MARSHALL	
7	Gunnar HALLE	
8	Ian OLNEY	
9	Graeme SHARP	
10	Mike MILLIGAN	
11	Paul BERNARD	
	Substitutes	
12	Craig FLEMING	
14	Neil McDONALD	
Gk	John KEELEY	

EVERTON
Salmon Pink & Blue stripes, Salmon Pink shorts   Goals

1	Neville SOUTHALL ❑	
2	Alan HARPER	
3	Andy HINCHCLIFFE	
4	John EBBRELL	
5	Dave WATSON	
6	Gary ABLETT	
7	Robert WARZYCHA	
8	Barry HORNE	
9	Paul RIDEOUT	
10	Mo JOHNSTON ‡	
11	PREKI †	
	Substitutes	
12	Peter BEAGRIE †56	
14	Tony COTTEE ‡74	
Gk	Jason KEARTON	

Date　　Saturday 17 October 1992
Venue　　Stamford Bridge, 3.00pm

CHELSEA (1) 2
IPSWICH TOWN (0) 1

Attendance　16,702
Referee　　Brian HILL
Linesmen　　K.J. Hawkes, I.A. Madge

CHELSEA
Blue shirts, Blue shorts　　　　　　　　　Goals

1	Kevin HITCHCOCK	
2	Gareth HALL	28
3	Frank SINCLAIR	
4	Andy TOWNSEND ❑	
5	David LEE	
6	Mal DONAGHY	
7	Graham STUART †	
8	Robert FLECK	
9	Mick HARFORD ❑	78
10	Eddie NEWTON	
11	Dennis WISE	
	Substitutes	
12	Graeme LE SAUX †75	
14	Craig BURLEY	
Gk	Alec CHAMBERLAIN	

IPSWICH TOWN
White shirts, White shorts　　　　　　　　Goals

1	Clive BAKER	
2	Phil WHELAN †	
3	Neil THOMPSON	
4	Mick STOCKWELL	
5	John WARK	
6	David LINIGHAN	
7	Geraint WILLIAMS	
8	Paul GODDARD ‡	
9	Gavin JOHNSON	
10	Jason DOZZELL	
11	Chris KIWOMYA	
	Substitutes	
12	Steve WHITTON †71	79
14	Steve PALMER ‡75	
Gk	Jason WINTERS	

Date　　Saturday 17 October 1992
Venue　　Selhurst Park, 3.00pm

CRYSTAL PALACE (0) 0
MANCHESTER CITY (0) 0

Attendance　14,005
Referee　　Martin BODENHAM
Linesmen　　M.D. Dearing, G.T. Pearson

CRYSTAL PALACE
Red & Blue striped shirts, Red shorts　　　Goals

1	Nigel MARTYN	
2	Richard SHAW	
3	Lee SINNOTT	
4	Gareth SOUTHGATE	
5	Eric YOUNG	
6	Simon OSBORN	
7	Paul WILLIAMS	
8	Chris COLEMAN	
9	Chris ARMSTRONG	
10	John SALAKO	
11	Eddie McGOLDRICK ‡	
	Substitutes	
12	Geoff THOMAS	
14	Stan COLLYMORE ‡76	
Gk	Paul HEALD	

MANCHESTER CITY
White shirts, White shorts　　　　　　　　Goals

1	Tony COTON	
2	Ian BRIGHTWELL	
3	Terry PHELAN	
4	Steve McMAHON	
5	Keith CURLE	
6	Andy HILL	
7	David WHITE	
8	Garry FLITCROFT	
9	Niall QUINN	
10	Fitzroy SIMPSON	
11	Rick HOLDEN	
	Substitutes	
12	Peter REID	
14	Mike SHERON	
Gk	Martyn MARGETSON	

Date Saturday 17 October 1992
Venue Goodison Park, 3.00pm

EVERTON (1) 1
COVENTRY CITY (1) 1

Attendance 17,587
Referee Bob HAMER
Linesmen J. Hilditch, J.B. Robinson

EVERTON
Blue shirts, White shorts   Goals

1	Neville SOUTHALL	
2	Robert WARZYCHA †	
3	Andy HINCHCLIFFE	
4	Martin KEOWN	
5	Dave WATSON	
6	Gary ABLETT	
7	Billy KENNY	
8	Peter BEARDSLEY	
9	Tony COTTEE	
10	Barry HORNE ‡	
11	Peter BEAGRIE	28
	Substitutes	
12	PREKI †81	
14	Ian SNODIN ‡88	
Gk	Jason KEARTON	

COVENTRY CITY
Red shirts, White shorts   Goals

1	Steve OGRIZOVIC	
2	Brian BORROWS	
3	Kenny SANSOM	
4	Peter ATHERTON	
5	Andy PEARCE	
6	Peter NDLOVU	44
7	Lloyd McGRATH	
8	Lee HURST	
9	Terry FLEMING	
10	Stewart ROBSON	
11	John WILLIAMS	
	Substitutes	
12	Phil BABB	
14	Tony SHERIDAN	
Gk	Jonathan GOULD	

Date Saturday 17 October 1992
Venue Elland Road, 3.00pm

LEEDS UNITED (1) 3
SHEFFIELD UNITED (0) 1

Attendance 29,706
Referee Ray LEWIS
Linesmen P.D. Harding, T, Lynch

LEEDS UNITED
White shirts, White shorts   Goals

1	John LUKIC	
2	Jon NEWSOME	
3	Tony DORIGO	
4	David BATTY ❏	
5	Chris FAIRCLOUGH	
6	Chris WHYTE	78
7	Gordon STRACHAN	
8	Eric CANTONA ❏ †	
9	Lee CHAPMAN	36
10	Gary McALLISTER	
11	Gary SPEED	74
	Substitutes	
12	Carl SHUTT †84	
14	Scott SELLARS	
Gk	Mervyn DAY	

SHEFFIELD UNITED
Red & White striped shirts, Black shorts   Goals

1	Alan KELLY	
2	Mitch WARD ❏	
3	Tom COWAN	
4	John GANNON	
5	Brian GAYLE	
6	Paul BEESLEY	53
7	Carl BRADSHAW ❏	
8	Paul ROGERS	
9	Adrian LITTLEJOHN ❏ †	
10	Brian DEANE ❏	
11	Alan CORK	
	Substitutes	
12	Ian BRYSON †53	
14	Charlie HARTFIELD	
Gk	Simon TRACEY	

Date	Saturday 17 October 1992
Venue	Carrow Road, 3.00pm

NORWICH CITY (0) 2
QPR (0) 1

Attendance	16,009
Referee	Dermot GALLAGHER
Linesmen	B.L. Polkey, M.G. Wright

NORWICH CITY
Yellow shirts, Green shorts   Goals

1	Bryan GUNN	
2	Ian CULVERHOUSE	
3	Mark BOWEN	53p
4	Ian BUTTERWORTH	
5	John POLSTON	
6	Daryl SUTCH	
7	Ian CROOK	
8	David PHILLIPS	
9	Mark ROBINS ‡	
10	Jeremy GOSS	
11	Chris SUTTON	64
	Substitutes	
12	Rob NEWMAN	
14	Lee POWER ‡75	
Gk	Mark WALTON	

QPR
Blue & White hooped shirts, White shorts   Goals

1	Jan STEJSKAL	
2	David BARDSLEY ❑	
3	Clive WILSON	
4	Ray WILKINS	
5	Darren PEACOCK	
6	Alan McDONALD	
7	Andy IMPEY	
8	Ian HOLLOWAY	
9	Dennis BAILEY	
10	Gary PENRICE †	
11	Andy SINTON ‡	
	Substitutes	
12	Bradley ALLEN †68	77
14	Danny MADDIX ‡82	
Gk	Tony ROBERTS	

Date	Saturday 17 October 1992
Venue	City Ground, 3.00pm

NOTTINGHAM FOREST (0) 0
ARSENAL (1) 1

Attendance	24,862
Referee	Joe WORRALL
Linesmen	G.I. Grandidge, G.R. Hamblin

NOTTINGHAM FOREST
Red shirts, White shorts   Goals

1	Mark CROSSLEY	
2	Gary CHARLES	
3	Stuart PEARCE	
4	Roy KEANE	
5	Carl TILER	
6	Ray McKINNON ‡	
7	Gary CROSBY	
8	Scot GEMMILL	
9	Nigel CLOUGH	
10	Gary BANNISTER	
11	Thorvaldur ORLYGSSON	
	Substitutes	
12	Steve CHETTLE	
14	Kingsley BLACK ‡67	
Gk	Andy MARRIOTT	

ARSENAL
Yellow shirts, Blue shorts   Goals

1	David SEAMAN	
2	Lee DIXON	
3	Nigel WINTERBURN	
4	David HILLIER	
5	Steve BOULD ❑	
6	Tony ADAMS	
7	John JENSEN †	
8	Ian WRIGHT ‡	
9	Alan SMITH	38
10	Paul MERSON	
11	Kevin CAMPBELL	
	Substitutes	
12	Colin PATES †83	
14	Anders LIMPAR ‡75	
Gk	Alan MILLER	

Date	Saturday 17 October 1992
Venue	Hillsborough, 3.00pm

SHEFFIELD WEDNESDAY (2) 2
OLDHAM ATHLETIC (1) 1

Attendance	24,485
Referee	Ron GROVES
Linesmen	N.S. Barry, D.E. Binsley

SHEFFIELD WEDNESDAY
Blue & White striped shirts, Black shorts   Goals

1	Chris WOODS	
2	Paul WARHURST	
3	Nigel WORTHINGTON	
4	Carlton PALMER ❏	9
5	Peter SHIRTLIFF	
6	Viv ANDERSON	
7	John HARKES	
8	Chris WADDLE †	
9	David HIRST ‡	
10	Chris BART-WILLIAMS	
11	Mark BRIGHT	17
	Substitutes	
12	Gordon WATSON †82	
14	Danny WILSON ‡58	
Gk	Kevin PRESSMAN	

OLDHAM ATHLETIC
Green shirts, Green shorts   Goals

1	Jon HALLWORTH	
2	Gunnar HALLE	
3	Neil POINTON	
4	Nick HENRY	
5	Richard JOBSON	
6	Steve REDMOND ❏	
7	Andy BARLOW †	
8	Ian OLNEY ❏	
9	Graeme SHARP	
10	Mike MILLIGAN	44
11	Paul BERNARD	
	Substitutes	
12	Neil ADAMS †38	
14	Craig FLEMING	
Gk	John KEELEY	

Date	Saturday 17 October 1992
Venue	The Dell, 3.00pm

SOUTHAMPTON (0) 2
WIMBLEDON (0) 2

Attendance	11,221
Referee	Keren BARRATT
Linesmen	R.E. Budden, M.R. Sims

SOUTHAMPTON
Red & White striped shirts, Black shorts   Goals

1	Tim FLOWERS	
2	Jason DODD	
3	Francis BENALI †	
4	Terry HURLOCK	
5	Kenneth MONKOU	
6	Steve WOOD	
7	Perry GROVES	83
8	Glenn COCKERILL	
9	Paul MOODY ‡	
10	Iain DOWIE	57
11	Micky ADAMS	
	Substitutes	
12	Neil MADDISON †78	
14	Lee POWELL ‡56	
Gk	Ian ANDREWS	

WIMBLEDON
Blue shirts, Blue shirts   Goals

1	Neil SULLIVAN	
2	Warren BARTON	
3	Roger JOSEPH	
4	Vinnie JONES	
5	Alan McLEARY	
6	Scott FITZGERALD ❏	
7	Paul MILLER	
8	Robbie EARLE	
9	John FASHANU	
10	Steve COTTERILL	50, 67
11	Andy CLARKE	
	Substitutes	
12	Lawrie SANCHEZ	
14	Gary ELKINS	
Gk	Hans SEGERS	

Date	Saturday 17 October 1992
Venue	White Hart Lane, 3.00pm

TOTTENHAM HOTSPUR (0) 2
MIDDLESBROUGH (2) 2

Attendance	24,735
Referee	Paul DUKIN
Linesmen	J.A. Elwin, M. Stobbart

TOTTENHAM HOTSPUR
White shirts, Navy Blue shorts   Goals

1	Ian WALKER	
2	Justin EDINBURGH	
3	Pat VAN DEN HAUWE	
4	Vinny SAMWAYS	
5	David TUTTLE †	
6	Neil RUDDOCK	
7	Steve SEDGLEY	
8	Gordon DURIE	
9	Darren ANDERTON ‡	
10	Teddy SHERINGHAM	70p
11	Paul ALLEN	
	Substitutes	
12	NAYIM †55	
14	Nick BARMBY ‡63	73
Gk	Erik THORSTVEDT	

MIDDLESBROUGH
Red shirts, White shorts   Goals

1	Stephen PEARS	
2	Chris MORRIS	
3	Jimmy PHILLIPS	
4	Alan KERNAGHAN	
5	Derek WHYTE	
6	Jon GITTENS	
7	Bernie SLAVEN †	
8	Robbie MUSTOE	1
9	Paul WILKINSON	32
10	Tommy WRIGHT	
11	Mark PROCTOR	
	Substitutes	
12	Curtis FLEMING †73	
14	Graham KAVANAGH	
Gk	Andy COLLETT	

Date	Sunday 18 October 1992
Venue	Old Trafford, 4.00pm

MANCHESTER UNITED (0) 2
LIVERPOOL (2) 2

Attendance	33,243
Referee	Keith HACKETT
Linesmen	U.D Rennie, K.M. Lynch

MANCHESTER UNITED
Red shirts, White shorts   Goals

1	Peter SCHMEICHEL	
2	Paul PARKER	
3	Denis IRWIN	
4	Steve BRUCE	
5	Darren FERGUSON	
6	Gary PALLISTER	
7	Andrei KANCHELSKIS ‡	
8	Paul INCE	
9	Brian McCLAIR	
10	Mark HUGHES	78, 90
11	Ryan GIGGS	
	Substitutes	
12	Mike PHELAN	
14	Clayton BLACKMORE ‡66	
Gk	Gary WALSH	

LIVERPOOL
Green shirts, Green shorts   Goals

1	Bruce GROBBELAAR	
2	Mike MARSH	
3	David BURROWS	
4	Steve NICOL	
5	Torben PIECHNIK	
6	Don HUTCHISON	23
7	Steve McMANAMAN	
8	Jamie REDKNAPP †	
9	Ian RUSH ❑	44
10	Jan MOLBY ‡	
11	Ronnie ROSENTHAL	
	Substitutes	
12	Michael THOMAS †72	
14	Nick TANNER ‡82	
Gk	David JAMES	

Date	Monday 19 October 1992
Venue	Villa Park, 7.45pm

ASTON VILLA (0) 0
BLACKBURN ROVERS (0) 0

Attendance	30,398
Referee	Howard KING
Linesmen	P.M. Roberts, A. Streets

ASTON VILLA
Claret & Blue shirts, White shorts — Goals

1	Nigel SPINK	
2	Earl BARRETT	
3	Steve STAUNTON	
4	Shaun TEALE	
5	Paul McGRATH	
6	Kevin RICHARDSON	
7	Ray HOUGHTON	
8	Garry PARKER	
9	Dean SAUNDERS	
10	Dalian ATKINSON	
11	Stephen FROGGATT †	
	Substitutes	
12	Bryan SMALL †45	
14	Dwight YORKE	
Gk	Mark BOSNICH	

BLACKBURN ROVERS
Blue & White shirts, Blue shorts — Goals

1	Bobby MIMMS	
2	David MAY	
3	Alan WRIGHT	
4	Tim SHERWOOD	
5	Colin HENDRY	
6	Kevin MORAN	
7	Stuart RIPLEY	
8	Gordon COWANS	
9	Alan SHEARER	
10	Mike NEWELL	
11	Jason WILCOX	
	Substitutes	
12	Nicky MARKER	
14	Roy WEGERLE	
Gk	Darren COLLIER	

Date	Wednesday 21 October 1992
Venue	City Ground, 7.30pm

NOTTINGHAM FOREST (0) 1
MIDDLESBROUGH (0) 0

Attendance	16,897
Referee	Mike PECK
Linesmen	P. Mewall, M. Warren

NOTTINGHAM FOREST
Red shirts, White shorts — Goals

1	Mark CROSSLEY	
2	Gary CHARLES	
3	Stuart PEARCE	
4	Roy KEANE	
5	Carl TILER	
6	Thorvaldur ORLYGSSON	
7	Gary CROSBY	
8	Scot GEMMILL	
9	Nigel CLOUGH	
10	Gary BANNISTER ‡	
11	Kingsley BLACK	66
	Substitutes	
12	Steve CHETTLE	
14	Lee GLOVER ‡45	
Gk	Andy MARRIOTT	

MIDDLESBROUGH
White shirts, Black shorts — Goals

1	Stephen PEARS	
2	Chris MORRIS	
3	Jimmy PHILLIPS	
4	Alan KERNAGHAN	
5	Derek WHYTE	
6	Jon GITTENS	
7	Bernie SLAVEN	
8	Graham KAVANAGH ❑ †	
9	Paul WILKINSON	
10	Tommy WRIGHT	
11	Mark PROCTOR	
	Substitutes	
12	Curtis FLEMING †77	
14	Alan MOORE	
Gk	Andy COLLETT	

Date	Saturday 24 October 1992
Venue	Highbury Stadium, 3.00pm

ARSENAL (1) 2
EVERTON (0) 0

Attendance	28,052
Referee	Keith HACKETT
Linesmen	W.M. Jordan, D.C. Madgwick

ARSENAL
Red & White shirts, White shirts   Goals

1	David SEAMAN	
2	Lee DIXON †	
3	Nigel WINTERBURN	
4	David HILLIER	
5	Steve BOULD	
6	Tony ADAMS	
7	John JENSEN	
8	Ian WRIGHT ‡	5
9	Alan SMITH	
10	Paul MERSON	
11	Kevin CAMPBELL	
	Substitutes	
12	Colin PATES †30	
14	Anders LIMPAR ‡38	58
Gk	Alan MILLER	

EVERTON
Blue shirts, Blue shorts   Goals

1	Neville SOUTHALL	
2	Ian SNODIN ‡	
3	Andy HINCHCLIFFE †	
4	Martin KEOWN	
5	Dave WATSON	
6	Gary ABLETT ❏	
7	Robert WARZYCHA	
8	Peter BEARDSLEY	
9	Tony COTTEE	
10	Barry HORNE	
11	Peter BEAGRIE ❏	
	Substitutes	
12	Paul RIDEOUT †53	
14	Alan HARPER ‡66	
Gk	Jason KEARTON	

Date	Saturday 24 October 1992
Venue	Ewood Park, 3.00pm

BLACKBURN ROVERS (0) 0
MANCHESTER UNITED (0) 0

Attendance	20,305
Referee	Mike REED
Linesmen	A.J. Hill, A. Streets

BLACKBURN ROVERS
Blue & White shirts, White shorts   Goals

1	Bobby MIMMS	
2	David MAY	
3	Alan WRIGHT	
4	Tim SHERWOOD ❏	
5	Colin HENDRY	
6	Kevin MORAN	
7	Stuart RIPLEY ‡	
8	Gordon COWANS	
9	Alan SHEARER	
10	Mike NEWELL	
11	Jason WILCOX	
	Substitutes	
12	Nicky MARKER	
14	Roy WEGERLE ‡80	
Gk	Darren COLLIER	

MANCHESTER UNITED
Red shirts, White shorts   Goals

1	Peter SCHMEICHEL	
2	Paul PARKER	
3	Denis IRWIN	
4	Steve BRUCE ❏	
5	Darren FERGUSON †	
6	Gary PALLISTER	
7	Clayton BLACKMORE ❏	
8	Paul INCE	
9	Brian McCLAIR	
10	Mark HUGHES	
11	Ryan GIGGS	
	Substitutes	
12	Andrei KANCHELSKIS †75	
14	Neil WEBB	
Gk	Gary WALSH	

Date	Saturday 24 October 1992
Venue	Highfield Road, 3.00pm

COVENTRY CITY (0) 1
CHELSEA (1) 2

Attendance	15,626
Referee	Mike PECK
Linesmen	J. McGrath, K.M. Lynch

COVENTRY CITY
Sky Blue shirts, Sky Blue shorts   Goals

1	Steve OGRIZOVIC	
2	Brian BORROWS	
3	Kenny SANSOM	
4	Peter ATHERTON	
5	Andy PEARCE	
6	Peter NDLOVU	
7	Lloyd McGRATH ‡	
8	Lee HURST	
9	Robert ROSARIO	58
10	Stewart ROBSON	
11	John WILLIAMS	
	Substitutes	
12	Phil BABB	
14	Paul WILLIAMS ‡38	
Gk	Jonathan GOULD	

CHELSEA
Blue shirts, Blue shorts (tbc)   Goals

1	Kevin HITCHCOCK	
2	Gareth HALL ❑	
3	Frank SINCLAIR ❑	
4	Andy TOWNSEND	
5	David LEE	
6	Mal DONAGHY	
7	Graham STUART	70
8	Robert FLECK	
9	Mick HARFORD	32
10	Eddie NEWTON	
11	Darren BARNARD ‡	
	Substitutes	
12	Craig BURLEY	
14	Graeme LE SAUX ‡69	
Gk	Alec CHAMBERLAIN	

Date	Saturday 24 October 1992
Venue	Portman Road, 3.00pm

IPSWICH TOWN (0) 2
CRYSTAL PALACE (0) 2

Attendance	17,861
Referee	Gerald ASHBY
Linesmen	J.F. Moore, M.G. Wright

IPSWICH TOWN
Blue & White shirts, White shorts   Goals

1	Clive BAKER	
2	Gavin JOHNSON	
3	Neil THOMPSON	
4	Mick STOCKWELL	
5	John WARK	
6	David LINIGHAN	
7	Geraint WILLIAMS	
8	Paul GODDARD †	
9	Steve WHITTON	
10	Jason DOZZELL	72, 83
11	Chris KIWOMYA	
	Substitutes	
12	David GREGORY †81	
14	Phil WHELAN	
Gk	Jason WINTERS	

CRYSTAL PALACE
Red & Blue striped shirts, Red shorts   Goals

1	Nigel MARTYN ❑	
2	Richard SHAW	
3	Lee SINNOTT	
4	Gareth SOUTHGATE	
5	Eric YOUNG	
6	Simon OSBORN	
7	Chris COLEMAN	75
8	Paul WILLIAMS	
9	Chris ARMSTRONG	60
10	John SALAKO	
11	Eddie McGOLDRICK	
	Substitutes	
12	Geoff THOMAS	
14	Stan COLLYMORE	
Gk	Paul HEALD	

Date	Saturday 24 October 1992
Venue	Maine Road, 3.00pm

MANCHESTER CITY (0) 1
SOUTHAMPTON (0) 0

Attendance	20,089
Referee	Philip DON
Linesmen	T. Heilbron, P.J. Robinson

MANCHESTER CITY
Light Blue shirts, White shorts   Goals

1	Tony COTON	
2	Ian BRIGHTWELL	
3	Terry PHELAN	
4	Steve McMAHON ❑	
5	Keith CURLE	
6	Andy HILL	
7	David WHITE	
8	Mike SHERON	74
9	Niall QUINN	
10	Fitzroy SIMPSON	
11	Rick HOLDEN	
	Substitutes	
12	Peter REID	
14	Garry FLITCROFT	
Gk	Martyn MARGETSON	

SOUTHAMPTON
Red & White striped shirts, Black shorts   Goals

1	Tim FLOWERS	
2	Jason DODD	
3	Francis BENALI ‡	
4	Terry HURLOCK ❑ †	
5	Kenneth MONKOU	
6	Richard HALL	
7	Matthew LE TISSIER	
8	Glenn COCKERILL	
9	Perry GROVES	
10	Iain DOWIE ❑	
11	Micky ADAMS	
	Substitutes	
12	Paul MOODY †79	
14	Neil MADDISON ‡79	
Gk	Ian ANDREWS	

Date	Saturday 24 October 1992
Venue	Ayresome Park, 3.00pm

MIDDLESBROUGH (1) 1
SHEFFIELD WEDNESDAY (1) 1

Attendance	18,414
Referee	Philip WRIGHT
Linesmen	N.S. Barry, D.S. Oliver

MIDDLESBROUGH
Red shirts, White shorts   Goals

1	Stephen PEARS	
2	Chris MORRIS	
3	Jimmy PHILLIPS	
4	Alan KERNAGHAN	
5	Curtis FLEMING	
6	Jon GITTENS	
7	Bernie SLAVEN ❑	
8	Mark PROCTOR	
9	Paul WILKINSON	34
10	Graham KAVANAGH	
11	Tommy WRIGHT	
	Substitutes	
12	Alan MOORE	
14	Nicholas PEVERELL	
Gk	Andy COLLETT	

SHEFFIELD WEDNESDAY
Blue & White striped shirts, Black shorts   Goals

1	Chris WOODS	
2	John HARKES	
3	Nigel WORTHINGTON	
4	Carlton PALMER	
5	Nigel PEARSON	
6	Viv ANDERSON	
7	Graham HYDE	
8	Chris WADDLE	
9	Mark BRIGHT	29
10	Chris BART-WILLIAMS	
11	Paul WARHURST †	
	Substitutes	
12	Gordon WATSON †45	
14	Danny WILSON	
Gk	Kevin PRESSMAN	

Date	Saturday 24 October 1992
Venue	Boundary Park, 3.00pm

OLDHAM ATHLETIC (1) 1
ASTON VILLA (0) 1

Attendance	13,457
Referee	Rodger GIFFORD
Linesmen	T.A. Atkinson, R.R. Rawson

OLDHAM ATHLETIC
Blue shirts, Blue shorts — Goals

		Goals
1	Jon HALLWORTH	
2	Gunnar HALLE	
3	Neil POINTON	
4	Nick HENRY	
5	Richard JOBSON	
6	Steve REDMOND	
7	Ian OLNEY ‡	19
8	Ian MARSHALL	
9	Graeme SHARP	
10	Mike MILLIGAN	
11	Paul BERNARD	
	Substitutes	
12	Neil ADAMS	
14	Neil McDONALD ‡70	
Gk	John KEELEY	

ASTON VILLA
White shirts, Black shorts — Goals

		Goals
1	Nigel SPINK	
2	Earl BARRETT	
3	Steve STAUNTON	
4	Shaun TEALE	
5	Paul McGRATH	
6	Kevin RICHARDSON	
7	Ray HOUGHTON	
8	Dwight YORKE ‡	
9	Dean SAUNDERS	
10	Dalian ATKINSON	81
11	Bryan SMALL	
	Substitutes	
12	Mark BLAKE	
14	Dave FARRELL ‡75	
Gk	Mark BOSNICH	

Date	Saturday 24 October 1992
Venue	Loftus Road, 3.00pm

QPR (0) 2
LEEDS UNITED (0) 1

Attendance	19,326
Referee	Howard KING
Linesmen	R.J. Harris, P.A. Josper

QPR
Blue & White hooped shirts, White shorts — Goals

		Goals
1	Jan STEJSKAL	
2	David BARDSLEY	73
3	Clive WILSON	
4	Ray WILKINS	
5	Darren PEACOCK	
6	Alan McDONALD	
7	Andy IMPEY	
8	Ian HOLLOWAY	
9	Les FERDINAND	85
10	Bradley ALLEN	
11	Andy SINTON	
	Substitutes	
12	Simon BARKER	
14	Danny MADDIX	
Gk	Tony ROBERTS	

LEEDS UNITED
Yellow shirts, Yellow shorts — Goals

		Goals
1	John LUKIC	
2	Jon NEWSOME	
3	Tony DORIGO	
4	David BATTY	
5	Chris FAIRCLOUGH	
6	Chris WHYTE	
7	Gordon STRACHAN	57
8	Rod WALLACE †	
9	Lee CHAPMAN	
10	Gary McALLISTER ‡	
11	Gary SPEED	
	Substitutes	
12	Carl SHUTT †78	
14	David ROCASTLE ‡87	
Gk	Mervyn DAY	

Date	Saturday 24 October 1992
Venue	Bramall Lane, 3.00pm

SHEFFIELD UNITED (0) 0
NOTTINGHAM FOREST (0) 0

Attendance	19,152
Referee	Robbie HART
Linesmen	P. Rejer, E. Lomas

SHEFFIELD UNITED
Red & White striped shirts, White shorts · Goals

1	Simon TRACEY	
2	Mitch WARD	
3	Tom COWAN	
4	John GANNON	
5	Brian GAYLE	
6	PAul BEESLEY	
7	Carl BRADSHAW	
8	Jamie HOYLAND	
9	Adrian LITTLEJOHN †	
10	Brian DEANE	
11	Ian BRYSON	
	Substitutes	
12	Glyn HODGES †71	
14	Alan CORK	
Gk	Alan KELLY	

NOTTINGHAM FOREST
White shirts, Black shorts · Goals

1	Mark CROSSLEY	
2	Gary CHARLES	
3	Stuart PEARCE	
4	Roy KEANE	
5	Carl TILER	
6	Thorvaldur ORLYGSSON	
7	Gary CROSBY	
8	Scot GEMMILL ❑	
9	Nigel CLOUGH	
10	Lee GLOVER	
11	Kingsley BLACK	
	Substitutes	
12	Steve CHETTLE	
14	Steve STONE	
Gk	Andy MARRIOTT	

Date	Sunday 25 October 1992
Venue	Anfield, 3.00pm

LIVERPOOL (2) 4
NORWICH CITY (1) 1

Attendance	36,318
Referee	Ray LEWIS
Linesmen	P.D. Harding, T. Lynch

LIVERPOOL
Red shirts, Red shorts · Goals

1	Bruce GROBBELAAR	
2	Mike MARSH †	
3	David BURROWS	52
4	Steve NICOL ❑	
5	Torben PIECHNIK	
6	Don HUTCHISON	20
7	Steve McMANAMAN	
8	Mark WALTERS	89p
9	Ronnie ROSENTHAL	
10	Jamie REDKNAPP	
11	Michael THOMAS	15
	Substitutes	
12	Mark WRIGHT †68	
14	Paul STEWART	
Gk	David JAMES	

NORWICH CITY
Yellow shirts, Green shorts · Goals

1	Bryan GUNN	
2	Ian CULVERHOUSE	
3	Mark BOWEN	
4	Ian BUTTERWORTH ❑	2
5	John POLSTON	
6	Rob NEWMAN ❑	
7	Ian CROOK	
8	David PHILLIPS	
9	Mark ROBINS †	
10	Jeremy GOSS ❑ ‡	
11	Chris SUTTON ❑	
	Substitutes	
12	Daryl SUTCH †61	
14	Ruel FOX ‡61	
Gk	Mark WALTON	

Date	Sunday 25 October 1992
Venue	Selhurst Park, 4.00pm

WIMBLEDON (1) 1
TOTTENHAM HOTSPUR (0) 1

Attendance	8,628
Referee	Allan GUNN
Linesmen	M.D. Dearing, K.J. Hawkes

WIMBLEDON
Blue shirts, Blue shorts   Goals

1	Hans SEGERS	
2	Warren BARTON	
3	Roger JOSEPH	
4	Vinnie JONES ❏	
5	Alan McLEARY	
6	Scott FITZGERALD	
7	Terry GIBSON †	38
8	Robbie EARLE	
9	John FASHANU	
10	Steve COTTERILL	
11	Andy CLARKE ‡	
	Substitutes	
12	Brian McALLISTER †79	
14	Dean HOLDSWORTH ‡67	
Gk	Neil SULLIVAN	

TOTTENHAM HOTSPUR
White shirts, White shorts   Goals

1	Ian WALKER ‡	
2	Justin EDINBURGH	
3	Dean AUSTIN	
4	Vinny SAMWAYS	
5	Gary MABBUTT	
6	Neil RUDDOCK ❏	
7	Steve SEDGLEY	
8	Gordon DURIE †	
9	NAYIM	
10	Teddy SHERINGHAM	
11	Paul ALLEN	
	Substitutes	
12	David HOWELLS	
14	Nick BARMBY †45	48
Gk	Erik THORSTVEDT ‡45	

Date	Saturday 31 October 1992
Venue	Stamford Bridge, 3.00pm

CHELSEA (1) 1
SHEFFIELD UNITED (1) 2

Attendance	13,763
Referee	David ALLISON
Linesmen	W.J. Norbury, M. Stobbart

CHELSEA
Blue shirts, Blue shorts   Goals

1	Kevin HITCHCOCK	
2	Gareth HALL	
3	Frank SINCLAIR	
4	Andy TOWNSEND	41
5	David LEE	
6	Mal DONAGHY	
7	Graham STUART ‡	
8	Robert FLECK †	
9	Mick HARFORD	
10	Eddie NEWTON	
11	Dennis WISE	
	Substitutes	
12	Joe ALLON †69	
14	Graeme LE SAUX ‡59	
Gk	Alec CHAMBERLAIN	

SHEFFIELD UNITED
Red & White striped shirts, White shorts   Goals

1	Simon TRACEY	
2	Kevin GAGE	
3	Tom COWAN	
4	John GANNON †	
5	Brian GAYLE	
6	Paul BEESLEY	
7	Mitch WARD	
8	Paul ROGERS	
9	Adrian LITTLEJOHN ❏	40
10	Brian DEANE	57
11	Glyn HODGES	
	Substitutes	
12	Jamie HOYLAND †76	
14	Alan CORK	
Gk	Alan KELLY	

Date	Saturday 31 October 1992
Venue	Goodison Park, 3.00pm

EVERTON (0) 1
MANCHESTER CITY (2) 3

Attendance	20,242
Referee	Joe WORRALL
Linesmen	D.E. Binsley, G.I. Grandidge

EVERTON
Blue shirts, White shorts   Goals

1	Neville SOUTHALL	
2	Matthew JACKSON	
3	Gary ABLETT	
4	Billy KENNY	
5	Dave WATSON	
6	Martin KEOWN	
7	Robert WARZYCHA	
8	Stuart BARLOW	
9	Paul RIDEOUT	
10	Barry HORNE †	
11	Peter BEAGRIE	
	Substitutes	
12	PREKI †60	
14	Andy HINCHCLIFFE	
Gk	Jason KEARTON	

MANCHESTER CITY
White shirts, Light Blue shorts   Goals

1	Tony COTON	
2	Ian BRIGHTWELL	68og
3	Terry PHELAN	
4	Steve McMAHON	
5	Keith CURLE	
6	Andy HILL	
7	David WHITE	19
8	Mike SHERON	12, 62
9	Niall QUINN ‡	
10	Fitzroy SIMPSON †	
11	Rick HOLDEN	
	Substitutes	
12	Peter REID †56	
14	Garry FLITCROFT ‡87	
Gk	Martyn MARGETSON	

Date	Saturday 31 October 1992
Venue	Elland Road, 3.00pm

LEEDS UNITED (0) 2
COVENTRY CITY (1) 2

Attendance	28,018
Referee	Brian HILL
Linesmen	J. Hilditch, R. Pearson

LEEDS UNITED
White shirts, White shorts   Goals

1	John LUKIC	
2	Jon NEWSOME	
3	Tony DORIGO	
4	David BATTY †	
5	Chris FAIRCLOUGH	90
6	Chris WHYTE	
7	Gordon STRACHAN	
8	Rod WALLACE ‡	
9	Lee CHAPMAN	70
10	Gary McALLISTER	12og
11	Gary SPEED	
	Substitutes	
12	David ROCASTLE †28	
14	Eric CANTONA ‡58	
Gk	Mervyn DAY	

COVENTRY CITY
Sky Blue shirts, Sky Blue shorts   Goals

1	Steve OGRIZOVIC	
2	Brian BORROWS	
3	Kenny SANSOM	
4	Peter ATHERTON	
5	Peter BILLING	
6	Peter NDLOVU	77
7	Tony SHERIDAN †	
8	Lee HURST	
9	Paul WILLIAMS	
10	Stewart ROBSON	
11	John WILLIMAS	
	Substitutes	
12	Phil BABB †71	
14	Terry FLEMING	
Gk	Jonathan GOULD	

Date	Saturday 31 October 1992
Venue	Old Trafford, 3.00pm

MANCHESTER UNITED (0) 0
WIMBLEDON (0) 1

Attendance	32,622
Referee	Kelvin MORTON
Linesmen	A.N. Butler, M.A. Cooper

MANCHESTER UNITED
Red shirts, White shorts   Goals

1	Peter SCHMEICHEL	
2	Paul PARKER	
3	Clayton BLACKMORE	
4	Steve BRUCE	
5	Darren FERGUSON ❏	
6	Gary PALLISTER	
7	Andrei KANCHELSKIS †	
8	Paul INCE	
9	Brian McCLAIR	
10	Mark HUGHES	
11	Ryan GIGGS	
	Substitutes	
12	Bryan ROBSON †67	
14	Mike PHELAN	
Gk	Gary WALSH	

WIMBLEDON
Blue shirts, Blue shorts   Goals

1	Hans SEGERS	
2	Warren BARTON	
3	Roger JOSEPH	
4	Vinnie JONES	
5	Alan McLEARY	
6	Brian McALLISTER ❏	
7	Terry GIBSON ❏	
8	Robbie EARLE	
9	Dean HOLDSWORTH	
10	Lawrie SANCHEZ ❏	79
11	Gerald DOBBS †	
	Substitutes	
12	Andy CLARKE †82	
14	Steve COTTERILL	
Gk	Neil SULLIVAN	

Date	Saturday 31 October 1992
Venue	Carrow Road, 3.00pm

NORWICH CITY (0) 1
MIDDLESBROUGH (0) 1

Attendance	14,499
Referee	Steve LODGE
Linesmen	G. Butland, G.R. Hamblin

NORWICH CITY
Yellow shirts, Green shorts   Goals

1	Bryan GUNN	
2	Chris SUTTON †	
3	Mark BOWEN	
4	Ian BUTTERWORTH	
5	John POLSTON ‡	
6	Daryl SUTCH	86
7	Ian CROOK	
8	Rob NEWMAN	
9	Mark ROBINS	
10	Jeremy GOSS	
11	David PHILLIPS	
	Substitutes	
12	Ruel FOX †73	
14	Darren BECKFORD ‡84	
Gk	Mark WALTON	

MIDDLESBROUGH
Red shirts, White shorts   Goals

1	Stephen PEARS	
2	Curtis FLEMING	
3	Jimmy PHILLIPS	
4	Alan KERNAGHAN	
5	Derek WHYTE	
6	Jon GITTENS	
7	Tommy WRIGHT †	
8	Willie FALCONER	
9	Paul WILKINSON	64
10	Mark PROCTOR	
11	John HENDRIE	
	Substitutes	
12	Chris MORRIS †32	
14	Bernie SLAVEN	
Gk	Ian IRONSIDE	

Date	Saturday 31 October 1992
Venue	City Ground, 3.00pm

NOTTINGHAM FOREST (0) 0
IPSWICH TOWN (1) 1

Attendance	21,411
Referee	Martin BODENHAM
Linesmen	A. Black, M.A. Riley

NOTTINGHAM FOREST
Red shirts, White shorts   Goals

1	Mark CROSSLEY	
2	Brian LAWS	
3	Stuart PEARCE	
4	Roy KEANE	
5	Carl TILER	
6	Thorvaldur ORLYGSSON ‡	
7	Gary CROSBY	
8	Scot GEMMILL	
9	Nigel CLOUGH	
10	Lee GLOVER	
11	Kingsley BLACK	
	Substitutes	
12	Steve CHETTLE	
14	Gary BANNISTER ‡72	
Gk	Andy MARRIOTT	

IPSWICH TOWN
Blue & White shirts, Blue shorts   Goals

1	Clive BAKER	
2	Phil WHELAN	
3	Neil THOMPSON	
4	Mick STOCKWELL	
5	John WARK	
6	David LINIGHAN	
7	Geraint WILLIAMS ❑	
8	Steve PALMER	
9	Gavin JOHNSON ‡	
10	Jason DOZZELL	6
11	Chris KIWOMYA	
	Substitutes	
12	Paul GODDARD	
14	Neil GREGORY ‡89	
Gk	Jason WINTERS	

Date	Saturday 31 October 1992
Venue	Hillsborough, 3.00pm

SHEFFIELD WEDNESDAY (0) 0
BLACKBURN ROVERS (0) 0

Attendance	31,044
Referee	Ray LEWIS
Linesmen	W.J. Nattrass, P. Newall

SHEFFIELD WEDNESDAY
Blue & White striped shirts, Black shorts   Goals

1	Chris WOODS	
2	John HARKES	
3	Nigel WORTHINGTON	
4	Carlton PALMER	
5	Nigel PEARSON	
6	Viv ANDERSON ❑	
7	Danny WILSON ❑	
8	Chris WADDLE	
9	David HIRST	
10	Mark BRIGHT	
11	John SHERIDAN	
	Substitutes	
12	Gordon WATSON	
14	Chris BART-WILLIAMS	
Gk	Kevin PRESSMAN	

BLACKBURN ROVERS
Red & Black striped shirts, White shorts   Goals

1	Bobby MIMMS	
2	David MAY ❑	
3	Alan WRIGHT	
4	Tim SHERWOOD	
5	Colin HENDRY	
6	Kevin MORAN ❑	
7	Mark ATKINS †	
8	Gordon COWANS	
9	Alan SHEARER	
10	Mike NEWELL ❑	
11	Jason WILCOX ‡	
	Substitutes	
12	Tony DOBSON †73	
14	Roy WEGERLE ‡54	
Gk	Darren COLLIER	

Date	Saturday 31 October 1992
Venue	The Dell, 3.00pm

SOUTHAMPTON (0) 1
OLDHAM ATHLETIC (0) 0

Attendance	10,827
Referee	Paul DURKIN
Linesmen	R.J. Harris, A. Schneider

SOUTHAMPTON
Red & White striped shirts, Black shorts   Goals

1	Tim FLOWERS	
2	Jeff KENNA	
3	Micky ADAMS	
4	Terry HURLOCK ❏	
5	Richard HALL	58
6	Kenneth MONKOU	
7	Matthew LE TISSIER	
8	Glenn COCKERILL	
9	Neil MADDISON	
10	Iain DOWIE ❏	
11	Francis BENALI	
	Substitutes	
12	Tommy WIDDRINGTON	
14	Lee POWELL	
Gk	Ian ANDREWS	

OLDHAM ATHLETIC
Blue shirts, Blue shorts   Goals

1	Jon HALLWORTH	
2	Neil McDONALD	
3	Neil POINTON	
4	Nick HENRY	
5	Richard JOBSON	
6	Steve REDMOND	
7	Gunnar HALLE †	
8	Ian MARSHALL	
9	Graeme SHARP	
10	Mike MILLIGAN	
11	Paul BERNARD	
	Substitutes	
12	Neil ADAMS †65	
14	Craig FLEMING	
Gk	John KEELEY	

Date	Saturday 31 October 1992
Venue	White Hart Lane, 3.00pm

TOTTENHAM HOTSPUR (0) 2
LIVERPOOL (0) 0

Attendance	32,917
Referee	Gerald ASHBY
Linesmen	J.F. Moore, M.E. Alexander

TOTTENHAM HOTSPUR
White shirts, Navy Blue shorts   Goals

1	Erik THORSTVEDT	
2	Justin EDINBURGH	
3	Dean AUSTIN ❏ ‡	
4	Nick BARMBY †	
5	Gary MABBUTT	
6	Neil RUDDOCK	72
7	Steve SEDGLEY	
8	Gordon DURIE	
9	NAYIM	63
10	Teddy SHERINGHAM	
11	Paul ALLEN	
	Substitutes	
12	David HOWELLS ‡72	
14	Andy TURNER †82	
Gk	Kevin DEARDEN	

LIVERPOOL
Red shirts, Red shorts   Goals

1	David JAMES	
2	Mike MARSH	
3	David BURROWS	
4	Torben PIECHNIK ❏	
5	Mark WRIGHT	
6	Don HUTCHISON ❏	
7	Steve McMANAMAN	
8	Mark WALTERS ❏ †	
9	Ian RUSH	
10	Jamie REDKNAPP	
11	Michael THOMAS	
	Substitutes	
12	Nicky TANNER †78	
14	Paul STEWART ‡73	
Gk	Mike HOOPER	

LEAGUE TABLE

Up to and including 31.10.92

		P	W	D	L	F	A	Pts
1	Blackburn Rovers	14	7	6	1	24	9	27
2	Norwich City	14	8	3	3	24	25	27
3	Queen's Park Rangers	13	6	5	2	20	13	23
4	Arsenal	13	7	2	4	17	12	23
5	Coventry City	14	6	5	3	18	15	23
6	Aston Villa	13	5	6	2	21	15	21
7	Manchester United	14	5	6	3	14	11	21
8	Ipswich Town	14	4	8	2	20	18	20
9	Manchester City	14	5	4	5	17	14	19
10	Chelsea	14	5	4	5	19	18	19
11	Middlesbrough	14	4	6	4	23	19	18
12	Leeds United	14	4	6	4	25	23	18
13	Sheffield Wednesday	14	4	5	5	16	17	17
14	Liverpool	14	4	4	6	20	23	16
15	Sheffield United	14	4	4	6	14	19	16
16	Oldham Athletic	14	3	6	5	21	23	15
17	Tottenham Hotspur	14	3	6	5	14	22	15
18	Wimbledon	14	3	5	6	18	21	14
19	Southampton	14	3	5	6	12	17	14
20	Everton	14	3	4	7	12	19	13
21	Crystal Palace	13	1	8	4	17	21	11
22	Nottingham Forest	14	2	4	8	11	23	10

LEADING SCORERS

Alan SHEARER	Blackburn Rovers	12
Lee CHAPMAN	Leeds United	8
David WHITE	Manchester City	8
Paul WILKINSON	Middlesbrough	8
Ian WRIGHT	Arsenal	8

LEAGUE GOALSCORING FIGURES

Running Totals

Date	Games	Goals	Average	Games	Goals	Average
03.10.92	10	40	4.00	119	325	2.73
04.10.92	1	1	1.00	120	326	2.72
17.10.92	9	24	2.67	129	350	2.71
18.10.92	1	4	4.00	130	354	2.72
19.10.92	1	0	0.00	131	354	2.70
21.10.92	1	1	1.00	132	355	2.69
24.10.92	9	17	1.89	141	372	2.64
25.10.92	2	7	3.50	143	379	2.65
31.10.92	9	18	2.00	152	397	2.61

Date Sunday 1 November 1992
Venue Villa Park, 4.00pm

ASTON VILLA (1) 2
QPR (0) 0

Attendance 20,140
Referee Mike PECK
Linesmen E.J. Walsh, B.A. Wigginton

ASTON VILLA
Claret & Blue shirts, White shorts   Goals

1	Nigel SPINK	
2	Earl BARRETT	
3	Steve STAUNTON	
4	Shaun TEALE	
5	Paul McGRATH	
6	Kevin RICHARDSON	
7	Ray HOUGHTON	
8	Garry PARKER	
9	Dean SAUNDERS	43
10	Dalian ATKINSON ‡	79
11	Dave FARRELL †	
	Substitutes	
12	Dwight YORKE ‡89	
14	Bryan SMALL †59	
Gk	Mark BOSNICH	

QPR
Red & Black hooped shirts, Red shorts   Goals

1	Tony ROBERTS	
2	David BARDSLEY	
3	Clive WILSON	
4	Ray WILKINS	
5	Darren PEACOCK	
6	Alan McDONALD	
7	Andy IMPEY †	
8	Ian HOLLOWAY	
9	Les FERDINAND	
10	Bradley ALLEN	
11	Simon BARKER	
	Substitutes	
12	Dennis BAILEY †80	
14	Danny MADDIX	
Gk	Jan STEJSKAL	

Date	Monday 2 November 1992
Venue	Stamford Bridge, 3.00pm

CRYSTAL PALACE (0) 1
ARSENAL (1) 2

Attendance	20,734
Referee	Vic CALLOW
Linesmen	M.K. Bullivant, W.M. Jordan

CRYSTAL PALACE
Red & Blue striped shirts, Red shorts   Goals

1	Nigel MARTYN	
2	Richard SHAW	
3	Lee SINNOTT ‡	
4	Gareth SOUTHGATE	
5	Eric YOUNG	
6	Andy THORN	
7	Simon OSBORN	
8	Paul WILLIAMS	
9	Chris ARMSTRONG †	
10	John SALAKO	
11	Eddie McGOLDRICK	69
	Substitutes	
12	Chris COLEMAN ‡86	
14	Geoff THOMAS †71	
Gk	Paul HEALD	

ARSENAL
Yellow shirts, Blue shorts   Goals

1	David SEAMAN	
2	Lee DIXON	
3	Steve MORROW	
4	David HILLIER	
5	Steve BOULD	
6	Tony ADAMS	
7	John JENSEN ❑	
8	Ian WRIGHT ‡	73
9	Alan SMITH	
10	Paul MERSON	5
11	Kevin CAMPBELL	
	Substitutes	
12	Pal LYDERSEN	
14	Anders LIMPAR ‡88	
Gk	Alan MILLER	

Date	Saturday 7 November 1992
Venue	Highbury Stadium, 3.00pm

ARSENAL (3) 3
COVENTRY CITY (0) 0

Attendance	27,693
Referee	Joe WORRALL
Linesmen	C. Jones, I.M.D. Mitchell

ARSENAL
Red & White shirts, White shorts   Goals

1	David SEAMAN	
2	Lee DIXON	
3	Steve MORROW	
4	David HILLIER	
5	Steve BOULD	
6	Tony ADAMS	
7	John JENSEN	
8	Ian WRIGHT	30
9	Alan SMITH	8
10	Paul MERSON	
11	Kevin CAMPBELL ‡	45
	Substitutes	
12	Pal LYDERSEN	
14	Anders LIMPAR ‡73	
Gk	Alan MILLER	

COVENTRY CITY
Sky Blue shirts, Sky Blue shorts   Goals

1	Steve OGRIZOVIC	
2	Brian BORROWS †	
3	Kenny SANSOM	
4	Peter ATHERTON	
5	Peter BILLING	
6	Peter NDLOVU	
7	Craig MIDDLETON	
8	Lee HURST	
9	Robert ROSARIO	
10	Phil BABB	
11	John WILLIAMS	
	Substitutes	
12	Terry FLEMING †78	
14	Paul WILLIAMS	
Gk	Jonathan GOULD	

Date	Saturday 7 November 1992
Venue	Villa Park, 3.00pm

ASTON VILLA (1) 1
MANCHESTER UNITED (0) 0

Attendance	39,063
Referee	David ELLERAY
Linesmen	A.N. Butler, M.A. Cooper

ASTON VILLA
Claret & Blue shirts, White shorts   Goals

1	Nigel SPINK	
2	Earl BARRETT	
3	Steve STAUNTON	
4	Shaun TEALE	
5	Paul McGRATH	
6	Kevin RICHARDSON	
7	Ray HOUGHTON	
8	Garry PARKER	
9	Dean SAUNDERS	
10	Dalian ATKINSON	12
11	Bryan SMALL	
	Substitutes	
12	Dwight YORKE	
14	Cyrille REGIS	
Gk	Mark BOSNICH	

MANCHESTER UNITED
Blue shirts, Blue shorts   Goals

1	Peter SCHMEICHEL	
2	Paul PARKER	
3	Clayton BLACKMORE	
4	Steve BRUCE	
5	Darren FERGUSON †	
6	Gary PALLISTER	
7	Bryan ROBSON ❑	
8	Paul INCE	
9	Lee SHARPE	
10	Mark HUGHES	
11	Ryan GIGGS	
	Substitutes	
12	Brian McCLAIR †80	
14	Andrei KANCHELSKIS	
Gk	Fraser DIGBY	

Date	Saturday 7 November 1992
Venue	Ewood Park, 3.00pm

BLACKBURN ROVERS (0) 0
TOTTENHAM HOTSPUR (0) 2

Attendance	17,305
Referee	Keren BARRATT
Linesmen	T.A. Atkinson, P.D. Harding

BLACKBURN ROVERS
Blue & White shirts, White shorts   Goals

1	Bobby MIMMS	
2	David MAY †	
3	Alan WRIGHT	
4	Tim SHERWOOD ❑	
5	Colin HENDRY	
6	Kevin MORAN	
7	Mark ATKINS	
8	Gordon COWANS ‡	
9	Alan SHEARER	
10	Mike NEWELL	
11	Stuart RIPLEY	
	Substitutes	
12	Chris PRICE †70	
14	Roy WEGERLE ‡70	
Gk	Darren COLLIER	

TOTTENHAM HOTSPUR
Yellow shirts, Yellow shorts   Goals

1	Erik THORSTVEDT	
2	Justin EDINBURGH	
3	Dean AUSTIN	
4	Vinny SAMWAYS	
5	Gary MABBUTT	
6	Neil RUDDOCK	
7	David HOWELLS	67
8	Gordon DURIE	
9	NAYIM	
10	Teddy SHERINGHAM	81p
11	Paul ALLEN	
	Substitutes	
12	Nick BARMBY	
14	Jason CUNDY	
Gk	Ian WALKER	

Date	Saturday 7 November 1992
Venue	Stamford Bridge, 3.00pm

CHELSEA (2) 3
CRYSTAL PALACE (0) 1

Attendance	17,141
Referee	Ron GROVES
Linesmen	W.J. Norbury, P.A. Josper

CHELSEA
Blue shirts, Blue shorts   Goals

1	Kevin HITCHCOCK	
2	Gareth HALL	
3	Frank SINCLAIR ‡	
4	Andy TOWNSEND	
5	David LEE	
6	Mal DONAGHY	
7	Graham STUART	40
8	Robert FLECK	
9	Mick HARFORD	58
10	Eddie NEWTON	
11	Dennis WISE	
	Substitutes	
12	Craig BURLEY	
14	Graeme LE SAUX ‡62	
Gk	Nicky COLGAN	

CRYSTAL PALACE
Red & Blue striped shirts, Red shorts   Goals

1	Nigel MARTYN	
2	Richard SHAW	4og
3	Lee SINNOTT ❑ ■	
4	Gareth SOUTHGATE	
5	Eric YOUNG	70
6	Andy THORN	
7	Simon OSBORN	
8	Paul WILLIAMS ❑ †	
9	Chris ARMSTRONG	
10	John SALAKO	
11	Eddie McGOLDRICK ❑	
	Substitutes	
12	Chris COLEMAN †60	
14	Stan COLLYMORE	
Gk	Paul HEALD	

Date	Saturday 7 November 1992
Venue	Portman Road, 3.00pm

IPSWICH TOWN (0) 0
SOUTHAMPTON (0) 0

Attendance	15,722
Referee	Roger DILKES
Linesmen	J.A. Elwin, A. Schneider

IPSWICH TOWN
Blue & White shirts, White shorts   Goals

1	Clive BAKER	
2	Gavin JOHNSON	
3	Neil THOMPSON	
4	Mick STOCKWELL	
5	John WARK	
6	David LINIGHAN	
7	Geraint WILLIAMS	
8	Steve PALMER †	
9	Steve WHITTON	
10	Jason DOZZELL	
11	Chris KIWOMYA	
	Substitutes	
12	Paul GODDARD †70	
14	Phil WHELAN	
Gk	Jason WINTERS	

SOUTHAMPTON
Red & White striped shirts, Black shorts   Goals

1	Tim FLOWERS	
2	Jeff KENNA	
3	Micky ADAMS ❑	
4	Terry HURLOCK	
5	Richard HALL	
6	Kenneth MONKOU	
7	Matthew LE TISSIER	
8	Glenn COCKERILL	
9	Iain DOWIE	
10	Neil MADDISON	
11	Francis BENALI	
	Substitutes	
12	Tommy WIDDRINGTON	
14	Jason DODD	
Gk	Ian ANDREWS	

Date	Saturday 7 November 1992
Venue	Anfield, 3.00pm

LIVERPOOL (3) 4
MIDDLESBROUGH (1) 1

Attendance	34,974
Referee	Dermot GALLAGHER
Linesmen	U.D. Rennie, P.R. Richards

LIVERPOOL
Red shirts, Red shorts   Goals

1	Mike HOOPER	
2	Mike MARSH	
3	David BURROWS	
4	Steve NICOL	
5	Torben PIECHNIK	
6	Don HUTCHISON	
7	Steve McMANAMAN	45
8	Jamie REDKNAPP	
9	Ian RUSH	89
10	Ronnie ROSENTHAL	9, 38
11	Michael THOMAS	
	Substitutes	
12	Rob JONES	
14	Nick TANNER	
Gk	David JAMES	

MIDDLESBROUGH
White shirts, Black shorts   Goals

1	Stephen PEARS	
2	Curtis FLEMING	
3	Jimmy PHILLIPS	41
4	Alan KERNAGHAN ‡	
5	Derek WHYTE	
6	Jon GITTENS	
7	Robbie MUSTOE	
8	Willie FALCONER	
9	Paul WILKINSON	
10	Mark PROCTOR †	
11	John HENDRIE	
	Substitutes	
12	Bernie SLAVEN †75	
14	Chris MORRIS ‡14	
Gk	Ian IRONSIDE	

Date	Saturday 7 November 1992
Venue	Maine Road, 3.00pm

MANCHESTER CITY (2) 4
LEEDS UNITED (0) 0

Attendance	27,255
Referee	Kelvin MORTON
Linesmen	P.M. Roberts, J.B. Robinson

MANCHESTER CITY
Light Blue shirts, White shorts   Goals

1	Tony COTON	
2	Ian BRIGHTWELL	80
3	Terry PHELAN	
4	Steve McMAHON	
5	Keith CURLE	
6	Andy HILL	75
7	David WHITE	37
8	Mike SHERON	13
9	Niall QUINN	
10	Fitzroy SIMPSON ❏	
11	Rick HOLDEN	
	Substitutes	
12	Peter REID	
14	Garry FLITCROFT	
Gk	Martyn MARGETSON	

LEEDS UNITED
Yellow shirts, Yellow shorts   Goals

1	Mervyn DAY	
2	Jon NEWSOME	
3	David WETHERALL	
4	Steve HODGE †	
5	Chris FAIRCLOUGH	
6	Chris WHYTE	
7	Gordon STRACHAN ❏	
8	Eric CANTONA	
9	Rod WALLACE ❏	
10	Gary McALLISTER	
11	Gary SPEED	
	Substitutes	
12	Lee CHAPMAN †56	
14	David ROCASTLE	
Gk	Paul PETTINGER	

Date	Saturday 7 November 1992
Venue	City Ground, 3.00pm

NOTTINGHAM FOREST (0) 0
EVERTON (0) 1

Attendance	20,941
Referee	Steve LODGE
Linesmen	E.B. Crompton, P. Rejer

NOTTINGHAM FOREST
Red shirts, White shorts   Goals

1	Mark CROSSLEY
2	Brian LAWS
3	Stuart PEARCE
4	Steve CHETTLE
5	Carl TILER
6	Roy KEANE
7	Thorvaldur ORLYGSSON
8	Scot GEMMILL
9	Nigel CLOUGH
10	Lee GLOVER
11	Ian WOAN
	Substitutes
12	Gary BANNISTER
14	Gary CROSBY
Gk	Andy MARRIOTT

EVERTON
Blue shirts, Blue shorts   Goals

1	Neville SOUTHALL	
2	Matthew JACKSON	
3	Gary ABLETT	
4	Ian SNODIN	
5	Dave WATSON	
6	Martin KEOWN	
7	Alan HARPER †	
8	Peter BEARDSLEY	
9	Paul RIDEOUT	52
10	Barry HORNE ❏	
11	John EBBRELL	
	Substitutes	
12	Robert WARZYCHA †67	
14	Stuart BARLOW	
Gk	Jason KEARTON	

Date	Saturday 7 November 1992
Venue	Selhurst Park, 3.00pm

WIMBLEDON (0) 0
QPR (2) 2

Attendance	6,771
Referee	Philip DON
Linesmen	M.E. Alexander, M.D. Dearing

WIMBLEDON
Blue shirts, Blue shorts   Goals

1	Hans SEGERS
2	Warren BARTON
3	Roger JOSEPH
4	Vinnie JONES
5	Alan McLEARY
6	Brian McALLISTER
7	Terry GIBSON †
8	Robbie EARLE
9	Dean HOLDSWORTH
10	Lawrie SANCHEZ ‡
11	Gerald DOBBS
	Substitutes
12	Andy CLARKE †69
14	Steve COTTERILL ‡69
Gk	Neil SULLIVAN

QPR
Red & Black hooped shirts, Black shorts   Goals

1	Tony ROBERTS	
2	David BARDSLEY	
3	Clive WILSON	
4	Ray WILKINS ❏	42
5	Darren PEACOCK	
6	Alan McDONALD	
7	Andy IMPEY	
8	Ian HOLLOWAY	
9	Les FERDINAND	
10	Bradley ALLEN	25
11	Andy SINTON	
	Substitutes	
12	Simon BARKER	
14	Danny MADDIX	
Gk	Jan STEJSKAL	

Date	Sunday 8 November 1992
Venue	Bramall Lane, 4.00pm

SHEFFIELD UNITED (0) 1
SHEFFIELD WEDNESDAY (0) 1

Attendance	30,039
Referee	Mike REED
Linesmen	R.H. Andrews, E. Lomas

SHEFFIELD UNITED
Red & White striped shirts, White shorts   Goals

1	Alan KELLY	
2	Kevin GAGE	
3	Tom COWAN	
4	John GANNON	
5	Brian GAYLE	
6	Paul BEESLEY	
7	Carl BRADSHAW	
8	Paul ROGERS	
9	Adrian LITTLEJOHN	61
10	Brian DEANE	
11	Mitch WARD †	
	Substitutes	
12	Glyn HODGES †87	
14	Jamie HOYLAND	
Gk	Phil KITE	

SHEFFIELD WEDNESDAY
Blue & White striped shirts, Black shorts   Goals

1	Chris WOODS	
2	Roger NILSSON	
3	Nigel WORTHINGTON	
4	Carlton PALMER	
5	Nigel PEARSON	
6	Chris BART-WILLIAMS	
7	Danny WILSON	
8	Chris WADDLE	
9	David HIRST ❏	84
10	Mark BRIGHT ❏	
11	John SHERIDAN †	
	Substitutes	
12	Paul WARHURST †67	
14	John HARKES	
Gk	Kevin PRESSMAN	

Date	Monday 9 November 1992
Venue	Boundary Park, 7.30pm

OLDHAM ATHLETIC (2) 2
NORWICH CITY (2) 3

Attendance	11,018
Referee	Robbie HART
Linesmen	J. McGrath, E.J. Walsh

OLDHAM ATHLETIC
Blue shirts, Blue shorts   Goals

1	Jon HALLWORTH	
2	Gunnar HALLE	
3	Neil POINTON	
4	Nick HENRY	
5	Richard JOBSON	
6	Steve REDMOND	
7	Ian OLNEY †	
8	Ian MARSHALL	43
9	Graeme SHARP	25
10	Mike MILLIGAN	
11	Paul BERNARD	
	Substitutes	
12	Neil ADAMS †58	
14	Neil McDONALD	
Gk	Jason KEELEY	

NORWICH CITY
Yellow shirts, Green shorts   Goals

1	Bryan GUNN	
2	Ian CULVERHOUSE ❏	
3	Mark BOWEN	
4	Ian BUTTERWORTH	
5	John POLSTON	
6	Daryl SUTCH	
7	Ian CROOK	
8	Darren BECKFORD ‡	
9	Mark ROBINS	14, 27, 90
10	Ruel FOX	
11	David PHILLIPS	
	Substitutes	
12	Rob NEWMAN	
14	Chris SUTTON ‡88	
Gk	Mark WALTON	

Date	Saturday 21 November 1992
Venue	Highfield Road, 3.00pm

COVENTRY CITY (1) 2
MANCHESTER CITY (0) 3

Attendance	14,590
Referee	Paul DURKIN
Linesmen	D.T. Colwell, B.L. Polkey

COVENTRY CITY
Sky Blue shirts, Sky Blue shorts   Goals

1	Steve OGRIZOVIC	
2	Brian BORROWS	
3	Kenny SANSOM	
4	Peter ATHERTON	
5	Andy PEARCE	
6	Peter NDLOVU	
7	Stewart ROBSON	
8	Lee HURST	
9	Robert ROSARIO	
10	Mick QUINN	13, 49
11	John WILLIAMS ‡	
	Substitutes	
12	Peter BILLING	
14	Phil BABB ‡66	
Gk	Jonathan GOULD	

MANCHESTER CITY
Purple shirts, Purple shorts   Goals

1	Tony COTON	
2	Ian BRIGHTWELL ‡	
3	Terry PHELAN	
4	Steve McMAHON	
5	Keith CURLE	78p
6	Andy HILL	
7	David WHITE	
8	Mike SHERON	56
9	Niall QUINN	66
10	Fitzroy SIMPSON	
11	Rick HOLDEN	
	Substitutes	
12	Garry FLITCROFT	
14	David BRIGHTWELL ‡45	
Gk	Martyn MARGETSON	

Date	Saturday 21 November 1992
Venue	Selhurst Park, 3.00pm

CRYSTAL PALACE (1) 1
NOTTINGHAM FOREST (0) 1

Attendance	15,330
Referee	Keith HACKETT
Linesmen	W.M. Jordan, D.C. Madgwick

CRYSTAL PALACE
Red & Blue striped shirts, Red shorts   Goals

1	Nigel MARTYN	
2	John HUMPHREY	
3	Richard SHAW	
4	Gareth SOUTHGATE	
5	Eric YOUNG	
6	Andy THORN	
7	Simon OSBORN	
8	Paul WILLIAMS	
9	Chris ARMSTRONG	23
10	Paul MORTIMER †	
11	Eddie McGOLDRICK	
	Substitutes	
12	Chris COLEMAN †77	
14	George NDAH	
Gk	Andrew WOODMAN	

NOTTINGHAM FOREST
White shirts, Black shorts   Goals

1	Mark CROSSLEY	
2	Brian LAWS	
3	Stuart PEARCE	
4	Steve CHETTLE	
5	Carl TILER	
6	Roy KEANE ❑	
7	Gary BANNISTER	84
8	Scot GEMMILL	
9	Nigel CLOUGH	
10	Lee GLOVER	
11	Ian WOAN	
	Substitutes	
12	Kingsley BLACK	
14	Terry WILSON	
Gk	Andy MARRIOTT	

Date	Saturday 21 November 1992
Venue	Goodison Park, 3.00pm

EVERTON (0) 0
CHELSEA (1) 1

Attendance	17,418
Referee	Mike REED
Linesmen	M.A. Riley, M. Warren

EVERTON
Blue shirts, White shorts — Goals

1	Neville SOUTHALL	
2	Matthew JACKSON	
3	Gary ABLETT	
4	Ian SNODIN	
5	Dave WATSON ❑	
6	Martin KEOWN	
7	Alan HARPER ‡	
8	Peter BEARDSLEY	
9	Paul RIDEOUT	
10	Barry HORNE †	
11	Andy HINCHCLIFFE	
	Substitutes	
12	Stuart BARLOW †53	
14	Robert WARZYCHA ‡72	
Gk	Jason KEARTON	

CHELSEA
White shirts, Red shorts — Goals

1	Kevin HITCHCOCK	
2	Gareth HALL	
3	Frank SINCLAIR	
4	Andy TOWNSEND	
5	David LEE	
6	Mal DONAGHY	
7	Graham STUART ❑	
8	Robert FLECK ❑	45
9	Mick HARFORD ❑	
10	Eddie NEWTON ❑	
11	Dennis WISE ❑	
	Substitutes	
12	Erland JOHNSEN	
14	Graeme LE SAUX	
Gk	Nick COLGAN	

Date	Saturday 21 November 1992
Venue	Elland Road, 3.00pm

LEEDS UNITED (0) 3
ARSENAL (0) 0

Attendance	30,516
Referee	Robbie HART
Linesmen	J. McGrath, R. Pearson

LEEDS UNITED
White shirts, White shorts — Goals

1	John LUKIC	
2	Jon NEWSOME	
3	Tony DORIGO	
4	David ROCASTLE	
5	Chris FAIRCLOUGH	51
6	Chris WHYTE	
7	Gordon STRACHAN	
8	Rod WALLACE †	
9	Lee CHAPMAN	56
10	Gary McALLISTER	87
11	Gary SPEED	
	Substitutes	
12	Carl SHUTT †83	
14	Ray WALLACE	
Gk	Mervyn DAY	

ARSENAL
Red & White shirts, White shorts — Goals

1	David SEAMAN ‡	
2	Lee DIXON	
3	Steve MORROW	
4	David HILLIER †	
5	Steve BOULD	
6	Tony ADAMS	
7	John JENSEN	
8	Ian WRIGHT	
9	Kevin CAMPBELL	
10	Paul MERSON ❑	
11	Anders LIMPAR	
	Substitutes	
12	Andy LINIGHAN	
14	Ray PARLOUR †46	
Gk	Alan MILLER ‡51	

Date	Saturday 21 November 1992
Venue	Old Trafford, 3.00pm

MANCHESTER UNITED (3) 3
OLDHAM ATHLETIC (0) 0

Attendance	33,497
Referee	Allan GUNN
Linesmen	M. Fletcher, B. Lowe

MANCHESTER UNITED
Red shirts, White shorts   Goals

1	Peter SCHMEICHEL	
2	Paul PARKER	
3	Denis IRWIN †	
4	Steve BRUCE	
5	Lee SHARPE	
6	Gary PALLISTER	
7	Bryan ROBSON	
8	Paul INCE ‡	
9	Brian McCLAIR	10, 28
10	Mark HUGHES	11
11	Ryan GIGGS	
	Substitutes	
12	Mike PHELAN †77	
14	Nicky BUTT ‡65	
Gk	Fraser DIGBY	

OLDHAM ATHLETIC
Blue shirts, Blue shorts   Goals

1	Jon HALLWORTH	
2	Gunnar HALLE	
3	Neil POINTON	
4	Nick HENRY	
5	Richard JOBSON ❑	
6	Steve REDMOND	
7	Neil McDONALD	
8	Ian MARSHALL	
9	Graeme SHARP †	
10	Mike MILLIGAN	
11	Neil ADAMS ❑	
	Substitutes	
12	Ian OLNEY †62	
14	Paul BERNARD	
Gk	Paul GERRARD	

Date	Saturday 21 November 1992
Venue	Ayresome Park, 3.00pm

MIDDLESBROUGH (0) 2
WIMBLEDON (0) 0

Attendance	14,524
Referee	Joe WORRALL
Linesmen	D.E. Binsley, G.I. Grandidge

MIDDLESBROUGH
Red shirts, White shorts   Goals

1	Stephen PEARS	
2	Curtis FLEMING	
3	Jimmy PHILLIPS †	
4	Jon GITTENS	
5	Derek WHYTE	
6	Robbie MUSTOE	
7	Willie FALCONER	
8	Jamie POLLOCK ‡	
9	Paul WILKINSON	
10	John HENDRIE	49
11	Chris MORRIS	56
	Substitutes	
12	Mark PROCTOR †73	
14	Graham KAVANAGH ‡85	
Gk	Ian IRONSIDE	

WIMBLEDON
Blue shirts, Blue shorts   Goals

1	Hans SEGERS	
2	Warren BARTON	
3	Roger JOSEPH	
4	Vinnie JONES ❑	
5	John SCALES	
6	Brian McALLISTER	
7	Terry GIBSON	
8	Robbie EARLE	
9	Dean HOLDSWORTH	
10	Gerald DOBBS †	
11	Paul McGEE ‡	
	Substitutes	
12	Steve COTTERILL †64	
14	Paul MILLER ‡64	
Gk	Neil SULLIVAN	

Date	Saturday 21 November 1992
Venue	Carrow Road, 3.00pm

NORWICH CITY (0) 2
SHEFFIELD UNITED (0) 1

Attendance	14,874
Referee	Mike PECK
Linesmen	M.K. Bullivant, M. Stobbart

NORWICH CITY
Yellow shirts, Green shorts   Goals

1	Bryan GUNN	
2	Ian CULVERHOUSE	
3	Mark BOWEN	
4	Ian BUTTERWORTH	
5	John POLSTON	
6	Daryl SUTCH	
7	Ian CROOK	
8	Darren BECKFORD	
9	Mark ROBINS	80
10	Ruel FOX	
11	David PHILLIPS	
	Substitutes	
12	Chris SUTTON	
14	Gary MEGSON	
Gk	Mark WALTON	

SHEFFIELD UNITED
Red & White striped shirts, White shorts   Goals

1	Alan KELLY	
2	Kevin GAGE	
3	Tom COWAN	
4	John GANNON	
5	John PEMBERTON	
6	Paul BEESLEY	60og
7	Mitch WARD †	
8	Paul ROGERS	
9	Adrian LITTLEJOHN ‡	
10	Brian DEANE	
11	Glyn HODGES	
	Substitutes	
12	Chris KAMARA †76	
14	Alan CORK ‡63	71
Gk	Phil KITE	

Date	Saturday 21 November 1992
Venue	Hillsborough, 3.00pm

SHEFFIELD WEDNESDAY (1) 1
IPSWICH TOWN (0) 1

Attendance	24,270
Referee	Keren BARRATT
Linesmen	N.S. Barry, J. Hilditch

SHEFFIELD WEDNESDAY
Blue & White striped shirts, Black shorts   Goals

1	Chris WOODS	
2	Roland NILSSON	
3	Nigel WORTHINGTON ❑	
4	Carlton PALMER	
5	Nigel PEARSON	
6	Paul WARHURST ‡	
7	Danny WILSON	
8	Chris WADDLE	
9	David HIRST	
10	Mark BRIGHT	
11	John SHERIDAN	
	Substitutes	
12	John HARKES	
14	Chris BART-WILLIAMS ‡66	
Gk	Kevin PRESSMAN	

IPSWICH TOWN
White shirts, White shorts   Goals

1	Clive BAKER	
2	Phil WHELAN ❑	
3	Neil THOMPSON	16og
4	Mick STOCKWELL	
5	Gavin JOHNSON	
6	David LINIGHAN	
7	Geraint WILLIAMS	
8	Paul GODDARD	
9	Steve PALMER	
10	Jason DOZZELL	
11	Chris KIWOMYA	74
	Substitutes	
12	Steve WHITTON	
14	Eddie YOUDS	
Gk	Jason WINTERS	

Date	Saturday 21 November 1992
Venue	White Hart Lane, 3.00pm

TOTTENHAM HOTSPUR (0) 0
ASTON VILLA (0) 0

Attendance	32,852
Referee	Jim BORRETT
Linesmen	G.P. Barber, W.J. Norbury

TOTTENHAM HOTSPUR
White shirts, Navy Blue shorts   Goals

1	Erik THORSTVEDT	
2	Justin EDINBURGH	
3	Dean AUSTIN	
4	Vinny SAMWAYS	
5	Gary MABBUTT	
6	Neil RUDDOCK ❑	
7	David HOWELLS	
8	Gordon DURIE ‡	
9	NAYIM	
10	Teddy SHERINGHAM	
11	Paul ALLEN †	
	Substitutes	
12	Jason CUNDY †78	
14	Nick BARMBY ‡45	
Gk	Ian WALKER	

ASTON VILLA
Claret & Blue shirts, White shorts   Goals

1	Nigel SPINK	
2	Earl BARRETT	
3	Steve STAUNTON	
4	Shaun TEALE ❑ †	
5	Paul McGRATH	
6	Kevin RICHARDSON	
7	Ray HOUGHTON	
8	Garry PARKER ‡	
9	Dean SAUNDERS	
10	Dalian ATKINSON	
11	Bryan SMALL	
	Substitutes	
12	Ugo EHIOGU †71	
14	Cyrille REGIS ‡84	
Gk	Mark BOSNICH	

Date	Sunday 22 November 1992
Venue	The Dell, 4.00pm

SOUTHAMPTON (1) 1
BLACKBURN ROVERS (1) 1

Attendance	16,626
Referee	Martin BODENHAM
Linesmen	I.A. Madge, G.T. Pearson

SOUTHAMPTON
Red & White shirts, Black shorts   Goals

1	Tim FLOWERS	
2	Jeff KENNA	
3	Micky ADAMS	
4	Terry HURLOCK	
5	Richard HALL	
6	Kenneth MONKOU	
7	Matthew LE TISSIER	22
8	Glenn COCKERILL	
9	Neil MADDISON ‡	
10	Iain DOWIE	
11	Francis BENALI	
	Substitutes	
12	Perry GROVES	
14	Nicky BANGER ‡62	
Gk	Ian ANDREWS	

BLACKBURN ROVERS
Blue & White shirts, White shorts   Goals

1	Bobby MIMMS	
2	David MAY	
3	Tony DOBSON	
4	Tim SHERWOOD	
5	Colin HENDRY	
6	Kevin MORAN	38
7	Stuart RIPLEY	
8	Gordon COWANS	
9	Alan SHEARER	
10	Mike NEWELL	
11	Jason WILCOX ‡	
	Substitutes	
12	Nick MARKER	
14	Roy WEGERLE ‡68	
Gk	Darren COLLIER	

Date	Monday 23 November 1992
Venue	Loftus Road, 7.45pm

QPR (0) 0
LIVERPOOL (0) 1

Attendance	21,056
Referee	Roger MILFORD
Linesmen	J.A. Elwin, G.T. Pearson

QPR
Blue & White hooped shirts, White shorts — Goals

1	Tony ROBERTS	
2	David BARDSLEY	
3	Clive WILSON	
4	Ray WILKINS	
5	Darren PEACOCK	
6	Alan McDONALD	
7	Andy IMPEY	
8	Ian HOLLOWAY	
9	Les FERDINAND	
10	Bradley ALLEN	
11	Andy SINTON	
	Substitutes	
12	Simon BARKER	
14	Danny MADDIX	
Gk	Jan STEJSKAL	

LIVERPOOL
Red shirts, Red shorts — Goals

1	Mike HOOPER	
2	Mike MARSH	
3	David BURROWS	
4	Steve NICOL	
5	Torben PIECHNIK	
6	Don HUTCHISON	
7	Steve McMANAMAN	
8	Jamie REDKNAPP ❑	
9	Ian RUSH †	
10	Rob JONES	
11	Ronnie ROSENTHAL	87
	Substitutes	
12	John BARNES †17	
14	Mark WRIGHT	
Gk	Bruce GROBBELAAR	

Date	Saturday 28 November 1992
Venue	Highbury Stadium, 3.00pm

ARSENAL (0) 0
MANCHESTER UNITED (1) 1

Attendance	29,739
Referee	Howard KING
Linesmen	J.A. Elwin, D. Orr

ARSENAL
Red & White shirts, White shorts — Goals

1	David SEAMAN	
2	Lee DIXON	
3	Steve MORROW	
4	David HILLIER	
5	Steve BOULD	
6	Tony ADAMS ❑	
7	John JENSEN †	
8	Ian WRIGHT	
9	Kevin CAMPBELL	
10	Paul MERSON	
11	Anders LIMPAR ‡	
	Substitutes	
12	Ray PARLOUR †67	
14	Mark FLATTS ‡85	
Gk	Alan MILLER	

MANCHESTER UNITED
Blue shirts, Blue shorts — Goals

1	Peter SCMEICHEL	
2	Paul PARKER	
3	Denis IRWIN	
4	Steve BRUCE	
5	Lee SHARPE	
6	Gary PALLISTER	
7	Bryan ROBSON	
8	Paul INCE	
9	Brian McCLAIR	
10	Mark HUGHES ❑	27
11	Ryan GIGGS	
	Substitutes	
12	Andrei KANCHELSKIS	
14	Mike PHELAN	
Gk	Fraser DIGBY	

Date	Saturday 28 November 1992
Venue	Villa Park, 3.00pm

ASTON VILLA (1) 2
NORWICH CITY (2) 3

Attendance	28,837
Referee	Alf BUKSH
Linesmen	J. Leech, B.A. Wigginton

ASTON VILLA
Claret & Blue shirts, White shorts   Goals

1	Nigel SPINK	
2	Earl BARRETT	
3	Steve STAUNTON	
4	Ugo EHIOGU †	
5	Paul McGRATH	
6	Kevin RICHARDSON	
7	Ray HOUGHTON	45
8	Garry PARKER	46
9	Dean SAUNDERS	
10	Dalian ATKINSON	
11	Bryan SMALL	
	Substitutes	
12	Cyrille REGIS †80	
14	Dariusz KUBICKI	
Gk	Mark BOSNICH	

NORWICH CITY
Yellow shirts, Green shorts   Goals

1	Bryan GUNN	
2	Ian CULVERHOUSE	
3	Mark BOWEN	
4	Ian BUTTERWORTH	
5	John POLSTON	
6	Daryl SUTCH	49
7	Ian CROOK	
8	Darren BECKFORD †	30
9	Mark ROBINS	
10	Ruel FOX	
11	David PHILLIPS	17
	Substitutes	
12	Chris SUTTON ❏ †73	
14	Gary MEGSON	
Gk	Mark WALTON	

Date	Saturday 28 November 1992
Venue	Ewood Park, 3.00pm

BLACKBURN ROVERS (1) 1
QPR (0) 0

Attendance	15,850
Referee	Keith HACKETT
Linesmen	M. Warren, P. Newall

BLACKBURN ROVERS
Blue & White shirts, White shorts   Goals

1	Bobby MIMMS	
2	Chris PRICE	
3	Alan WRIGHT	
4	Tim SHERWOOD	
5	Colin HENDRY	
6	Kevin MORAN	
7	Stuart RIPLEY	
8	Gordon COWANS	
9	Alan SHEARER ‡	17
10	Mike NEWELL	
11	Jason WILCOX †	
	Substitutes	
12	Nick MARKER †79	
14	Roy WEGERLE ‡47	
Gk	Matt DICKINS	

QPR
Black & Red hooped shirts, Black shorts   Goals

1	Jan STEJSKAL	
2	David BARDSLEY	
3	Clive WILSON	
4	Ray WILKINS	
5	Darren PEACOCK	
6	Alan McDONALD	
7	Andy IMPEY	
8	Ian HOLLOWAY	
9	Les FERDINAND	
10	Dennis BAILEY †	
11	Andy SINTON	
	Substitutes	
12	Gary PENRICE †46	
14	Danny MADDIX	
Gk	Tony ROBERTS	

Date Saturday 28 November 1992
Venue Portman Road, 3.00pm

IPSWICH TOWN (0) 1
EVERTON (0) 0

Attendance 18,032
Referee Brian HILL
Linesmen M.G. Wright, G.T. Barber

IPSWICH TOWN
Blue & White shirts, White shorts   Goals

1	Clive BAKER	
2	Phil WHELAN	
3	Neil THOMPSON	
4	Mick STOCKWELL	
5	Gavin JOHNSON	72
6	David LINIGHAN	
7	Geraint WILLIAMS	
8	Paul GODDARD	
9	Steve WHITTON ‡	
10	Jason DOZZELL	
11	Chris KIWOMYA	
	Substitutes	
12	Eddie YOUDS	
14	Steve PALMER ‡85	
Gk	Jason WINTERS	

EVERTON
Salmon Pink & Blue stripes, Blue shorts   Goals

1	Neville SOUTHALL	
2	Alan HARPER	
3	Gary ABLETT ❏	
4	Ian SNODIN ‡	
5	Dave WATSON	
6	Martin KEOWN	
7	Billy KENNY	
8	Peter BEARDSLEY	
9	Stuart BARLOW	
10	Tony COTTEE †	
11	Andy HINCHCLIFFE	
	Substitutes	
12	Robert WARZYCHA †70	
14	Paul RIDEOUT ‡82	
Gk	Jason KEARTON	

Date Saturday 28 November 1992
Venue Anfield, 3.00pm

LIVERPOOL (3) 5
CRYSTAL PALACE (0) 0

Attendance 36,380
Referee Steve LODGE
Linesmen E.B. Crompton, P. Rejer

LIVERPOOL
Red shirts, Red shorts   Goals

1	Mike HOOPER	
2	Mike MARSH	9
3	David BURROWS	
4	Steve NICOL	
5	Torben PIECHNIK	
6	Don HUTCHISON	72
7	Steve McMANAMAN	7, 18
8	Jamie REDKNAPP	
9	Ronnie ROSENTHAL †	62
10	John BARNES	
11	Rob JONES	
	Substitutes	
12	Paul STEWART †75	
14	Mark WRIGHT	
Gk	Bruce GROBBELAAR	

CRYSTAL PALACE
Yellow shirts, Blue shorts   Goals

1	Nigel MARTYN	
2	John HUMPHREY	
3	Richard SHAW	
4	Gareth SOUTHGATE	
5	Eric YOUNG ❏	
6	Andy THORN	
7	Simon OSBORN	
8	Lee SINNOTT ‡	
9	Chris ARMSTRONG	
10	Paul WILLIAMS †	
11	Eddie McGOLDRICK ❏	
	Substitutes	
12	Chris COLEMAN †63	
14	George NDAH ‡73	
Gk	Andy WOODMAN	

Date   Saturday 28 November 1992
Venue   Maine Road, 3.00pm

MANCHESTER CITY (0) 0
TOTTENHAM HOTSPUR (0) 1

Attendance 25,496
Referee   David ALLISON
Linesmen   R. Pearson, P.R. Richards

MANCHESTER CITY
Light Blue shirts, White shorts   Goals

1	Tony COTON	
2	David BRIGHTWELL	
3	Terry PHELAN	
4	Steve McMAHON	
5	Keith CURLE	
6	Andy HILL	
7	David WHITE	
8	Mike SHERON	
9	Niall QUINN	
10	Fitzroy SIMPSON †	
11	Rick HOLDEN	
	Substitutes	
12	Garry FLITCROFT †86	
14	Peter REID	
Gk	Martyn MARGETSON	

TOTTENHAM HOTSPUR
Yellow shirts, Yellow shorts   Goals

1	Erik THORSTVEDT	
2	Justin EDINBURGH	
3	Dean AUSTIN	
4	Vinny SAMWAYS ❏	
5	Gary MABBUTT	
6	Neil RUDDOCK	
7	David HOWELLS †	
8	Nick BARMBY ‡	
9	NAYIM	
10	Teddy SHERINGHAM	
11	Kevin WATSON	77
	Substitutes	
12	Jason CUNDY †32	
14	Paul MORAN ‡79	
Gk	Ian WALKER	

Date   Saturday 28 November 1992
Venue   City Ground, 3.00pm

NOTTINGHAM FOREST (1) 1
SOUTHAMPTON (1) 2

Attendance 19,942
Referee   David ELLERAY
Linesmen   A.N. Butler, M.A. Cooper

NOTTINGHAM FOREST
Red shirts, White shorts   Goals

1	Mark CROSSLEY	
2	Brian LAWS ❏	
3	Stuart PEARCE	
4	Steve CHETTLE	
5	Carl TILER	
6	Roy KEANE	
7	Gary BANNISTER †	
8	Scot GEMMILL	
9	Nigel CLOUGH	43
10	Neil WEBB	
11	Ian WOAN	
	Substitutes	
12	Lee GLOVER †65	
14	Kingsley BLACK	
Gk	Andy MARRIOTT	

SOUTHAMPTON
Blue shirts, Blue shorts   Goals

1	Tim FLOWERS	
2	Jeff KENNA	
3	Micky ADAMS	63
4	Terry HURLOCK ❏ †	
5	Richard HALL	
6	Kenneth MONKOU ❏	
7	Matthew LE TISSIER	21
8	Glenn COCKERILL ❏	
9	Iain DOWIE	
10	Neil MADDISON	
11	Francis BENALI	
	Substitutes	
12	Perry GROVES ❏ †59	
14	Tommy WIDDRINGTON	
Gk	Ian ANDREWS	

Date	Saturday 28 November 1992
Venue	Boundary Park, 3.00pm

OLDHAM ATHLETIC (3) 4
MIDDLESBROUGH (1) 1

Attendance	12,401
Referee	Kelvin MORTON
Linesmen	P.M. Roberts, J.B. Robinson

OLDHAM ATHLETIC
Blue shirts, Blue shorts   Goals

		Goals
1	John KEELEY	
2	Gunnar HALLE	21
3	Neil POINTON	24
4	Nick HENRY	
5	Richard JOBSON	
6	Steve REDMOND	
7	Neil ADAMS	60
8	Ian OLNEY	
9	Graeme SHARP	28
10	Mike MILLIGAN	
11	Mark BRENNAN	
	Substitutes	
12	Roger PALMER	
14	Paul BERNARD	
Gk	Paul GERRARD	

MIDDLESBROUGH
Red shirts, White shorts   Goals

		Goals
1	Stephen PEARS	
2	Curtis FLEMING ❑	
3	Gary PARKINSON	
4	Robbie MUSTOE	
5	Derek WHYTE	
6	Jon GITTENS ❑	
7	Willie FALCONER	15
8	Craig HIGNETT ‡	
9	Paul WILKINSON	
10	Mark PROCTOR †	
11	Tommy WRIGHT	
	Substitutes	
12	Jamie POLLOCK †65 ❑	
14	Graham KAVANAGH ‡62	
Gk	Ian IRONSIDE	

Date	Saturday 28 November 1992
Venue	Bramall Lane, 3.00pm

SHEFFIELD UNITED (1) 1
COVENTRY CITY (1) 1

Attendance	15,625
Referee	Philip DON
Linesmen	T. Heilbron, P.J. Robinson

SHEFFIELD UNITED
Red & White striped shirts, White shorts   Goals

		Goals
1	Alan KELLY	
2	Carl BRADSHAW ❑ ■	
3	Tom COWAN ❑	
4	John GANNON †	
5	John PEMBERTON ❑	
6	Paul BEESLEY	
7	Mitch WARD	
8	Paul ROGERS	
9	Alan CORK ‡	
10	Brian DEANE	
11	Glyn HODGES	
	Substitutes	
12	Chris KAMARA †89	
14	Adrian LITTLEJOHN ‡75	
Gk	Danny WAINWRIGHT	

COVENTRY CITY
Sky Blue shirts, Sky Blue shorts   Goals

		Goals
1	Steve OGRIZOVIC	
2	Brian BORROWS	
3	Phil BABB	
4	Peter ATHERTON	
5	Andy PEARCE	37og
6	Peter NDLOVU	
7	Stewart ROBSON	
8	Lee HURST	
9	Robert ROSARIO ❑	
10	Mick QUINN	7
11	Kevin GALLACHER ❑ ‡	
	Substitutes	
12	Peter BILLING	
14	John WILLIAMS ‡77	
Gk	Jonathan GOULD	

Date	Saturday 28 November 1992
Venue	Selhurst Park, 3.00pm

WIMBLEDON (0) 1
SHEFFIELD WEDNESDAY (1) 1

Attendance	5,740
Referee	Roger MILFORD
Linesmen	J.F. Moore, P.A. Josper

WIMBLEDON
Blue shirts, Blue shorts · Goals

1	Hans SEGERS	
2	Warren BARTON	
3	Roger JOSEPH	
4	Vinnie JONES	89p
5	John SCALES	
6	Brian McALLISTER	
7	Dean BLACKWELL	
8	Robbie EARLE	
9	Dean HOLDSWORTH	
10	Lawrie SANCHEZ	
11	Paul MILLER †	
	Substitutes	
12	Terry GIBSON †69	
14	Paul McGEE	
Gk	Neil SULLIVAN	

SHEFFIELD WEDNESDAY
Yellow shirts, Yellow shorts · Goals

1	Chris WOODS	
2	Roland NILSSON	
3	Nigel WORTHINGTON	
4	Viv ANDERSON	
5	Chris BART-WILLIAMS	14
6	Paul WARHURST	
7	Danny WILSON †	
8	Chris WADDLE	
9	David HIRST	
10	Mark BRIGHT	
11	John SHERIDAN	
	Substitutes	
12	John HARKES †65	
14	Peter SHIRTLIFF	
Gk	Kevin PRESSMAN	

Date	Sunday 29 November 1992
Venue	Stamford Bridge, 4.00pm

CHELSEA (0) 1
LEEDS UNITED (0) 0

Attendance	24,345
Referee	Martin BODENHAM
Linesmen	R.J. Harris, K.J. Hawkes

CHELSEA
Blue shirts, Blue shorts · Goals

1	Kevin HITCHCOCK	
2	Gareth HALL	
3	Frank SINCLAIR	
4	Andy TOWNSEND	87
5	David LEE	
6	Mal DONAGHY	
7	Graham STUART	
8	Robert FLECK	
9	Mick HARFORD	
10	Eddie NEWTON	
11	Dennis WISE	
	Substitutes	
12	Erland JOHNSEN	
14	Graeme LE SAUX	
Gk	Nick COLGAN	

LEEDS UNITED
White shirts, White shorts · Goals

1	John LUKIC	
2	Jon NEWSOME	
3	Tony DORIGO	
4	David ROCASTLE	
5	Chris FAIRCLOUGH	
6	Chris WHYTE	
7	Gordon STRACHAN	
8	Rod WALLACE	
9	Lee CHAPMAN	
10	Gary McALLISTER	
11	Gary SPEED	
	Substitutes	
12	Carl SHUTT	
14	Ray WALLACE	
Gk	Mervyn DAY	

LEAGUE TABLE

Up to and including 29.11.92

		P	W	D	L	F	A	Pts
1	Norwich City	17	11	3	3	32	30	36
2	Blackburn Rovers	17	8	7	2	26	12	31
3	Arsenal	17	9	2	6	22	17	29
4	Aston Villa	17	7	7	3	26	18	28
5	Chelsea	17	8	4	5	24	19	28
6	Manchester United	17	7	6	4	18	12	27
7	Queen's Park Rangers	17	7	5	5	22	17	26
8	Manchester City	17	7	4	6	24	17	25
9	Liverpool	17	7	4	6	30	24	25
10	Ipswich Town	17	5	10	2	22	19	25
11	Coventry City	17	6	6	5	21	22	24
12	Tottenham Hotspur	17	5	7	5	17	22	22
13	Leeds United	17	5	6	6	28	28	21
14	Middlesbrough	17	5	6	6	27	27	21
15	Sheffield Wednesday	17	4	8	5	19	20	20
16	Southampton	17	4	7	6	15	19	19
17	Oldham Athletic	17	4	6	7	27	30	18
18	Sheffield United	17	4	6	7	17	23	18
19	Everton	17	4	4	9	13	21	16
20	Wimbledon	17	3	6	8	19	26	15
21	Crystal Palace	17	1	9	7	20	32	12
22	Nottingham Forest	17	2	5	10	13	27	11

LEADING SCORERS

Alan SHEARER	Blackburn Rovers	13
Mark ROBINS	Norwich City	10
Ian WRIGHT	Arsenal	10
Dalian ATKINSON	Aston Villa	9
Lee CHAPMAN	Leeds United	9
David WHITE	Manchester City	9

LEAGUE GOALSCORING FIGURES

Running Totals

Date	Games	Goals	Average	Games	Goals	Average
01.11.92	1	2	2.00	153	399	2.61
02.11.92	1	3	3.00	154	402	2.61
0/.11.92	9	22	2.44	163	424	2.60
08.11.92	1	2	2.00	164	426	2.60
09.11.92	1	5	5.00	165	431	2.61
21.11.92	9	21	2.33	174	452	2.60
22.11.92	1	2	2.00	175	454	2.59
23.11.92	1	1	1.00	176	455	2.58
28.11.92	10	26	2.60	186	481	2.59
29.11.92	1	1	1.00	187	482	2.58

Date   Saturday 5 December 1992
Venue   Highfield Road, 3.00pm

COVENTRY CITY (1) 2
IPSWICH TOWN (1) 2

Attendance   11,294
Referee   Keith HACKETT
Linesmen   N.S. Barry, T.J. Stevens

COVENTRY CITY
Sky Blue shirts, Sky Blue shorts   Goals

1	Steve OGRIZOVIC	
2	Brian BORROWS	
3	Phil BABB	
4	Peter ATHERTON	
5	Andy PEARCE †	
6	Peter NDLOVU	
7	Stewart ROBSON ‡	
8	Lee HURST	
9	Robert ROSARIO	
10	Mick QUINN	54
11	Kevin GALLACHER	16
	Substitutes	
12	Lloyd McGRATH †45	
14	John WILLIAMS ‡78	
Gk	Jonathan GOULD	

IPSWICH TOWN
Red & Black striped shirts, Black shorts   Goals

1	Clive BAKER	
2	Phil WHELAN ❏ ‡	
3	Neil THOMPSON	
4	Mick STOCKWELL	
5	John WARK †	
6	David LINIGHAN	
7	Gavin JOHNSON	
8	Paul GODDARD	
9	Steve WHITTON	70p
10	Jason DOZZELL ❏	
11	Chris KIWOMYA	13
	Substitutes	
12	Eddie YOUDS †60 ❏	
14	Vlado BOZINOSKI ‡75	
Gk	Jason WINTERS	

Date	Saturday 5 December 1992
Venue	Selhurst Park, 3.00pm

CRYSTAL PALACE (1) 2
SHEFFIELD UNITED (0) 0

Attendance	12,361
Referee	Howard KING
Linesmen	I.M.D. Mitchell, G.T. Pearson

CRYSTAL PALACE
Red & Blue striped shirts, Red shorts Goals

1	Nigel MARTYN	
2	John HUMPHREY	
3	Richard SHAW	
4	Gareth SOUTHGATE	76
5	Eric YOUNG	
6	Andy THORN	
7	Simon OSBORN †	
8	George NDAH	
9	Chris ARMSTRONG	43
10	Chris COLEMAN	
11	Eddie McGOLDRICK	
	Substitutes	
12	Bobby BOWRY †85	
14	Grant WATTS	
Gk	Andy WOODMAN	

SHEFFIELD UNITED
Yellow shirts, White shorts Goals

1	Alan KELLY	
2	Carl BRADSHAW ‡	
3	David BARNES	
4	John GANNON	
5	John PEMBERTON	
6	Paul BEESLEY	
7	Kevin GAGE †	
8	Paul ROGERS	
9	Jamie HOYLAND	
10	Brian DEANE	
11	Glyn HODGES	
	Substitutes	
12	Alan CORK †72	
14	Adrian LITTLEJOHN ‡69	
Gk	Ken VEYSEY	

Date	Saturday 5 December 1992
Venue	Elland Road, 3.00pm

LEEDS UNITED (0) 1
NOTTINGHAM FOREST (1) 4

Attendance	29,364
Referee	Alf BUKSH
Linesmen	J. Leech, W.J. Nattrass

LEEDS UNITED
White shirts, White shorts Goals

1	John LUKIC	
2	Jon NEWSOME	
3	Tony DORIGO	
4	David ROCASTLE ‡	
5	Chris FAIRCLOUGH	
6	Ray WALLACE †	
7	Gordon STRACHAN	
8	Rod WALLACE	
9	Lee CHAPMAN	
10	Gary McALLISTER	
11	Gary SPEED ❑	87
	Substitutes	
12	Carl SHUTT †65	
14	Steve HODGE ‡65	
Gk	Mervyn DAY	

NOTTINGHAM FOREST
Red shirts, Red shorts Goals

1	Mark CROSSLEY	
2	Brian LAWS	
3	Stuart PEARCE	
4	Steve CHETTLE	
5	Carl TILER	
6	Roy KEANE	53, 67
7	Neil WEBB	
8	Scot GEMMILL	
9	Nigel CLOUGH	27
10	Lee GLOVER ‡	
11	Ian WOAN †	
	Substitutes	
12	Kingsley BLACK †14	54
14	Gary BANNISTER ‡77	
Gk	Andy MARRIOTT	

Date	Saturday 5 December 1992
Venue	Ayresome Park, 3.00pm

MIDDLESBROUGH (0) 3
BLACKBURN ROVERS (1) 2

Attendance	20,096
Referee	Brian HILL
Linesmen	R. Pearson, M.A. Riley

MIDDLESBROUGH
Red shirts, White shorts | Goals

1	Stephen PEARS		
2	Curtis FLEMING		
3	Jimmy PHILLIPS	74og	
4	Nicky MOHAN		
5	Derek WHYTE		
6	Robbie MUSTOE †		
7	John HENDRIE	52, 55, 66	
8	Andy PEAKE ❏		
9	Paul WILKINSON ❏		
10	Craig HIGNETT ‡		
11	Tommy WRIGHT		
	Substitutes		
12	Jamie POLLOCK †45		
14	Mark PROCTOR ‡77		
Gk	Ian IRONSIDE		

BLACKBURN ROVERS
Blue & White shirts, Blue shorts | Goals

1	Bobby MIMMS		
2	Chris PRICE		
3	Alan WRIGHT		
4	Tim SHERWOOD		
5	Colin HENDRY		
6	Kevin MORAN ❏		
7	Stuart RIPLEY †		
8	Gordon COWANS		
9	Alan SHEARER		
10	Mike NEWELL		
11	Jason WILCOX	44	
	Substitutes		
12	Roy WEGERLE †68		
14	Nick MARKER		
Gk	Darren COLLIER		

Date	Saturday 5 December 1992
Venue	Carrow Road, 3.00pm

NORWICH CITY (0) 2
WIMBLEDON (0) 1

Attendance	14,161
Referee	Ron GROVES
Linesmen	W.J. Norbury, A. Schneider

NORWICH CITY
Yellow shirts, Green shorts | Goals

1	Bryan GUNN		
2	Ian CULVERHOUSE		
3	Mark BOWEN		
4	Ian BUTTERWORTH		
5	John POLSTON		
6	Daryl SUTCH ‡		
7	Ian CROOK		
8	Darren BECKFORD †		
9	Mark ROBINS ❏	77	
10	Ruel FOX		
11	David PHILLIPS	88	
	Substitutes		
12	Chris SUTTON †71		
14	Gary MEGSON ‡75		
Gk	Mark WALTON		

WIMBLEDON
Blue shirts, Blue shorts | Goals

1	Hans SEGERS		
2	Steve TALBOYS		
3	Roger JOSEPH		
4	Vinnie JONES †		
5	John SCALES		
6	Brian McALLISTER ❏		
7	Dean BLACKWELL		
8	Robbie EARLE		
9	Dean HOLDSWORTH ‡		
10	Lawrie SANCHEZ ❏	53	
11	Paul MILLER ❏		
	Substitutes		
12	John FASHANU †62		
14	Terry GIBSON ‡76		
Gk	Neil SULLIVAN		

Date	Saturday 5 December 1992
Venue	Loftus Road, 3.00pm

QPR (2) 3
OLDHAM ATHLETIC (1) 2

Attendance	11,800
Referee	Steve LODGE
Linesmen	G.R. Hamblin, B.A. Wigginton

QPR
Blue & White hooped shirts, White shorts — Goals

1	Jan STEJSKAL	
2	David BARDSLEY	
3	Clive WILSON	
4	Ray WILKINS	
5	Darren PEACOCK	
6	Alan McDONALD	
7	Andy IMPEY ❑	
8	Ian HOLLOWAY ❑	
9	Les FERDINAND ‡	24, 52
10	Gary PENRICE	33
11	Andy SINTON †	
	Substitutes	
12	Bradley ALLEN †19	
14	Danny MADDIX ‡76	
Gk	Tony ROBERTS	

OLDHAM ATHLETIC
Red & White shirts, Red shorts — Goals

1	Paul GERRARD	
2	Gunnar HALLE ❑	
3	Neil POINTON	
4	Nick HENRY	
5	Richard JOBSON	
6	Steve REDMOND	
7	Neil ADAMS	41
8	Ian OLNEY	46
9	Graeme SHARP	
10	Mike MILLIGAN	
11	Mark BRENNAN ❑ †	
	Substitutes	
12	Roger PALMER †72	
14	Craig FLEMING	
Gk	Ian GRAY	

Date	Saturday 5 December 1992
Venue	Hillsborough, 3.00pm

SHEFFIELD WEDNESDAY (1) 1
ASTON VILLA (1) 2

Attendance	29,964
Referee	Robbie HART
Linesmen	M. Warren, J. McGrath

SHEFFIELD WEDNESDAY
Blue & White striped shirts, Black shorts — Goals

1	Chris WOODS	
2	Roger NILSSON	
3	Nigel WORTHINGTON	
4	Carlton PALMER	
5	Viv ANDERSON	
6	Paul WARHURST	
7	John HARKES †	
8	Chris WADDLE	
9	David HIRST	
10	Mark BRIGHT	26
11	John SHERIDAN ‡	
	Substitutes	
12	Chris BART-WILLIAMS †77	
14	Gordon WATSON ‡80	
Gk	Kevin PRESSMAN	

ASTON VILLA
Claret & Blue shirts, White shorts — Goals

1	Mark BOSNICH	
2	Earl BARRETT	
3	Steve STAUNTON ❑	
4	Neil COX	
5	Paul McGRATH	
6	Kevin RICHARDSON	
7	Dwight YORKE	
8	Garry PARKER	
9	Dean SAUNDERS	
10	Dalian ATKINSON	19, 67
11	Bryan SMALL	
	Substitutes	
12	Matthias BREITKREUTZ	
14	Cyrille REGIS	
Gk	Michael OAKES	

Date	Saturday 5 December 1992
Venue	The Dell, 3.00pm

SOUTHAMPTON (1) 2
ARSENAL (0) 0

Attendance	17,286
Referee	John KEY
Linesmen	M.E. Alexander, M. Stobbart

SOUTHAMPTON
Red & White striped shirts, Black shorts — Goals

		Goals
1	Tim FLOWERS	
2	Jeff KENNA	
3	Micky ADAMS	
4	Terry HURLOCK	
5	Richard HALL ❑	
6	Kenneth MONKOU	
7	Matthew LE TISSIER ‡	
8	Glenn COCKERILL †	
9	Iain DOWIE ❑	53
10	Neil MADDISON	16
11	Francis BENALI	
	Substitutes	
12	Nicky BANGER ‡69	
14	Perry GROVES †72	
Gk	Ian ANDREWS	

ARSENAL
Yellow shirts, Blue shorts — Goals

		Goals
1	David SEAMAN	
2	Lee DIXON †	
3	Steve MORROW	
4	David HILLIER	
5	Steve BOULD	
6	Tony ADAMS	
7	Ray PARLOUR	
8	Ian WRIGHT ❑	
9	Kevin CAMPBELL	
10	Paul MERSON	
11	Mark FLATTS ‡	
	Substitutes	
12	John JENSEN †25	
14	Anders LIMPAR ‡69	
Gk	Alan MILLER	

Date	Saturday 5 December 1992
Venue	White Hart Lane, 3.00pm

TOTTENHAM HOTSPUR (0) 1
CHELSEA (0) 2

Attendance	31,540
Referee	Roger DILKES
Linesmen	M.D. Dearing, M.G. Wright

TOTTENHAM HOTSPUR
White shirts, Navy Blue shorts — Goals

		Goals
1	Erik THORSTVEDT	
2	Dean AUSTIN	
3	Justin EDINBURGH	
4	Vinny SAMWAYS	
5	Gary MABBUTT	
6	Neil RUDDOCK	
7	Jason CUNDY	
8	Nick BARMBY †	
9	NAYIM	
10	Teddy SHERINGHAM	
11	Kevin WATSON ‡	
	Substitutes	
12	Sol CAMPBELL †68	88
14	Darren ANDERTON ‡68	
Gk	Kevin DEARDEN	

CHELSEA
Blue shirts, Blue shorts — Goals

		Goals
1	Kevin HITCHCOCK	
2	Gareth HALL	
3	Frank SINCLAIR	
4	Andy TOWNSEND	
5	David LEE	
6	Mal DONAGHY	
7	Graham STUART	
8	Robert FLECK ‡	
9	Graeme LE SAUX	
10	Eddie NEWTON	76, 85
11	Dennis WISE	
	Substitutes	
12	Erland JOHNSEN	
14	Craig BURLEY ‡61	
Gk	Nick COLGAN	

Date	Sunday 6 December 1992
Venue	Old Trafford, 4.00pm

MANCHESTER UNITED (1) 2
MANCHESTER CITY (0) 1

Attendance	35,408
Referee	Gerald ASHBY
Linesmen	R.H. Andrews, U.D. Rennie

MANCHESTER UNITED
Red shirts, White shorts   Goals

1	Peter SCHMEICHEL	
2	Paul PARKER	
3	Denis IRWIN	
4	Steve BRUCE	
5	Lee SHARPE	
6	Gary PALLISTER	
7	Bryan ROBSON	
8	Paul INCE	20
9	Brian McCLAIR	
10	Mark HUGHES	73
11	Ryan GIGGS †	
	Substitutes	
12	Eric CANTONA †45	
14	Mike PHELAN	
Gk	Fraser DIGBY	

MANCHESTER CITY
Light Blue shirts, Light Blue shorts   Goals

1	Tony COTON	
2	Ian BRIGHTWELL	
3	Terry PHELAN ❏	
4	Steve McMAHON ❏	
5	Keith CURLE	
6	Andy HILL	
7	David WHITE	
8	Mike SHERON ‡	
9	Niall QUINN	74
10	Fitzroy SIMPSON †	
11	Rick HOLDEN ❏	
	Substitutes	
12	Peter REID †54	
14	Garry FLITCROFT ‡65	
Gk	Martyn MARGETSON	

Date	Monday 7 December 1992
Venue	Goodison Park, 7.45pm

EVERTON (0) 2
LIVERPOOL (0) 1

Attendance	35,826
Referee	Martin BODENHAM
Linesmen	M. Fletcher, M.A. Riley

EVERTON
Blue shirts, White shorts   Goals

1	Neville SOUTHALL	
2	Barry HORNE	
3	Gary ABLETT	
4	Ian SNODIN ‡	
5	Dave WATSON	
6	Martin KEOWN	
7	Billy KENNY	
8	Peter BEARDSLEY	84
9	Stuart BARLOW	
10	Mo JOHNSTON	63
11	David UNSWORTH †	
	Substitutes	
12	Peter BEAGRIE †46	
14	Paul RIDEOUT ‡75	
Gk	Jason KEARTON	

LIVERPOOL
Red shirts, Red shorts   Goals

1	Mike HOOPER	
2	Mike MARSH	
3	Mark WRIGHT	62
4	Steve NICOL	
5	Torben PIECHNIK	
6	Don HUTCHISON ‡	
7	Steve McMANAMAN	
8	Jamie REDKNAPP	
9	Ronnie ROSENTHAL †	
10	John BARNES	
11	Rob JONES	
	Substitutes	
12	Mark WALTERS †70	
14	Paul STEWART ‡75	
Gk	Bruce GROBBELAAR	

Date	Friday 11 December 1992
Venue	Ayresome Park, 7.30pm

MIDDLESBROUGH (0) 0
CHELSEA (0) 0

Attendance	15,559
Referee	Keren BARRATT
Linesmen	B. Lowe, U.D. Rennie

MIDDLESBROUGH
Red shirts, White shorts   Goals

1	Stephen PEARS	
2	Curtis FLEMING	
3	Jimmy PHILLIPS ❑	
4	Nicky MOHAN	
5	Derek WHYTE	
6	Jamie POLLOCK †	
7	John HENDRIE	
8	Andy PEAKE	
9	Paul WILKINSON	
10	Craig HIGNETT	
11	Tommy WRIGHT	
	Substitutes	
12	Graham KAVANAGH †77	
14	Mark PROCTOR	
Gk	Ian IRONSIDE	

CHELSEA
Blue shirts, Blue shorts   Goals

1	Kevin HITCHCOCK	
2	Gareth HALL	
3	Frank SINCLAIR ❑	
4	Andy TOWNSEND	
5	David LEE	
6	Mal DONAGHY	
7	Graham STUART	
8	Robert FLECK	
9	Graham LE SAUX	
10	Eddie NEWTON	
11	Dennis WISE	
	Substitutes	
12	Craig BURLEY	
14	Erland JOHNSEN	
Gk	Nick COLGAN	

Date	Saturday 12 December 1992
Venue	Villa Park, 3.00pm

ASTON VILLA (1) 2
NOTTINGHAM FOREST (1) 1

Attendance	29,015
Referee	Joe WORRALL
Linesmen	A. Black, C. Jones

ASTON VILLA
Claret & Blue shirts, White shorts   Goals

1	Nigel SPINK	
2	Earl BARRETT	
3	Steve STAUNTON	
4	Shaun TEALE	
5	Paul McGRATH	47
6	Kevin RICHARDSON	
7	Ray HOUGHTON	
8	Garry PARKER	
9	Dean SAUNDERS	
10	Cyrille REGIS	33
11	Neil COX	
	Substitutes	
12	Dwight YORKE	
14	Matthias BREITKREUTZ	
Gk	Michael OAKES	

NOTTINGHAM FOREST
White shirts, Black shorts   Goals

1	Mark CROSSLEY	
2	Brian LAWS	
3	Stuart PEARCE	
4	Steve CHETTLE	
5	Carl TILER	
6	Roy KEANE	9
7	Neil WEBB	
8	Scot GEMMILL	
9	Nigel CLOUGH	
10	Lee GLOVER ‡	
11	Kingsley BLACK	
	Substitutes	
12	Gary BANNISTER	
14	Thorvaldur ORLYGSSON ‡77	
Gk	Andy MARRIOTT	

Date	Saturday 12 December 1992
Venue	Portman Road, 3.00pm

IPSWICH TOWN (0) 3
MANCHESTER CITY (1) 1

Attendance	16,833
Referee	Ray LEWIS
Linesmen	J.A. Elwin, J.F. Moore

IPSWICH TOWN
Blue & White shirts, White shorts · Goals

1	Clive BAKER	
2	Phil WHELAN	
3	Neil THOMPSON	
4	Mick STOCKWELL	57
5	John WARK	
6	David LINIGHAN	
7	Gavin JOHNSON	61
8	Paul GODDARD	88
9	Steve WHITTON	
10	Jason DOZZELL	
11	Bontcho GUENTCHEV †	
	Substitutes	
12	Eddie YOUDS †84	
14	Vlado BOZINOSKI	
Gk	Jason WINTERS	

MANCHESTER CITY
White shirts, Light Blue shorts · Goals

1	Tony COTON	
2	Ian BRIGHTWELL	
3	Terry PHELAN ❑	
4	Steve McMAHON ❑	
5	Keith CURLE	
6	Andy HILL †	
7	David WHITE	
8	Peter REID	
9	Niall QUINN	
10	Garry FLITCROFT ❑	37
11	Rick HOLDEN	
	Substitutes	
12	Mike SHERON †89	
14	Fitzroy SIMPSON	
Gk	Martyn MARGETSON	

Date	Saturday 12 December 1992
Venue	Elland Road, 3.00pm

LEEDS UNITED (1) 3
SHEFFIELD WEDNESDAY (1) 1

Attendance	29,770
Referee	Jim BORRETT
Linesmen	M.A. Riley, E.J. Walsh

LEEDS UNITED
White shirts, White shorts · Goals

1	John LUKIC	
2	Jon NEWSOME	
3	Tony DORIGO	
4	David ROCASTLE ‡	
5	Chris FAIRCLOUGH	
6	Chris WHYTE ❑	
7	Gordon STRACHAN	
8	Rod WALLACE ❑ †	
9	Lee CHAPMAN ❑	46
10	Gary McALLISTER	
11	Gary SPEED	32
	Substitutes	
12	Imre VARADI †77	79
14	Steve HODGE ‡86	
Gk	Mervyn DAY	

SHEFFIELD WEDNESDAY
Yellow shirts, Black shorts · Goals

1	Chris WOODS	
2	Roland NILSSON	37
3	Nigel WORTHINGTON	
4	Carlton PALMER	
5	Nigel PEARSON	
6	Paul WARHURST	
7	John HARKES	
8	Chris WADDLE †	
9	David HIRST	
10	Mark BRIGHT ❑	
11	John SHERIDAN ❑	
	Substitutes	
12	Chris BART-WILLIAMS †86	
14	Gordon WATSON	
Gk	Kevin PRESSMAN	

Date	Saturday 12 December 1992
Venue	Old Trafford, 3.00pm

MANCHESTER UNITED (0) 1
NORWICH CITY (0) 0

Attendance	34,500
Referee	Roger MILFORD
Linesmen	M.A. Riley, E.J. Walsh

MANCHESTER UNITED
Red shirts, White shorts — Goals

1	Peter SCHMEICHEL	
2	Paul PARKER	
3	Denis IRWIN	
4	Steve BRUCE	
5	Lee SHARPE	
6	Gary PALLISTER	
7	Eric CANTONA	
8	Paul INCE	
9	Brian McCLAIR	
10	Mark HUGHES	59
11	Ryan GIGGS	
	Substitutes	
12	Andrei KANCHELSKIS	
14	Clayton BLACKMORE	
Gk	Fraser DIGBY	

NORWICH CITY
Yellow shirts, Green shorts — Goals

1	Bryan GUNN	
2	Ian CULVERHOUSE	
3	Mark BOWEN	
4	Ian BUTTERWORTH	
5	John POLSTON	
6	Daryl SUTCH	
7	Ian CROOK ‡	
8	Darren BECKFORD †	
9	Mark ROBINS	
10	Ruel FOX	
11	David PHILLIPS	
	Substitutes	
12	Chris SUTTON †75	
14	Gary MEGSON ‡16	
Gk	Andy MARSHALL	

Date	Saturday 12 December 1992
Venue	Loftus Road, 3.00pm

QPR (1) 1
CRYSTAL PALACE (0) 3

Attendance	14,571
Referee	Robbie HART
Linesmen	R.E. Budden, W.J. Norbury

QPR
Blue & White hooped shirts, White shorts — Goals

1	Jan STEJSKAL	
2	David BARDSLEY	
3	Clive WILSON	
4	Ray WILKINS	
5	Darren PEACOCK	
6	Alan McDONALD	
7	Andy IMPEY	
8	Ian HOLLOWAY	
9	Les FERDINAND	
10	Gary PENRICE	26
11	Andy SINTON	
	Substitutes	
12	Bradley ALLEN	
14	Danny MADDIX	
Gk	Tony ROBERTS	

CRYSTAL PALACE
Red & Blue striped shirts, Red shorts — Goals

1	Nigel MARTYN	
2	John HUMPHREY	
3	Richard SHAW	
4	Gareth SOUTHGATE	
5	Eric YOUNG	
6	Andy THORN	
7	Simon OSBORN	
8	George NDAH ‡	
9	Chris ARMSTRONG ❑	71
10	Chris COLEMAN †	
11	Eddie McGOLDRICK	46, 89
	Substitutes	
12	Bobby BOWRY †10	
14	Grant WATTS ‡64	
Gk	Andy WOODMAN	

Date	Saturday 12 December 1992
Venue	Bramall Lane, 3.00pm

SHEFFIELD UNITED (1) 1
EVERTON (0) 0

Attendance	16,266
Referee	Kelvin MORTON
Linesmen	D.E. Binsley, P.M. Roberts

SHEFFIELD UNITED
Red & White striped shirts, White shorts   Goals

1	Alan KELLY	
2	Kevin GAGE	
3	David BARNES	
4	John GANNON	
5	John PEMBERTON	
6	Paul BEESLEY	
7	Mitch WARD ❏ †	
8	Paul ROGERS	
9	Adrian LITTLEJOHN	34
10	Brian DEANE	
11	Glyn HODGES ‡	
	Substitutes	
12	Alan CORK †70	
14	Jamie HOYLAND ‡83	
Gk	Ken VEYSEY	

EVERTON
Blue shirts, Blue shorts   Goals

1	Neville SOUTHALL	
2	Matthew JACKSON †	
3	Gary ABLETT	
4	Ian SNODIN	
5	Dave WATSON	
6	Martin KEOWN	
7	Barry HORNE	
8	Peter BEARDSLEY	
9	Stuart BARLOW	
10	Mo JOHNSTON	
11	PREKI ‡	
	Substitutes	
12	Paul RIDEOUT †58	
14	Peter BEAGRIE ‡58	
Gk	Jason KEARTON	

Date	Saturday 12 December 1992
Venue	The Dell, 3.00pm

SOUTHAMPTON (1) 2
COVENTRY CITY (2) 2

Attendance	12,306
Referee	Bob NIXON
Linesmen	R.J. Harris, K.J. Hawkes

SOUTHAMPTON
Red & White striped shirts, Black shorts   Goals

1	Tim FLOWERS	
2	Jeff KENNA	
3	Micky ADAMS ❏	
4	Terry HURLOCK	
5	Richard HALL	
6	Steve WOOD	
7	Matthew LE TISSIER	
8	Perry GROVES	
9	Iain DOWIE	61
10	Neil MADDISON	9
11	Francis BENALI	
	Substitutes	
12	Jason DODD	
14	Nicky BANGER	
Gk	Ian ANDREWS	

COVENTRY CITY
Sky Blue shirts, Sky Blue shorts   Goals

1	Steve OGRIZOVIC	
2	Brian BORROWS	
3	Phil BABB	
4	Peter ATHERTON	
5	Kenny SANSOM	
6	Peter NDLOVU	
7	Lloyd McGRATH	
8	Lee HURST	
9	Robert ROSARIO ❏	
10	Mick QUINN	6, 25
11	Kevin GALLACHER	
	Substitutes	
12	John WILLIAMS	
14	David BUSST	
Gk	Jonathan GOULD	

Date	Saturday 12 December 1992
Venue	White Hart Lane, 3.00pm

TOTTENHAM HOTSPUR (1) 1
ARSENAL (0) 0

Attendance	33,709
Referee	Alf BUKSH
Linesmen	M.K. Bullivant, A. Schneider

TOTTENHAM HOTSPUR
White shirts, Navy Blue shorts   Goals

1	Erik THORSTVEDT	
2	Dean AUSTIN	
3	Justin EDINBURGH	
4	Vinny SAMWAYS	
5	Gary MABBUTT	
6	Neil RUDDOCK ❏	
7	David HOWELLS	
8	Gordon DURIE ❏ ‡	
9	NAYIM	
10	Teddy SHERINGHAM	
11	Paul ALLEN	20
	Substitutes	
12	Gudni BERGSSON	
14	Nick BARMBY ‡75	
Gk	Ian WALKER	

ARSENAL
Red & White shirts, White shorts   Goals

1	David SEAMAN	
2	Pal LYDERSEN	
3	Nigel WINTERBURN	
4	David HILLIER	
5	Steve BOULD ❏	
6	Tony ADAMS ❏	
7	John JENSEN ❏ ‡	
8	Ian WRIGHT	
9	Kevin CAMPBELL	
10	Paul MERSON	
11	Ray PARLOUR	
	Substitutes	
12	David O'LEARY	
14	Anders LIMPAR ‡80	
Gk	Alan MILLER	

Date	Saturday 12 December 1992
Venue	Selhurst Park, 3.00pm

WIMBLEDON (3) 5
OLDHAM ATHLETIC (0) 2

Attendance	3,386
Referee	Keith HACKETT
Linesmen	W.M. Jordan, D.C. Madgwick

WIMBLEDON
Blue shirts, Blue shorts   Goals

1	Hans SEGERS	
2	Neal ARDLEY	18, 26
3	Roger JOSEPH	
4	Vinnie JONES	
5	John SCALES	
6	Brian McALLISTER	
7	Dean BLACKWELL	
8	Robbie EARLE	
9	Dean HOLDSWORTH	22, 52
10	Lawrie SANCHEZ	
11	Andy CLARKE	51
	Substitutes	
12	Steve TALBOYS	
14	John FASHANU	
Gk	Neil SULLIVAN	

OLDHAM ATHLETIC
Red & White shirts, White shorts   Goals

1	Paul GERRARD	
2	Gunnar HALLE	
3	Neil POINTON	
4	Nick HENRY	
5	Richard JOBSON ❏	
6	Steve REDMOND ‡	
7	Neil ADAMS †	
8	Ian OLNEY	
9	Graeme SHARP	
10	Mike MILLIGAN	63
11	Mark BRENNAN	46
	Substitutes	
12	Roger PALMER †70	
14	Craig FLEMING ‡45	
Gk	John KEELEY	

Date	Sunday 13 December 1992	
Venue	Anfield, 4.00pm	

LIVERPOOL (0) 2
BLACKBURN ROVERS (0) 1

Attendance	43,688	
Referee	Philip DON	
Linesmen	T.A. Atkinson, M.A. Cooper	

LIVERPOOL
Red shirts, Red shorts   Goals

1	Mike HOOPER	
2	Mike MARSH	
3	Mark WRIGHT	
4	Steve NICOL	
5	Torben PIECHNIK	
6	Ronnie ROSENTHAL †	
7	Steve McMANAMAN	
8	Jamie REDKNAPP	
9	Ian RUSH	
10	John BARNES	
11	Rob JONES	
	Substitutes	
12	Mark WALTERS †56	77, 85
14	Paul STEWART	
Gk	Bruce GROBBELAAR	

BLACKBURN ROVERS
Blue & White shirts, White shorts   Goals

1	Bobby MIMMS	
2	David MAY	
3	Alan WRIGHT	
4	Mark ATKINS	
5	Colin HENDRY	
6	Kevin MORAN	
7	Tim SHERWOOD	
8	Gordon COWANS †	
9	Alan SHEARER	80
10	Mike NEWELL	
11	Jason WILCOX ‡	
	Substitutes	
12	Stuart RIPLEY †79	
14	Roy WEGERLE ‡79	
Gk	Darren COLLIER	

Date	Saturday 19 December 1992	
Venue	Highbury Stadium, 3.00pm	

ARSENAL (0) 1
MIDDLESBROUGH (1) 1

Attendance	23,197	
Referee	Steve LODGE	
Linesmen	G.R. Hamblin, B.A. Wigginton	

ARSENAL
Red & White shirts, White shorts   Goals

1	David SEAMAN	
2	Pal LYDERSEN	
3	Nigel WINTERBURN	
4	David HILLIER	
5	Andy LINIGHAN	
6	Tony ADAMS	
7	Mark FLATTS	
8	Ian WRIGHT	81
9	Alan SMITH	
10	Paul MERSON †	
11	Ray PARLOUR ‡	
	Substitutes	
12	John JENSEN †45	
14	Kevin CAMPBELL ‡77	
Gk	Alan MILLER	

MIDDLESBROUGH
White shirts, Black shorts   Goals

1	Stephen PEARS	
2	Curtis FLEMING	
3	Jimmy PHILLIPS	
4	Nicky MOHAN ❏	
5	Derek WHYTE	
6	Jamie POLLOCK	
7	John HENDRIE	
8	Andy PEAKE	
9	Paul WILKINSON	34
10	Craig HIGNETT †	
11	Tommy WRIGHT ‡	
	Substitutes	
12	Willie FALCONER †64	
14	Mark PROCTOR ‡87	
Gk	Ian IRONSIDE	

Date	Saturday 19 December 1992
Venue	Ewood Park, 3.00pm

BLACKBURN ROVERS (1) 1
SHEFFIELD UNITED (0) 0

Attendance	16,057
Referee	Dermot GALLAGHER
Linesmen	T. Heilbron, J.B. Robinson

BLACKBURN ROVERS
Blue & White shirts, White shorts   Goals

1	Bobby MIMMS	
2	David MAY	
3	Alan WRIGHT	
4	Mark ATKINS	
5	Colin HENDRY	
6	Kevin MORAN	27
7	Stuart RIPLEY ❏ ‡	
8	Gordon COWANS	
9	Alan SHEARER ❏	
10	Mike NEWELL	
11	Jason WILCOX	
	Substitutes	
12	Tim SHERWOOD	
14	Tony DOBSON ‡70	
Gk	Darren COLLIER	

SHEFFIELD UNITED
Yellow shirts, Black shorts   Goals

1	Alan KELLY	
2	Kevin GAGE	
3	David BARNES ❏	
4	John GANNON ❏ †	
5	John PEMBERTON ❏	
6	Paul BEESLEY	
7	Carl BRADSHAW ‡	
8	Paul ROGERS	
9	Jamie HOYLAND	
10	Brian DEANE	
11	Glyn HODGES ❏	
	Substitutes	
12	Adrian LITTLEJOHN †72	
14	Mitch WARD ‡79	
Gk	Ken VEYSEY	

Date	Saturday 19 December 1992
Venue	Stamford Bridge, 3.00pm

CHELSEA (0) 1
MANCHESTER UNITED (0) 1

Attendance	34,496
Referee	Ray LEWIS
Linesmen	J.A. Elwin, J.F. Moore

CHELSEA
Blue shirts, Blue shorts   Goals

1	Kevin HITCHCOCK	
2	Gareth HALL	
3	Frank SINCLAIR	
4	Andy TOWNSEND	
5	David LEE	67
6	Mal DONAGHY	
7	Graham STUART	
8	Robert FLECK ❏ ‡	
9	Graeme LE SAUX	
10	Eddie NEWTON	
11	Dennis WISE	
	Substitutes	
12	Craig BURLEY	
14	Mick HARFORD ‡63	
Gk	Nick COLGAN	

MANCHESTER UNITED
Red shirts, White shorts   Goals

1	Peter SCHMEICHEL	
2	Paul PARKER	
3	Denis IRWIN	
4	Steve BRUCE	
5	Mike PHELAN †	
6	Gary PALLISTER ❏	
7	Eric CANTONA	71
8	Paul INCE	
9	Brian McCLAIR	
10	Mark HUGHES ❏	
11	Lee SHARPE	
	Substitutes	
12	Andrei KANCHELSKIS †83	
14	Clayton BLACKMORE	
Gk	Fraser DIGBY	

Date   Saturday 19 December 1992
Venue   Highfield Road, 3.00pm

COVENTRY CITY (1) 5
LIVERPOOL (0) 1

Attendance   19,779
Referee   Kelvin MORTON
Linesmen   B.L. Polkey, E.J. Walsh

COVENTRY CITY
Sky Blue shirts, Sky Blue shorts   Goals

1	Jonathan GOULD	
2	Brian BORROWS	37p, 54
3	Phil BABB	
4	Peter ATHERTON	
5	Kenny SANSOM	
6	John WILLIAMS	
7	Lloyd McGRATH	
8	Lee HURST	
9	Robert ROSARIO	
10	Mick QUINN	71, 74
11	Kevin GALLACHER	61
	Substitutes	
12	Andy PEARCE	
14	Sean FLYNN	
Gk	Martin DAVIES	

LIVERPOOL
Red shirts, Red shorts   Goals

1	Mike HOOPER	
2	Mike MARSH	
3	Rob JONES †	
4	Stig Inge BJORNEBYE	
5	Torben PIECHNIK	
6	Mark WRIGHT	
7	Paul STEWART	
8	Jamie REDKNAPP ❑ ■	64
9	Ian RUSH	
10	John BARNES	
11	Mark WALTERS	
	Substitutes	
12	Don HUTCHISON †61 ❑	
14	Ronnie ROSENTHAL	
Gk	David JAMES	

Date   Saturday 19 December 1992
Venue   Goodison Park, 3.00pm

EVERTON (2) 2
SOUTHAMPTON (1) 1

Attendance   14,051
Referee   Mike PECK
Linesmen   A. Streets, M. Warren

EVERTON
Blue shirts, White shorts   Goals

1	Neville SOUTHALL	
2	Ian SNODIN	
3	Gary ABLETT	
4	Barry HORNE	
5	Dave WATSON	
6	Martin KEOWN	
7	Robert WARZYCHA	
8	Peter BEARDSLEY	11p
9	Paul RIDEOUT	36
10	Billy KENNY	
11	Peter BEAGRIE	
	Substitutes	
12	David UNSWORTH	
14	Stuart BARLOW	
Gk	Jason KEARTON	

SOUTHAMPTON
Red & White striped shirts, Black shorts   Goals

1	Tim FLOWERS	
2	Jeff KENNA	
3	Micky ADAMS	
4	Terry HURLOCK ❑	
5	Richard HALL	
6	Kenneth MONKOU ‡	
7	Matthew LE TISSIER ❑	5
8	Perry GROVES	
9	Iain DOWIE ❑ †	
10	Neil MADDISON	
11	Francis BENALI	
	Substitutes	
12	Kerry DIXON †63	
14	Jason DODD ‡71	
Gk	Ian ANDREWS	

Date	Saturday 19 December 1992
Venue	Maine Road, 3.00pm

MANCHESTER CITY (0) 1
ASTON VILLA (1) 1

Attendance	23,525
Referee	Ray BIGGER
Linesmen	A.N. Butler, A.J. Hill

MANCHESTER CITY
Light Blue shirts, White Shorts   Goals

1	Tony COTON	
2	Ian BRIGHTWELL	
3	Terry PHELAN ❑	
4	Steve McMAHON	
5	Keith CURLE ❑	
6	Andy HILL	
7	David WHITE	
8	Peter REID †	
9	Niall QUINN	
10	Garry FLITCROFT	58
11	Rick HOLDEN	
	Substitutes	
12	Mike SHERON †57	
14	Fitzroy SIMPSON	
Gk	Martyn MARGETSON	

ASTON VILLA
Claret & Blue shirts, White shorts   Goals

1	Nigel SPINK	
2	Earl BARRETT	
3	Steve STAUNTON	
4	Shaun TEALE	
5	Paul McGRATH	
6	Kevin RICHARDSON	
7	Ray HOUGHTON	
8	Garry PARKER	34
9	Dean SAUNDERS	
10	Dalian ATKINSON ‡	
11	Dwight YORKE	
	Substitutes	
12	Neil COX	
14	Matthias BREITKREUTZ ‡61	
Gk	Mark BOSNICH	

Date	Saturday 19 December 1992
Venue	Boundary Park, 3.00pm

OLDHAM ATHLETIC (1) 2
TOTTENHAM HOTSPUR (0) 1

Attendance	11,735
Referee	Roger MILFORD
Linesmen	R.R. Rawson, P.R. Richards

OLDHAM ATHLETIC
Blue shirts, Blue shorts   Goals

1	Paul GERRARD	
2	Gunnar HALLE	
3	Andy BARLOW	
4	Paul BERNARD	
5	Richard JOBSON	
6	Craig FLEMING	
7	Neil ADAMS	
8	Ian OLNEY	90
9	Graeme SHARP	29
10	Mike MILLIGAN	
11	Mark BRENNAN	
	Substitutes	
12	Andy RITCHIE	
14	Steve REDMOND	
Gk	John KEELEY	

TOTTENHAM HOTSPUR
White shirts, Navy Blue shorts   Goals

1	Erik THORSTVEDT	
2	Dean AUSTIN	
3	Justin EDINBURGH ❑	
4	Vinny SAMWAYS	
5	Gary MABBUTT	
6	Neil RUDDOCK	
7	David HOWELLS	
8	Gordon DURIE	
9	NAYIM ‡	
10	Teddy SHERINGHAM	61
11	Paul ALLEN	
	Substitutes	
12	Gudni BERGSSON	
14	Nick BARMBY ‡37	
Gk	Ian WALKER	

Date	Saturday 19 December 1992
Venue	Hillsborough, 3.00pm

SHEFFIELD WEDNESDAY (1) 1
QPR (0) 0

Attendance	23,164
Referee	Joe WORRALL
Linesmen	D.E. Binsley, G.I. Grandidge

SHEFFIELD WEDNESDAY
Blue & White striped shirts, Black shorts   Goals

1	Chris WOODS	
2	Roland NILSSON	
3	Nigel WORTHINGTON	
4	Carlton PALMER	
5	Viv ANDERSON	
6	Paul WARHURST †	
7	Danny WILSON	
8	Chris WADDLE	
9	David HIRST	
10	Mark BRIGHT	39
11	John SHERIDAN	
	Substitutes	
12	Chris BART-WILLIAMS †26	
14	Gordon WATSON	
Gk	Kevin PRESSMAN	

QPR
Red & Black hooped shirts, Red shorts   Goals

1	Tony ROBERTS	
2	David BARDSLEY	
3	Clive WILSON	
4	Ray WILKINS	
5	Darren PEACOCK	
6	Alan McDONALD ❏	
7	Andy IMPEY †	
8	Ian HOLLOWAY	
9	Les FERDINAND	
10	Gary PENRICE	
11	Andy SINTON	
	Substitutes	
12	Simon BARKER †74	
14	Danny MADDIX	
Gk	Jan STEJSKAL	

Date	Sunday 20 December 1992
Venue	Selhurst Park, 1.00pm

CRYSTAL PALACE (1) 1
LEEDS UNITED (0) 0

Attendance	14,462
Referee	Allan GUNN
Linesmen	M.E. Alexander, D. Orr

CRYSTAL PALACE
Red & Blue striped shirts, Red shorts   Goals

1	Nigel MARTYN	
2	John HUMPHREY	
3	Richard SHAW	
4	Gareth SOUTHGATE ‡	
5	Eric YOUNG	
6	Andy THORN	30
7	Simon OSBORN	
8	Geoff THOMAS	
9	Chris ARMSTRONG	
10	Simon RODGER	
11	Eddie McGOLDRICK	
	Substitutes	
12	Grant WATTS	
14	Bobby BOWRY ‡79	
Gk	Andy WOODMAN	

LEEDS UNITED
White shirts, White shorts   Goals

1	John LUKIC	
2	Jon NEWSOME	
3	Tony DORIGO	
4	David ROCASTLE	
5	Chris FAIRCLOUGH	
6	Chris WHYTE ❏ ‡	
7	Gordon STRACHAN	
8	Rod WALLACE †	
9	Lee CHAPMAN	
10	Gary McALLISTER	
11	Gary SPEED	
	Substitutes	
12	Imre VARADI †73	
14	Steve HODGE ‡60	
Gk	Mervyn DAY	

Date	Sunday 20 December 1992
Venue	City Ground, 3.00pm

NOTTINGHAM FOREST (1) 1
WIMBLEDON (1) 1

Attendance	19,362
Referee	Robbie HART
Linesmen	E.B. Crompton, J. McGrath

NOTTINGHAM FOREST
Red shirts, White shorts   Goals

1	Mark CROSSLEY	
2	Brian LAWS	
3	Stuart PEARCE	
4	Steve CHETTLE	
5	Carl TILER	
6	Roy KEANE	
7	Gary CROSBY	
8	Scot GEMMILL	
9	Nigel CLOUGH	5
10	Neil WEBB	
11	Kingsley BLACK	
	Substitutes	
12	Gary BANNISTER	
14	Ian WOAN	
Gk	Andy MARRIOTT	

WIMBLEDON
Blue shirts, Blue shorts   Goals

1	Hans SEGERS	
2	Neal ARDLEY ❏ ‡	
3	Roger JOSEPH	
4	Vinnie JONES	
5	John SCALES	
6	Brian McALLISTER ❏	
7	Dean BLACKWELL	
8	Robbie EARLE	
9	Dean HOLDSWORTH	
10	Steve TALBOYS	
11	Andy CLARKE †	13
	Substitutes	
12	John FASHANU †75	
14	Paul MILLER ‡60	
Gk	Neil SULLIVAN	

Date	Monday 21 December 1992
Venue	Carrow Road, 7.45pm

NORWICH CITY (0) 0
IPSWICH TOWN (0) 2

Attendance	20,032
Referee	David ELLERAY
Linesmen	W.M. Jordan, P.A. Josper

NORWICH CITY
Yellow shirts, Green shorts   Goals

1	Bryan GUNN	
2	Ian CULVERHOUSE	
3	Mark BOWEN	
4	Ian BUTTERWORTH ‡	
5	John POLSTON	
6	Daryl SUTCH	
7	Gary MEGSON	
8	Darren BECKFORD †	
9	Mark ROBINS	
10	Ruel FOX	
11	David PHILLIPS	
	Substitutes	
12	Chris SUTTON †57	
14	Rob NEWMAN ‡45	
Gk	Mark WALTON	

IPSWICH TOWN
Blue & White shirts, White shorts   Goals

1	Clive BAKER	
2	Gavin JOHNSON	
3	Neil THOMPSON	87
4	Mick STOCKWELL	
5	John WARK	
6	David LINIGHAN	
7	Geraint WILLIAMS	
8	Paul GODDARD †	
9	Steve WHITTON	
10	Jason DOZZELL	
11	Chris KIWOMYA	51
	Substitutes	
12	Phil WHELAN †81	
14	Bontcho GUENTCHEV	
Gk	Jason WINTERS	

Date	Saturday 26 December 1992
Venue	Highbury Stadium, 12 noon

ARSENAL (0) 0
IPSWICH TOWN (0) 0

Attendance	26,198
Referee	Roger MILFORD
Linesmen	G. Butland, K.J. Hawkes

ARSENAL
Red & White shirts, White shorts   Goals

1	David SEAMAN	
2	Pal LYDERSEN	
3	Nigel WINTERBURN	
4	David HILLIER	
5	Steve BOULD ❑	
6	Andy LINIGHAN	
7	John JENSEN †	
8	Ian WRIGHT	
9	Alan SMITH	
10	Kevin CAMPBELL ‡	
11	Mark FLATTS	
	Substitutes	
12	David O'LEARY †76	
14	Anders LIMPAR ‡76	
Gk	Alan MILLER	

IPSWICH TOWN
Blue & White shirts, Blue shorts   Goals

1	Clive BAKER	
2	Gavin JOHNSON	
3	Neil THOMPSON	
4	Mick STOCKWELL	
5	John WARK	
6	David LINIGHAN	
7	Geraint WILLIAMS	
8	Paul GODDARD ‡	
9	Steve WHITTON †	
10	Jason DOZZELL	
11	Chris KIWOMYA	
	Substitutes	
12	Phil WHELAN †55	
14	Bontcho GUENTCHEV ‡60	
Gk	Jason WINTERS	

Date	Saturday 26 December 1992
Venue	Ewood Park, 3.00pm

BLACKBURN ROVERS (2) 3
LEEDS UNITED (1) 1

Attendance	19,910
Referee	Steve LODGE
Linesmen	M. Fletcher, P. Rejer

BLACKBURN ROVERS
Blue & White shirts, White shorts   Goals

1	Bobby MIMMS	
2	David MAY	
3	Alan WRIGHT	
4	Mark ATKINS	
5	Colin HENDRY	
6	Kevin MORAN	
7	Stuart RIPLEY	
8	Gordon COWANS	
9	Alan SHEARER †	45, 58
10	Mike NEWELL	
11	Jason WILCOX	8
	Substitutes	
12	Tim SHERWOOD †83	
14	Nick MARKER	
Gk	Darren COLLIER	

LEEDS UNITED
Yellow shirts, Yellow shorts   Goals

1	John LUKIC	
2	Mel STERLAND †	
3	Tony DORIGO	
4	David BATTY	
5	Chris FAIRCLOUGH	
6	Chris WHYTE	
7	Gordon STRACHAN ❑	
8	Imre VARADI	
9	Lee CHAPMAN	
10	Gary McALLISTER	37
11	Gary SPEED	
	Substitutes	
12	Jon NEWSOME †71	
14	Carl SHUTT	
Gk	Mervyn DAY	

Date	Saturday 26 December 1992
Venue	Stamford Bridge, 12 noon

CHELSEA (0) 1
SOUTHAMPTON (1) 1

Attendance	18,344
Referee	Allan GUNN
Linesmen	G.P. Barber, D. Orr

CHELSEA
Blue shirts, Blue shorts — Goals

		Goals
1	Kevin HITCHCOCK	
2	Gareth HALL	
3	Frank SINCLAIR	
4	Andy TOWNSEND	
5	David LEE	
6	Mal DONAGHY	
7	Graham STUART	
8	Robert FLECK ‡	
9	Graeme LE SAUX †	
10	Eddie NEWTON	89
11	Dennis WISE	
	Substitutes	
12	Craig BURLEY †79	
14	John SPENCER ‡73	
Gk	Dmitri KHARIN	

SOUTHAMPTON
Red & White striped shirts, Black shorts — Goals

		Goals
1	Tim FLOWERS	
2	Jeff KENNA	
3	Micky ADAMS ❏	
4	Terry HURLOCK	
5	Richard HALL	
6	Kenneth MONKOU	
7	Matthew LE TISSIER ❏	
8	Perry GROVES ‡	
9	Iain DOWIE	2
10	Neil MADDISON	
11	Francis BENALI	
	Substitutes	
12	Kerry DIXON	
14	Jason DODD ‡45	
Gk	Ian ANDREWS	

Date	Saturday 26 December 1992
Venue	Highfield Road, 12 noon

COVENTRY CITY (0) 3
ASTON VILLA (0) 0

Attendance	24,245
Referee	Roger DILKES
Linesmen	P.M. Roberts, J.B. Robinson

COVENTRY CITY
Sky Blue shirts, Sky Blue shorts — Goals

		Goals
1	Jonathan GOULD	
2	Brian BORROWS	
3	Phil BABB	
4	Peter ATHERTON ❏	
5	Kenny SANSOM	
6	John WILLIAMS	
7	Lloyd McGRATH	
8	Lee HURST	
9	Robert ROSARIO	59
10	Mick QUINN ❏ †	52, 55
11	Kevin GALLACHER ‡	
	Substitutes	
12	Andy PEARCE †89	
14	Peter NDLOVU ‡82	
Gk	Steve OGRIZOVIC	

ASTON VILLA
Claret & Blue shirts, Blue shorts — Goals

		Goals
1	Nigel SPINK	
2	Earl BARRETT	
3	Steve STAUNTON	
4	Shaun TEALE	
5	Paul McGRATH	
6	Kevin RICHARDSON	
7	Ray HOUGHTON	
8	Garry PARKER †	
9	Dean SAUNDERS	
10	Cyrille REGIS ‡	
11	Bryan SMALL	
	Substitutes	
12	Neil COX †83	
14	Stefan BEINLICH ‡75	
Gk	Mark BOSNICH	

Date	Saturday 26 December 1992
Venue	Selhurst Park, 12 noon

CRYSTAL PALACE (2) 2
WIMBLEDON (0) 0

Attendance	16,825
Referee	Ray LEWIS
Linesmen	J.A. Elwin, J.F. Moore

Crystal Palace
Red & Blue striped shirts, Red shorts   Goals

1	Nigel MARTYN	
2	John HUMPHREY	
3	Richard SHAW	
4	Gareth SOUTHGATE †	
5	Eric YOUNG	
6	Andy THORN	
7	Chris COLEMAN	3
8	Geoff THOMAS	37
9	Chris ARMSTRONG	
10	Simon RODGER	
11	Eddie McGOLDRICK	
	Substitutes	
12	Simon OSBORN †86	
14	Grant WATTS	
Gk	Andy WOODMAN	

WIMBLEDON
White shirts, Black shorts   Goals

1	Hans SEGERS	
2	Dean HOLDSWORTH	
3	Roger JOSEPH ‡	
4	Vinnie JONES ❑	
5	John SCALES	
6	Brian McALLISTER ❑ ■	
7	Dean BLACKWELL †	
8	Robbie EARLE	
9	John FASHANU ❑	
10	Lawrie SANCHEZ	
11	Andy CLARKE	
	Substitutes	
12	Steve TALBOYS †67	
14	Neal ARDLEY ‡53	
Gk	Neil SULLIVAN	

Date	Saturday 26 December 1992
Venue	Goodison Park, 3.00pm

EVERTON (0) 2
MIDDLESBROUGH (0) 2

Attendance	24,391
Referee	Ron GROVES
Linesmen	A. Black, E. Lomas

EVERTON
Blue shirts, White shorts   Goals

1	Neville SOUTHALL	
2	Ian SNODIN †	
3	David UNSWORTH	
4	Barry HORNE	
5	Dave WATSON	
6	Gary ABLETT	
7	Robert WARZYCHA ‡	
8	Peter BEARDSLEY	66p
9	Paul RIDEOUT	47
10	Billy KENNY ❑	
11	Peter BEAGRIE	
	Substitutes	
12	PREKI †61	
14	Stuart BARLOW ‡85	
Gk	Jason KEARTON	

MIDDLESBROUGH
Red shirts, White shorts   Goals

1	Stephen PEARS	
2	Curtis FLEMING	
3	Jimmy PHILLIPS	
4	Nicky MOHAN	
5	Derek WHYTE	
6	Jamie POLLOCK ❑ †	
7	John HENDRIE	
8	Andy PEAKE	
9	Paul WILKINSON	
10	Craig HIGNETT	49, 82
11	Tommy WRIGHT	
	Substitutes	
12	Willie FALCONER †74	
14	Mark PROCTOR	
Gk	Ian IRONSIDE	

Date	Saturday 26 December 1992
Venue	Maine Road, 3.00pm

MANCHESTER CITY (1) 2
SHEFFIELD UNITED (0) 0

Attendance	27,455
Referee	Keren BARRATT
Linesmen	T.A. Atkinson, T. Lynch

MANCHESTER CITY
Light Blue shirts, White shorts   Goals

1	Tony COTON	
2	Ian BRIGHTWELL	
3	Terry PHELAN	
4	Steve McMAHON	
5	Keith CURLE	
6	Andy HILL	
7	David WHITE	20, 55
8	Mike SHERON	
9	Niall QUINN	
10	Garry FLITCROFT	
11	Rick HOLDEN	
	Substitutes	
12	Peter REID	
14	David BRIGHTWELL	
Gk	Martyn MARGETSON	

SHEFFIELD UNITED
Red & White shirts, Black shorts   Goals

1	Alan KELLY	
2	Chris KAMARA	
3	David BARNES	
4	John GANNON ❏	
5	John PEMBERTON	
6	Paul BEESLEY	
7	Mitch WARD †	
8	Paul ROGERS	
9	Carl BRADSHAW ❏	
10	Brian DEANE ‡	
11	Glyn HODGES	
	Substitutes	
12	Alan CORK †63	
14	Jamie HOYLAND ‡77	
Gk	Ken VEYSEY	

Date	Saturday 26 December 1992
Venue	Carrow Road, 3.00pm

NORWICH CITY (0) 0
TOTTENHAM HOTSPUR (0) 0

Attendance	19,413
Referee	John MARTIN
Linesmen	M.D. Dearing, G.T. Pearson

NORWICH CITY
Yellow shirts, Green shorts   Goals

1	Bryan GUNN	
2	Ian CULVERHOUSE	
3	Mark BOWEN	
4	Rob NEWMAN	
5	John POLSTON	
6	Gary MEGSON	
7	Ian CROOK	
8	Chris SUTTON	
9	Mark ROBINS	
10	Ruel FOX	
11	David PHILLIPS	
	Substitutes	
12	Darren BECKFORD	
14	Daryl SUTCH	
Gk	Mark WALTON	

TOTTENHAM HOTSPUR
White shirts, Navy Blue shorts   Goals

1	Erik THORSTVEDT	
2	Dean AUSTIN ❏	
3	Justin EDINBURGH	
4	Vinny SAMWAYS ❏	
5	Gary MABBUTT	
6	Neil RUDDOCK	
7	David HOWELLS	
8	Nick BARMBY ‡	
9	Darren ANDERTON	
10	Teddy SHERINGHAM	
11	Paul ALLEN	
	Substitutes	
12	Gudni BERGSSON	
14	Paul MORAN ‡83	
Gk	Ian WALKER	

Date	Saturday 26 December 1992
Venue	Hillsborough, 12 noon

SHEFFIELD WEDNESDAY (2) 3
MANCHESTER UNITED (0) 3

Attendance	37,708
Referee	Alf BUKSH
Linesmen	J. Leech, W.J. Nattrass

SHEFFIELD WEDNESDAY
Blue & White striped shirts, Black shorts   Goals

1	Chris WOODS	
2	Roland NILSSON	
3	Nigel WORTHINGTON	
4	Carlton PALMER	
5	Viv ANDERSON	
6	Peter SHIRTLIFF	
7	Danny WILSON ‡	
8	Chris WADDLE	
9	David HIRST	2
10	Mark BRIGHT ❑	6
11	John SHERIDAN	62
	Substitutes	
12	Chris BART-WILLIAMS	
14	John HARKES ‡73	
Gk	Kevin PRESSMAN	

MANCHESTER UNITED
Red shirts, White shorts   Goals

1	Peter SCHMEICHEL	
2	Paul PARKER	
3	Denis IRWIN	
4	Steve BRUCE ❑	
5	Lee SHARPE	
6	Gary PALLISTER	
7	Eric CANTONA	84
8	Paul INCE	
9	Brian McCLAIR	67, 80
10	Mark HUGHES ❑	
11	Ryan GIGGS †	
	Substitutes	
12	Andrei KANCHELSKIS †68	
14	Mike PHELAN	
Gk	Fraser DIGBY	

Date	Monday 28 December 1992
Venue	Villa Park, 7.30pm

ASTON VILLA (1) 1
ARSENAL (0) 0

Attendance	35,170
Referee	Martin BODENHAM
Linesmen	I.A. Madge, D.C. Richards

ASTON VILLA
Claret & Blue shirts, White shorts   Goals

1	Nigel SPINK	
2	Earl BARRETT	
3	Steve STAUNTON	
4	Shaun TEALE	
5	Paul McGRATH	
6	Kevin RICHARDSON	
7	Ray HOUGHTON	
8	Garry PARKER	
9	Dean SAUNDERS	45p
10	Dwight YORKE	
11	Stephen FROGGATT †	
	Substitutes	
12	Neil COX †74	
14	Stefan BEINLICH	
Gk	Mark BOSNICH	

ARSENAL
Yellow shirts, Blue shorts   Goals

1	David SEAMAN	
2	Pal LYDERSEN	
3	Nigel WINTERBURN	
4	David HILLIER †	
5	Steve BOULD	
6	Andy LINIGHAN	
7	David O'LEARY	
8	Ian WRIGHT	
9	Alan SMITH	
10	Kevin CAMPBELL	
11	Ray PARLOUR ‡	
	Substitutes	
12	Anders LIMPAR †66	
14	Mark FLATTS ‡45	
Gk	Alan MILLER	

Date	Monday 28 December 1992
Venue	Portman Road, 3.00pm

IPSWICH TOWN (0) 2
BLACKBURN ROVERS (0) 1

Attendance	21,431
Referee	Allan GUNN
Linesmen	G.P. Barber, D. Orr

IPSWICH TOWN
Blue & White shirts, White shorts   Goals

1	Clive BAKER	
2	Gavin JOHNSON	
3	Neil THOMPSON	
4	Mick STOCKWELL	
5	John WARK	
6	David LINIGHAN	
7	Geraint WILLIAMS	
8	Bontcho GUENTCHEV	79
9	Steve WHITTON	
10	Jason DOZZELL	
11	Chris KIWOMYA	81
	Substitutes	
12	Phil WHELAN	
14	Paul GODDARD	
Gk	Jason WINTERS	

BLACKBURN ROVERS
Red & Black striped shirts, Black shorts   Goals

1	Bobby MIMMS	
2	David MAY	
3	Alan WRIGHT	
4	Mark ATKINS ‡	
5	Colin HENDRY ❑	
6	Nick MARKER	
7	Tim SHERWOOD	
8	Gordon COWANS	
9	Roy WEGERLE	72
10	Mike NEWELL	
11	Jason WILCOX †	
	Substitutes	
12	Stuart RIPLEY †85	
14	Tony DOBSON ‡80	
Gk	Darren COLLIER	

Date	Monday 28 December 1992
Venue	Elland Road, 3.00pm

LEEDS UNITED (0) 0
NORWICH CITY (0) 0

Attendance	30,282
Referee	Philip DON
Linesmen	G.I. Grandidge, T. Heilbron

LEEDS UNITED
White shirts, White shorts   Goals

1	John LUKIC	
2	Mel STERLAND	
3	Tony DORIGO	
4	David BATTY	
5	Chris FAIRCLOUGH	
6	David WETHERALL †	
7	Gordon STRACHAN ❑	
8	Imre VARADI	
9	Lee CHAPMAN ❑	
10	Gary McALLISTER	
11	Gary SPEED	
	Substitutes	
12	Jon NEWSOME †80	
14	Rod WALLACE	
Gk	Mervyn DAY	

NORWICH CITY
Yellow shirts, Green shorts   Goals

1	Bryan GUNN	
2	Ian CULVERHOUSE	
3	Mark BOWEN	
4	Rob NEWMAN †	
5	John POLSTON	
6	Gary MEGSON	
7	Ian CROOK	
8	Chris SUTTON	
9	Mark ROBINS	
10	Ruel FOX	
11	David PHILLIPS	
	Substitutes	
12	Daryl SUTCH †68	
14	Colin WOODTHORPE	
Gk	Mark WALTON	

Date	Monday 28 December 1992
Venue	Anfield, 3.00pm

LIVERPOOL (0) 1
MANCHESTER CITY (1) 1

Attendance	43,037
Referee	David ALLISON
Linesmen	R.R. Rawson, P.R. Richards

LIVERPOOL
Red shirts, Red shorts   Goals

1	Mike HOOPER	
2	Mike MARSH	
3	Rob JONES	
4	Steve NICOL	
5	Torben PIECHNIK	
6	Stig Inge BJORNEBYE	
7	Steve McMANAMAN	
8	Jamie REDKNAPP	
9	Ian RUSH	49
10	John BARNES	
11	Mark WALTERS	
	Substitutes	
12	Don HUTCHISON	
14	Michael THOMAS	
Gk	Bruce GROBBELAAR	

MANCHESTER CITY
Light Blue shirts, White shorts   Goals

1	Tony COTON	
2	Ian BRIGHTWELL	
3	Terry PHELAN	
4	Steve McMAHON ❏	
5	Keith CURLE	
6	Andy HILL	
7	David WHITE	
8	Mike SHERON †	
9	Niall QUINN	39
10	Garry FLITCROFT	
11	Rick HOLDEN	
	Substitutes	
12	Peter REID †59	
14	David BRIGHTWELL	
Gk	Martyn MARGETSON	

Date	Monday 28 December 1992
Venue	Old Trafford, 3.00pm

MANCHESTER UNITED (2) 5
COVENTRY CITY (0) 0

Attendance	36,025
Referee	Ron GROVES
Linesmen	M. Warren, D.S. Oliver

MANCHESTER UNITED
Red shirts, White shorts   Goals

1	Peter SCHMEICHEL	
2	Paul PARKER	
3	Denis IRWIN	83
4	Steve BRUCE ‡	
5	Lee SHARPE	78
6	Gary PALLISTER	
7	Eric CANTONA	64p
8	Paul INCE	
9	Brian McCLAIR	
10	Mark HUGHES	40
11	Ryan GIGGS †	6
	Substitutes	
12	Andrei KANCHELSKIS †79	
14	Mike PHELAN ‡59	
Gk	Fraser DIGBY	

COVENTRY CITY
Sky Blue shirts, Sky Blue shorts   Goals

1	Jonathon GOULD	
2	Brian BORROWS	
3	Phil BABB	
4	Peter ATHERTON	
5	Kenny SANSOM	
6	John WILLIAMS ‡	
7	Lloyd McGRATH ❏	
8	Lee HURST	
9	Robert ROSARIO	
10	Mick QUINN	
11	Kevin GALLACHER	
	Substitutes	
12	Andy PEAKE	
14	Peter NDLOVU ‡45	
Gk	Steve OGRIZOVIC	

Date	Monday 28 December 1992
Venue	Ayresome Park, 3.00pm

MIDDLESBROUGH (0) 0
CRYSTAL PALACE (1) 1

Attendance	21,123
Referee	Keith HACKETT
Linesmen	N.S. Barry, A.J. Hill

MIDDLESBROUGH
Red shirts, White shorts — Goals

1	Stephen PEARS	
2	Curtis FLEMING ‡	
3	Jimmy PHILLIPS	
4	Nicky MOHAN	
5	Derek WHYTE	
6	Jamie POLLOCK †	
7	John HENDRIE	
8	Andy PEAKE	
9	Paul WILKINSON	
10	Craig HIGNETT	
11	Tommy WRIGHT	
	Substitutes	
12	Willie FALCONER †64	
14	Mark PROCTOR ‡74	
Gk	Ian IRONSIDE	

CRYSTAL PALACE
Yellow shirts, Light Blue shorts — Goals

1	Nigel MARTYN	
2	John HUMPHREY	
3	Richard SHAW	
4	Chris COLEMAN	
5	Eric YOUNG ❏	
6	Andy THORN †	
7	Simon OSBORN	63
8	Geoff THOMAS	
9	Chris ARMSTRONG	
10	Simon RODGER	
11	Eddie McGOLDRICK	
	Substitutes	
12	Bobby BOWRY †55	
14	Grant WATTS	
Gk	Andy WOODMAN	

Date	Monday 28 December 1992
Venue	Loftus Road, 3.00pm

QPR (1) 4
EVERTON (0) 2

Attendance	14,802
Referee	Gerald ASHBY
Linesmen	M.E. Alexander, M.K. Bullivant

QPR
Blue & White hooped shirts, White shorts — Goals

1	Tony ROBERTS	
2	David BARDSLEY	
3	Clive WILSON	
4	Ray WILKINS	
5	Darren PEACOCK	
6	Alan McDONALD	
7	Simon BARKER	
8	Ian HOLLOWAY	
9	Les FERDINAND	
10	Gary PENRICE	46
11	Andy SINTON	27, 51, 88
	Substitutes	
12	Andy IMPEY	
14	Danny MADDIX	
Gk	Jan STEJSKAL	

EVERTON
Salmon Pink & Blue striped shirts, Blue shorts — Goals

1	Neville SOUTHALL ■	
2	Iain JENKINS	
3	Gary ABLETT	
4	Barry HORNE	
5	Dave WATSON	
6	Martin KEOWN	
7	Robert WARZYCHA ‡	
8	Peter BEARDSLEY	
9	Paul RIDEOUT ■	
10	Billy KENNY	
11	Peter BEAGRIE †	
	Substitutes	
12	Stuart BARLOW †48	65, 72
14	PREKI	
Gk	Jason KEARTON ‡22	

Date	Monday 28 December 1992
Venue	The Dell, 3.00pm

SOUTHAMPTON (0) 1
SHEFFIELD WEDNESDAY (0) 2

Attendance 17,426
Referee Roger MILFORD
Linesmen R.E. Budden, R.J. Harris

SOUTHAMPTON
Red & White striped shirts, Black shorts   Goals

1	Tim FLOWERS	
2	Jeff KENNA	
3	Micky ADAMS	
4	Terry HURLOCK	
5	Richard HALL	
6	Kenneth MONKOU	80
7	Matthew LE TISSIER	
8	Jason DODD	
9	Iain DOWIE	
10	Neil MADDISON	
11	Francis BENALI †	
	Substitutes	
12	Nicky BANGER †58	
14	Tommy WIDDRINGTON	
Gk	Ian ANDREWS	

SHEFFIELD WEDNESDAY
Yellow shirts, Yellow shorts   Goals

1	Chris WOODS	
2	Roland NILSSON	
3	Nigel WORTHINGTON	
4	Carlton PALMER	
5	Viv ANDERSON ❑	
6	Peter SHIRTLIFF	
7	Danny WILSON	
8	Chris WADDLE	
9	David HIRST	63
10	Mark BRIGHT	
11	John SHERIDAN	12p
	Substitutes	
12	Chris BART-WILLIAMS	
14	John HARKES	
Gk	Kevin PRESSMAN	

Date	Monday 28 December 1992
Venue	White Hart Lane, 1.00pm

TOTTENHAM HOTSPUR (1) 2
NOTTINGHAM FOREST (0) 1

Attendance 32,118
Referee Mike REED
Linesmen G.R. Hamblin, C. Jones

TOTTENHAM HOTSPUR
White shirts, Navy Blue shorts   Goals

1	Erik THORSTVEDT	
2	Dean AUSTIN	
3	Justin EDINBURGH	
4	Vinny SAMWAYS	
5	Gary MABBUTT	85
6	Neil RUDDOCK	
7	David HOWELLS	
8	Nick BARMBY ‡	35
9	Darren ANDERTON †	
10	Teddy SHERINGHAM	
11	Paul ALLEN	
	Substitutes	
12	Paul MORAN †65	
14	Gudni BERGSSON ‡89	
Gk	Ian WALKER	

NOTTINGHAM FOREST
Red shirts, Red shorts   Goals

1	Mark CROSSLEY	
2	Brian LAWS	
3	Stuart PEARCE	
4	Steve CHETTLE	
5	Carl TILER	
6	Roy KEANE	
7	Gary CROSBY	
8	Scot GEMMILL	73
9	Nigel CLOUGH	
10	Neil WEBB	
11	Kingsley BLACK †	
	Substitutes	
12	Ian WOAN †67	
14	Lee GLOVER	
Gk	Andy MARRIOTT	

Date   Monday 28 December 1992
Venue   Selhurst Park, 3.00pm

WIMBLEDON (0) 0
CHELSEA (0) 0

Attendance 14,687
Referee   David ELLERAY
Linesmen   P.A. Josper, M.G. Wright

WIMBLEDON
Blue shirts, Blue shorts   Goals

1	Hans SEGERS
2	Roger JOSEPH
3	Brian McALLISTER
4	Vinnie JONES ❑
5	John SCALES
6	Dean BLACKWELL
7	Neal ARDLEY †
8	Robbie EARLE
9	John FASHANU
10	Lawrie SANCHEZ ❑
11	Andy CLARKE ‡

Substitutes

12	Steve TALBOYS †67
14	Paul MILLER ‡67
Gk	Neil SULLIVAN

CHELSEA
White shirts, Red shorts   Goals

1	Kevin HITCHCOCK
2	Gareth HALL
3	Frank SINCLAIR
4	Andy TOWNSEND
5	David LEE
6	Mal DONAGHY
7	Graham STUART
8	Robert FLECK
9	Andy MYERS
10	Eddie NEWTON
11	Dennis WISE

Substitutes

12	Craig BURLEY
14	John SPENCER
Gk	Dmitri KHARIN

LEAGUE TABLE

Up to and including 28.12.92	P	W	D	L	F	A	Pts
1 Norwich City	22	12	5	5	34	34	41
2 Manchester United	22	10	8	4	30	17	38
3 Aston Villa	22	10	8	4	32	24	38
4 Blackburn Rovers	22	10	7	5	34	20	37
5 Ipswich Town	22	8	12	2	31	23	36
6 Chelsea	22	9	8	5	28	22	35
7 Queen's Park Rangers	21	9	5	7	30	25	32
8 Coventry City	22	8	8	6	33	32	32
9 Arsenal	22	9	4	9	23	22	31
10 Manchester City	22	8	6	8	30	24	30
11 Liverpool	21	8	5	8	35	33	29
12 Tottenham Hotspur	22	7	8	7	22	27	29
13 Middlesbrough	22	6	9	7	29	29	27
14 Sheffield Wednesday	22	6	9	7	33	33	27
15 Crystal Palace	22	6	9	7	29	33	27
16 Leeds United	22	6	7	9	33	37	25
17 Southampton	22	5	9	8	22	26	24
18 Everton	22	6	5	11	21	30	23
19 Oldham Athletic	20	5	6	9	33	39	21
20 Sheffield United	21	5	6	10	18	28	21
21 Wimbledon	22	4	8	10	26	33	20
22 Nottingham Forest	21	3	6	12	20	33	15

LEADING SCORERS

Alan SHEARER	Blackburn Rovers	16
Dalian ATKINSON	Aston Villa	11
Mark ROBINS	Norwich City	11
David WHITE	Manchester City	11
Ian WRIGHT	Arsenal	11

LEAGUE GOALSCORING FIGURES

Running Totals

Date	Games	Goals	Average	Games	Goals	Average
05.12.92	9	32	3.56	196	514	2.62
06.12.92	1	3	3.00	197	517	2.62
07.12.92	1	3	3.00	198	520	2.63
11.12.92	1	0	0.00	199	520	2.61
12.12.92	9	29	3.22	208	549	2.64
13.12.92	1	3	3.00	209	552	2.64
19.12.92	8	20	2.50	217	572	2.64
20.12.92	2	3	1.50	219	575	2.63
21.12.92	1	2	2.00	220	577	2.62
26.12.92	9	23	2.56	229	600	2.62
28.12.92	10	24	2.40	239	624	2.61

Date   Saturday 9 January 1993
Venue   Highbury Stadium, 3.00pm

ARSENAL (1) 1
SHEFFIELD UNITED (0) 1

Attendance   23,818
Referee   Gerald ASHBY
Linesmen   M.E. Alexander, D.C. Richards

ARSENAL
Red & White Shirts, White shorts   Goals

1	David SEAMAN	
2	Lee DIXON	
3	Nigel WINTERBURN	
4	David HILLIER	43
5	Andy LINIGHAN	
6	Tony ADAMS	
7	John JENSEN	
8	Ian WRIGHT	
9	Alan SMITH	
10	Paul MERSON †	
11	Anders LIMPAR	
	Substitutes	
12	David O'LEARY †81	
14	Kevin CAMPBELL	
Gk	Alan MILLER	

SHEFFIELD UNITED
White shirts, Black shorts   Goals

1	Alan KELLY	
2	Kevin GAGE	
3	David BARNES	
4	John GANNON ‡	
5	John PEMBERTON	
6	Paul BEESLEY	
7	Chris KAMARA ❏	
8	Paul ROGERS †	
9	Adrian LITTLEJOHN	87
10	Brian DEANE	
11	Glyn HODGES	
	Substitutes	
12	Jamie HOYLAND †81	
14	Alan CORK ‡63	
Gk	Ken VEYSEY	

Date   Saturday 9 January 1993
Venue   Ewood Park, 3.00pm

BLACKBURN ROVERS (0) 0
WIMBLEDON (0) 0

Attendance   14,504
Referee   Robbie HART
Linesmen   J. McGrath, E.J. Walsh

BLACKBURN ROVERS
Blue & White shirts, White shorts   Goals

1	Bobby MIMMS	
2	David MAY	
3	Alan WRIGHT	
4	Tim SHERWOOD	
5	Colin HENDRY	
6	Kevin MORAN ‡	
7	Stuart RIPLEY	
8	Nicky MARKER	
9	Roy WEGERLE	
10	Mike NEWELL	
11	Jason WILCOX	
	Substitutes	
12	Mark ATKINS	
14	Patrik ANDERSSON ‡30	
Gk	Darren COLLIER	

WIMBLEDON
Red shirts, Red shorts   Goals

1	Hans SEGERS	
2	Roger JOSEPH	
3	Gary ELKINS	
4	Vinnie JONES ❏	
5	John SCALES ❏	
6	Dean BLACKWELL	
7	Greg BERRY	
8	Robbie EARLE	
9	John FASHANU ❏	
10	Lawrie SANCHEZ	
11	Andy CLARKE	
	Substitutes	
12	Steve TALBOYS	
14	Steve COTTERILL	
Gk	Neil SULIVAN	

Date	Saturday 9 January 1993
Venue	Stamford Bridge, 3.00pm

CHELSEA (0) 2
MANCHESTER CITY (2) 4

Attendance	15,939
Referee	Vic CALLOW
Linesmen	G.P. Barber, G. Butland

CHELSEA
Blue shirts, Blue shorts — Goals

1	Kevin HITCHCOCK	
2	Steve CLARKE ‡	
3	Frank SINCLAIR	
4	Andy TOWNSEND ❏	
5	David LEE	
6	Mal DONAGHY	
7	Graham STUART	77
8	Robert FLECK	
9	Mick HARFORD	
10	Eddie NEWTON	
11	Graeme LE SAUX	
	Substitutes	
12	Craig BURLEY	
14	John SPENCER ‡65	83
Gk	Nick COLGAN	

MANCHESTER CITY
White shirts, White shorts — Goals

1	Tony COTON	
2	Ray RANSON	
3	Terry PHELAN	54
4	Steve McMAHON ❏	
5	Keith CURLE	
6	David BRIGHTWELL	
7	David WHITE	26
8	Mike SHERON	29, 87
9	Niall QUINN	
10	Garry FLITCROFT	
11	Rick HOLDEN	
	Substitutes	
12	Adie MIKE	
14	Peter REID	
Gk	Martyn MARGETSON	

Date	Saturday 9 January 1993
Venue	Highfield Road, 3.00pm

COVENTRY CITY (0) 0
NOTTINGHAM FOREST (0) 1

Attendance	15,264
Referee	Martin BODENHAM
Linesmen	M. Fletcher, R.J. Harris

COVENTRY CITY
Sky Blue shirts, Sky Blue shorts — Goals

1	Steve OGRIZOVIC	
2	Brian BORROWS	
3	Phil BABB	
4	Peter ATHERTON	
5	Kenny SANSOM †	
6	John WILLIAMS	
7	Lloyd McGRATH ❏	
8	Lee HURST	
9	Robert ROSARIO	
10	Mick QUINN	
11	Kevin GALLACHER	
	Substitutes	
12	Andy PEARCE †80	
14	Michael GYNN	
Gk	Jonathan GOULD	

NOTTINGHAM FOREST
Red shirts, White shorts — Goals

1	Mark CROSSLEY	
2	Brian LAWS	
3	Stuart PEARCE	
4	Steve CHETTLE	
5	Carl TILER	
6	Roy KEANE	
7	Scot GEMMILL	
8	Nigel CLOUGH	
9	Neil WEBB	
10	Ian WOAN	65
11	Gary BANNISTER	
	Substitutes	
12	Thorvaldur ORLYGSSON	
14	Steve STONE	
Gk	Andy MARRIOTT	

Date	Saturday 9 January 1993
Venue	Selhurst Park, 3.00pm

CRYSTAL PALACE (0) 0
EVERTON (0) 2

Attendance	13,227
Referee	Roger MILFORD
Linesmen	W.J. Norbury, M. Stobbart

CRYSTAL PALACE
Red & Blue striped shirts, Red shorts   Goals

1	Nigel MARTYN ❑	
2	John HUMPHREY	
3	Bobby BOWRY †	
4	Chris COLEMAN	
5	Eric YOUNG	
6	Andy THORN ‡	
7	Grant WATTS	
8	Geoff THOMAS	
9	Chris ARMSTRONG	
10	Simon RODGER	
11	Eddie McGOLDRICK	
	Substitutes	
12	George NDAH †68	
14	Richard NEWMAN ‡45	
Gk	Andy WOODMAN	

EVERTON
White shirts, White shorts   Goals

1	Neville SOUTHALL	
2	Matthew JACKSON	50
3	Gary ABLETT	
4	Ian SNODIN ❑	
5	Dave WATSON	
6	Martin KEOWN	
7	PREKI	
8	Peter BEARDSLEY	85
9	Paul RIDEOUT †	
10	Billy KENNY	
11	John EBBRELL	
	Substitutes	
12	Stuart BARLOW †57	
14	Robert WARZYCHA	
Gk	Jason KEARTON	

Date	Saturday 9 January 1993
Venue	Portman Road, 3.00pm

IPSWICH TOWN (0) 1
OLDHAM ATHLETIC (1) 2

Attendance	15,025
Referee	Ken REDFERN
Linesmen	A.P. D'Urso, I.M.D. Mitchell

IPSWICH TOWN
Blue & White shirts, White shorts   Goals

1	Clive BAKER	
2	Gavin JOHNSON	
3	Neil THOMPSON ‡	
4	Mick STOCKWELL	
5	John WARK	
6	David LINIGHAN	
7	Geraint WILLIAMS	
8	Bontcho GUENTCHEV	
9	Steve WHITTON	
10	Jason DOZZELL	
11	Chris KIWOMYA	60
	Substitutes	
12	Phil WHELAN	
14	Paul GODDARD ‡71	
Gk	Craig FORREST	

OLDHAM ATHLETIC
Red & White shirts, Red shorts   Goals

1	Paul GERRARD	
2	Gunnar HALLE	
3	Andy BARLOW ❑	
4	Paul BERNARD	51
5	Richard JOBSON	
6	Craig FLEMING	
7	Nick HENRY	
8	Ian OLNEY ❑	
9	Ian MARSHALL †	
10	Mike MILLIGAN	
11	Mark BRENNAN ‡	16
	Substitutes	
12	Graeme SHARP †63	
14	Steve REDMOND ‡63	
Gk	John KEELEY	

Date	Saturday 9 January 1993
Venue	Elland Road, 3.00pm

LEEDS UNITED (0) 2
SOUTHAMPTON (1) 1

Attendance	26,071
Referee	Ron GROVES
Linesmen	T.A. Atkinson, P. Rejer

LEEDS UNITED
White Shirts, White shorts   Goals

1	John LUKIC	
2	Mel STERLAND ‡	
3	Tony DORIGO	
4	Rod WALLACE	
5	Chris FAIRCLOUGH	
6	David WETHERALL	
7	Gordon STRACHAN †	
8	Carl SHUTT	
9	Lee CHAPMAN	50
10	Gary McALLISTER	
11	Gary SPEED	72
	Substitutes	
12	David ROCASTLE †45	
14	Jon NEWSOME ‡83	
Gk	Mervyn DAY	

SOUTHAMPTON
Blue shirts, Blue shorts   Goals

1	Tim FLOWERS	
2	Jeff KENNA	
3	Micky ADAMS	
4	Terry HURLOCK	
5	Richard HALL ❑	
6	Kenneth MONKOU ❑	
7	Matthew LE TISSIER	
8	Glenn COCKERILL	
9	Kerry DIXON	19
10	Neil MADDISON	
11	Francis BENALI ‡	
	Substitutes	
12	Perry GROVES	
14	Nicky BANGER ‡80	
Gk	Ian ANDREWS	

Date	Saturday 9 January 1993
Venue	Anfield, 3.00pm

LIVERPOOL (1) 1
ASTON VILLA (0) 2

Attendance	40,826
Referee	Keith HACKETT
Linesmen	R. Pearson, T.J. Stevens

LIVERPOOL
Red shirts, Red shorts   Goals

1	Mike HOOPER	
2	Mike MARSH	
3	Rob JONES	
4	Paul STEWART	
5	Torben PIECHNIK	
6	Stig Inge BJORNEBYE	
7	Steve McMANAMAN	
8	Jamie REDKNAPP †	
9	Ronnie ROSENTHAL ‡	
10	John BARNES	42
11	Michael THOMAS	
	Substitutes	
12	Don HUTCHISON †78	
14	Mark WALTERS ‡70	
Gk	David JAMES	

ASTON VILLA
White shirts, Black shorts   Goals

1	Nigel SPINK	
2	Earl BARRETT	
3	Steve STAUNTON	
4	Shaun TEALE ❑	
5	Paul McGRATH	
6	Kevin RICHARDSON	
7	Ray HOUGHTON	
8	Garry PARKER	54
9	Dean SAUNDERS	64
10	Dalian ATKINSON †	
11	Dwight YORKE	
	Substitutes	
12	Stephen FROGGATT †46 ‡	
14	Neil COX ‡87	
Gk	Mark BOSNICH	

Date	Saturday 9 January 1993
Venue	Old Trafford, 3.00pm

MANCHESTER UNITED (1) 4
TOTTENHAM HOTSPUR (0) 1

Attendance	35,648
Referee	Mike PECK
Linesmen	M. Warren, A. Streets

MANCHESTER UNITED
Red shirts, White shorts   Goals

1	Peter SCHMEICHEL	
2	Paul PARKER	58
3	Denis IRWIN	52
4	Steve BRUCE	
5	Lee SHARPE	
6	Gary PALLISTER	
7	Eric CANTONA	40
8	Paul INCE ‡	
9	Brian McCLAIR	53
10	Mark HUGHES	
11	Ryan GIGGS †	
	Substitutes	
12	Andrei KANCHELSKIS †74	
14	Mike PHELAN ‡67	
Gk	Les SEALEY	

TOTTENHAM HOTSPUR
White shirts, Navy Blue shorts   Goals

1	Erik THORSTVEDT	
2	Dean AUSTIN †	
3	Justin EDINBURGH	
4	Vinny SAMWAYS	
5	Gary MABBUTT	
6	Neil RUDDOCK	
7	David HOWELLS	
8	Nick BARMBY	88
9	NAYIM ‡	
10	Teddy SHERINGHAM	
11	Paul ALLEN	
	Substitutes	
12	Gudni BERGSSON †81	
14	Darren ANDERTON ‡70	
Gk	Ian WALKER	

Date	Saturday 9 January 1993
Venue	Ayresome Park, 3.00pm

MIDDLESBROUGH (0) 0
QPR (0) 1

Attendance	15,616
Referee	Roger DILKES
Linesmen	E. Lomas, R.R. Rawson

MIDDLESBROUGH
Red shirts, White shorts   Goals

1	Stephen PEARS	
2	Curtis FLEMING	
3	Jimmy PHILLIPS	
4	Nicky MOHAN	
5	Jon GITTENS ❑	
6	Jamie POLLOCK ❑	
7	Craig HIGNETT	
8	Andy PEAKE	
9	Paul WILKINSON	
10	Tommy WRIGHT †	
11	John HENDRIE	
	Substitutes	
12	Willie FALCONER †65	
14	Mark PROCTOR	
Gk	Ian IRONSIDE	

QPR
Blue & White hooped shirts, Blue shorts   Goals

1	Tony ROBERTS	
2	David BARDSLEY ❑	
3	Rufus BREVETT	
4	Clive WILSON	
5	Darren PEACOCK	
6	Alan McDONALD	
7	Andy IMPEY	
8	Simon BARKER	
9	Les FERDINAND ❑	72
10	Gary PENRICE †	
11	Andy SINTON ‡	
	Substitutes	
12	Bradley ALLEN †29	
14	Danny MADDIX ‡45	
Gk	Jan STEJSKAL	

Date	Sunday 10 January 1993
Venue	Hillsborough, 4.00pm

SHEFFIELD WEDNESDAY (1) 1
NORWICH CITY (0) 0

Attendance	23,360
Referee	David ALLISON
Linesmen	W.J. Nattrass, P.R. Richards

SHEFFIELD WEDNESDAY
Blue & White striped shirts, Black shorts — Goals

		Goals
1	Chris WOODS	
2	Roland NILSSON	
3	Nigel WORTHINGTON	42
4	John HARKES	
5	Viv ANDERSON ‡	
6	Peter SHIRTLIFF	
7	Danny WILSON	
8	Chris WADDLE	
9	David HIRST †	
10	Mark BRIGHT	
11	John SHERIDAN	
	Substitutes	
12	Chris BART-WILLIAMS †85	
14	Paul WARHURST ‡45	
Gk	Kevin PRESSMAN	

NORWICH CITY
Yellow shirts, Green shorts — Goals

		Goals
1	Bryan GUNN	
2	Ian CULVERHOUSE	
3	Mark BOWEN	
4	Ian BUTTERWORTH	
5	John POLSTON	
6	Gary MEGSON	
7	Ian CROOK	
8	Lee POWER	
9	Mark ROBINS †	
10	Ruel FOX	
11	David PHILLIPS	
	Substitutes	
12	Daryl SUTCH †37	
14	Colin WOODTHORPE	
Gk	Mark WALTON	

Date	Saturday 16 January 1993
Venue	Goodison Park, 3.00pm

EVERTON (1) 2
LEEDS UNITED (0) 0

Attendance	21,031
Referee	David ELLERAY
Linesmen	A.N. Butler, M.A. Cooper

EVERTON
Blue shirts, White shorts — Goals

		Goals
1	Neville SOUTHALL	
2	Matthew JACKSON	
3	Gary ABLETT	
4	John EBBRELL	
5	Dave WATSON	
6	Martin KEOWN ❏	
7	PREKI	
8	Peter BEARDSLEY	
9	Tony COTTEE †	30, 49
10	Barry HORNE	
11	Peter BEAGRIE ‡	
	Substitutes	
12	Stuart BARLOW †71	
14	Alan HARPER ‡71	
Gk	Jason KEARTON	

LEEDS UNITED
White shirts, White shorts — Goals

		Goals
1	Mervyn DAY	
2	Jon NEWSOME †	
3	Tony DORIGO	
4	David BATTY	
5	David WETHERALL	
6	Chris WHYTE	
7	Gordon STRACHAN ‡	
8	Carl SHUTT	
9	Lee CHAPMAN	
10	Gary McALLISTER	
11	Gary SPEED	
	Substitutes	
12	Chris FAIRCLOUGH †66	
14	Rod WALLACE ‡66	
Gk	John LUKIC	

Date	Saturday 16 January 1993
Venue	Maine Road, 3.00pm

MANCHESTER CITY (0) 0
ARSENAL (0) 1

Attendance	25,047
Referee	Keith BURGE
Linesmen	P. Rejer, M.A. Riley

MANCHESTER CITY
Light Blue shirts, White shorts   Goals

1	Tony COTON	
2	Ray RANSON	
3	Terry PHELAN	
4	Fitzroy SIMPSON	
5	Keith CURLE	
6	David BRIGHTWELL	
7	David WHITE	
8	Mike SHERON	
9	Niall QUINN	
10	Garry FLITCROFT ❑	
11	Rick HOLDEN	
	Substitutes	
12	Peter REID	
14	Adie MIKE	
Gk	Martyn MARGETSON	

ARSENAL
Red & White shirts, White shorts   Goals

1	David SEAMAN	
2	Lee DIXON ❑	
3	Nigel WINTERBURN	
4	David HILLIER	
5	Steve BOULD	
6	Tony ADAMS	
7	John JENSEN ❑	
8	Kevin CAMPBELL	
9	Alan SMITH	
10	Paul MERSON	79
11	Mark FLATTS	
	Substitutes	
12	David O'LEARY	
14	Jimmy CARTER	
Gk	Alan MILLER	

Date	Saturday 16 January 1993
Venue	Carrow Road, 3.00pm

NORWICH CITY (1) 1
COVENTRY CITY (0) 1

Attendance	13,613
Referee	Allan GUNN
Linesmen	A.P. D'Urso, M.D. Dearing

NORWICH CITY
Yellow shirts, Green shorts   Goals

1	Bryan GUNN	
2	Ian CULVERHOUSE	
3	Mark BOWEN	
4	Ian BUTTERWORTH	
5	John POLSTON ‡	
6	Jeremy GOSS	
7	Ian CROOK †	
8	Darren BECKFORD	
9	Chris SUTTON	13
10	Ruel FOX	
11	David PHILLIPS	
	Substitutes	
12	Daryl SUTCH †26	
14	Colin WOODTHORPE ‡86	
Gk	Mark WALTON	

COVENTRY CITY
Sky Blue shirts, Sky Blue shorts   Goals

1	Steve OGRIZOVIC	
2	Brian BORROWS	
3	Phil BABB	
4	Peter ATHERTON	
5	David BUSST	
6	John WILLIAMS	
7	Chris GREENMAN ‡	
8	Michael GYNN	
9	Robert ROSARIO	
10	Mick QUINN	57
11	Kevin GALLACHER	
	Substitutes	
12	Terry FLEMING	
14	Keith ROWLAND ‡46	
Gk	Jonathan GOULD	

Date	Saturday 16 January 1993
Venue	City Ground, 3.00pm

NOTTINGHAM FOREST (1) 3
CHELSEA (0) 0

Attendance	23,249
Referee	Paul DURKIN
Linesmen	J.B. Robinson, P.J. Robinson

NOTTINGHAM FOREST
Red shirts, White shorts — Goals

1	Mark CROSSLEY	
2	Brian LAWS	
3	Stuart PEARCE	
4	Steve CHETTLE	
5	Carl TILER	
6	Roy KEANE	
7	Gary BANNISTER	9, 58
8	Scot GEMMILL †	
9	Nigel CLOUGH	
10	Neil WEBB	
11	Ian WOAN	
	Substitutes	
12	Thorvaldur ORLYGSSON †84	89
14	Gary CROSBY	
Gk	Andy MARRIOTT	

CHELSEA
Blue shirts, Blue shorts — Goals

1	Kevin HITCHCOCK	
2	Gareth HALL	
3	Frank SINCLAIR ❏	
4	Andy TOWNSEND	
5	Erland JOHNSEN	
6	Mal DONAGHY	
7	Graham STUART	
8	Craig BURLEY	
9	Mick HARFORD †	
10	Eddie NEWTON	
11	Graeme LE SAUX ‡	
	Substitutes	
12	Robert FLECK †72	
14	John SPENCER ‡72	
Gk	Dmitri KHARIN	

Date	Saturday 16 January 1993
Venue	Boundary Park, 3.00pm

OLDHAM ATHLETIC (0) 0
BLACKBURN ROVERS (0) 1

Attendance	13,742
Referee	Alf BUKSH
Linesmen	J. Leach, W.J. Nattrass

OLDHAM ATHLETIC
Blue shirts, Blue shorts — Goals

1	Paul GERRARD	
2	Gunnar HALLE	
3	Neil POINTON	
4	Paul BERNARD	
5	Richard JOBSON ❏	
6	Craig FLEMING	
7	Neil ADAMS	
8	Ian OLNEY	
9	Ian MARSHALL	
10	Mike MILLIGAN	
11	Steve REDMOND	
	Substitutes	
12	Roger PALMER	
14	Neil TOLSON	
Gk	John KEELEY	

BLACKBURN ROVERS
Black & Red striped shirts, Black shorts — Goals

1	Bobby MIMMS	
2	David MAY ❏	
3	Alan WRIGHT	
4	Tim SHERWOOD	
5	Colin HENDRY	
6	Kevin MORAN	
7	Stuart RIPLEY	80
8	Gordon COWANS ❏	
9	Roy WEGERLE ❏	
10	Mike NEWELL	
11	Jason WILCOX	
	Substitutes	
12	Mark ATKINS	
14	Nick MARKER	
Gk	Darren COLLIER	

Date	Saturday 16 January 1993
Venue	Bramall Lane, 3.00pm

SHEFFIELD UNITED (1) 3
IPSWICH TOWN (0) 0

Attendance	16,758
Referee	David ALLISON
Linesmen	J. Hilditch, T. Lynch

SHEFFIELD UNITED
Red & White striped shirts, White shorts   Goals

1	Alan KELLY	
2	Kevin GAGE	
3	David BARNES	
4	Jamie HOYLAND	
5	Brian GAYLE	
6	Paul BEESLEY	
7	Chris KAMARA	
8	Franz CARR	
9	Alan CORK ‡	
10	Brian DEANE	31, 72, 75
11	Glyn HODGES	
	Substitutes	
12	Mitch WARD	
14	Ian BRYSON ‡80	
Gk	Phil KITE	

IPSWICH TOWN
Blue & White shirts, Blue shorts   Goals

1	Clive BAKER	
2	Gavin JOHNSON ‡	
3	Neil THOMPSON	
4	Mick STOCKWELL †	
5	Phil WHELAN	
6	David LINIGHAN	
7	Geraint WILLIAMS	
8	Bontcho GUENTCHEV	
9	Steve WHITTON	
10	Jason DOZZELL	
11	Chris KIWOMYA	
	Substitutes	
12	Eddie YOUDS †82	
14	Vlado BOZINOSKI ‡70	
Gk	Craig FORREST	

Date	Saturday 16 January 1993
Venue	The Dell, 3.00pm

SOUTHAMPTON (0) 1
CRYSTAL PALACE (0) 0

Attendance	13,397
Referee	Philip DON
Linesmen	G.P. Barber, A. Schneider

SOUTHAMPTON
Red & White striped shirts, Black shorts   Goals

1	Tim FLOWERS	
2	Jason DODD	
3	Micky ADAMS ❑	
4	Terry HURLOCK	
5	Richard HALL	
6	Kenneth MONKOU	
7	Matthew LE TISSIER	
8	Glenn COCKERILL	
9	Iain DOWIE	
10	Neil MADDISON	50
11	Perry GROVES ‡	
	Substitutes	
12	Francis BENALI	
14	Nicky BANGER ‡67	
Gk	Ian ANDREWS	

CRYSTAL PALACE
Yellow shirts, Light Blue shorts   Goals

1	Nigel MARTYN	
2	John HUMPHREY ❑	
3	Lee SINNOTT	
4	Chris COLEMAN	
5	Grant WATTS †	
6	Andy THORN ❑ ‡	
7	George NDAH	
8	Geoff THOMAS	
9	Chris ARMSTRONG	
10	Simon RODGER	
11	Eddie McGOLDRICK	
	Substitutes	
12	Bobby BOWRY †77	
14	Dean GORDON ‡69	
Gk	Andy WOODMAN	

Date	Saturday 16 January 1993
Venue	White Hart Lane, 3.00pm

TOTTENHAM HOTSPUR (0) 0
SHEFFIELD WEDNESDAY (0) 2

Attendance	25,702
Referee	Kelvin MORTON
Linesmen	I.A. Madge, G.T. Pearson

TOTTENHAM HOTSPUR
White shirts, Navy Blue shorts   Goals

1	Erik THORSTVEDT	
2	Dean AUSTIN	
3	Justin EDINBURGH ‡	
4	Vinny SAMWAYS	
5	Gary MABBUTT	
6	Neil RUDDOCK	
7	David HOWELLS †	
8	Nick BARMBY	
9	Darren ANDERTON	
10	Teddy SHERINGHAM	
11	Paul ALLEN	
	Substitutes	
12	John HENDRY ‡75	
14	Gudni BERGSSON †75	
Gk	Ian WALKER	

SHEFFIELD WEDNESDAY
Yellow shirts, Yellow shorts   Goals

1	Chris WOODS	
2	Roland NILSSON	
3	Nigel WORTHINGTON	
4	John HARKES	
5	Nigel PEARSON	
6	Peter SHIRTLIFF	
7	Graham HYDE ‡	
8	Chris WADDLE	
9	David HIRST	88
10	Mark BRIGHT	54
11	John SHERIDAN	
	Substitutes	
12	Chris BART-WILLIAMS	
14	Paul WARHURST ‡85	
Gk	Kevin PRESSMAN	

Date	Saturday 16 January 1993
Venue	Selhurst Park, 3.00pm

WIMBLEDON (1) 2
LIVERPOOL (0) 0

Attendance	11,294
Referee	Roger DILKES
Linesmen	S.G. Tomlin, I.M.D. Mitchell

WIMBLEDON
Blue shirts, Blue shorts   Goals

1	Hans SEGERS	
2	Roger JOSEPH	
3	Gary ELKINS	
4	Steve COTTERILL	64
5	John SCALES	
6	Dean BLACKWELL	
7	Neal ARDLEY	
8	Robbie EARLE	
9	John FASHANU †	36p
10	Lawrie SANCHEZ	
11	Andy CLARKE ‡	
	Substitutes	
12	Dean HOLDSWORTH †90	
14	Steve TALBOYS ‡72	
Gk	Neil SULLIVAN	

LIVERPOOL
Red shirts, Red shorts   Goals

1	David JAMES	
2	Mike MARSH	
3	Rob JONES	
4	Paul STEWART	
5	Torben PIECHNIK †	
6	Mark WRIGHT	
7	Mark WALTERS ‡	
8	Jamie REDKNAPP	
9	Don HUTCHISON	
10	David BARNES	
11	Stig Inge BJORNEBYE	
	Substitutes	
12	Steve HARKNESS †38	
14	Ronnie ROSENTHAL ‡76	
Gk	Mike HOOPER	

Date	Sunday 17 January 1993
Venue	Villa Park, 4.00pm

ASTON VILLA (3) 5
MIDDLESBROUGH (0) 1

Attendance	19,977
Referee	Keith COOPER
Linesmen	R.H. Andrews, M.J. Holohan

ASTON VILLA
Claret & Blue shirts, White shorts · Goals

		Goals
1	Nigel SPINK	
2	Earl BARRETT	
3	Steve STAUNTON	
4	Shaun TEALE	68
5	Paul McGRATH †	32
6	Kevin RICHARDSON	
7	Ray HOUGHTON	
8	Garry PARKER	26
9	Dean SAUNDERS	58
10	Dwight YORKE	44
11	Stephen FROGGATT ‡	
	Substitutes	
12	Neil COX †82	
14	Stefan BEINLICH ‡70	
Gk	Mark BOSNICH	

MIDDLESBROUGH
White shirts, Black shorts · Goals

		Goals
1	Stephen PEARS	
2	Nicky MOHAN	
3	Jimmy PHILLIPS	
4	Derek WHYTE †	
5	Jon GITTENS	
6	Willie FALCONER	
7	Graham KAVANAGH ‡	
8	Andy PEAKE	
9	Paul WILKINSON	
10	Tommy WRIGHT	
11	John HENDRIE	
	Substitutes	
12	Jamie POLLOCK †67	
14	Craig HIGNETT ‡45	82
Gk	Ian IRONSIDE	

Date	Monday 18 January 1993
Venue	Loftus Road, 7.45pm

QPR (1) 1
MANCHESTER UNITED (1) 3

Attendance	21,142
Referee	John MARTIN
Linesmen	A.P. D'Urso, J.A. Elwin

QPR
Blue & White hooped shirts, White shorts · Goals

		Goals
1	Tony ROBERTS	
2	David BARDSLEY	
3	Clive WILSON	
4	Simon BARKER ❑	
5	Darren PEACOCK †	
6	Alan McDONALD ❑	
7	Andy IMPEY	
8	Ian HOLLOWAY	
9	Dennis BAILEY	
10	Bradley ALLEN	42
11	Andy SINTON	
	Substitutes	
12	Garry THOMPSON †70	
14	Rufus BREVETT	
Gk	Jan STEJSKAL	

MANCHESTER UNITED
Red shirts, Black shorts · Goals

		Goals
1	Peter SCHMEICHEL	
2	Paul PARKER	
3	Denis IRWIN	
4	Steve BRUCE	
5	Lee SHARPE	
6	Gary PALLISTER	
7	Andrei KANCHELSKIS	48
8	Paul INCE	26
9	Brian McCLAIR	
10	Mark HUGHES ‡	
11	Ryan GIGGS	30
	Substitutes	
12	Craig LAWTON	
14	Mike PHELAN ‡9	
Gk	Les SEALEY	

Date	Saturday 23 January 1993
Venue	Highfield Road, 5.00pm

COVENTRY CITY (3) 3
OLDHAM ATHLETIC (0) 0

Attendance	10,544
Referee	Ray LEWIS
Linesmen	J.A. Elwin, M.J. Holohan

● *Game brought forward from 10 February 1993.*

COVENTRY CITY
Sky Blue shirts, Sky Blue shorts   Goals

1	Steve OGRIZOVIC	
2	Brian BORROWS	
3	Phil BABB	
4	Peter ATHERTON	
5	David BUSST	
6	John WILLIAMS	
7	Peter NDLOVU	12
8	Michael GYNN	
9	Robert ROSARIO	
10	Mick QUINN ❏	
11	Kevin GALLACHER ‡	6, 18
	Substitutes	
12	Peter BILLING	
14	Keith ROWLAND ‡40	
Gk	Jonathan GOULD	

OLDHAM ATHLETIC
Red & White shirts, White shorts   Goals

1	Paul GERRARD	
2	Gunnar HALLE	
3	Neil POINTON †	
4	Paul BERNARD	
5	Richard JOBSON ❏	
6	Craig FLEMING ❏	
7	Roger PALMER	
8	Ian OLNEY	
9	Ian MARSHALL	
10	Mike MILLIGAN ❏	
11	Steve REDMOND	
	Substitutes	
12	Neil ADAMS †57	
14	Chris MAKIN	
Gk	Ian GRAY	

Date	Tuesday 26 January 1993
Venue	Ewood Park, 7.45pm

BLACKBURN ROVERS (1) 2
COVENTRY CITY (2) 5

Attendance	15,215
Referee	Ked REDFERN
Linesmen	T. Heilbron, J. Hilditch

BLACKBURN ROVERS
Blue & White shirts, White shorts   Goals

1	Bobby MIMMS	
2	David MAY	19og
3	Alan WRIGHT †	
4	Tim SHERWOOD	
5	Colin HENDRY	71
6	Nicky MARKER	
7	Stuart RIPLEY	
8	Gordon COWANS ‡	
9	Roy WEGERLE	
10	Mike NEWELL	13
11	Jason WILCOX	
	Substitutes	
12	Mark ATKINS †47	
14	Patrik ANDERSSON ‡69	
Gk	Darren COLLIER	

COVENTRY CITY
Red shirts, White shorts   Goals

1	Steve OGRIZOVIC	
2	Brian BORROWS	
3	Phil BABB	
4	Peter ATHERTON	
5	David BUSST	
6	John WILLIAMS	48
7	Peter NDLOVU	
8	Michael GYNN	
9	Robert ROSARIO	
10	Mick QUINN	85, 89
11	Lee HURST	44
	Substitutes	
12	Peter BILLING	
14	Keith ROWLAND	
Gk	Jonathan GOULD	

Date	Tuesday 26 January 1993
Venue	Ayresome Park, 7.30pm

MIDDLESBROUGH (1) 2
SOUTHAMPTON (0) 1

Attendance	13,921
Referee	Peter FOAKES
Linesmen	N.S. Barry, U.D. Rennie

MIDDLESBROUGH
Red shirts, White shorts   Goals

1	Stephen PEARS	
2	Curtis FLEMING	
3	Jimmy PHILLIPS	
4	Chris MORRIS	
5	Nicky MOHAN	24
6	Willie FALCONER ■	
7	Tommy WRIGHT	
8	Jamie POLLOCK ❑	
9	Paul WILKINSON	71
10	Andy PEAKE	
11	John HENDRIE	
	Substitutes	
12	Craig HIGNETT	
14	Jon GITTENS	
Gk	Ian IRONSIDE	

SOUTHAMPTON
Blue shirts, Blue shorts   Goals

1	Tim FLOWERS	
2	Jason DODD	
3	Micky ADAMS	
4	Terry HURLOCK ■	
5	Richard HALL	
6	Kevin MOORE	
7	Matthew LE TISSIER ❑	58
8	Francis BENALI ❑	
9	Iain DOWIE	
10	Neil MADDISON	
11	Perry GROVES ‡	
	Substitutes	
12	Jeff KENNA	
14	Nicky BANGER ‡7	
Gk	Ian ANDREWS	

Date	Tuesday 26 January 1993
Venue	Boundary Park, 7.30pm

OLDHAM ATHLETIC (0) 0
MANCHESTER CITY (0) 1

Attendance	14,903
Referee	Jim BORRETT
Linesmen	P.M. Roberts, J. McGrath

OLDHAM ATHLETIC
Blue shirts, Blue shorts   Goals

1	Paul GERRARD	
2	Gunnar HALLE	
3	Craig FLEMING	
4	Paul BERNARD	
5	Richard JOBSON	
6	Ian MARSHALL ❑	
7	Roger PALMER	
8	Ian OLNEY	
9	Andy RITCHIE †	
10	Mike MILLIGAN	
11	Neil ADAMS	
	Substitutes	
12	Paul MOULDEN †79	
14	Steve REDMOND	
Gk	Ian GRAY	

MANCHESTER CITY
White shirts, Light Blue shorts   Goals

1	Tony COTON ❑	
2	Ray RANSON ❑	
3	Terry PHELAN	
4	Steve McMAHON ❑	
5	Michel VONK	
6	Fitzroy SIMPSON ❑	
7	David WHITE	
8	Mike SHERON	
9	Niall QUINN ❑	77
10	Garry FLITCROFT	
11	Rick HOLDEN	
	Substitutes	
12	Peter REID	
14	Kare INGEBRIGTSEN	
Gk	Martyn MARGETSON	

Date	Tuesday 26 January 1993		*Date*	Wednesday 27 January 1993
Venue	Selhurst Park, 8.00pm		*Venue*	Villa Park, 7.45pm

WIMBLEDON (0) 1
EVERTON (0) 3

Attendance	3,039
Referee	Keith HACKETT
Linesmen	W.M. Jordan, D.C. Madgwick

WIMBLEDON
Blue shirts, Blue shorts   Goals

1	Hans SEGERS	
2	Roger JOSEPH	
3	Gary ELKINS	
4	Vinnie JONES	
5	John SCALES	
6	Dean BLACKWELL	
7	Neal ARDLEY	
8	Robbie EARLE	
9	John FASHANU	75
10	Lawrie SANCHEZ ❑ †	
11	Dean HOLDSWORTH	
	Substitutes	
12	Andy CLARKE †67	
14	Steve TALBOYS	
Gk	Neil SULLIVAN	

EVERTON
White shirts, White shorts   Goals

1	Neville SOUTHALL	
2	Matthew JACKSON	
3	Gary ABLETT	
4	Ian SNODIN	73
5	Dave WATSON	
6	Martin KEOWN	
7	Alan HARPER	
8	Peter BEARDSLEY	
9	Tony COTTEE	61, 71
10	Barry HORNE	
11	PREKI †	
	Substitutes	
12	Stuart BARLOW †63	
14	Billy KENNY	
Gk	Jason KEARTON	

ASTON VILLA (0) 3
SHEFFIELD UNITED (0) 1

Attendance	20,266
Referee	Keith BURGE
Linesmen	K.J. Hawkes, J. Leech

ASTON VILLA
Claret & Blue shirts, White shorts   Goals

1	Nigel SPINK	
2	Earl BARRETT	
3	Steve STAUNTON	
4	Shaun TEALE	
5	Paul McGRATH	54
6	Kevin RICHARDSON	89
7	Matthias BREITKREUTZ †	
8	Garry PARKER	
9	Dean SAUNDERS	58
10	Dwight YORKE ‡	
11	Bryan SMALL	
	Substitutes	
12	Neil COX †80	
14	Stefan BEINLICH ‡74	
Gk	Michael OAKES	

SHEFFIELD UNITED
White shirts, Black shorts   Goals

1	Alan KELLY	
2	Kevin GAGE	
3	David BARNES ❑	
4	Jamie HOYLAND	
5	Brian GAYLE	
6	Paul BEESLEY ❑	
7	Franz CARR ❑ †	
8	Charlie HARTFIELD ‡	
9	Chris KAMARA ❑	
10	Brian DEANE	74
11	Glyn HODGES	
	Substitutes	
12	Carl BRADSHAW †82	
14	Alan CORK ‡61	
Gk	Mel REES	

Date	Wednesday 27 January 1993
Venue	Old Trafford, 8.00pm

MANCHESTER UNITED (0) 2
NOTTINGHAM FOREST (0) 0

Attendance	36,085
Referee	Joe WORRALL
Linesmen	D.E. Binsley, G.I. Grandidge

MANCHESTER UNITED
Red shirts, White shorts   Goals

1	Peter SCHMEICHEL	
2	Paul PARKER	
3	Denis IRWIN	
4	Steve BRUCE	
5	Lee SHARPE	
6	Gary PALLISTER	
7	Eric CANTONA	
8	Paul INCE	47
9	Brian McCLAIR	
10	Mark HUGHES	68
11	Ryan GIGGS	
	Substitutes	
12	Andrei KANCHELSKIS	
14	Mike PHELAN	
Gk	Les SEALEY	

NOTTINGHAM FOREST
White shirts, Black shorts   Goals

1	Mark CROSSLEY	
2	Brian LAWS	
3	Brett WILLIAMS	
4	Steve CHETTLE	
5	Carl TILER	
6	Roy KEANE †	
7	Gary BANNISTER	
8	Scot GEMMILL	
9	Nigel CLOUGH	
10	Neil WEBB	
11	Ian WOAN ‡	
	Substitutes	
12	Gary CROSBY †75	
14	Thorvaldur ORLYGSSON ‡75	
Gk	Andy MARRIOTT	

Date	Wednesday 27 January 1993
Venue	Carrow Road, 7.45pm

NORWICH CITY (2) 4
CRYSTAL PALACE (2) 2

Attendance	13,543
Referee	Vic CALLOW
Linesmen	B.L. Polkey, M.G. Wright

NORWICH CITY
Yellow shirts, Green shorts   Goals

1	Bryan GUNN	
2	Ian CULVERHOUSE	
3	Mark BOWEN	
4	Ian BUTTERWORTH	
5	John POLSTON ❏	
6	Gary MEGSON	
7	Jeremy GOSS	50
8	Lee POWER	9, 89
9	Chris SUTTON	26
10	Ruel FOX	
11	David PHILLIPS	
	Substitutes	
12	Mark ROBINS	
14	Colin WOODTHORPE	
Gk	Mark WALTON	

CRYSTAL PALACE
Red & Blue striped shirts, Red shorts   Goals

1	Nigel MARTYN	
2	John HUMPHREY ‡	
3	Richard SHAW	
4	Chris COLEMAN	
5	Lee SINNOTT	
6	Andy THORN	
7	Simon OSBORN	
8	Geoff THOMAS	45
9	Chris ARMSTRONG	2
10	Simon RODGER	
11	Eddie McGOLDRICK	
	Substitutes	
12	Bobby BOWRY	
14	George NDAH ‡75	
Gk	Andy WOODMAN	

Date	Wednesday 27 January 1993
Venue	Loftus Road, 7.45pm

QPR (0) 1
CHELSEA (0) 1

Attendance	15,806
Referee	Tony WARD
Linesmen	W.J. Norbury, D. Orr

QPR
Blue & White hooped shirts, White shorts · Goals

1	Tony ROBERTS	
2	David BARDSLEY	
3	Rufus BREVETT	
4	Simon BARKER	
5	Danny MADDIX	
6	Alan McDONALD	
7	Clive WILSON ‡	
8	Ian HOLLOWAY	
9	Les FERDINAND	
10	Bradley ALLEN	88
11	Andy IMPEY	
	Substitutes	
12	Darren PEACOCK	
14	Devon WHITE ‡73 ❑	
Gk	Jan STEJSKAL	

CHELSEA
Blue shirts, Blue shorts · Goals

1	Dmitri KHARIN	
2	Gareth HALL	
3	Frank SINCLAIR ❑	
4	Andy TOWNSEND †	
5	Andy MYERS	
6	Mal DONAGHY	
7	Graham STUART	
8	John SPENCER	47
9	Mick HARFORD ❑	
10	Eddie NEWTON	
11	Graeme LE SAUX ❑	
	Substitutes	
12	Steve CLARKE †46	
14	Robert FLECK	
Gk	Gerry PEYTON	

Date	Wednesday 27 January 1993
Venue	White Hart Lane, 7.30pm

TOTTENHAM HOTSPUR (0) 0
IPSWICH TOWN (0) 2

Attendance	23,738
Referee	Steve LODGE
Linesmen	G.R. Hamblin, B.A. Wigginton

TOTTENHAM HOTSPUR
White shirts, Navy Blue shorts · Goals

1	Erik THORSTVEDT	
2	Dean AUSTIN ❑ ‡	i
3	Justin EDINBURGH ❑	
4	Vinny SAMWAYS	
5	Gary MABBUTT	
6	Neil RUDDOCK	
7	Nick BARMBY	
8	Gordon DURIE †	
9	Darren ANDERTON	
10	Teddy SHERINGHAM	
11	Paul ALLEN	
	Substitutes	
12	David HOWELLS †34 ❑	
14	Pat VAN DEN HAUWE ‡78	
Gk	Ian WALKER	

IPSWICH TOWN
Blue & White shirts, White shorts · Goals

1	Clive BAKER	
2	Gavin JOHNSON	
3	Neil THOMPSON	
4	Geraint WILLIAMS	
5	Phil WHELAN	
6	David LINIGHAN	
7	Frank YALLOP	47
8	Bontcho GUENTCHEV	79
9	Vlado BOZINOSKI ❑	
10	Jason DOZZELL ❑	
11	Chris KIWOMYA	
	Substitutes	
12	Eddie YOUDS	
14	Paul GODDARD	
Gk	Craig FORREST	

Date	Saturday 30 January 1993
Venue	Stamford Bridge, 3.00pm

CHELSEA (0) 0
SHEFFIELD WEDNESDAY (1) 2

Attendance	16,261
Referee	Peter FOULKES
Linesmen	R.E. Budden, P.A. Josper

CHELSEA
Blue shirts, Blue shorts   Goals

1	Dmitri KHARIN †	
2	Gareth HALL ❑	
3	Frank SINCLAIR	
4	Andy TOWNSEND	
5	Andy MYERS ‡	
6	Mal DONAGHY	
7	Graham STUART	
8	John SPENCER	
9	Mick HARFORD	
10	Eddie NEWTON	
11	Graeme LE SAUX	
	Substitutes	
12	Steve CLARKE ‡45	
14	Robert FLECK	
Gk	Gerry PEYTON †45	

SHEFFIELD WEDNESDAY
Yellow shirts, Yellow shorts   Goals

1	Chris WOODS	
2	Roland NILSSON †	
3	Nigel WORTHINGTON	
4	Carlton PALMER	
5	John HARKES ❑	89
6	Peter SHIRTLIFF	
7	Danny WILSON	
8	Chris WADDLE	
9	Paul WARHURST	3
10	Chris BART-WILLIAMS	
11	John SHERIDAN	
	Substitutes	
12	Nigel PEARSON †75	
14	Graham HYDE	
Gk	Kevin PRESSMAN	

Date	Saturday 30 January 1993
Venue	Highfield Road, 3.00pm

COVENTRY CITY (0) 0
WIMBLEDON (1) 2

Attendance	11,774
Referee	Rodger GIFFORD
Linesmen	M.J. Holohan, C. Jones

COVENTRY CITY
Sky Blue shirts, Sky Blue shorts   Goals

1	Steve OGRIZOVIC	
2	Brian BORROWS	
3	Phil BABB	
4	Peter ATHERTON	
5	David BUSST	
6	John WILLIAMS	
7	Peter BILLING †	
8	Michael GYNN	
9	Robert ROSARIO	
10	Niall QUINN	
11	Lee HURST	
	Substitutes	
12	Sean FLYNN †64	
14	Andy PEARCE	
Gk	Jonathan GOULD	

WIMBLEDON
White shirts, Black shorts   Goals

1	Hans SEGERS	
2	Roger JOSEPH	
3	Brian McALLISTER	
4	Vinnie JONES	
5	John SCALES	
6	Dean BLACKWELL	
7	Neal ARDLEY	
8	Robbie EARLE	
9	John FASHANU	
10	Dean HOLDSWORTH	4
11	Andy CLARKE ‡	55
	Substitutes	
12	Lawrie SANCHEZ	
14	Gerald DOBBS ‡85	
Gk	Neil SULLIVAN	

Date	Saturday 30 January 1993
Venue	Selhurst Park, 3.00pm

CRYSTAL PALACE (0) 1
TOTTENHAM HOTSPUR (3) 3

Attendance	20,937
Referee	David ELLERAY
Linesmen	M.K. Bullivant, R.J. Harris

CRYSTAL PALACE
Red & Blue striped shirts, Red shorts   Goals

1	Nigel MARTYN	
2	Lee SINNOTT	
3	Richard SHAW	
4	Chris COLEMAN	
5	Eric YOUNG	
6	Andy THORN ❑	
7	Simon OSBORN	
8	Geoff THOMAS ‡	
9	Chris ARMSTRONG	
10	Simon RODGER	
11	Eddie McGOLDRICK	
	Substitutes	
12	John HUMPHREY	
14	George NDAH ‡45	
Gk	Andy WOODMAN	

TOTTENHAM HOTSPUR
White shirts, Navy Blue shorts   Goals

1	Erik THORSTVEDT	
2	Dean AUSTIN	
3	Justin EDINBURGH	
4	Vinny SAMWAYS	
5	Gary MABBUTT	
6	Neil RUDDOCK	54og
7	David HOWELLS	
8	Andy GRAY ❑ ‡	26
9	Darren ANDERTON	
10	Teddy SHERINGHAM	15, 30
11	Paul ALLEN	
	Substitutes	
12	Andy TURNER	
14	Pat VAN DEN HAUWE ‡73	
Gk	Ian WALKER	

Date	Saturday 30 January 1993
Venue	Goodison Park, 3.00pm

EVERTON (0) 0
NORWICH CITY (1) 1

Attendance	20,301
Referee	Ray LEWIS
Linesmen	P.D. Harding, T. Lynch

EVERTON
Blue shirts, White shorts   Goals

1	Neville SOUTHALL	
2	Matthew JACKSON	
3	Alan HARPER	
4	Ian SNODIN †	
5	Dave WATSON	
6	Gary ABLETT ❑	
7	PREKI ‡	
8	Peter BEARDSLEY	
9	Tony COTTEE	
10	Barry HORNE	
11	Billy KENNY	
	Substitutes	
12	Paul RIDEOUT †46	
14	Stuart BARLOW ‡68	
Gk	Jason KEARTON	

NORWICH CITY
Yellow shirts, Green shorts   Goals

1	Bryan GUNN	
2	Ian CULVERHOUSE	
3	Mark BOWEN	
4	Ian BUTTERWORTH	
5	John POLSTON	
6	Gary MEGSON	
7	Jeremy GOSS ❑	
8	Lee POWER †	
9	Chris SUTTON	16
10	Ruel FOX	
11	David PHILLIPS	
	Substitutes	
12	Mark ROBINS †82	
14	Colin WOODTHORPE	
Gk	Mark WALTON	

Date	Saturday 30 January 1993
Venue	Portman Road, 3.00pm

IPSWICH TOWN (1) 2
MANCHESTER UNITED (0) 1

Attendance	22,068
Referee	John KEY
Linesmen	J.F. Moore, M. Stobbart

IPSWICH TOWN
Blue & White shirts, White shorts   Goals

1	Clive BAKER	
2	Gavin JOHNSON	
3	Neil THOMPSON	
4	Geraint WILLIAMS	
5	Phil WHELAN	
6	David LINIGHAN	
7	Frank YALLOP	47
8	Bontcho GUENTCHEV †	
9	Vlado BOZINOSKI ‡	
10	Jason DOZZELL ❑	
11	Chris KIWOMYA	20
	Substitutes	
12	John WARK †88	
14	Mick STOCKWELL ‡88	
Gk	Craig FORREST	

MANCHESTER UNITED
Red shirts, Black shorts   Goals

1	Peter SCHMEICHEL	
2	Paul PARKER	
3	Denis IRWIN	
4	Steve BRUCE	
5	Lee SHARPE †	
6	Gary PALLISTER ❑	
7	Eric CANTONA	
8	Paul INCE	
9	Brian McCLAIR	85
10	Mark HUGHES ❑	
11	Ryan GIGGS	
	Substitutes	
12	Andrei KANCHELSKIS †67	
14	Mike PHELAN	
Gk	Les SEALEY	

Date	Saturday 30 January 1993
Venue	Elland Road, 3.00pm

LEEDS UNITED (0) 3
MIDDLESBROUGH (0) 0

Attendance	30,344
Referee	John MARTIN
Linesmen	A.J. Hill, P. Newall

LEEDS UNITED
White shirts, White shorts   Goals

1	John LUKIC	
2	David WETHERALL ❑	
3	Tony DORIGO	
4	David BATTY	81
5	Chris FAIRCLOUGH	90
6	Chris WHYTE	
7	Gordon STRACHAN	
8	Carl SHUTT ‡	
9	Rod WALLACE †	
10	Gary McALLISTER	
11	Gary SPEED	
	Substitutes	
12	Frank STRANDLI †57	69
14	David ROCASTLE ‡88	
Gk	Mervyn DAY	

MIDDLESBROUGH
Red shirts, White shorts   Goals

1	Stephen PEARS	
2	Curtis FLEMING	
3	Jimmy PHILLIPS	
4	Chris MORRIS	
5	Nicky MOHAN	
6	Willie FALCONER	
7	Tommy WRIGHT †	
8	Jamie POLLOCK ❑	
9	Paul WILKINSON	
10	Andy PEAKE	
11	John HENDRIE	
	Substitutes	
12	Craig HIGNETT †72	
14	Jon GITTENS	
Gk	Ian IRONSIDE	

Date	Saturday 30 January 1993
Venue	Maine Road, 3.00pm

MANCHESTER CITY (1) 3
BLACKBURN ROVERS (2) 2

Attendance	29,122
Referee	Mike PECK
Linesmen	A. Streets, M. Warren

MANCHESTER CITY
Light Blue shirts, White shorts   Goals

1	Tony COTON	
2	Ray RANSON	
3	Terry PHELAN	14og
4	Steve McMAHON ❏	
5	Keith CURLE	74p
6	Michel VONK ❏	
7	David WHITE	78
8	Mike SHERON	33
9	Niall QUINN	
10	Fitzroy SIMPSON †	
11	Rick HOLDEN	
	Substitutes	
12	Kare INGEBRIGTSEN †45	
14	Peter REID	
Gk	Martyn MARGETSON	

BLACKBURN ROVERS
Red & Black shirts, Black shorts   Goals

1	Bobby MIMMS	
2	Nick MARKER	
3	Tony DOBSON	
4	Tim SHERWOOD	
5	Colin HENDRY	
6	Kevin MORAN ‡	
7	Patrik ANDERSSON	
8	Mark ATKINS	
9	Roy WEGERLE ❏	
10	Mike NEWELL	4
11	Jason WILCOX	
	Substitutes	
12	Gordon COWANS	
14	Simon IRELAND ‡81	
Gk	Darren COLLIER	

Date	Saturday 30 January 1993
Venue	City Ground, 3.00pm

NOTTINGHAM FOREST (1) 2
OLDHAM ATLETIC (0) 0

Attendance	21,240
Referee	Philip DON
Linesmen	D.T. Colwell, E.B. Crompton

NOTTINGHAM FOREST
Red shirts, White shorts   Goals

1	Mark CROSSLEY	
2	Brian LAWS	
3	Brett WILLIAMS	
4	Steve CHETTLE	
5	Carl TILER ❏	
6	Roy KEANE ❏	
7	Gary BANNISTER ❏	
8	Scot GEMMILL	
9	Nigel CLOUGH	
10	Neil WEBB	
11	Ian WOAN	14, 59
	Substitutes	
12	Gary CROSBY	
14	Thorvaldur ORLYGSSON	
Gk	Andy MARRIOTT	

OLDHAM ATHLETIC
Blue shirts, Blue shorts   Goals

1	Paul GERRARD	
2	Gunnar HALLE	
3	Neil POINTON †	
4	Craig FLEMING	
5	Richard JOBSON	
6	Ian MARSHALL	
7	Roger PALMER	
8	Ian OLNEY	
9	Mark BRENNAN ❏	
10	Mike MILLIGAN	
11	Neil ADAMS	
	Substitutes	
12	Andy RITCHIE †45	
14	Neil TOLSON	
Gk	Ian GRAY	

Date	Saturday 30 January 1993
Venue	Bramall Lane, 3.00pm

SHEFFIELD UNITED (0) 1
QPR (1) 2

Attendance	16,366
Referee	Vic CALLOW
Linesmen	A. Black, T. Heilbron

SHEFFIELD UNITED
Red & White shirts, White shorts   Goals

1	Alan KELLY	
2	Kevin GAGE †	
3	David BARNES	
4	Jamie HOYLAND	88
5	Brian GAYLE	
6	Paul BEESLEY	
7	Carl BRADSHAW	
8	Chris KAMARA	
9	Adrian LITTLEJOHN	
10	Brian DEANE	
11	Glyn HODGES	
	Substitutes	
12	Mitch WARD †70	
14	Alan CORK	
Gk	Phil KITE	

QPR
Blue & White hooped shirts, Blue shorts   Goals

1	Tony ROBERTS	
2	David BARDSLEY	
3	Rufus BREVETT	
4	Simon BARKER	
5	Danny MADDIX	
6	Alan McDONALD	
7	Clive WILSON †	
8	Ian HOLLOWAY	75
9	Les FERDINAND	
10	Bradley ALLEN	19
11	Andy IMPEY	
	Substitutes	
12	Darren PEACOCK †64	
14	Devon WHITE	
Gk	Jan STEJSKAL	

Date	Saturday 30 January 1993
Venue	The Dell, 3.00pm

SOUTHAMPTON (1) 2
ASTON VILLA (0) 0

Attendance	19,087
Referee	Philip WRIGHT
Linesmen	W.M. Jordan, S.G. Tomlin

SOUTHAMPTON
Red & White striped shirts, Black shorts   Goals

1	Tim FLOWERS	
2	Jason DODD	
3	Micky ADAMS	
4	Terry HURLOCK	
5	Richard HALL	
6	Kevin MOORE	
7	Matthew LE TISSIER ❏	
8	Nicky BANGER	39
9	Iain DOWIE	63
10	Neil MADDISON	
11	Francis BENALI	
	Substitutes	
12	Jeff KENNA	
14	Lee POWELL	
Gk	Ian ANDREWS	

ASTON VILLA
Claret & Blue shirts, White shorts   Goals

1	Nigel SPINK	
2	Earl BARRETT	
3	Steve STAUNTON	
4	Shaun TEALE	
5	Paul McGRATH	
6	Kevin RICHARDSON ❏	
7	Matthias BREITKREUTZ †	
8	Garry PARKER	
9	Dean SAUNDERS	
10	Dwight YORKE	
11	Bryan SMALL ‡	
	Substitutes	
12	Neil COX †68	
14	Stefan BEINLICH ‡69	
Gk	Michael OAKES	

Date   Sunday 31 January 1993
Venue   Highbury Stadium, 3.00pm

ARSENAL (0) 0
LIVERPOOL (0) 1

Attendance   27,580
Referee   Keith COOPER
Linesmen   A.P. D'URSO, D. Orr

ARSENAL
Red & White shirts, White shorts   Goals

1	David SEAMAN
2	Lee DIXON
3	Nigel WINTERBURN ▢ ■
4	David HILLIER †
5	Andy LINIGHAN
6	Tony ADAMS
7	Jimmy CARTER
8	Kevin CAMPBELL
9	Alan SMITH
10	Paul MERSON
11	Ray PARLOUR

Substitutes

12	David O'LEARY †13 ‡
14	Neil HEANEY ‡83
Gk	Alan MILLER

LIVERPOOL
Green shirts, Green shorts   Goals

1	David JAMES	
2	Mike MARSH †	
3	Rob JONES	
4	Steve NICOL	
5	Mark WRIGHT	
6	Stig Inge BJORNEBYE	
7	Steve McMANAMAN	
8	Jamie REDKNAPP	
9	Ian RUSH	
10	John BARNES	59p
11	Paul STEWART ▢	

Substitutes

12	Don HUTCHISON †47
14	Mark WALTERS
Gk	Mike HOOPER

LEAGUE TABLE

Up to and including 31.01.93		P	W	D	L	F	A	Pts
1	Norwich City	26	14	6	6	40	38	48
2	Manchester United	26	13	8	5	40	21	47
3	Aston Villa	26	13	8	5	42	29	47
4	Ipswich Town	26	10	12	4	36	29	42
5	Blackburn Rovers	26	11	8	7	39	28	41
6	Manchester City	26	11	6	9	38	29	39
7	Queen's Park Rangers	25	11	6	8	35	30	39
8	Coventry City	27	10	9	8	42	38	39
9	Sheffield Wednesday	25	9	9	7	32	29	36
10	Chelsea	26	9	9	8	31	32	36
11	Arsenal	25	10	5	10	25	24	35
12	Liverpool	24	9	5	10	37	37	32
13	Everton	26	9	5	12	28	32	32
14	Tottenham Hotspur	26	8	8	10	26	36	32
15	Leeds United	25	8	7	10	38	40	31
16	Southampton	26	7	9	10	27	30	30
17	Middlesbrough	26	7	9	10	36	43	30
18	Wimbledon	26	6	9	11	31	36	27
19	Crystal Palace	26	6	9	11	32	43	27
20	Sheffield United	25	6	7	12	24	34	25
21	Nottingham Forest	25	6	6	13	26	35	24
22	Oldham Athletic	25	6	6	13	35	47	24

LEADING SCORERS

Alan SHEARER	Blackburn Rovers	16
Mick QUINN	Coventry City	13
David WHITE	Manchester City	13

LEAGUE GOALSCORING FIGURES

Running Totals

Date	Games	Goals	Average	Games	Goals	Average
09.01.93	10	26	2.60	249	650	2.61
10.01.93	1	1	1.00	250	651	2.60
16.01.93	9	17	1.89	259	668	2.58
17.01.93	1	6	6.00	260	674	2.59
18.01.93	1	4	4.00	261	678	2.60
23.01.93	1	3	3.00	262	681	2.60
26.01.93	4	15	3.75	266	696	2.62
27.01.93	5	16	3.20	271	712	2.63
30.01.93	10	27	2.70	281	739	2.63
31.01.93	1	1	1.00	282	740	2.62

Date	Tuesday 2 February 1993
Venue	Ewood Park, 7.30pm

BLACKBURN ROVERS (1) 1
CRYSTAL PALACE (1) 2

Attendance	14,163
Referee	Philip WRIGHT
Linesmen	U.D. Rennie, B. Lowe

BLACKBURN ROVERS
Blue & White shirts, White shorts   Goals

1	Bobby MIMMS	
2	Mark ATKINS	
3	Alan WRIGHT	
4	Tim SHERWOOD	
5	Colin HENDRY ❏	
6	Nicky MARKER †	
7	Stuart RIPLEY	
8	Gordon COWANS ‡	
9	Roy WEGERLE	16
10	Mike NEWELL	
11	Jason WILCOX	
	Substitutes	
12	Patrik ANDERSSON †80	
14	Henning BERG ‡70	
Gk	Darren COLLIER	

CRYSTAL PALACE
Yellow shirts, Light Blue shorts   Goals

1	Nigel MARTYN	
2	Lee SINNOTT	
3	Richard SHAW	
4	Chris COLEMAN ❏	
5	Eric YOUNG	
6	Andy THORN	
7	Simon OSBORN	
8	Bobby BOWRY	
9	Chris ARMSTRONG	9
10	Simon RODGER	59
11	Eddie McGOLDRICK	
	Substitutes	
12	John HUMPHREY	
14	George NDAH	
Gk	Andy WOODMAN	

Date	Saturday 6 February 1993
Venue	Villa Park, 3.00pm

ASTON VILLA (2) 2
IPSWICH TOWN (0) 0

Attendance	25,395
Referee	Paul DURKIN
Linesmen	R.J. Harris, I.A. Madge

ASTON VILLA
Claret & Blue shirts, White shorts   Goals

1	Mark BOSNICH	
2	Earl BARRETT	
3	Steve STAUNTON	
4	Shaun TEALE	
5	Paul McGRATH	
6	Kevin RICHARDSON	
7	Ray HOUGHTON	
8	Garry PARKER	
9	Dean SAUNDERS	42
10	Dwight YORKE ‡	32
11	Stephen FROGGATT †	
	Substitutes	
12	Neil COX †80	
14	Stefan BEINLICH ‡85	
Gk	Michael OAKES	

IPSWICH TOWN
Blue & White shirts, Blue shorts   Goals

1	Clive BAKER	
2	Phil WHELAN	
3	Neil THOMPSON	
4	Mick STOCKWELL ❏	
5	John WARK	
6	David LINIGHAN †	
7	Geraint WILLIAMS ❏	
8	Bontcho GUENTCHEV	
9	Steve WHITTON	
10	Jason DOZZELL	
11	Chris KIWOMYA	
	Substitutes	
12	Gavin JOHNSON †45	
14	Frank YALLOP	
Gk	Craig FORREST	

Date	Saturday 6 February 1993
Venue	Anfield, 3.00pm

LIVERPOOL (0) 0
NOTTINGHAM FOREST (0) 0

Attendance	40,463
Referee	Keren BARRATT
Linesmen	W.J. Nattrass, T. Heilbron

LIVERPOOL
Red shirts, Red shorts   Goals

1	David JAMES	
2	Mike MARSH †	
3	Rob JONES	
4	Steve NICOL	
5	Mark WRIGHT	
6	Stig Inge BJORNEBYE	
7	Steve McMANAMAN	
8	Jamie REDKNAPP	
9	Ian RUSH	
10	John BARNES	
11	Paul STEWART	
	Substitutes	
12	Mark WALTERS †81	
14	Don HUTCHISON	
Gk	Mike HOOPER	

NOTTINGHAM FOREST
White shirts, Black shorts   Goals

1	Mark CROSSLEY	
2	Brian LAWS	
3	Brett WILLIAMS	
4	Steve CHETTLE	
5	Carl TILER	
6	Roy KEANE ❏	
7	Gary BANNISTER	
8	Scot GEMMILL	
9	Nigel CLOUGH	
10	Thorvaldur ORLYGSSON	
11	Ian WOAN	
	Substitutes	
12	Gary CROSBY	
14	Gary CHARLES	
Gk	Andy MARRIOTT	

Date	Saturday 6 February 1993
Venue	Old Trafford, 3.00pm

MANCHESTER UNITED (0) 2
SHEFFIELD UNITED (1) 1

Attendance	36,156
Referee	Martin BODENHAM
Linesmen	M.A. Riley, M. Fletcher

MANCHESTER UNITED
Red shirts, White shorts   Goals

1	Peter SCHMEICHEL	
2	Paul PARKER	
3	Denis IRWIN	
4	Steve BRUCE	
5	Lee SHARPE	
6	Gary PALLISTER	
7	Eric CANTONA	80
8	Paul INCE	
9	Brian McCLAIR	64
10	Mark HUGHES	
11	Ryan GIGGS †	
	Substitutes	
12	Andrei KANCHELSKIS †70	
14	Mike PHELAN	
Gk	Les SEALEY	

SHEFFIELD UNITED
Yellow shirts, Black shorts   Goals

1	Alan KELLY	
2	Mitch WARD	
3	Tom COWAN	
4	Jamie HOYLAND	
5	Brian GAYLE	
6	Paul BEESLEY	
7	Franz CARR	7
8	Chris KAMARA ‡	
9	Ian BRYSON †	
10	Brian DEANE	
11	Charlie HARTFIELD ❏	
	Substitutes	
12	Alan CORK †75	
14	Carl BRADSHAW ‡67 ❏	
Gk	Phil KITE	

Date	Saturday 6 February 1993	
Venue	Ayresome Park, 3.00pm	

MIDDLESBROUGH (0) 0
COVENTRY CITY (0) 2

Attendance	14,008	
Referee	Jim BORRETT	
Linesmen	J. Leech, J. McGrath	

MIDDLESBROUGH
Red shirts, White shorts   Goals

1	Stephen PEARS	
2	Chris MORRIS ‡	
3	Jimmy PHILLIPS	
4	Nicky MOHAN ❏	
5	Jon GITTENS ❏	
6	Willie FALCONER	
7	Bernie SLAVEN	
8	Craig HIGNETT	
9	Paul WILKINSON	
10	Andy PEAKE	
11	John HENDRIE †	
	Substitutes	
12	Tommy WRIGHT †7	
14	Jamie POLLOCK ‡74	
Gk	Ian IRONSIDE	

COVENTRY CITY
Sky Blue shirts, Sky Blue shorts   Goals

1	Steve OGRIZOVIC	
2	Brian BORROWS	
3	Phil BABB	
4	Peter ATHERTON	
5	Andy PEARCE ❏	
6	John WILLIAMS	
7	Peter NDLOVU	67
8	Michael GYNN	
9	Robert ROSARIO	
10	Mick QUINN ❏	79
11	Lee HURST	
	Substitutes	
12	David BUSST	
14	Sean FLYNN	
Gk	Jonathan GOULD	

Date	Saturday 6 February 1993	
Venue	Boundary Park, 3.00pm	

OLDHAM ATHLETIC (1) 3
CHELSEA (0) 1

Attendance	11,762	
Referee	Roger MILFORD	
Linesmen	T.A. Atkinson, A.J. Hill	

OLDHAM ATHLETIC
Blue shirts, Blue shorts   Goals

1	Paul GERRARD	
2	Craig FLEMING	
3	Gunnar HALLE	
4	Nick HENRY	38
5	Steve REDMOND	
6	Ian MARSHALL	
7	Neil ADAMS	61
8	Ian OLNEY	
9	Andy RITCHIE	
10	Mike MILLIGAN	
11	Mark BRENNAN	71
	Substitutes	
12	Roger PALMER	
14	Neil TOLSON	
Gk	Ian GRAY	

CHELSEA
White shirts, Red shorts   Goals

1	Kevin HITCHCOCK	
2	Gareth HALL	
3	Frank SINCLAIR	
4	Andy TOWNSEND	
5	David LEE	
6	Mal DONAGHY	
7	Graham STUART †	
8	John SPENCER	
9	Mick HARFORD	89
10	Eddie NEWTON	
11	Graeme LE SAUX ❏ ‡	
	Substitutes	
12	Robert FLECK †63	
14	Paul BERNARD ‡63	
Gk	Gerry PEYTON	

Date	Saturday 6 February 1993
Venue	Loftus Road, 3.00pm

QPR (0) 1
MANCHESTER CITY (0) 1

Attendance	13,003
Referee	Mike REED
Linesmen	D. Orr, M.G. Wright

QPR
Blue & White hooped shirts, White shorts   Goals

1	Tony ROBERTS	
2	David BARDSLEY	
3	Rufus BREVETT	
4	Simon BARKER	
5	Danny MADDIX	
6	Alan McDONALD	
7	Clive WILSON	66p
8	Andy IMPEY	
9	Les FERDINAND	
10	Bradley ALLEN	
11	Andy SINTON	
	Substitutes	
12	Darren PEACOCK	
14	Devon WHITE	
Gk	Jan STEJSKAL	

MANCHESTER CITY
Purple shirts, Purple shorts   Goals

1	Andy DIBBLE	
2	Ray RANSON ❑	
3	Terry PHELAN	
4	Steve McMAHON †	
5	Keith CURLE	
6	Michel VONK	
7	David WHITE	
8	Mike SHERON	77
9	Niall QUINN ‡	
10	Fitzroy SIMPSON ❑	
11	Rick HOLDEN	
	Substitutes	
12	Peter REID †69	
14	Kare INGEBRIGTSEN ‡29	
Gk	Tony COTON	

Date	Saturday 6 February 1993
Venue	Hillsborough, 3.00pm

SHEFFIELD WEDNESDAY (2) 3
EVERTON (0) 1

Attendance	24,979
Referee	Kelvin MORTON
Linesmen	P.J. Robinson, R. Pearson

SHEFFIELD WEDNESDAY
Blue & White striped shirts, Black shorts   Goals

1	Chris WOODS	
2	Roland NILSSON	
3	Nigel WORTHINGTON	
4	Carlton PALMER	
5	John HARKES	17
6	Peter SHIRTLIFF	
7	Danny WILSON ‡	
8	Chris WADDLE	62
9	Paul WARHURST	16
10	Nigel JEMSON †	
11	John SHERIDAN	
	Substitutes	
12	Graham HYDE †31	
14	Nigel PEARSON ‡66	
Gk	Kevin PRESSMAN	

EVERTON
Salmon Pink & Blue striped shirts, Salmon Pink shorts   Goals

1	Neville SOUTHALL ■	
2	Matthew JACKSON	
3	Kenny SANSOM	
4	Ian SNODIN ❑	
5	Dave WATSON ❑	
6	Gary ABLETT ❑	
7	Robert WARZYCHA †	
8	Peter BEARDSLEY	
9	Tony COTTEE	83
10	Billy KENNY	
11	PREKI ‡	
	Substitutes	
12	Stuart BARLOW †45	
14	Alan HARPER	
Gk	Jason KEARTON ‡43	

Date	Saturday 6 February 1993
Venue	Selhurst Park, 3.00pm

WIMBLEDON (0) 1
LEEDS UNITED (0) 0

Attendance	6,704
Referee	Vic CALLOW
Linesmen	G.P. Barber, B.A. Wiggington

WIMBLEDON
Blue shirts, Blue shorts — Goals

1	Hans SEGERS	
2	Roger JOSEPH	
3	Brian McALLISTER	
4	Lawrie SANCHEZ ❏	
5	John SCALES	
6	Gary ELKINS	
7	Neal ARDLEY	
8	Robbie EARLE ‡	
9	John FASHANU	
10	Dean HOLDSWORTH	61
11	Gerald DOBBS †	
	Substitutes	
12	Andy CLARKE †80	
14	Steve TALBOYS ‡80	
Gk	Neil SULLIVAN	

LEEDS UNITED
White shirts, White shorts — Goals

1	John LUKIC	
2	Scott SELLARS	
3	Tony DORIGO	
4	David BATTY	
5	Jon NEWSOME	
6	Chris WHYTE	
7	David ROCASTLE ‡	
8	Frank STRANDLI †	
9	Lee CHAPMAN	
10	Gary McALLISTER	
11	Gary SPEED	
	Substitutes	
12	Carl SHUTT †45	
14	Rob BOWMAN ‡78	
Gk	Mervyn DAY	

Date	Sunday 7 February 1993
Venue	White Hart Lane, 1.00pm

TOTTENHAM HOTSPUR (0) 4
SOUTHAMPTON (1) 2

Attendance	20,098
Referee	Ken REDFERN
Linesmen	D.C. Madgwick, S.G. Tomlin

TOTTENHAM HOTSPUR
White shirts, Navy Blue shorts — Goals

1	Erik THORSTVEDT	
2	Dean AUSTIN	
3	Justin EDINBURGH	
4	Vinny SAMWAYS	
5	Gary MABBUTT	
6	Neil RUDDOCK	
7	David HOWELLS †	
8	Nick BARMBY ‡	56
9	Darren ANDERTON	57
10	Teddy SHERINGHAM	54, 59
11	Paul ALLEN	
	Substitutes	
12	Andy GRAY †18	
14	Pat VAN DEN HAUWE ‡63	
Gk	Ian WALKER	

SOUTHAMPTON
Blue shirts, White shorts — Goals

1	Tim FLOWERS	
2	Jason DODD	
3	Micky ADAMS	
4	Terry HURLOCK ❏	
5	Richard HALL	66
6	Kenneth MONKOU	
7	Matthew LE TISSIER	
8	Nicky BANGER	
9	Iain DOWIE	21
10	Neil MADDISON	
11	Francis BENALI ■	
	Substitutes	
12	Jeff KENNA	
14	Kerry DIXON	
Gk	Ian ANDREWS	

Date	Monday 8 February 1993
Venue	Elland Road, 7.45pm

LEEDS UNITED (0) 0
MANCHESTER UNITED (0) 0

Attendance	34,166
Referee	Kelvin MORTON
Linesmen	J. McGrath, J.B. Robinson

LEEDS UNITED
White shirts, White shorts   Goals

1	John LUKIC	
2	Scott SELLARS ‡	
3	Tony DORIGO	
4	David BATTY	
5	Jon NEWSOME	
6	Chris WHYTE	
7	Rob BOWMAN	
8	Carl SHUTT †	
9	Lee CHAPMAN	
10	Gary McALLISTER	
11	Gary SPEED	
	Substitutes	
12	Frank SRANDLI †77	
14	Steve HODGE ‡85	
Gk	Mervyn DAY	

MANCHESTER UNITED
Red shirts, Black shorts   Goals

1	Peter SCHMEICHEL	
2	Paul PARKER	
3	Denis IRWIN	
4	Steve BRUCE	
5	Lee SHARPE	
6	Gary PALLISTER ❏	
7	Eric CANTONA ❏	
8	Paul INCE	
9	Brian McCLAIR	
10	Mark HUGHES	
11	Ryan GIGGS †	
	Substitutes	
12	Andrei KANCHELSKIS †72	
14	Mike PHELAN	
Gk	Les SEALEY	

Date	Tuesday 9 February 1993
Venue	Portman Road, 7.45pm

IPSWICH TOWN (1) 1
QPR (0) 1

Attendance	17,354
Referee	Roger MILFORD
Linesmen	W.J. Norbury, D.C. Madgwick

IPSWICH TOWN
Blue & White shirts, White shorts   Goals

1	Clive BAKER	
2	Gavin JOHNSON	
3	Neil THOMPSON	40
4	Mick STOCKWELL	
5	John WARK	
6	David LINIGHAN	
7	Geraint WILLIAMS	
8	Bontcho GUENTCHEV	
9	Steve WHITTON ❏	
10	Jason DOZZELL	
11	Chris KIWOMYA ‡	
	Substitutes	
12	Phil WHELAN	
14	Vlado BOZINOSKI ‡45	
Gk	Craig FORREST	

QPR
Red & Black hooped shirts, Red shorts   Goals

1	Tony ROBERTS	
2	David BARDSLEY	
3	Rufus BREVETT	
4	Maurice DOYLE ‡	
5	Danny MADDIX	
6	Alan McDONALD	
7	Clive WILSON	
8	Andy IMPEY †	
9	Les FERDINAND	
10	Bradley ALLEN	
11	Andy SINTON	
	Substitutes	
12	Darren PEACOCK †86	
14	Devon WHITE ‡56	80
Gk	Jan STEJSKAL	

Date	Tuesday 9 February 1993
Venue	Bramall Lane, 7.45pm

SHEFFIELD UNITED (1) 2
MIDDLESBROUGH (0) 0

Attendance	15,184
Referee	Tony WARD
Linesmen	D.E. Binsley, G.I. Grandidge

SHEFFIELD UNITED
Red & White striped shirts, White shorts   Goals

1	Alan KELLY	
2	Mitch WARD	
3	Tom COWAN	
4	Jamie HOYLAND	
5	Brian GAYLE	
6	Paul BEESLEY	
7	Franz CARR ‡	38
8	Charlie HARTFIELD	
9	Adrian LITTLEJOHN †	
10	Brian DEANE ❏	60
11	Glyn HODGES	
	Substitutes	
12	Alan CORK †75	
14	Carl BRADSHAW ‡83	
Gk	Phil KITE	

MIDDLESBROUGH
White shirts, Black shorts   Goals

1	Stephen PEARS †	
2	Curtis FLEMING	
3	Gary PARKINSON	
4	Derek WHYTE	.
5	Nicky MOHAN	
6	Jon GITTENS	
7	Bernie SLAVEN	
8	Jamie POLLOCK ❏	
9	Tommy WRIGHT	
10	Andy PEAKE ‡	
11	Craig HIGNETT	
	Substitutes	
12	Mark PROCTOR ‡16	
14	Graham KAVANAGH	
Gk	Ian IRONSIDE †45	

Date	Wednesday 10 February 1993
Venue	Highbury Stadium, 7.45pm

ARSENAL (0) 0
WIMBLEDON (1) 1

Attendance	18,253
Referee	Philip DON
Linesmen	P.A. Josper, M.D. Dearing

ARSENAL
Red & White shirts, White shorts   Goals

1	David SEAMAN	
2	Martin KEOWN	
3	Nigel WINTERBURN	
4	David HILLIER	
5	Andy LINIGHAN	
6	Tony ADAMS	
7	Ian SELLEY ❏	
8	Ian WRIGHT	
9	Alan SMITH †	
10	Paul MERSON ‡	
11	Kevin CAMPBELL	
	Substitutes	
12	Steve MORROW †84	
14	Jimmy CARTER ‡69	
Gk	Alan MILLER	

WIMBLEDON
Blue shirts, Blue shorts   Goals

1	Hans SEGERS	
2	Roger JOSEPH	
3	Gary ELKINS	
4	Steve TALBOYS ‡	
5	John SCALES	
6	Scott FITZGERALD	
7	Neal ARDLEY	
8	Robbie EARLE	
9	John FASHANU	
10	Dean HOLDSWORTH	19
11	Gerald DOBBS ❏	
	Substitutes	
12	Andy CLARKE	
14	Peter FEAR ‡38	
Gk	Neil SULIVAN	

Date	Wednesday 10 February 1993
Venue	Stamford Bridge, 7.30pm

CHELSEA (0) 0
LIVERPOOL (0) 0

Attendance	20,981
Referee	John MARTIN
Linesmen	A.P. D'Urso, S.G. Tomlin

CHELSEA
Blue shirts, Blue shorts   Goals

1	Kevin HITCHCOCK	
2	Gareth HALL ❑	
3	Frank SINCLAIR	
4	Andy TOWNSEND	
5	David LEE	
6	Mal DONAGHY	
7	David HOPKIN †	
8	Robert FLECK ‡	
9	Mick HARFORD	
10	Eddie NEWTON	
11	Paul BERNARD	
	Substitutes	
12	Graham STUART †66	
14	John SPENCER ‡85	
Gk	Dave BEASANT	

LIVERPOOL
Red shirts, Red shorts   Goals

1	David JAMES	
2	Mike MARSH ❑	
3	Rob JONES	
4	Steve NICOL	
5	Mark WRIGHT	
6	Stig Inge BJORNEBYE	
7	Steve McMANAMAN	
8	Ronnie ROSENTHAL †	
9	Ian RUSH	
10	John BARNES	
11	Paul STEWART	
	Substitutes	
12	Don HUTCHISON †45	
14	Mark WALTERS	
Gk	Mike HOOPER	

Date	Wednesday 10 February 1993
Venue	Selhurst Park, 8.00pm

CRYSTAL PALACE (1) 1
ASTON VILLA (0) 0

Attendance	12,270
Referee	Ken REDFERN
Linesmen	A. Schneider, G. Butland

CRYSTAL PALACE
Red & Blue striped shirts, Red shorts   Goals

1	Nigel MARTYN	
2	Bobby BOWRY	9
3	Richard SHAW †	
4	Chris COLEMAN ‡	
5	Eric YOUNG	
6	Andy THORN	
7	Simon OSBORN	
8	Geoff THOMAS	
9	Chris ARMSTRONG	
10	Simon RODGER	
11	Eddie McGOLDRICK	
	Substitutes	
12	John HUMPHREY †71	
14	Paul WILLIAMS ‡83	
Gk	Andy WOODMAN	

ASTON VILLA
White shirts, Blue shorts   Goals

1	Mark BOSNICH	
2	Earl BARRETT	
3	Steve STAUNTON	
4	Shaun TEALE	
5	Paul McGRATH	
6	Kevin RICHARDSON	
7	Ray HOUGHTON	
8	Garry PARKER ‡	
9	Dean SAUNDERS	
10	Dwight YORKE	
11	Stephen FROGGATT	
	Substitutes	
12	Neil COX	
14	Stefan BEINLICH ‡79	
Gk	Nigel SPINK	

Date Wednesday 10 February 1993
Venue Goodison Park, 7.30pm

EVERTON (1) 1
TOTTENHAM HOTSPUR (1) 2

Attendance 16,164
Referee Keren BARRATT
Linesmen T.A. Atkinson, M.A. Riley

EVERTON
Blue shirts, White shorts   Goals

1	Neville SOUTHALL	
2	Alan HARPER ‡	
3	Kenny SANSOM	29
4	Matthew JACKSON	
5	Dave WATSON	
6	Gary ABLETT	
7	Billy KENNY †	
8	Peter BEARDSLEY	
9	Tony COTTEE	
10	Paul RIDEOUT	
11	Barry HORNE	
	Substitutes	
12	PREKI †30	
14	Mo JOHNSTON ‡62	
Gk	Jason KEARTON	

TOTTENHAM HOTSPUR
White shirts, Navy Blue shorts   Goals

1	Erik THORSTVEDT	
2	Dean AUSTIN ‡	
3	Justin EDINBURGH	
4	Vinny SAMWAYS	
5	Gary MABBUTT	26
6	Neil RUDDOCK ❏	
7	David HOWELLS	
8	Andy GRAY †	
9	Darren ANDERTON	
10	Teddy SHERINGHAM	
11	Paul ALLEN	69
	Substitutes	
12	NAYIM †67	
14	Pat VAN DEN HAUWE ‡51	
Gk	Ian WALKER	

Date Wednesday 10 February 1993
Venue The Dell, 7.30pm

SOUTHAMPTON (2) 3
NORWICH CITY (0) 0

Attendance 12,969
Referee Joe WORRALL
Linesmen I.M.D. Mitchell, G.T. Pearson

SOUTHAMPTON
Red & White striped shirts, Black shorts   Goals

1	Tim FLOWERS	
2	Jeff KENNA	
3	Micky ADAMS	25
4	Tommy WIDDRINGTON	
5	Richard HALL	9
6	Kenneth MONKOU	
7	Matthew LE TISSIER †	
8	Jason DODD	
9	Iain DOWIE	
10	Neil MADDISON	
11	Francis BENALI	
	Substitutes	
12	Nicky BANGER †69	79
14	Lee POWELL	
Gk	Ian ANDREWS	

NORWICH CITY
Yellow shirts, Green shorts   Goals

1	Bryan GUNN	
2	Ian CULVERHOUSE	
3	Mark BOWEN	
4	Ian BUTTERWORTH	
5	John POLSTON	
6	Gary MEGSON	
7	Jeremy GOSS	
8	Lee POWER	
9	Mark ROBINS †	
10	Ruel FOX	
11	David PHILLIPS	
	Substitutes	
12	Daryl SUTCH †76	
14	Andrew JOHNSON	
Gk	Mark WALTON	

Date	Saturday 13 February 1993
Venue	Stamford Bridge, 3.00pm

CHELSEA (0) 0
ASTON VILLA (1) 1

Attendance	20,081
Referee	Mike PECK
Linesmen	M. Stobbart, M. Bullivant

CHELSEA
Blue shirts, Blue shorts   Goals

1	Kevin HITCHCOCK	
2	Gareth HALL	
3	Frank SINCLAIR	
4	Andy TOWNSEND ❏	
5	David LEE	
6	Mal DONAGHY ‡	
7	David HOPKIN †	
8	Robert FLECK	
9	Mick HARFORD	
10	Eddie NEWTON	
11	Dennis WISE	
	Substitutes	
12	Graham STUART †58	
14	John SPENCER ‡76	
Gk	Dave BEASANT	

ASTON VILLA
White shirts, Black shorts   Goals

1	Mark BOSNICH	
2	Earl BARRETT	
3	Steve STAUNTON	
4	Shaun TEALE	
5	Paul McGRATH	
6	Kevin RICHARDSON	
7	Ray HOUGHTON	22
8	Garry PARKER †	
9	Dean SAUNDERS ❏	
10	Dalian ATKINSON ‡	
11	Stephen FROGGATT	
	Substitutes	
12	Neil COX †83	
14	Dwight YORKE ‡61	
Gk	Nigel SPINK	

Date	Saturday 13 February 1993
Venue	Elland Road, 3.00pm

LEEDS UNITED (1) 2
OLDHAM ATHLETIC (0) 0

Attendance	27,654
Referee	Roger DILKES
Linesmen	R.H. Andrews, B. Lowe

LEEDS UNITED
White shirts, White shorts   Goals

1	John LUKIC	
2	Scott SELLARS †	
3	Tony DORIGO	
4	David BATTY	
5	Jon NEWSOME	
6	Chris WHYTE	
7	Rob BOWMAN	
8	Rod WALLACE	
9	Lee CHAPMAN	79
10	Gary McALLISTER	18p
11	Gary SPEED	
	Substitutes	
12	Carl SHUTT †76 ‡	
14	Steve HODGE ‡80	
Gk	Mervyn DAY	

OLDHAM ATHLETIC
Blue shirts, Blue shorts   Goals

1	Paul GERRARD	
2	Craig FLEMING	
3	Gunnar HALLE	
4	Nick HENRY †	
5	Steve REDMOND	
6	Ian MARSHALL	
7	Paul BERNARD	
8	Ian OLNEY	
9	Andy RITCHIE ‡	
10	Mike MILLIGAN	
11	Mark BRENNAN	
	Substitutes	
12	Roger PALMER †56	
14	Neil TOLSON ‡70	
Gk	Ian GRAY	

Date	Saturday 13 February 1993
Venue	The Dell, 5.00pm

SOUTHAMPTON (1) 2
LIVERPOOL (0) 1

Attendance	17,216
Referee	Alf BUKSH
Linesmen	G.Butland, B.A. Wigginton

SOUTHAMPTON
Red & White striped shirts, Black shorts   Goals

1	Tim FLOWERS	
2	Jeff KENNA †	
3	Micky ADAMS ❏	
4	Tommy WIDDRINGTON	
5	Richard HALL	
6	Kenneth MONKOU ❏	
7	Matthew LE TISSIER	
8	Jason DODD	
9	Iain DOWIE	
10	Neil MADDISON	23
11	Francis BENALI	
	Substitutes	
12	Nicky BANGER †67	73
14	Kevin MOORE	
Gk	Ian ANDREWS	

LIVERPOOL
Green shirts, Green shorts   Goals

1	David JAMES	
2	Mike MARSH †	
3	Rob JONES	
4	Steve NICOL	
5	Mark WRIGHT	
6	Stig Inge BJORNEBYE	
7	Steve McMANAMAN	
8	Don HUTCHISON	61
9	Ian RUSH	
10	David BARNES	
11	Paul STEWART	
	Substitutes	
12	Jamie REDKNAPP †45	
14	Mark WALTERS	
Gk	Mike HOOPER	

Date	Saturday 20 February 1993
Venue	Villa Park, 3.00pm

ASTON VILLA (2) 2
EVERTON (1) 1

Attendance	33,913
Referee	Tony WARD
Linesmen	B.L. Polkey, E.J. Walsh

ASTON VILLA
Claret & Blue shirts, White shorts   Goals

1	Mark BOSNICH	
2	Earl BARRETT	18
3	Steve STAUNTON	
4	Shaun TEALE ❏	
5	Paul McGRATH	
6	Kevin RICHARDSON	
7	Ray HOUGHTON	
8	Neil COX ❏	12
9	Dean SAUNDERS ❏	
10	Dwight YORKE	
11	Stefan BEINLICH	
	Substitutes	
12	Cyrille REGIS	
14	Bryan SMALL	
Gk	Nigel SPINK	

EVERTON
White shirts, Blue shorts   Goals

1	Jason KEARTON	
2	Matthew JACKSON	
3	Kenny SANSOM	
4	Ian SNODIN ❏	
5	Dave WATSON	
6	Gary ABLETT	
7	Robert WARZYCHA †	
8	Peter BEARDSLEY	24p
9	Tony COTTEE ❏	
10	Mo JOHNSTON ‡	
11	Barry HORNE	
	Substitutes	
12	Stuart BARLOW †50	
14	PREKI ‡75	
Gk	Stephen REEVES	

Date	Saturday 20 February 1993
Venue	Anfield, 3.00pm

LIVERPOOL (0) 0
IPSWICH TOWN (0) 0

Attendance	36,680
Referee	Allan GUNN
Linesmen	A. Streets, M. Warren

LIVERPOOL
Red shirts, Red shorts   Goals

1	David JAMES	
2	Jamie REDKNAPP	
3	Rob JONES	
4	Steve NICOL	
5	Mark WRIGHT	
6	Stig Inge BJORNEBYE †	
7	Steve McMANAMAN	
8	Don HUTCHISON ‡	
9	Ian RUSH	
10	John BARNES	
11	Paul STEWART	
	Substitutes	
12	Mike MARSH †44	
14	Mark WALTERS ‡82	
Gk	Mike HOOPER	

IPSWICH TOWN
Blue & White shirts, White shorts   Goals

1	Clive BAKER	
2	Gavin JOHNSON	
3	Neil THOMPSON	
4	Mick STOCKWELL	
5	John WARK	
6	David LINIGHAN	
7	Geraint WILLIAMS	
8	Bontcho GUENTCHEV	
9	Steve WHITTON	
10	Jason DOZZELL	
11	Chris KIWOMYA	
	Substitutes	
12	Phil WHELAN	
14	Paul GODDARD	
Gk	Craig FORREST	

Date	Saturday 20 February 1993
Venue	Old Trafford, 3.00pm

MANCHESTER UNITED (0) 2
SOUTHAMPTON (0) 1

Attendance	36,257
Referee	Ray LEWIS
Linesmen	T. Lynch, P. Harding

MANCHESTER UNITED
Red shirts, White shorts   Goals

1	Peter SCHMEICHEL	
2	Paul PARKER	
3	Denis IRWIN	
4	Steve BRUCE	
5	Lee SHARPE	
6	Gary PALLISTER	
7	Eric CANTONA ❏	
8	Paul INCE	
9	Brian McCLAIR	
10	Mark HUGHES ❏	
11	Ryan GIGGS	82, 83
	Substitutes	
12	Andrei KANCHELSKIS	
14	Mike PHELAN	
Gk	Les SEALEY	

SOUTHAMPTON
Blue shirts, Blue shorts   Goals

1	Tim FLOWERS	
2	Jeff KENNA	
3	Micky ADAMS	
4	Tommy WIDDRINGTON ❏	
5	Richard HALL ❏	
6	Kenneth MONKOU	
7	Matthew LE TISSIER †	
8	Jason DODD	
9	Iain DOWIE	
10	Neil MADDISON	
11	Francis BENALI	
	Substitutes	
12	Nicky BANGER †65	77
14	Kevin MOORE	
Gk	Ian ANDREWS	

Date	Saturday 20 February 1993
Venue	Ayresome Park, 3.00pm

MIDDLESBROUGH (0) 1
NOTTINGHAM FOREST (0) 2

Attendance	15,639
Referee	David ELLERAY
Linesmen	R.H. Andrews, A.N. Butler

MIDDLESBROUGH
Red shirts, White shorts   Goals

1	Stephen PEARS	
2	Gary PARKINSON †	
3	Jimmy PHILLIPS	59
4	Derek WHYTE	
5	Jon GITTENS	
6	Andy PEAKE ❏	
7	Bernie SLAVEN	
8	Craig HIGNETT ‡	
9	Paul WILKINSON	
10	Chris KAMARA	
11	Tommy WRIGHT	
	Substitutes	
12	Chris MORRIS †72	
14	Graham KAVANAGH ‡72	
Gk	Ian IRONSIDE	

NOTTINGHAM FOREST
White shirts, Black shorts   Goals

1	Mark CROSSLEY	
2	Gary CHARLES	
3	Steve CHETTLE	
4	Steve STONE	68
5	Carl TILER ❏	
6	Roy KEANE ❏	
7	Thorvaldur ORLYGSSON	
8	Scot GEMMILL	
9	Nigel CLOUGH	58
10	Gary BANNISTER	
11	Ian WOAN	
	Substitutes	
12	Gary CROSBY	
14	Craig ARMSTRONG	
Gk	Andy MARRIOTT	

Date	Saturday 20 February 1993
Venue	Carrow Road, 3.00pm

NORWICH CITY (2) 2
MANCHESTER CITY (0) 1

Attendance	16,386
Referee	Brian HILL
Linesmen	P.A. Vosper, G.P. Barber

NORWICH CITY
Yellow shorts, Green shorts   Goals

1	Bryan GUNN	
2	Ian CULVERHOUSE	
3	Mark BOWEN	
4	Ian BUTTERWORTH	
5	John POLSTON	
6	Gary MEGSON ❏	
7	Jeremy GOSS †	
8	Lee POWER ‡	29
9	Mark ROBINS	28
10	Ruel FOX	
11	David PHILLIPS	
	Substitutes	
12	Daryl SUTCH †60	
14	Andrew JOHNSON ‡89	
Gk	Mark WALTON	

MANCHESTER CITY
Light Blue shirts, White shorts   Goals

1	Tony COTON	
2	Ray RANSON ❏	
3	Terry PHELAN †	
4	Kare INGEBRIGTSEN ‡	
5	Keith CURLE	
6	Michel VONK	
7	David WHITE	
8	Mike SHERON	46
9	Niall QUINN	
10	Garry FLITCROFT	
11	Rick HOLDEN	
	Substitutes	
12	Andy HILL †44	
14	Mike QUIGLEY ‡81	
Gk	Andy DIBBLE	

Date	Saturday 20 February 1993
Venue	Boundary Park, 3.00pm

OLDHAM ATHLETIC (0) 0
ARSENAL (0) 1

Attendance	12,311
Referee	Keith HACKETT
Linesmen	R.R. Rawson, T.J. Stevens

OLDHAM ATHLETIC
Blue shirts, Blue shorts   Goals

1	Paul GERRARD	
2	Craig FLEMING	
3	Gunnar HALLE	
4	Nick HENRY	
5	Richard JOBSON	
6	Ian MARSHALL	
7	Neil ADAMS	
8	Ian OLNEY †	
9	Andy RITCHIE	
10	Mike MILLIGAN	
11	Mark BRENNAN	
	Substitutes	
12	Paul MOULDEN †45	
14	Steve REDMOND	
Gk	Ian GRAY	

ARSENAL
Red & White shirts, White shorts   Goals

1	David SEAMAN	
2	Martin KEOWN	
3	Steve MORROW	
4	David HILLIER	
5	Andy LINIGHAN	50
6	Tony ADAMS	
7	John JENSEN	
8	Ian SELLEY	
9	Kevin CAMPBELL	
10	Paul MERSON	
11	Anders LIMPAR ‡	
	Substitutes	
12	Pal LYDERSEN	
14	Jimmy CARTER ‡78	
Gk	Jim WILL	

Date	Saturday 20 February 1993
Venue	Loftus Road, 3.00pm

QPR (2) 2
COVENTRY CITY (0) 0

Attendance	12,453
Referee	Paul DURKIN
Linesmen	D.C. Richards, C. Jones

QPR
Blue & White hooped shirts, White shorts   Goals

1	Tony ROBERTS	
2	David BARDSLEY	
3	Rufus BREVETT	
4	Simon BARKER	
5	Darren PEACOCK	41
6	Karl READY	
7	Clive WILSON	
8	Andy IMPEY	
9	Les FERDINAND ❏	
10	Bradley ALLEN	
11	Andy SINTON	
	Substitutes	
12	Alan McCARTHY	
14	Maurice DOYLE	
Gk	Jan STEJSKAL	

COVENTRY CITY
Red shirts, White shorts   Goals

1	Steve OGRIZOVIC	
2	Brian BORROWS	
3	Phil BABB	
4	Peter ATHERTON	
5	Andy PEARCE	34og
6	John WILLIAMS	
7	Peter NDLOVU	
8	Michael GYNN ‡	
9	Robert ROSARIO	
10	Mick QUINN	
11	Lee HURST ❏	
	Substitutes	
12	David BUSST	
14	Stewart ROBSON ‡62	
Gk	Jonathan GOULD	

Date	Saturday 20 February 1993
Venue	Hillsborough, 3.00pm

SHEFFIELD WEDNESDAY (1) 2
CRYSTAL PALACE (0) 1

Attendance	26,459
Referee	Mike REED
Linesmen	D.S. Oliver, E. Lomas

SHEFFIELD WEDNESDAY
Blue & White striped shirts, Black shorts   Goals

1	Chris WOODS	
2	Roland NILSSON	
3	Nigel WORTHINGTON	
4	Carlton PALMER	
5	John HARKES	
6	Peter SHIRTLIFF	
7	Danny WILSON	71
8	Chris WADDLE	
9	Paul WARHURST ❑	27
10	Chris BART-WILLIAMS †	
11	John SHERIDAN	
	Substitutes	
12	Nigel JEMSON †58	
14	Viv ANDERSON	
Gk	Kevin PRESSMAN	

CRYSTAL PALACE
Yellow shirts, Light Blue shorts   Goals

1	Nigel MARTYN	
2	John HUMPHREY	
3	Richard SHAW	
4	Bobby BOWRY	
5	Eric YOUNG	
6	Andy THORN	
7	Simon OSBORN	
8	Paul WILLIAMS †	
9	Chris ARMSTRONG	62
10	Simon RODGER	
11	Eddie McGOLDRICK	
	Substitutes	
12	Chris COLEMAN †45	
14	Gareth SOUTHGATE	
Gk	Andy WOODMAN	

Date	Saturday 20 February 1993
Venue	White Hart Lane, 3.00pm

TOTTENHAM HOTSPUR (2) 4
LEEDS UNITED (0) 0

Attendance	32,040
Referee	Gerald ASHBY
Linesmen	M.E. Alexander, W.M. Jordan

TOTTENHAM HOTSPUR
White shirts, Navy Blue shorts   Goals

1	Erik THORSTVEDT	
2	Dean AUSTIN	
3	Justin EDINBURGH	
4	Vinny SAMWAYS	
5	Gary MABBUTT	
6	Neil RUDDOCK	48
7	David HOWELLS †	
8	Nick BARMBY ‡	
9	Darren ANDERTON	
10	Teddy SHERINGHAM	8, 37, 67p
11	Paul ALLEN	
	Substitutes	
12	Andy GRAY †8	
14	Pat VAN DEN HAUWE ‡72	
Gk	Ian WALKER	

LEEDS UNITED
Yellow shirts, Yellow shorts   Goals

1	John LUKIC	
2	Rob BOWMAN	
3	Tony DORIGO	
4	David BATTY	
5	Jon NEWSOME	
6	Chris WHYTE	
7	Steve HODGE	
8	Rod WALLACE †	
9	Lee CHAPMAN ‡	
10	Gary McALLISTER	
11	Gary SPEED	
	Substitutes	
12	David ROCASTLE †63 ❑	
14	Frank STRANDLI ‡85	
Gk	Mervyn DAY	

Date	Saturday 20 February 1993
Venue	Selhurst Park, 3.00pm

WIMBLEDON (2) 2
SHEFFIELD UNITED (0) 0

Attendance	3,979
Referee	Robbie HART
Linesmen	W.J. Norbury, R.E. Budden

WIMBLEDON
Blue shirts, Blue shorts — Goals

1	Hans SEGERS	
2	Roger JOSEPH	
3	Gary ELKINS	
4	Vinnie JONES	
5	John SCALES	
6	Brian McALLISTER ❑	
7	Neal ARDLEY	
8	Robbie EARLE	
9	John FASHANU	1
10	Dean HOLDSWORTH	
11	Gerald DOBBS	44
	Substitutes	
12	Steve COTTERILL	
14	Dean BLACKWELL	
Gk	Neil SULLIVAN	

SHEFFIELD UNITED
White shirts, Black shorts — Goals

1	Alan KELLY	
2	Mitch WARD	
3	Tom COWAN	
4	John GANNON	
5	Brian GAYLE	
6	Paul BEESLEY ‡	
7	Franz CARR †	
8	Paul ROGERS	
9	Jamie HOYLAND	
10	Brian DEANE	
11	Adrian LITTLEJOHN	
	Substitutes	
12	Glyn HODGES †58	
14	Alan CORK ‡58	
Gk	Phil KITE	

Date	Sunday 21 February 1993
Venue	Ewood Park, 4.00pm

BLACKBURN ROVERS (1) 2
CHELSEA (0) 0

Attendance	14,780
Referee	David ALLISON
Linesmen	J. Hilditch, P. Newall

BLACKBURN ROVERS
Blue & White shirts, White shorts — Goals

1	Bobby MIMMS	
2	David MAY	
3	Tony DOBSON	
4	Tim SHERWOOD	
5	Colin HENDRY	
6	Kevin MORAN †	
7	Stuart RIPLEY	
8	Patrik ANDERSSON	
9	Roy WEGERLE	
10	Mike NEWELL	8, 63
11	Jason WILCOX	
	Substitutes	
12	Mark ATKINS †65	
14	Steve LIVINGSTONE	
Gk	Darren COLLIER	•

CHELSEA
Blue shirts, Blue shorts — Goals

1	Kevin HITCHCOCK	
2	Gareth HALL ❑	
3	Frank SINCLAIR ■	
4	Andy TOWNSEND	
5	David LEE	
6	Anthony BARNESS	
7	Robert FLECK	
8	Tony CASCARINO	
9	Mick HARFORD	
10	Eddie NEWTON ‡	
11	Graeme LE SAUX †	
	Substitutes	
12	Mal DONAGHY †48	
14	Graham STUART ‡80	
Gk	Dave BEASANT	

Date	Monday 22 February 1993
Venue	Bramall Lane, 7.30pm

SHEFFIELD UNITED (1) 2
OLDHAM ATHLETIC (0) 0

Attendance	14,628
Referee	Gerald ASHBY
Linesmen	J. Hilditch, R. Pearson

● *Was scheduled for 29 December - postponed frozen pitch.*

SHEFFIELD UNITED
Red & White striped shirts, Black shorts   Goals

1	Alan KELLY	
2	Mitch WARD	
3	Tom COWAN	
4	Jamie HOYLAND	
5	Brian GAYLE	
6	Paul BEESLEY	
7	Carl BRADSHAW	
8	Charlie HARTFIELD †	
9	Ian BRYSON	
10	Brian DEANE ❑	
11	Adrian LITTLEJOHN	77
	Substitutes	
12	John GANNON †24	45
14	Alan CORK	
Gk	Phil KITE	

OLDHAM ATHLETIC
Blue shirts, Blue shorts   Goals

1	Paul GERRARD	
2	Craig FLEMING	
3	Neil POINTON †	
4	Nick HENRY	
5	Richard JOBSON	
6	Steve REDMOND	
7	Neil ADAMS ❑	
8	Paul MOULDEN ‡	
9	Ian MARSHALL	
10	Mike MILLIGAN	
11	Mark BRENNAN	
	Substitutes	
12	Roger PALMER †37	
14	Neil TOLSON ‡78	
Gk	Ian GRAY	

Date	Tuesday 23 February 1993
Venue	Maine Road, 7.45pm

MANCHESTER CITY (0) 1
SHEFFIELD WEDNESDAY (0) 2

Attendance	23,619
Referee	Martin BODENHAM
Linesmen	B.L. Polkey, E.J. Walsh

● *From 10 February*

MANCHESTER CITY
Light Blue shirts, White shorts   Goals

1	Tony COTON	
2	Ray RANSON	
3	Andy HILL	
4	Mike QUIGLEY	
5	Keith CURLE	
6	Michel VONK	
7	David WHITE	
8	Mike SHERON	
9	Niall QUINN ❑	84
10	Garry FLITCROFT	
11	Adie MIKE †	
	Substitutes	
12	David BRIGHTWELL †77	
14	Kare INGEBRIGTSEN	
Gk	Andy DIBBLE	

SHEFFIELD WEDNESDAY
Yellow shirts, Black shorts   Goals

1	Chris WOODS	
2	Roland NILSSON	
3	Nigel WORTHINGTON	
4	Carlton PALMER	
5	John HARKES	
6	Peter SHIRTLIFF	
7	Danny WILSON ‡	
8	Chris WADDLE	
9	Paul WARHURST	82
10	Chris BART-WILLIAMS †	
11	John SHERIDAN	
	Substitutes	
12	Mark BRIGHT †70	
14	Viv ANDERSON ‡43	72
Gk	Kevin PRESSMAN	

Date	Wednesday 24 February 1993
Venue	Highbury Stadium, 7.45pm

ARSENAL (0) 0
LEEDS UNITED (0) 0

Attendance	21,061
Referee	Ken REDFERN
Linesmen	W.J. Norbury, A.P. D'Urso

● *Game brought forward from 9 March*

ARSENAL
Red & White shirts, White shorts   Goals

1	David SEAMAN	
2	Martin KEOWN	
3	Nigel WINTERBURN	
4	David HILLIER	
5	Andy LINIGHAN	
6	Tony ADAMS	
7	Ian SELLEY	
8	Ian WRIGHT	
9	Alan SMITH	
10	Paul MERSON	
11	Anders LIMPAR ‡	
	Substitutes	
12	Steve MORROW	
14	Kevin CAMPBELL ‡81	
Gk	Jim WILL	

LEEDS UNITED
Yellow shirts, Yellow shorts   Goals

1	John LUKIC	
2	Chris FAIRCLOUGH	
3	Tony DORIGO ❑	
4	David BATTY	
5	David WETHERALL	
6	Chris WHYTE ❑	
7	Gordon STRACHAN ‡	
8	Rod WALLACE	
9	Frank STRANDLI ❑	
10	Brian McALLISTER †	
11	Gary SPEED	
	Substitutes	
12	Jon NEWSOME †45	
14	Lee CHAPMAN ‡70	
Gk	Mervyn DAY	

Date	Wednesday 24 February 1993
Venue	City Ground, 7.30pm

NOTTINGHAM FOREST (0) 1
QPR (0) 0

Attendance	22,436
Referee	Rodger GIFFORD
Linesmen	A. Streets, J. Hilditch

● *Was scheduled for Boxing Day - postponed frozen pitch.*

NOTTINGHAM FOREST
Red shirts, White shorts   Goals

1	Mark CROSSLEY	
2	Gary CHARLES	
3	Steve CHETTLE	
4	Steve STONE	
5	Carl TILER	
6	Roy KEANE	
7	Gary CROSBY	70
8	Scot GEMMILL	
9	Nigel CLOUGH	
10	Gary BANNISTER	
11	Ian WOAN	
	Substitutes	
12	Kingsley BLACK	
14	Craig ARMSTRONG	
Gk	Andy MARRIOTT	

QPR
Blue & White hooped shirts, Blue shorts   Goals

1	Tony ROBERTS	
2	David BARDSLEY	
3	Rufus BREVETT	
4	Simon BARKER	
5	Darren PEACOCK	
6	Danny MADDIX ❑	
7	Clive WILSON	
8	Andy IMPEY	
9	Les FERDINAND	
10	Bradley ALLEN †	
11	Andy SINTON	
	Substitutes	
12	Dennis BAILEY †72	
14	Karl READY	
Gk	Jan STEJSKAL	

Date	Saturday 27 February 1993
Venue	Villa Park, 3.00pm

ASTON VILLA (0) 1
WIMBLEDON (0) 0

Attendance	34,496
Referee	Steve LODGE
Linesmen	P. Rejer, A. Black

ASTON VILLA
Claret & Blue shirts, White shorts   Goals

1	Mark BOSNICH	
2	Earl BARRETT	
3	Steve STAUNTON	
4	Shaun TEALE	
5	Paul McGRATH	
6	Kevin RICHARDSON	
7	Ray HOUGHTON	
8	Neil COX	
9	Dean SAUNDERS	
10	Dwight YORKE	79
11	Cyrille REGIS	
	Substitutes	
12	Stefan BEINLICH	
14	Bryan SMALL	
Gk	Nigel SPINK	

WIMBLEDON
Blue shirts, Blue shorts   Goals

1	Hans SEGERS	
2	Roger JOSEPH	
3	Gary ELKINS	
4	Vinnie JONES	
5	John SCALES	
6	Brian McALLISTER	
7	Neal ARDLEY	
8	Robbie EARLE	
9	John FASHANU	
10	Steve COTTERILL	
11	Gerald DOBBS ‡	
	Substitutes	
12	Dean BLACKWELL	
14	Andy CLARKE ‡80	
Gk	Neil SULLIVAN	

Date	Saturday 27 February 1993
Venue	Selhurst Park, 3.00pm

CRYSTAL PALACE (0) 0
COVENTRY CITY (0) 0

Attendance	12,248
Referee	Peter FOAKES
Linesmen	J.F. Moore, M. Stobbart

CRYSTAL PALACE
Red & Blue striped shirts, Red shorts   Goals

1	Nigel MARTYN	
2	John HUMPHREY	
3	Richard SHAW †	
4	Chris COLEMAN	
5	Eric YOUNG	
6	Andy THORN	
7	Bobby BOWRY	
8	Geoff THOMAS	
9	Chris ARMSTRONG	
10	Simon RODGER	
11	Eddie McGOLDRICK	
	Substitutes	
12	George NDAH †68	
14	Gareth SOUTHGATE	
Gk	Andy WOODMAN	

COVENTRY CITY
Sky Blue shirts, Sky Blue shorts   Goals

1	Steve OGRIZOVIC	
2	Brian BORROWS	
3	Phil BABB ❑	
4	Peter ATHERTON	
5	Andy PEARCE	
6	John WILLIAMS	
7	Stewart ROBSON	
8	Michael GYNN †	
9	Robert ROSARIO ❑	
10	Mick QUINN	
11	David SMITH	
	Substitutes	
12	Sean FLYNN †79	
14	David BUSST	
Gk	Jonathan GOULD	

Date	Saturday 27 February 1993	
Venue	Goodison Park, 3.00pm	

EVERTON (1) 2
OLDHAM ATHLETIC (0) 2

Attendance	18,025
Referee	Keith COOPER
Linesmen	N.S. Barry, E.B. Crompton

EVERTON
Blue shirts, White shorts · Goals

1	Jason KEARTON	
2	Matthew JACKSON	
3	Kenny SANSOM	
4	Ian SNODIN	
5	Dave WATSON	
6	Gary ABLETT	
7	Billy KENNY	
8	Peter BEARDSLEY	20p
9	Tony COTTEE	
10	Barry HORNE ❏	
11	Stuart BARLOW †	61
	Substitutes	
12	Paul RIDEOUT †80	
14	PREKI	
Gk	Stephen REEVES	

OLDHAM ATHLETIC
Red & White shirts, Red shorts · Goals

1	Paul GERRARD	
2	Craig FLEMING	
3	Gunnar HALLE	
4	Nick HENRY	
5	Richard JOBSON	
6	Steve REDMOND	
7	Neil ADAMS	87p, 88
8	Andy RITCHIE ‡	
9	Ian MARSHALL	
10	Mike MILLIGAN ❏	
11	Mark BRENNAN ❏ †	
	Substitutes	
12	Roger PALMER †65	
14	Paul MOULDEN ‡38	
Gk	Ian GRAY	

Date	Saturday 27 February 1993	
Venue	Elland Road, 3.00pm	

LEEDS UNITED (0) 1
IPSWICH TOWN (0) 0

Attendance	28,848
Referee	M. REED
Linesmen	B. Lowe, U.D. Rennie

LEEDS UNITED
White shirts, White shorts · Goals

1	John LUKIC	
2	Jon NEWSOME	
3	Tony DORIGO	71p
4	David BATTY	
5	Chris FAIRCLOUGH ❏	
6	David WETHERALL	
7	Gordon STRACHAN	
8	Rod WALLACE	
9	Frank STRANDLI ❏ †	
10	Ray WALLACE	
11	Gary SPEED	
	Substitutes	
12	Lee CHAPMAN †77	
14	David ROCASTLE	
Gk	Mervyn DAY	

IPSWICH TOWN
Red & Black striped shirts, Black shorts · Goals

1	Clive BAKER	
2	Gavin JOHNSON ❏	
3	Neil THOMPSON	
4	Mick STOCKWELL	
5	John WARK	
6	David LINIGHAN	
7	Geraint WILLIAMS	
8	Bontcho GUENTCHEV †	
9	Steve WHITTON	
10	Jason DOZZELL	
11	Chris KIWOMYA ❏	
	Substitutes	
12	Paul GODDARD †81	
14	Phil WHELAN	
Gk	Craig FORREST	

Date	Saturday 27 February 1993
Venue	Old Trafford, 3.00pm

MANCHESTER UNITED (1) 3
MIDDLESBROUGH (0) 0

Attendance	36,251
Referee	Keith HACKETT
Linesmen	R.R. Rawson, T.J. Stevens

MANCHESTER UNITED
Red shirts, White shorts   Goals

1	Peter SCHMEICHEL	
2	Paul PARKER	
3	Denis IRWIN	79
4	Steve BRUCE	
5	Lee SHARPE	
6	Gary PALLISTER	
7	Eric CANTONA	85
8	Paul INCE	
9	Brian McCLAIR	
10	Mark HUGHES	
11	Ryan GIGGS	20
	Substitutes	
12	Andrei KANCHELSKIS	
14	Mike PHELAN	
Gk	Les SEALEY	

MIDDLESBROUGH
Blue shirts, Blue shorts   Goals

1	Stephen PEARS	
2	Chris MORRIS	
3	Jimmy PHILLIPS	
4	Derek WHYTE	
5	Nicky MOHAN	
6	Andy PEAKE	
7	John HENDRIE	
8	Robbie MUSTOE †	
9	Paul WILKINSON	
10	Chris KAMARA	
11	Tommy WRIGHT	
	Substitutes	
12	Bernie SLAVEN †72	
14	Alan KERNAGHAN	
Gk	Ian IRONSIDE	

Date	Saturday 27 February 1993
Venue	City Ground, 3.00pm

NOTTINGHAM FOREST (0) 0
MANCHESTER CITY (1) 2

Attendance	25,956
Referee	Alf BUKSH
Linesmen	G.R. Hamblin, K.J. Hawkes

NOTTINGHAM FOREST
Red shirts, White shorts   Goals

1	Mark CROSSLEY	
2	Gary CHARLES	
3	Steve CHETTLE	
4	Steve STONE †	
5	Carl TILER	
6	Roy KEANE	
7	Gary CROSBY	
8	Kingsley BLACK	
9	Nigel CLOUGH	
10	Lee GLOVER	
11	Ian WOAN	
	Substitutes	
12	Brian LAWS †22	
14	Craig ARMSTRONG	
Gk	Andy MARRIOTT	

MANCHESTER CITY
Light Blue shirts, Light Blue shorts   Goals

1	Tony COTON	
2	Ray RANSON	
3	Terry PHELAN	
4	Fitzroy SIMPSON	
5	Andy HILL	
6	Michel VONK	
7	David WHITE	19
8	Mike SHERON †	
9	Mick QUINN	
10	Garry FLITCROFT	89
11	Rick HOLDEN	
	Substitutes	
12	Mike QUIGLEY †89	
14	Adie MIKE	
Gk	Andy DIBBLE	

Date	Saturday 27 February 1993
Venue	Hillsborough, 3.00pm

SHEFFIELD WEDNESDAY (0) 1
LIVERPOOL (1) 1

Attendance	33,964
Referee	Vic CALLOW
Linesmen	T. Lynch, J. McGrath

SHEFFIELD WEDNESDAY
Blue & White shirts, Black shorts   Goals

1	Chris WOODS	
2	Roland NILSSON	
3	Nigel WORTHINGTON ❑ ■	
4	Carlton PALMER	
5	John HARKES	
6	Peter SHIRTLIFF ‡	
7	Graham HYDE †	
8	Chris WADDLE	
9	Paul WARHURST	
10	Mark BRIGHT	
11	John SHERIDAN	
	Substitutes	
12	Chris BART-WILLIAMS †89	
14	Viv ANDERSON ‡53	82
Gk	Kevin PRESSMAN	

LIVERPOOL
Red shirts, Red shorts   Goals

1	David JAMES	
2	Jamie REDKNAPP	
3	Rob JONES	
4	Steve NICOL	
5	Mark WRIGHT	
6	Stig Inge BJORNEBYE ❑ †	
7	Steve McMANAMAN	
8	Don HUTCHISON	20
9	Mark WALTERS	
10	David BARNES	
11	Paul STEWART	
	Substitutes	
12	Mike MARSH †45	
14	Ronnie ROSENTHAL	
Gk	Mike HOOPER	

Date	Saturday 27 February 1993
Venue	The Dell, 3.00pm

SOUTHAMPTON (3) 3
SHEFFIELD UNITED (1) 2

Attendance	13,814
Referee	Jim BORRETT
Linesmen	M.E. Alexander, W.M. Jordan

SOUTHAMPTON
Red & White striped shirts, Black shorts   Goals

1	Tim FLOWERS	
2	Jeff KENNA	5
3	Micky ADAMS	
4	Tommy WIDDRINGTON	
5	Richard HALL	
6	Kevin MOORE	2
7	Matthew LE TISSIER ❑	
8	Jason DODD	
9	Iain DOWIE	39
10	Neil MADDISON	
11	Nicky BANGER	
	Substitutes	
12	Glenn COCKERILL	
14	Matthew BOUND	
Gk	Ian ANDREWS	

SHEFFIELD UNITED
Yellow shirts, White shorts   Goals

1	Alan KELLY	
2	Mitch WARD	
3	Tom COWAN ‡	
4	John GANNON	
5	Brian GAYLE	37
6	Paul BEESLEY	
7	Michael LAKE	
8	Jamie HOYLAND †	
9	Alan CORK	
10	Brian DEANE ❑	
11	Adrian LITTLEJOHN	
	Substitutes	
12	Ian BRYSON †59	83
14	Carl BRADSHAW ‡16	
Gk	Phil KITE	

Date	Saturday 27 February 1993
Venue	White Hart Lane, 3.00pm

TOTTENHAM HOTSPUR (2) 3
QPR (0) 2

Attendance	32,341
Referee	David ELLERAY
Linesmen	M.K. Bullivant, R.J. Harris

TOTTENHAM HOTSPUR
White shirts, Navy Blue shorts   Goals

1	Erik THORSTVEDT	
2	Dean AUSTIN ❑	
3	Justin EDINBURGH	
4	Vinny SAMWAYS	
5	Gary MABBUTT	
6	Jason CUNDY	
7	Andy GRAY	
8	Nick BARMBY ‡	
9	Darren ANDERTON	61
10	Teddy SHERINGHAM	8, 34
11	Paul ALLEN	
	Substitutes	
12	Stuart NETHERCOTT	
14	NAYIM ‡88	
Gk	Kevin DEARDEN	

QPR
Red & Black hooped shirts, Red shorts   Goals

1	Tony ROBERTS	
2	David BARDSLEY	
3	Rufus BREVETT	
4	Simon BARKER ‡	
5	Darren PEACOCK	87
6	Alan McDONALD ❑	
7	Clive WILSON	
8	Danny MADDIX	
9	Les FERDINAND	
10	Devon WHITE	88
11	Andy SINTON	
	Substitutes	
12	Bradley ALLEN	
14	Andy IMPEY ‡21	
Gk	Jan STEJSKAL	

Date	Sunday 28 February 1993
Venue	Carrow Road, 4.00pm

NORWICH CITY (0) 0
BLACKBURN ROVERS (0) 0

Attendance	15,821
Referee	Philip DON
Linesmen	A.P. D'Urso, G. Butland

NORWICH CITY
Yellow shirts, Green shorts   Goals

1	Bryan GUNN	
2	Ian CULVERHOUSE	
3	Mark BOWEN	
4	Chris SUTTON	
5	John POLSTON	
6	David SMITH	
7	Daryl SUTCH	
8	Lee POWER	
9	Mark ROBINS	
10	Ruel FOX	
11	David PHILLIPS	
	Substitutes	
12	Colin WOODTHORPE	
14	Robert ULLATHORNE	
Gk	Mark WALTON	

BLACKBURN ROVERS
Blue & White shirts, Blue shorts   Goals

1	Bobby MIMMS	
2	David MAY ❑	
3	Tony DOBSON	
4	Tim SHERWOOD	
5	Colin HENDRY	
6	Kevin MORAN	
7	Stuart RIPLEY	
8	Patrik ANDERSSON	
9	Roy WEGERLE	
10	Mike NEWELL	
11	Jason WILCOX	
	Substitutes	
12	Mark ATKINS	
14	Steve LIVINGSTONE	
Gk	Darren COLLIER	

LEAGUE TABLE

Up to and including 28.02.93

		P	W	D	L	F	A	Pts
1	Aston Villa	31	17	8	6	48	31	59
2	Manchester United	30	16	9	5	47	23	57
3	Norwich City	29	15	7	7	42	42	52
4	Sheffield Wednesday	29	12	10	7	40	33	46
5	Blackburn Rovers	29	12	9	8	42	30	45
6	Queen's Park Rangers	30	12	8	10	41	36	44
7	Ipswich Town	30	10	14	6	37	33	44
8	Tottenham Hotspur	30	12	8	10	39	41	44
9	Manchester City	30	12	7	11	43	34	43
10	Coventry City	30	11	10	9	44	40	43
11	Arsenal	28	11	6	11	26	25	39
12	Southampton	31	10	9	12	38	39	39
13	Leeds United	31	10	9	12	41	45	39
14	Chelsea	30	9	10	11	32	38	37
15	Liverpool	29	9	9	11	39	40	36
16	Wimbledon	30	9	9	12	35	37	36
17	Crystal Palace	30	8	10	12	36	46	34
18	Everton	30	9	6	15	33	41	33
19	Nottingham Forest	29	8	7	14	29	38	31
20	Sheffield United	30	8	7	15	31	41	31
21	Middlesbrough	30	7	9	14	37	52	30
22	Oldham Athletic	30	7	7	16	40	55	28

LEADING SCORERS

Alan SHEARER	Blackburn Rovers	16
Teddy SHERINGHAM	Tottenham Hotspur	15
David WHITE	Manchester City	14
Mick QUINN	Coventry City	14

LEAGUE GOALSCORING FIGURES

Running Totals

Date	Games	Goals	Average	Games	Goals	Average
02.02.93	1	3	3.00	283	743	2.62
06.02.93	8	18	2.25	291	761	2.62
07.02.93	1	6	6.00	292	767	2.63
08.02.93	1	0	0.00	293	767	2.62
09.02.93	2	4	2.00	295	771	2.61
10.02.93	5	8	1.60	300	779	2.60
13.02.93	3	6	2.00	303	785	2.59
20.02.93	10	24	2.40	313	809	2.58
21.02.93	1	2	2.00	314	811	2.58
22.02.93	1	2	2.00	315	813	2.58
23.02.93	1	3	3.00	316	816	2.58
24.02.93	2	1	0.50	318	817	2.57
27.02.93	9	23	2.56	327	840	2.57
28.02.93	1	0	0.00	328	840	2.56

Date Monday 1 March 1993
Venue Stamford Bridge, 7.45pm

CHELSEA (0) 1
ARSENAL (0) 0

Attendance 17,725
Referee Tony WARD
Linesmen R.E. Budden, W.J. Norbury

CHELSEA
Blue shirts, Blue shorts — Goals

1	Dave BEASANT	
2	Gareth HALL	
3	Frank SINCLAIR	
4	Andy TOWNSEND	
5	Erland JOHNSEN	
6	Mal DONAGHY	
7	Graham STUART	81
8	Robert FLECK	
9	Mick HARFORD †	
10	Eddie NEWTON	
11	Darren BARNARD ‡	

Substitutes

12	John SPENCER †79
14	Damien MATTHEW ‡86
Gk	Kevin HITCHCOCK

ARSENAL
Red & White shirts, White shorts — Goals

1	David SEAMAN ▢
2	Lee DIXON
3	Steve MORROW
4	David HILLIER †
5	Andy LINIGHAN
6	Martin KEOWN
7	John JENSEN
8	Kevin CAMPBELL ‡
9	Alan SMITH
10	Paul MERSON
11	Mark FLATTS

Substitutes

12	Pal LYDERSEN †45
14	Jimmy CARTER ‡84
Gk	Alan MILLER

Date	Tuesday 2 March 1993
Venue	Portman Road, 7.45pm

IPSWICH TOWN (0) 0
MIDDLESBROUGH (1) 1

Attendance	15,430
Referee	Keren BARRATT
Linesmen	M.G. Wright, W.M. Jordan

● *Moved from February 13*

IPSWICH TOWN
Blue & White shirts, White shorts — Goals

1	Clive BAKER	
2	Frank YALLOP ‡	
3	Neil THOMPSON	
4	Mick STOCKWELL	
5	John WARK	
6	David LINIGHAN	
7	Geraint WILLIAMS	
8	Bontcho GUENTCHEV	
9	Steve WHITTON	
10	Vlado BOZINOSKI †	
11	Chris KIWOMYA	
	Substitutes	
12	Phil WHELAN †76	
14	Paul GODDARD ‡79	
Gk	Craig FORREST	

MIDDLESBROUGH
Red shirts, Black shorts — Goals

1	Ian IRONSIDE	
2	Chris MORRIS	
3	Jimmy PHILLIPS	
4	Alan KERNAGHAN	
5	Andy PEAKE	
6	Derek WHYTE	
7	John HENDRIE	
8	Robbie MUSTOE	
9	Paul WILKINSON	35
10	Chris KAMARA ‡	
11	Tommy WRIGHT	
	Substitutes	
12	Willie FALCONER ‡48	
14	Bernie SLAVEN	
Gk	Ben ROBERTS	

Date	Tuesday 2 March 1993
Venue	Bramall Lane, 7.45pm

SHEFFIELD UNITED (4) 6
TOTTENHAM HOTSPUR (0) 0

Attendance	16,654
Referee	Joe WORRALL
Linesmen	A.J. Hill, J. Leech

● *Moved from February 13*

SHEFFIELD UNITED
Red & White striped shirts, White shorts — Goals

1	Alan KELLY	
2	Kevin GAGE	
3	David BARNES †	
4	Jamie HOYLAND	
5	Brian GAYLE	
6	John PEMBERTON	
7	Franz CARR	13
8	Charlie HARTFIELD	
9	Ian BRYSON ‡	28, 29
10	Brian DEANE ❏	73
11	Glyn HODGES	
	Substitutes	
12	Paul ROGERS †70	87
14	Alan CORK ‡80	
Gk	Phil KITE	

TOTTENHAM HOTSPUR
Light Blue shirts, Light Blue shorts — Goals

1	Erik THORSTVEDT	
2	Dean AUSTIN	
3	Pat VAN DEN HAUWE ❏	
4	Vinny SAMWAYS	
5	Gary MABBUTT	
6	Jason CUNDY	
7	Andy GRAY †	21og
8	NAYIM ‡	
9	Darren ANDERTON	
10	Teddy SHERINGHAM	
11	Paul ALLEN	
	Substitutes	
12	John HENDRY †64	
14	Steve SEDGLEY ‡64	
Gk	Kevin DEARDEN	

Date	Wednesday 3 March 1993
Venue	Highfield Road, 7.30pm

COVENTRY CITY (1) 1
SHEFFIELD WEDNESDAY (0) 0

Attendance	13,206
Referee	Keith COOPER
Linesmen	P.J. Robinson, D.T. Colwell

● *Moved from 13 February*

COVENTRY CITY
Sky Blue shirts, Sky Blue shorts   Goals

1	Steve OGRIZOVIC	
2	Brian BORROWS	
3	Phil BABB	
4	Peter ATHERTON	
5	Andy PEARCE	
6	John WILLIAMS	
7	Peter NDLOVU	
8	Michael GYNN	43
9	Lloyd McGRATH ❑	
10	Mick QUINN	
11	Stewart ROBSON	
	Substitutes	
12	David BUSST	
14	Sean FLYNN	
Gk	Jonathan GOULD	

SHEFFIELD WEDNESDAY
Yellow shirts, Yellow shorts   Goals

1	Chris WOODS	
2	Phil KING	
3	Nigel WORTHINGTON	
4	Carlton PALMER	
5	Ryan JONES †	
6	Viv ANDERSON	
7	Graham HYDE ‡	
8	Chris WADDLE	
9	Paul WARHURST	
10	Mark BRIGHT	
11	John SHERIDAN	
	Substitutes	
12	Julian WATTS †84	
14	Nigel JEMSON ‡84	
Gk	Kevin PRESSMAN	

Date	Wednesday 3 March 1993
Venue	Goodison Park, 7.30pm

EVERTON (0) 2
BLACKBURN ROVERS (1) 1

Attendance	18,086
Referee	Peter FOAKES
Linesmen	J. Hilditch, M. Warren

EVERTON
Blue shirts, White shorts   Goals

1	Neville SOUTHALL	
2	Matthew JACKSON	
3	Kenny SANSOM	
4	Billy KENNY †	
5	Dave WATSON	
6	Gary ABLETT	
7	Mark WARD	
8	Peter BEARDSLEY	
9	Tony COTTEE	71
10	Barry HORNE	
11	John EBBRELL	
	Substitutes	
12	Stuart BARLOW †46	
14	PREKI	
Gk	Jason KEARTON	

BLACKBURN ROVERS
Red & Black striped shirts, Black shorts   Goals

1	Bobby MIMMS	
2	David MAY	42
3	Alan WRIGHT	
4	Tim SHERWOOD ■	
5	Colin HENDRY	56og
6	Nicky MARKER	
7	Stuart RIPLEY	
8	Patrik ANDERSSON ❑ †	
9	Roy WEGERLE ‡	
10	Mike NEWELL	
11	Jason WILCOX	
	Substitutes	
12	Steve LIVINGSTONE †75	
14	Mark ATKINS ‡65	
Gk	Darren COLLIER	

Date	Wednesday 3 March 1993
Venue	Carrow Road, 7.45pm

NORWICH CITY (1) 1
ARSENAL (0) 1

Attendance	14,820
Referee	John MARTIN
Linesmen	M.K. Bullivant, M. Stobbart

● *Moved from 6 February*

NORWICH CITY
Yellow shirts, Green shorts   Goals

1	Bryan GUNN	
2	Ian CULVERHOUSE	
3	Mark BOWEN	
4	Chris SUTTON	
5	John POLSTON	
6	David SMITH ❑	
7	Daryl SUTCH	
8	Lee POWER	
9	Mark ROBINS	
10	Ruel FOX	35
11	David PHILLIPS	
	Substitutes	
12	Colin WOODTHORPE	
14	Ian CROOK	
Gk	Mark WALTON	

ARSENAL
Red & White shirts, White shorts   Goals

1	David SEAMAN	
2	Lee DIXON	
3	Nigel WINTERBURN	
4	Paul DAVIS	
5	Andy LINIGHAN	
6	Martin KEOWN	
7	John JENSEN	
8	Ian WRIGHT ❑	81
9	Ray PARLOUR	
10	Jimmy CARTER	
11	Anders LIMPAR ‡	
	Substitutes	
12	Pal LYDERSEN	
14	Kevin CAMPBELL ‡70	
Gk	Alan MILLER	

Date	Wednesday 3 March 1993
Venue	City Ground, 7.30pm

NOTTINGHAM FOREST (1) 1
CRYSTAL PALACE (1) 1

Attendance	20,603
Referee	Jim BORRETT
Linesmen	P. Rejer, G.R. Hamblin

● *Brought forward from 10 March*

NOTTINGHAM FOREST
Red shirts, White shorts   Goals

1	Mark CROSSLEY	
2	Gary CHARLES	
3	Brian LAWS	
4	Steve CHETTLE	
5	Carl TILER	
6	Roy KEANE	24
7	Gary CROSBY	
8	Thorvaldur ORLYGSSON †	
9	Nigel CLOUGH	
10	Robert ROSARIO	
11	Ian WOAN	
	Substitutes	
12	Gary BANNISTER †72	
14	Kingsley BLACK	
Gk	Andy MARRIOTT	

CRYSTAL PALACE
Yellow shirts, Light Blue shorts   Goals

1	Nigel MARTYN	
2	Gareth SOUTHGATE	23
3	Dean GORDON †	
4	Chris COLEMAN	
5	Eric YOUNG ❑	
6	Andy THORN	
7	Bobby BOWRY ‡	
8	Geoff THOMAS	
9	Chris ARMSTRONG	
10	Simon RODGER	
11	Eddie McGOLDRICK	
	Substitutes	
12	John HUMPHREY †66	
14	George NDAH ‡78	
Gk	Andy WOODMAN	

Date	Saturday 6 March 1993
Venue	Anfield, 3.00pm

LIVERPOOL (0) 1
MANCHESTER UNITED (1) 2

Attendance	44,374
Referee	Roger MILFORD
Linesmen	P.J. Robinson, B.L. Polkey

LIVERPOOL
Red shirts, Red shorts   Goals

1	David JAMES	
2	Jamie REDKNAPP	
3	Rob JONES	
4	Steve NICOL	
5	Mark WRIGHT	
6	Stig Inge BJORNEBYE	
7	Steve McMANAMAN	
8	Don HUTCHISON	
9	Mark WALTERS ‡	
10	John BARNES	
11	Paul STEWART †	
	Substitutes	
12	Ian RUSH †44	50
14	David BURROWS ‡79	
Gk	Mike HOOPER	

MANCHESTER UNITED
Blue shirts, Blue shorts   Goals

1	Peter SCHMEICHEL	
2	Paul PARKER	
3	Denis IRWIN	
4	Steve BRUCE	
5	Lee SHARPE	
6	Gary PALLISTER	
7	Andrei KANCHELSKIS	
8	Paul INCE	
9	Brian McCLAIR	56
10	Mark HUGHES	42
11	Ryan GIGGS	
	Substitutes	
12	Dion DUBLIN	
14	Mike PHELAN	
Gk	Les SEALEY	

Date	Saturday 6 March 1993
Venue	Loftus Road, 3.00pm

QPR (2) 3
NORWICH CITY (1) 1

Attendance	13,892
Referee	Rodger GIFFORD
Linesmen	P.A. Josper, D.C. Richards

QPR
Blue & White hooped shirts, White shorts   Goals

1	Tony ROBERTS	
2	David BARDSLEY	
3	Rufus BREVETT	
4	Maurice DOYLE	
5	Danny MADDIX	
6	Alan McDONALD	
7	Andy IMPEY	
8	Clive WILSON	78
9	Les FERDINAND	18, 34
10	Devon WHITE †	
11	Michael MEAKER	
	Substitutes	
12	Bradley ALLEN †58	
14	Darren PEACOCK	
Gk	Jan STEJSKAL	

NORWICH CITY
Yellow shirts, Green shorts   Goals

1	Bryan GUNN	
2	Ian CULVERHOUSE	
3	Mark BOWEN	
4	Chris SUTTON	
5	Colin WOODTHORPE	
6	Daryl SUTCH	
7	Ian CROOK	
8	Lee POWER ‡	
9	Mark ROBINS	41
10	Ruel FOX	
11	David PHILLIPS	
	Substitutes	
12	David SMITH	
14	Jason MINETT ‡76	
Gk	Mark WALTON	

Date	Saturday 6 March 1993
Venue	Selhurst Park, 3.00pm

WIMBLEDON (1) 1
SOUTHAMPTON (1) 2

Attendance	4,534
Referee	Allan GUNN
Linesmen	M.D. Dearing, C. Jones

WIMBLEDON
Blue shirts, Blue shorts   Goals

1	Hans SEGERS	
2	Roger JOSEPH	
3	Gary ELKINS	
4	Vinnie JONES	
5	John SCALES	
6	Brian McALLISTER	
7	Neal ARDLEY	
8	Robbie EARLE	
9	John FASHANU	
10	Dean HOLDSWORTH	22
11	Andy CLARKE	
	Substitutes	
12	Greg BERRY	
14	Lawrie SANCHEZ	
Gk	Neil SULLIVAN	

SOUTHAMPTON
Red & White striped shirts, Black shorts   Goals

1	Tim FLOWERS	
2	Jeff KENNA	
3	Micky ADAMS	
4	Tommy WIDDRINGTON	
5	Kevin MOORE	73
6	Kenneth MONKOU	
7	Matthew LE TISSIER †	33
8	Glenn COCKERILL	
9	Iain DOWIE	
10	Neil MADDISON	
11	Jason DODD	
	Substitutes	
12	Nicky BANGER †78	
14	Matthew BOUND	
Gk	Ian ANDREWS	

Date	Sunday 7 March 1993
Venue	Highfield Road, 12.30pm

COVENTRY CITY (0) 0
EVERTON (1) 1

Attendance	11,285
Referee	David ELLERAY
Linesmen	M. Warren, T.J. Stevens

COVENTRY CITY
Sky Blue shirts, Sky Blue shorts   Goals

1	Steve OGRIZOVIC	
2	David BORROWS	
3	Phil BABB	
4	Peter ATHERTON	
5	Andy PEARCE	
6	John WILLIAMS ❏	
7	Peter NDLOVU	
8	Michael GYNN ‡	
9	Lloyd McGRATH	
10	Mick QUINN	
11	Sean FLYNN	
	Substitutes	
12	David BUSST	
14	Kevin GALLACHER ‡65	
Gk	Jonathan GOULD	

EVERTON
Salmon Pink & Blue stripes, Salmon Pink shorts   Goals

1	Neville SOUTHALL	
2	Matthew JACKSON	
3	Kenny SANSOM	
4	Ian SNODIN †	
5	Dave WATSON	
6	Gary ABLETT	
7	Mark WARD	8
8	Peter BEARDSLEY	
9	Tony COTTEE ❏	
10	Barry HORNE	
11	John EBBRELL	
	Substitutes	
12	PREKI †66	
14	Stuart BARLOW	
Gk	Jason KEARTON	

Date Tuesday 9 March 1993
Venue Ewood Park, 7.45pm

BLACKBURN ROVERS (0) 0
SOUTHAMPTON (0) 0

Attendance 13,566
Referee Steve LODGE
Linesmen B. Lowe, R. Pearson

BLACKBURN ROVERS
Blue & White shirts, White shorts   Goals

1	Bobby MIMMS	
2	David MAY	
3	Tony DOBSON	
4	Tim SHERWOOD	
5	Colin HENDRY	
6	Kevin MORAN †	
7	Stuart RIPLEY	
8	Mark ATKINS	
9	Roy WEGERLE	
10	Mike NEWELL	
11	Jason WILCOX	
	Substitutes	
12	Patrik ANDERSSON †80	
14	Steve LIVINGSTONE	
Gk	Darren COLLIER	

SOUTHAMPTON
Red & White striped shirts, Black shorts   Goals

1	Tim FLOWERS	
2	Jeff KENNA	
3	Micky ADAMS	
4	Tommy WIDDRINGTON	
5	Kevin MOORE ‡	
6	Kenneth MONKOU	
7	Matthew LE TISSIER †	
8	Glenn COCKERILL	
9	Iain DOWIE	
10	Neil MADDISON	
11	Jason DODD	
	Substitutes	
12	Nicky BANGER †80	
14	Matthew BOUND ‡86	
Gk	Ian ANDREWS	

Date Tuesday 9 March 1993
Venue Boundary Park, 7.30pm

OLDHAM ATHLETIC (1) 1
MANCHESTER UNITED (0) 0

Attendance 17,106
Referee Gerald ASHBY
Linesmen R.H. Andrews, U.D. Rennie

OLDHAM ATHLETIC
Blue shirts, Blue shorts   Goals

1	Paul GERRARD	
2	Gunnar HALLE ❑	
3	Neil POINTON ‡	
4	Nick HENRY ❑	
5	Richard JOBSON	
6	Craig FLEMING	
7	Neil ADAMS	26
8	Paul BERNARD	
9	Ian OLNEY	
10	Mike MILLIGAN	
11	Mark BRENNAN	
	Substitutes	
12	Roger PALMER	
14	Steve REDMOND ‡75	
Gk	John KEELEY	

MANCHESTER UNITED
Red shirts, White shorts   Goals

1	Peter SCHMEICHEL	
2	Paul PARKER	
3	Denis IRWIN	
4	Steve BRUCE	
5	Lee SHARPE	
6	Gary PALLISTER	
7	Andrei KANCHELSKIS †	
8	Paul INCE	
9	Brian McCLAIR	
10	Mark HUGHES ❑	
11	Ryan GIGGS	
	Substitutes	
12	Dion DUBLIN †73	
14	Mike PHELAN	
Gk	Les SEALEY	

Date	Tuesday 9 March 1993
Venue	Selhurst Park, 8.00pm

WIMBLEDON (1) 2
MIDDLESBROUGH (0) 0

Attendance	5,821
Referee	Mike REED
Linesmen	D. Orr, M.G. Wright

WIMBLEDON
Blue shirts, Blue shorts   Goals

1	Hans SEGERS	
2	Roger JOSEPH	
3	Gary ELKINS ❏	
4	Vinnie JONES ❏	
5	John SCALES	32
6	Brian McALLISTER	
7	Neal ARDLEY	
8	Robbie EARLE	
9	John FASHANU	
10	Dean HOLDSWORTH	74
11	Andy CLARKE †	
	Substitutes	
12	Greg BERRY †87	
14	Lawrie SANCHEZ	
Gk	Neil SULLIVAN	

MIDDLESBROUGH
Red shirts, White shorts   Goals

1	Stephen PEARS ❏	
2	Chris MORRIS	
3	Jimmy PHILLIPS ❏	
4	Alan KERNAGHAN	
5	Andy PEAKE ❏	
6	Derek WHYTE	
7	John HENDRIE	
8	Robbie MUSTOE ❏	
9	Paul WILKINSON	
10	Willie FALCONER	
11	Tommy WRIGHT †	
	Substitutes	
12	Bernie SLAVEN †72	
14	Nicky MOHAN	
Gk	Ian IRONSIDE	

Date	Wednesday 10 March 1993
Venue	Villa Park, 7.45pm

ASTON VILLA (0) 0
TOTTENHAM HOTSPUR (0) 0

Attendance	37,727
Referee	Keith HACKETT
Linesmen	J. Leech, B.T. Millership

ASTON VILLA
Claret & Blue shirts, White shorts   Goals

1	Mark BOSNICH	
2	Earl BARRETT	
3	Steve STAUNTON	
4	Shaun TEALE	
5	Paul McGRATH	
6	Kevin RICHARDSON	
7	Ray HOUGHTON	
8	Garry PARKER	
9	Dean SAUNDERS	
10	Dwight YORKE	
11	Tony DALEY ‡	
	Substitutes	
12	Neil COX	
14	Cyrille REGIS ‡85	
Gk	Nigel SPINK	

TOTTENHAM HOTSPUR
White shirts, Navy Blue shorts   Goals

1	Erik THORSTVEDT	
2	Dean AUSTIN	
3	Justin EDINBURGH	
4	Vinny SAMWAYS	
5	Gary MABBUTT	
6	Neil RUDDOCK	
7	Steve SEDGLEY ❏	
8	NAYIM	
9	Darren ANDERTON	
10	Teddy SHERINGHAM	
11	Andy GRAY †	
	Substitutes	
12	Andy TURNER †72	
14	Pat VAN DEN HAUWE	
Gk	Ian WALKER	

Date   Wednesday 10 March 1993
Venue   Stamford Bridge, 7.30pm

CHELSEA (1) 2
EVERTON (0) 1

Attendance   12,739
Referee   Martin BODENHAM
Linesmen   D.C. Madgwick, B.A. Wigginton

CHELSEA
Blue shirts, Blue shorts   Goals

1	Dave BEASANT	
2	Steve CLARKE	
3	David LEE	
4	Andy TOWNSEND	
5	Erland JOHNSEN	
6	Mal DONAGHY	
7	Graham STUART	39
8	Robert FLECK †	
9	Mick HARFORD ‡	
10	Eddie NEWTON	
11	Darren BARNARD	
	Substitutes	
12	John SPENCER †32	79
14	Tony CASCARINO ‡75	
Gk	Kevin HITCHCOCK	

EVERTON
Salmon Pink & Blue striped shirts, Salmon Pink shorts   Goals

1	Neville SOUTHALL	
2	Matthew JACKSON	
3	Andy HINCHCLIFFE	
4	Billy KENNY †	45
5	Dave WATSON	
6	Gary ABLETT ❑	
7	Mark WARD ❑	
8	Peter BEARDSLEY	
9	Tony COTTEE	
10	Barry HORNE	
11	Stuart BARLOW	
	Substitutes	
12	PREKI †82	
14	Kenny SANSOM	
Gk	Jason KEARTON	

Date   Wednesday 10 March 1993
Venue   Portman Road, 7.45pm

IPSWICH TOWN (0) 0
SHEFFIELD WEDNESDAY (0) 1

Attendance   16,538
Referee   Tony WARD
Linesmen   P.A. Josper, J.F. Moore

IPSWICH TOWN
Blue & White shirts, White shorts   Goals

1	Clive BAKER	
2	Gavin JOHNSON	
3	Eddie YOUDS ‡	
4	Mick STOCKWELL	
5	John WARK	
6	David LINIGHAN	
7	Phil WHELAN †	
8	Bontcho GUENTCHEV	
9	Steve WHITTON	
10	Jason DOZZELL	
11	Chris KIWOMYA	
	Substitutes	
12	Paul GODDARD †67	
14	Glenn PENNYFATHER ‡74	
Gk	Craig FORREST	

SHEFFIELD WEDNESDAY
Yellow shirts, Yellow shorts   Goals

1	Chris WOODS	
2	Phil KING ‡	
3	Nigel WORTHINGTON	
4	Simon STEWART ❑	
5	Julian WATTS	
6	Viv ANDERSON	
7	Graham HYDE	
8	Nigel JEMSON	
9	David HIRST †	35
10	Mark BRIGHT	
11	Ryan JONES	
	Substitutes	
12	Gordon WATSON †59	
14	Trevor FRANCIS ‡86	
Gk	Kevin PRESSMAN	

Date	Wednesday 10 March 1993
Venue	Anfield, 7.30pm

LIVERPOOL (0) 1
QPR (0) 0

Attendance	30,370
Referee	Keith BURGE
Linesmen	M.A. Cooper, A.J. Hill

LIVERPOOL
Red shirts, Red shorts   Goals

1	David JAMES	
2	Mike MARSH †	
3	Rob JONES	
4	Steve NICOL	
5	Mark WRIGHT	
6	Ronnie WHELAN	
7	Steve McMANAMAN	
8	Don HUTCHISON	
9	Ian RUSH	72
10	John BARNES	
11	David BURROWS	
	Substitutes	
12	Ronnie ROSENTHAL †67	
14	Istvan KOZMA	
Gk	Mike HOOPER	

QPR
Blue & White hooped shirts, White shorts   Goals

1	Tony ROBERTS	
2	David BARDSLEY	
3	Rufus BREVETT	
4	Maurice DOYLE	
5	Danny MADDIX ‡	
6	Alan McDONALD	
7	Andy IMPEY	
8	Clive WILSON	
9	Les FERDINAND ❏	
10	Devon WHITE	
11	Michael MEAKER	
	Substitutes	
12	Bradley ALLEN	
14	Darren PEACOCK ‡20 ❏	
Gk	Jan STEJSKAL	

Date	Wednesday 10 March 1993
Venue	Maine Road, 7.45pm

MANCHESTER CITY (1) 1
COVENTRY CITY (0) 0

Attendance	20,092
Referee	Paul DURKIN
Linesmen	LM.A. Riley, N.S. Barry

MANCHESTER CITY
Light Blue shirts, White shorts   Goals

1	Tony COTON	
2	Andy HILL	
3	Terry PHELAN	
4	Fitzroy SIMPSON	
5	Keith CURLE	
6	Michel VONK	
7	David WHITE	
8	Mike SHERON	
9	Niall QUINN	
10	Garry FLITCROFT	35
11	Rick HOLDEN	
	Substitutes	
12	Peter REID	
14	Ray RANSON	
Gk	Martyn MARGETSON	

COVENTRY CITY
Red shirts, White shorts   Goals

1	Steve OGRIZOVIC	
2	Brian BORROWS	
3	Phil BABB	
4	Peter ATHERTON	
5	David BUSST	
6	John WILLIAMS	
7	Peter NDLOVU	
8	Kevin GALLACHER	
9	Lloyd McGRATH	
10	Mick QUINN ‡	
11	Sean FLYNN	
	Substitutes	
12	Andy PEARCE	
14	Chris GREENMAN ‡45	
Gk	Jonathan GOULD	

Date	Wednesday 10 March 1993
Venue	Bramall Lane, 3.00pm

SHEFFIELD UNITED (0) 0
NORWICH CITY (0) 1

Attendance	15,583
Referee	Ray LEWIS
Linesmen	M. Warren, T.J. Stevens

SHEFFIELD UNITED
Red & White striped shirts, White shorts   Goals

1	Alan KELLY	
2	Kevin GAGE	
3	Mitch WARD	
4	Jamie HOYLAND	
5	Brian GAYLE ❑	
6	John PEMBERTON	
7	Franz CARR †	
8	Charlie HARTFIELD ❑ ‡	
9	Ian BRYSON	
10	Brian DEANE	
11	Glyn HODGES	
	Substitutes	
12	Carl BRADSHAW †58	
14	Adrian LITTLEJOHN ‡63	
Gk	Phil KITE	

NORWICH CITY
Yellow shirts, Green shorts   Goals

1	Bryan GUNN	
2	Ian CULVERHOUSE	
3	Mark BOWEN	
4	Chris SUTTON	
5	John POLSTON	
6	Daryl SUTCH †	
7	Ian CROOK	
8	Colin WOODTHORPE	
9	Mark ROBINS	
10	Ruel FOX	55
11	David PHILLIPS	
	Substitutes	
12	David SMITH †50	
14	Darren BECKFORD	
Gk	Mark WALTON	

Date	Saturday 13 March 1993
Venue	Highfield Road, 3.00pm

COVENTRY CITY (0) 0
ARSENAL (2) 2

Attendance	15,437
Referee	David ALLISON
Linesmen	D.T. Colwell, J. Hilditch

COVENTRY CITY
Sky Blue shirts, Sky Blue shorts   Goals

1	Steve OGRIZOVIC	
2	Brian BORROWS	
3	Phil BABB	
4	Peter ATHERTON	
5	David BUSST	
6	John WILLIAMS	
7	Peter NDLOVU	
8	Kevin GALLACHER	
9	David RENNIE	
10	Leigh JENKINSON †	
11	Sean FLYNN ‡	
	Substitutes	
12	Lloyd McGRATH †74	
14	Michael GYNN ‡74	
Gk	Jonathan GOULD	

ARSENAL
Red & White shirts, White shorts   Goals

1	David SEAMAN	
2	Lee DIXON	
3	Martin KEOWN	
4	Paul DAVIS	
5	Andy LINIGHAN	
6	Tony ADAMS	
7	Ray PARLOUR	
8	Ian WRIGHT ‡	29
9	Kevin CAMPBELL	28
10	Paul MERSON †	
11	Steve MORROW	
	Substitutes	
12	David HILLER †84	
14	Anders LIMPAR ‡64	
Gk	Alan MILLER	

Date   Saturday 13 March 1993
Venue   Goodison Park, 3.00pm

EVERTON (3) 3
NOTTINGHAM FOREST (0) 0

Attendance   21,271
Referee   Vic CALLOW
Linesmen   B. Lowe, R. Pearson

EVERTON
Blue shirts, White shorts   Goals

1	Neville SOUTHALL	
2	Matthew JACKSON	
3	Andy HINCHCLIFFE	38
4	Ian SNODIN ❑ †	
5	Dave WATSON ❑	
6	Gary ABLETT ❑	
7	Mark WARD	
8	Peter BEARDSLEY	
9	Tony COTTEE	15, 26
10	Billy KENNY	
11	PREKI ‡	
	Substitutes	
12	Stuart BARLOW †71	
14	Kenny SANSOM ‡78	
Gk	Jason KEARTON	

NOTTINGHAM FOREST
Red shirts, Red shorts   Goals

1	Mark CROSSLEY	
2	Gary CHARLES	
3	Brian LAWS	
4	Steve CHETTLE	
5	Carl TILER ❑	
6	Thorvaldur ORLYGSSON	
7	Gary CROSBY †	
8	Ray McKINNON	
9	Nigel CLOUGH	
10	Gary BANNISTER	
11	Ian WOAN ❑	
	Substitutes	
12	Lee GLOVER †79	
14	Brett WILLIAMS	
Gk	Andy MARRIOTT	

Date   Saturday 13 March 1993
Venue   Elland Road, 3.00pm

LEEDS UNITED (1) 1
MANCHESTER CITY (0) 0

Attendance   30,840
Referee   Keith HACKETT
Linesmen   A.J. Martin, B.T. Millership

LEEDS UNITED
White shirts, White shorts   Goals

1	John LUKIC	
2	David KERSLAKE	
3	Tony DORIGO	
4	David BATTY	
5	Chris FAIRCLOUGH ‡	
6	David WETHERALL	
7	David ROCASTLE	11
8	Rod WALLACE	
9	Frank STRANDLI †	
10	Steve HODGE	
11	Gary SPEED	
	Substitutes	
12	Lee CHAPMAN †57	
14	Jon NEWSOME ‡72	
Gk	Mervyn DAY	

Manchester City
Purple shirts, Purple shorts   Goals

1	Tony COTON	
2	Andy HILL	
3	Terry PHELAN	
4	Fitzroy SIMPSON	
5	Keith CURLE	
6	Michel VONK	
7	David WHITE	
8	Ray RANSON	
9	Niall QUINN ‡	
10	Garry FLITCROFT	
11	Rick HOLDEN ❑	
	Substitutes	
12	Peter REID	
14	Mike SHERON ‡68	
Gk	Andy DIBBLE	

Date	Saturday 13 March 1993
Venue	Ayresome Park, 3.00pm

MIDDLESBROUGH (1) 1
LIVERPOOL (1) 2

Attendance	22,463
Referee	Mike PECK
Linesmen	A. Streets, R.R. Rawson

MIDDLESBROUGH
Red shirts, White shorts   Goals

1	Ian IRONSIDE	
2	Chris MORRIS	
3	Jimmy PHILLIPS ❑	
4	Nicky MOHAN ❑	
5	Andy PEAKE ❑	
6	Derek WHYTE †	
7	John HENDRIE	
8	Robbie MUSTOE	
9	Paul WILKINSON	
10	Willie FALCONER	
11	Craig HIGNETT	
	Substitutes	
12	Tommy WRIGHT †83	
14	Bernie SLAVEN	
Gk	Ben ROBERTS	

LIVERPOOL
Green shirts, Green shorts   Goals

1	David JAMES	
2	David BURROWS	
3	Rob JONES	
4	Steve NICOL	15og
5	Mark WRIGHT	
6	Ronnie WHELAN	
7	Steve McMANAMAN ‡	
8	Don HUTCHISON ❑	11
9	Ian RUSH	81
10	John BARNES	
11	Ronnie ROSENTHAL †	
	Substitutes	
12	Mark WALTERS †45 ❑	
14	Jamie REDKNAPP ‡66	
Gk	Mike HOOPER	

Date	Saturday 13 March 1993
Venue	Carrow Road, 3.00pm

NORWICH CITY (1) 1
OLDHAM ATHLETIC (0) 0

Attendance	19,597
Referee	Roger MILFORD
Linesmen	P.J. Robinson, B.L. Polkey

NORWICH CITY
Yellow shirts, Green shorts   Goals

1	Bryan GUNN	
2	Ian CULVERHOUSE	
3	Mark BOWEN	
4	Chris SUTTON	
5	John POLSTON	
6	David SMITH	
7	Ian CROOK	
8	Colin WOODTHORPE	
9	Mark ROBINS †	
10	Ruel FOX	
11	David PHILLIPS	
	Substitutes	
12	Lee POWER †89	
14	Jeremy GOSS	
Gk	Mark WALTON	

OLDHAM ATHLETIC
Blue shirts, Blue shorts   Goals

1	Paul GERRARD	
2	Gunnar HALLE	
3	Neil POINTON	
4	Nick HENRY ‡	12og
5	Richard JOBSON	
6	Craig FLEMING	
7	Neil ADAMS †	
8	Paul BERNARD	
9	Ian OLNEY	
10	Mike MILLIGAN	
11	Mark BRENNAN	
	Substitutes	
12	Roger PALMER †66	
14	Steve REDMOND ‡85	
Gk	John KEELEY	

Date	Saturday 13 March 1993
Venue	Loftus Road, 3.00pm

QPR (1) 1
WIMBLEDON (1) 2

Attendance	12,270
Referee	Philip DON
Linesmen	M.G. Wright, M.K. Bullivant

QPR
Blue & White hooped shirts, White shorts   Goals

1	Tony ROBERTS †	
2	David BARDSLEY	
3	Rufus BREVETT	
4	Maurice DOYLE	
5	Darren PEACOCK	
6	Alan McDONALD	
7	Andy IMPEY	
8	Clive WILSON	
9	Les FERDINAND ‡	3
10	Bradley ALLEN	
11	Michael MEAKER ❏	
	Substitutes	
12	Devon WHITE ‡26	
14	Karl READY	
Gk	Jan STEJSKAL †18	

WIMBLEDON
Red shirts, Red shorts   Goals

1	Hans SEGERS	
2	Roger JOSEPH ❏	
3	Gary ELKINS	
4	Vinnie JONES ‡	
5	John SCALES	
6	Brian McALLISTER	
7	Neal ARDLEY	
8	Robbie EARLE	78
9	John FASHANU	7
10	Dean HOLDSWORTH	
11	Gerald DOBBS ❏	
	Substitutes	
12	Andy CLARKE	
14	Lawrie SANCHEZ ‡60	
Gk	Neil SULLIVAN	

Date	Saturday 13 March 1993
Venue	The Dell, 3.00pm

SOUTHAMPTON (1) 4
IPSWICH TOWN (2) 3

Attendance	15,428
Referee	David ELLERAY
Linesmen	R.J. Harris, S.G. Tomlin

SOUTHAMPTON
Red & White striped shirts, Black shorts   Goals

1	Tim FLOWERS	
2	Jeff KENNA	84
3	Micky ADAMS	
4	Tommy WIDDRINGTON †	
5	Richard HALL	17
6	Kenneth MONKOU	
7	Matthew LE TISSIER	65p, 90
8	Nicky BANGER	
9	Iain DOWIE	
10	Neil MADDISON	
11	Jason DODD	
	Substitutes	
12	Glenn COCKERILL †63	
14	Matthew BOUND	
Gk	Ian ANDREWS	

IPSWICH TOWN
Blue & White shirts, White shorts   Goals

1	Clive BAKER	
2	Gavin JOHNSON	
3	Phil WHELAN	
4	Mick STOCKWELL	
5	John WARK ❏	
6	David LINIGHAN	13
7	Frank YALLOP	
8	Bontcho GUENTCHEV	
9	Paul GODDARD †	35
10	Jason DOZZELL	
11	Chris KIWOMYA	87
	Substitutes	
12	Steve WHITTON †70	
14	Eddie YOUDS	
Gk	Craig FORREST	

Date	Sunday 14 March 1993
Venue	Old Trafford, 1.00pm

MANCHESTER UNITED (0) 1
ASTON VILLA (0) 1

Attendance	36,163
Referee	Allan GUNN
Linesmen	P.M. Roberts, J. Hilditch

MANCHESTER UNITED
Red shirts, White shorts   Goals

1	Peter SCHMEICHEL	
2	Paul PARKER	
3	Denis IRWIN	
4	Steve BRUCE	
5	Lee SHARPE	
6	Gary PALLISTER	
7	Eric CANTONA	
8	Paul INCE	
9	Brian McCLAIR	
10	Mark HUGHES	57
11	Ryan GIGGS	
	Substitutes	
12	Bryan ROBSON	
14	Andrei KANCHELSKIS	
Gk	Les SEALEY	

ASTON VILLA
White shirts, Black shorts   Goals

1	Mark BOSNICH	
2	Earl BARRETT	
3	Steve STAUNTON	53
4	Shaun TEALE ❑	
5	Paul McGRATH	
6	Kevin RICHARDSON	
7	Ray HOUGHTON	
8	Garry PARKER †	
9	Dean SAUNDERS	
10	Dwight YORKE	
11	Bryan SMALL	
	Substitutes	
12	Tony DALEY †66	
14	Neil COX	
Gk	Nigel SPINK	

Date	Monday 15 March 1993
Venue	Selhurst Park, 7.45pm

CRYSTAL PALACE (1) 1
CHELSEA (1) 1

Attendance	12,610
Referee	Keith COOPER
Linesmen	M.J. Holohan, J.A. Elwin

CRYSTAL PALACE
Red & Blue striped shirts, Red shorts   Goals

1	Nigel MARTYN	
2	John HUMPHREY †	
3	Gareth SOUTHGATE	
4	Chris COLEMAN ‡	
5	Eric YOUNG	
6	Dean GORDON	
7	Simon OSBORN	
8	Geoff THOMAS	
9	Chris ARMSTRONG ❑	41
10	Simon RODGER	
11	Eddie McGOLDRICK	
	Substitutes	
12	Richard SHAW †33	
14	George NDAH ‡75	
Gk	Andy WOODMAN	

CHELSEA
Blue shirts, Blue shorts   Goals

1	Dave BEASANT	
2	Steve CLARKE	
3	Frank SINCLAIR	
4	Andy TOWNSEND	
5	Erland JOHNSEN ❑	
6	Mal DONAGHY	
7	Graham STUART	4
8	John SPENCER	
9	Tony CASCARINO	
10	Eddie NEWTON	
11	Paul BERNARD	
	Substitutes	
12	Mick HARFORD	
14	David LEE	
Gk	Kevin HITCHCOCK	

Date   Wednesday 17 March 1993
Venue   City Ground, 7.30pm

NOTTINGHAM FOREST (0) 0
NORWICH CITY (1) 3

Attendance   20,799
Referee   Steve LODGE
Linesmen   P. Rejer, A. Black
● *Game scheduled for 13 February*

NOTTINGHAM FOREST
Red shirts, White shorts   Goals

1	Mark CROSSLEY	
2	Gary CHARLES	
3	Brian LAWS	
4	Steve CHETTLE	
5	Carl TILER	
6	Thorvaldur ORLYGSSON	
7	Gary CROSBY ‡	
8	Steve STONE	
9	Nigel CLOUGH	
10	Gary BANNISTER †	
11	Ian WOAN	
	Substitutes	
12	Kingsley BLACK ‡45	
14	Lee GLOVER †74	
Gk	Andy MARRIOTT	

NORWICH CITY
Yellow shirts, Green shorts   Goals

1	Bryan GUNN	
2	Ian CULVERHOUSE	
3	Mark BOWEN	
4	Chris SUTTON	
5	John POLSTON	
6	David SMITH	
7	Ian CROOK	78
8	Colin WOODTHORPE	
9	Mark ROBINS †	45
10	Ruel FOX	
11	David PHILLIPS	
	Substitutes	
12	Lee POWER †49	73
14	Jeremy GOSS	
Gk	Mark WALTON	

Date   Saturday 20 March 1993
Venue   Highbury Stadium, 3.00pm

ARSENAL (3) 4
SOUTHAMPTON (2) 3

Attendance   24,149
Referee   Keren BARRATT
Linesmen   R.J. Harris, D.C. Richards

ARSENAL
Red & White shirts, White shorts   Goals

1	David SEAMAN	
2	Martin KEOWN	
3	Nigel WINTERBURN	
4	Paul DAVIS †	
5	Andy LINIGHAN	15
6	Tony ADAMS	
7	Jimmy CARTER	20, 79
8	Steve MORROW	
9	Kevin CAMPBELL	
10	Paul MERSON	16
11	Anders LIMPAR ‡	
	Substitutes	
12	David HILLIER †60	
14	Paul DICKOV ‡67	
Gk	Alan MILLER	

SOUTHAMPTON
Blue shirts, Blue shorts   Goals

1	Tim FLOWERS	
2	Jeff KENNA	
3	Micky ADAMS	30
4	Terry HURLOCK ‡	
5	Richard HALL ❏	
6	Kenneth MONKOU ❏	
7	Matthew LE TISSIER	50
8	Glenn COCKERILL	
9	Iain DOWIE ❏	4
10	Neil MADDISON	
11	Francis BENALI †	
	Substitutes	
12	Nicky BANGER †45	
14	Jason DODD ‡83	
Gk	Ian ANDREWS	

Date	Saturday 20 March 1993
Venue	Villa Park, 3.00pm

ASTON VILLA (1) 2
SHEFFIELD WEDNESDAY (0) 0

Attendance	38,024
Referee	Roger MILFORD
Linesmen	K.J. Hawkes, A.J. Martin

ASTON VILLA
Claret & Blue shirts, White shorts   Goals

1	Mark BOSNICH	
2	Earl BARRETT	
3	Steve STAUNTON	
4	Shaun TEALE	
5	Paul McGRATH	
6	Kevin RICHARDSON	
7	Ray HOUGHTON	
8	Garry PARKER	
9	Dean SAUNDERS	
10	Dwight YORKE	2, 56
11	Cyrille REGIS	
	Substitutes	
12	Neil COX	
14	Bryan SMALL	
Gk	Nigel SPINK	

SHEFFIELD WEDNESDAY
Blue & White shirts, Black shorts   Goals

1	Chris WOODS	
2	Roland NILSSON	
3	Nigel WORTHINGTON	
4	Carlton PALMER	
5	Simon STEWART †	
6	Viv ANDERSON	
7	Danny WILSON	
8	Chris WADDLE	
9	Paul WARHURST	
10	Mark BRIGHT	
11	John SHERIDAN	
	Substitutes	
12	Graham HYDE †56	
14	Nigel JEMSON	
Gk	Kevin PRESSMAN	

Date	Saturday 20 March 1993
Venue	Ewood Park, 3.00pm

BLACKBURN ROVERS (1) 1
MIDDLESBROUGH (1) 1

Attendance	14,041
Referee	Gerald ASHBY
Linesmen	R.H. Andrews, E. Lomas

BLACKBURN ROVERS
Blue & White shirts, White shorts   Goals

1	Bobby MIMMS	
2	David MAY	
3	Henning BERG	
4	Lee MAKEL	
5	Colin HENDRY	
6	Kevin MORAN	
7	Stuart RIPLEY	
8	Mark ATKINS	23
9	Steve LIVINGSTONE	
10	Patrik ANDERSSON ‡	
11	Jason WILCOX	
	Substitutes	
12	Nick MARKER	
14	Roy WEGERLE ‡75	
Gk	Darren COLLIER	

MIDDLESBROUGH
Red shirts, Black shorts   Goals

1	Ian IRONSIDE	
2	Chris MORRIS ‡	
3	Jimmy PHILLIPS	
4	Nicky MOHAN ❏	
5	Andy PEAKE	
6	Derek WHYTE	
7	Tommy WRIGHT	
8	Robbie MUSTOE	
9	Paul WILKINSON	
10	Willie FALCONER	
11	John HENDRIE	32
	Substitutes	
12	Craig HIGNETT	
14	Chris KAMARA ‡77	
Gk	Andy COLLETT	

Date	Saturday 20 March 1993
Venue	Stamford Bridge, 3.00pm

CHELSEA (0) 1
TOTTENHAM HOTSPUR (1) 1

Attendance	25,157
Referee	Roger DILKES
Linesmen	M.K. Bullivant, W.M. Jordan

CHELSEA
Blue shirts, Blue shorts   Goals

1	Dave BEASANT	
2	Steve CLARKE	
3	Frank SINCLAIR	
4	Andy TOWNSEND	
5	Erland JOHNSEN	
6	Mal DONAGHY	
7	Graham STUART ‡	
8	John SPENCER	
9	Tony CASCARINO	52
10	Eddie NEWTON	
11	Dennis WISE ❑	
	Substitutes	
12	Gareth HALL	
14	Darren BARNARD ‡68	
Gk	Kevin HITCHCOCK	

TOTTENHAM HOTSPUR
White shirts, Navy Blue shorts   Goals

1	Erik THORSTVEDT	
2	Dean AUSTIN	
3	Justin EDINBURGH	
4	Andy GRAY ❑	
5	Stuart NETHERCOTT ❑	
6	Neil RUDDOCK	
7	Kevin WATSON ‡	
8	NAYIM	
9	Darren ANDERTON	
10	Teddy SHERINGHAM	31p
11	Andy TURNER †	
	Substitutes	
12	Danny HILL †73	
14	Gudni BERGSSON ‡68	
Gk	Kevin DEARDEN	

Date	Saturday 20 March 1993
Venue	Portman Road, 3.00pm

IPSWICH TOWN (0) 0
COVENTRY CITY (0) 0

Attendance	16,698
Referee	Joe WORRALL
Linesmen	G.P. Barber, I.M.D. Mitchell

IPSWICH TOWN
Blue & White shirts, White shorts   Goals

1	Clive BAKER	
2	Gavin JOHNSON	
3	Phil WHELAN	
4	Mick STOCKWELL	
5	John WARK	
6	David LINIGHAN	
7	Geraint WILLIAMS	
8	Bontcho GUENTCHEV	
9	Paul GODDARD †	
10	Jason DOZZELL	
11	Chris KIWOMYA	
	Substitutes	
12	Steve WHITTON †75	
14	Vlado BOZINOSKI	
Gk	Craig FORREST	

COVENTRY CITY
Red shirts, White shorts   Goals

1	Steve OGRIZOVIC	
2	Brian BORROWS	
3	Phil BABB	
4	Peter ATHERTON	
5	David BUSST	
6	John WILLIAMS	
7	Peter NDLOVU	
8	Kevin GALLACHER	
9	David RENNIE	
10	Mick QUINN	
11	Lee HURST	
	Substitutes	
12	Lloyd McGRATH	
14	Leigh JENKINSON	
Gk	Jonathan GOULD	

Date   Saturday 20 March 1993
Venue Anfield, 3.00pm

LIVERPOOL (0) 1
EVERTON (0) 0

Attendance 44,619
Referee   Philip DON
Linesmen   D.T. Colwell, J. Hilditch

LIVERPOOL
Red shirts, Red shorts   Goals

1	David JAMES	
2	David BURROWS	
3	Steve HARKNESS	
4	Steve NICOL	
5	Mark WRIGHT ‡	
6	Ronnie WHELAN	
7	Steve McMANAMAN †	
8	Don HUTCHISON	
9	Ian RUSH	
10	John BARNES	
11	Mark WALTERS	
	Substitutes	
12	Ronnie ROSENTHAL †74	90
14	Jan MOLBY ‡11	
Gk	Mike HOOPER	

EVERTON
Blue shirts, White shorts   Goals

1	Neville SOUTHALL	
2	Matthew JACKSON	
3	Andy HINCHCLIFFE	
4	Ian SNODIN ❑	
5	Dave WATSON	
6	Gary ABLETT	
7	Mark WARD †	
8	Peter BEARDSLEY	
9	Tony COTTEE	
10	Billy KENNY ‡	
11	John EBBRELL	
	Substitutes	
12	PREKI †63	
14	Stuart BARLOW ‡52	
Gk	Jason KEARTON	

Date   Saturday 20 March 1993
Venue Maine Road, 11.00am

MANCHESTER CITY (0) 1
MANCHESTER UNITED (0) 1

Attendance 37,136
Referee   Robbie HART
Linesmen   J. McGrath, E.J. Walsh

MANCHESTER CITY
Light Blue shirts, White shorts   Goals

1	Tony COTON	
2	Andy HILL ⟍	
3	Terry PHELAN	
4	Peter REID ❑	
5	Keith CURLE ❑	
6	Michel VONK	
7	David WHITE	
8	Mike SHERON	
9	Niall QUINN	57
10	Garry FLITCROFT	
11	Rick HOLDEN	
	Substitutes	
12	Mike QUIGLEY	
14	Kare INGEBRIGTSEN	
Gk	Martyn MARGETSON	

MANCHESTER UNITED
Red shirts, Black shorts   Goals

1	Peter SCHMEICHEL	
2	Paul PARKER	
3	Denis IRWIN	
4	Steve BRUCE	
5	Lee SHARPE	
6	Gary PALLISTER	
7	Eric CANTONA	68
8	Paul INCE	
9	Brian McCLAIR	
10	Mark HUGHES ❑	
11	Ryan GIGGS	
	Substitutes	
12	Bryan ROBSON	
14	Andrei KANCHELSKIS	
Gk	Les SEALEY	

Date   Saturday 20 March 1993
Venue   Boundary Park, 3.00pm

OLDHAM ATHLETIC (1) 2
QPR (0) 2

Attendance   10,946
Referee   Martin BODENHAM
Linesmen   M. Fletcher, M.A. Riley

OLDHAM ATHLETIC
Blue shirts, Blue shorts   Goals

1	Paul GERRARD	
2	Gunnar HALLE	
3	Neil POINTON ❏	
4	Nick HENRY	1
5	Richard JOBSON	
6	Craig FLEMING	
7	Neil ADAMS	88
8	Ian MARSHALL ‡	
9	Ian OLNEY	
10	Mike MILLIGAN	
11	Mark BRENNAN †	

Substitutes

12	Roger PALMER †45	
14	Paul BERNARD ‡17	
Gk	John KEELEY	

QPR
Black & Red hooped shirts, Black shorts   Goals

1	Tony ROBERTS	
2	David BARDSLEY	
3	Clive WILSON	
4	Maurice DOYLE	
5	Darren PEACOCK	
6	Alan McDONALD	
7	Andy IMPEY	
8	Ian HOLLOWAY	
9	Les FERDINAND ❏	
10	Bradley ALLEN	68
11	Andy SINTON ‡	73

Substitutes

12	Dennis BAILEY	
14	Karl READY ‡86	
Gk	Jan STEJSKAL	

Date   Saturday 20 March 1993
Venue   Bramall Lane, 3.00pm

SHEFFIELD UNITED (0) 0
CRYSTAL PALACE (1) 1

Attendance   18,857
Referee   John MARTIN
Linesmen   J.B. Robinson, R.R. Richards

SHEFFIELD UNITED
Red & White striped shirts, White shorts   Goals

1	Alan KELLY	
2	Tom COWAN	
3	Dane WHITEHOUSE	
4	Paul BEESLEY †	
5	Brian GAYLE	
6	John PEMBERTON	
7	Adrian LITTLEJOHN ❏	
8	Charlie HARTFIELD ‡	
9	Paul ROGERS	
10	Alan CORK	
11	Mitch WARD	

Substitutes

12	Carl BRADSHAW †69	
14	Jamie HOYLAND ‡62	
Gk	Phil KITE	

CRYSTAL PALACE
Yellow shirts, Light Blue shorts   Goals

1	Nigel MARTYN	
2	Richard SHAW	
3	Gareth SOUTHGATE	
4	Chris COLEMAN	44
5	Eric YOUNG ❏	
6	Andy THORN	
7	Simon OSBORN	
8	Geoff THOMAS	
9	Chris ARMSTRONG ■	
10	Simon RODGER	
11	Eddie McGOLDRICK ❏	

Substitutes

12	Paul WILLIAMS	
14	George NDAH	
Gk	Andy WOODMAN	

| *Date* | Saturday 20 March 1993 |
| *Venue* | Selhurst Park, 3.00pm |

WIMBLEDON (2) 3
NORWICH CITY (0) 0

Attendance	10,875
Referee	Keith COOPER
Linesmen	D.G. Madgwick, B.A. Wigginton

WIMBLEDON
Blue shirts, Blue shorts   Goals

1	Hans SEGERS	
2	Roger JOSEPH	
3	Gary ELKINS ❑	
4	Vinnie JONES ❑	
5	John SCALES	
6	Brian McALLISTER ❑	
7	Neal ARDLEY	29
8	Robbie EARLE	
9	John FASHANU	
10	Dean HOLDSWORTH	16, 82
11	Gerald DOBBS	
	Substitutes	
12	Andy CLARKE	
14	Lawrie SANCHEZ	
Gk	Perry DIGWEED	

NORWICH CITY
Yellow shirts, Green shorts   Goals

1	Bryan GUNN	
2	Ian CULVERHOUSE	
3	Mark BOWEN	
4	Chris SUTTON	
5	John POLSTON	
6	David SMITH	
7	Ian CROOK	
8	Colin WOODTHORPE ‡	
9	Mark ROBINS	
10	Ruel FOX	
11	David PHILLIPS	
	Substitutes	
12	Jeremy GOSS	
14	Lee POWER ‡68 ❑	
Gk	Mark WALTON	

| *Date* | Sunday 21 March 1993 |
| *Venue* | City Ground, 4.00pm |

NOTTINGHAM FOREST (1) 1
LEEDS UNITED (1) 1

Attendance	25,148
Referee	Ray LEWIS
Linesmen	J.A. Elwin, R.R. Rawson

NOTTINGHAM FOREST
Red shirts, White shorts   Goals

1	Mark CROSSLEY	
2	Gary CHARLES	
3	Steve CHETTLE	
4	Steve STONE	
5	Carl TILER ❑	
6	Roy KEANE	
7	Kingsley BLACK	
8	Gary BANNISTER	
9	Nigel CLOUGH ❑	25p
10	Robert ROSARIO	
11	Ian WOAN	
	Substitutes	
12	Brian LAWS	
14	Thorvaldur ORLYGSSON	
Gk	Andy MARRIOTT	

LEEDS UNITED
White shorts, White shorts   Goals

1	John LUKIC ❑	
2	David KERSLAKE	
3	Tony DORIGO	
4	David BATTY	
5	David WETHERALL ❑	
6	Jon NEWSOME	
7	David ROCASTLE	
8	Rod WALLACE ❑ ‡	13
9	Lee CHAPMAN	
10	Steve HODGE ❑	
11	Gary SPEED ❑	
	Substitutes	
12	Mark TINKLER	
14	Jamie FORRESTER ‡79	
Gk	Mervyn DAY	

Date	Monday 22 March 1993
Venue	Ayresome Park, 7.30pm

MIDDLESBROUGH (0) 2
OLDHAM ATHLETIC (2) 3

Attendance	12,290
Referee	Kelvin MORTON
Linesmen	P.M. Roberts, J.B. Robinson

MIDDLESBROUGH
Red shirts, White shorts   Goals

1	Ian IRONSIDE	
2	Curtis FLEMING	
3	Jimmy PHILLIPS	
4	Nicky MOHAN	83
5	Andy PEAKE †	
6	Derek WHYTE	
7	John HENDRIE	
8	Robbie MUSTOE	
9	Paul WILKINSON	
10	Willie FALCONER ❏	
11	Tommy WRIGHT	
	Substitutes	
12	Chris KAMARA †67	
14	Craig HIGNETT ‡45	88
Gk	Andy COLLETT	

OLDHAM ATHLETIC
Blue shirts, Blue shorts   Goals

1	Paul GERRARD	
2	Gunnar HALLE	
3	Neil POINTON	
4	Nick HENRY	
5	Richard JOBSON	
6	Craig FLEMING	
7	Neil ADAMS	
8	Andy RITCHIE ❏	85
9	Ian OLNEY	34
10	Mike MILLIGAN	
11	Paul BERNARD	29
	Substitutes	
12	Neil TOLSON	
14	Neil McDONALD	
Gk	John KEELEY	

Date	Tuesday 23 March 1993
Venue	Selhurst Park, 8.00pm

CRYSTAL PALACE (0) 1
LIVERPOOL (0) 1

Attendance	18,688
Referee	Roger DILKES
Linesmen	W.M. Jordan, M.K. Bullivant

CRYSTAL PALACE
Red & Blue striped shirts, Red shorts   Goals

1	Nigel MARTYN	
2	Richard SHAW ‡	
3	Gareth SOUTHGATE	
4	Chris COLEMAN	
5	Eric YOUNG	
6	Andy THORN	
7	Simon OSBORN	
8	Geoff THOMAS	
9	Chris ARMSTRONG	78
10	Simon RODGER	
11	Eddie McGOLDRICK	
	Substitutes	
12	Paul WILLIAMS	
14	George NDAH ‡74	
Gk	Andy WOODMAN	

LIVERPOOL
Green shirts, Green shorts   Goals

1	David JAMES	
2	David BURROWS ❏	
3	Steve HARKNESS	
4	Steve NICOL	
5	Mike MARSH	
6	Ronnie WHELAN	
7	Ronnie ROSENTHAL †	
8	Don HUTCHISON ❏	
9	Ian RUSH	49
10	John BARNES	
11	Mark WALTERS	
	Substitutes	
12	Steve McMANAMAN †64	
14	Stig Inge BJORNEBYE	
Gk	Mike HOOPER	

Date	Wednesday 24 March 1993
Venue	Highfield Road, 7.45pm

COVENTRY CITY (1) 1
SHEFFIELD UNITED (0) 3

Attendance	12,993
Referee	Philip WRIGHT
Linesmen	M.E. Alexander, B.A. Wigginton

COVENTRY CITY
Sky Blue shirts, Sky Blue shorts — Goals

		Goals
1	Steve OGRIZOVIC	
2	Brian BORROWS	
3	Phil BABB	
4	Peter ATHERTON	
5	David BUSST	
6	David RENNIE	
7	Peter NDLOVU	
8	Lee HURST	
9	Mick QUINN	
10	Michael GYNN	
11	John WILLIAMS	17
	Substitutes	
12	Lloyd McGRATH	
14	Leigh JENKINSON	
Gk	Jonathan GOULD	

SHEFFIELD UNITED
Red & White striped shirts, Black shorts — Goals

		Goals
1	Alan KELLY	
2	Kevin GAGE	
3	Tom COWAN ‡	
4	John GANNON	
5	Brian GAYLE	
6	John PEMBERTON	
7	Franz CARR †	
8	Dane WHITEHOUSE ❏	69
9	Alan CORK	
10	Brian DEANE	75
11	Mitch WARD	
	Substitutes	
12	Jamie HOYLAND †69	
14	Adrian LITTLEJOHN ‡45	87
Gk	Phil KITE	

Date	Wednesday 24 March 1993
Venue	Goodison Park, 7.30pm

EVERTON (1) 3
IPSWICH TOWN (0) 0

Attendance	15,638
Referee	Brian HILL
Linesmen	A. Streets, D.S. Oliver

EVERTON
Blue shirts, White shorts — Goals

		Goals
1	Neville SOUTHALL	
2	Paul HOLMES	
3	Andy HINCHCLIFFE	
4	Ian SNODIN †	
5	Dave WATSON	
6	Matthew JACKSON	49
7	Mark WARD ‡	
8	Peter BEARDSLEY	
9	Tony COTTEE	66
10	John EBBRELL	
11	Stuart BARLOW	18
	Substitutes	
12	Peter BEAGRIE †46	
14	Paul RIDEOUT ‡76	
Gk	Jason KEARTON	

IPSWICH TOWN
Red & Black striped shirts, Black shorts — Goals

		Goals
1	Clive BAKER	
2	Gavin JOHNSON	
3	Phil WHELAN †	
4	Mick STOCKWELL	
5	John WARK	
6	David LINIGHAN	
7	Geraint WILLIAMS	
8	Bontcho GUENTCHEV	
9	Paul GODDARD	
10	Jason DOZZELL	
11	Chris KIWOMYA	
	Substitutes	
12	Eddie YOUDS †61 ❏	
14	Vlado BOZINOSKI	
Gk	Andy PETTERSON	

Date	Wednesday 24 March, 1993
Venue	Elland Road, 7.30pm

LEEDS UNITED (1) 1
CHELSEA (0) 1

Attendance	28,135
Referee	Alan WILKIE
Linesmen	A. Black, I. Blanchard

LEEDS UNITED
White shirts, White shorts   Goals

1	John LUKIC	
2	David KERSLAKE	
3	Tony DORIGO †	
4	David BATTY	
5	David WETHERALL ❏	43
6	Jon NEWSOME	
7	David ROCASTLE	
8	Rod WALLACE	
9	Lee CHAPMAN ‡	
10	Steve HODGE	
11	Gary SPEED	
	Substitutes	
12	Gordon STRACHAN †44	
14	Frank STRANDLI ‡75	
Gk	Mervyn DAY	

CHELSEA
Blue shirts, Blue shorts   Goals

1	Dave BEASANT	
2	Steve CLARKE	
3	Frank SINCLAIR	
4	Andy TOWNSEND	
5	Erland JOHNSEN	
6	Mal DONAGHY	53
7	Graham STUART	
8	John SPENCER	
9	Tony CASCARINO ■	
10	Eddie NEWTON	
11	Dennis WISE ❏	
	Substitutes	
12	Gareth HALL	
14	Darren BARNARD	
Gk	Dmitri KHARIN	

Date	Wednesday 24 March 1993
Venue	Old Trafford, 8.00pm

MANCHESTER UNITED (0) 0
ARSENAL (0) 0

Attendance	37,301
Referee	Vic CALLOW
Linesmen	G.R. Hamblin, P. Rejer

MANCHESTER UNITED
Red shirts, White shorts   Goals

1	Peter SCHMEICHEL	
2	Paul PARKER	
3	Denis IRWIN	
4	Steve BRUCE	
5	Lee SHARPE	
6	Gary PALLISTER	
7	Eric CANTONA	
8	Paul INCE	
9	Brian McCLAIR	
10	Mark HUGHES †	
11	Ryan GIGGS	
	Substitutes	
12	Bryan ROBSON †77	
14	Andrei KANCHELSKIS	
Gk	Les SEALEY	

ARSENAL
Yellow shirts, Blue shorts   Goals

1	David SEAMAN	
2	Lee DIXON	
3	Martin KEOWN	
4	Steve MORROW	
5	Andy LINIGHAN	
6	Tony ADAMS †	
7	John JENSEN	
8	Ian WRIGHT	
9	Kevin CAMPBELL	
10	Paul MERSON	
11	Jimmy CARTER ‡	
	Substitutes	
12	David HILLIER †89	
14	Ray PARLOUR ‡60	
Gk	Alan MILLER	

Date	Wednesday 24 March 1993
Venue	Carrow Road, 7.45pm

NORWICH CITY (0) 1
ASTON VILLA (0) 0

Attendance	19,528
Referee	Robbie HART
Linesmen	W.J. Norbury, A. Schneider

NORWICH CITY
Yellow shirts, Green shorts   Goals

1	Bryan GUNN	
2	Ian CULVERHOUSE	
3	Mark BOWEN	
4	Chris SUTTON	
5	John POLSTON	81
6	Gary MEGSON	
7	Ian CROOK	
8	Jeremy GOSS	
9	Mark ROBINS †	
10	Ruel FOX	
11	David PHILLIPS	
	Substitutes	
12	Lee POWER †83	
14	Colin WOODTHORPE	
Gk	Mark WALTON	

ASTON VILLA
Claret & Blue shirts, White shorts   Goals

1	Mark BOSNICH	
2	Earl BARRETT	
3	Steve STAUNTON	
4	Shaun TEALE	
5	Paul McGRATH	
6	Kevin RICHARDSON	
7	Ray HOUGHTON	
8	Garry PARKER †	
9	Dean SAUNDERS	
10	Dwight YORKE	
11	Cyrille REGIS	
	Substitutes	
12	Tony DALEY †82	
14	Bryan SMALL	
Gk	Nigel SPINK	

Date	Wednesday 24 March 1993
Venue	Loftus Road, 7.45pm

QPR (0) 0
BLACKBURN ROVERS (1) 3

Attendance	10,677
Referee	Allan GUNN
Linesmen	C. Jones, D.C. Madgwick

QPR
Blue & White hooped shirts, White shorts   Goals

1	Tony ROBERTS	
2	David BARDSLEY	
3	Rufus BREVETT	
4	Clive WILSON	
5	Karl READY	
6	Alan McDONALD	
7	Andy IMPEY	
8	Ian HOLLOWAY	
9	Dennis BAILEY	
10	Bradley ALLEN	
11	Andy SINTON	
	Substitutes	
12	Maurice DOYLE	
14	Tony WITTER	
Gk	Jan STEJSKAL	

BLACKBURN ROVERS
Red & Black striped shirts, Black shorts   Goals

1	Bobby MIMMS	
2	Richard BROWN	
3	Tony DOBSON	
4	Henning BERG	
5	Colin HENDRY	
6	Kevin MORAN	55
7	Stuart RIPLEY	23
8	Gordon COWANS	
9	Mark ATKINS	65
10	Mike NEWELL	
11	Nicky MARKER	
	Substitutes	
12	Lee MAKEL	
14	Patrik ANDERSSON	
Gk	Darren COLLIER	

Date　　Wednesday 24 March 1993
Venue　　Hillsborough, 7.45pm

SHEFFIELD WEDNESDAY (0) 1
WIMBLEDON (0) 1

Attendance　20,918
Referee　　John LLOYD
Linesmen　　M.A. Cooper, T. Heilbron

SHEFFIELD WEDNESDAY
Blue & White striped shirts, Black shorts　　　　Goals

1	Chris WOODS	
2	Roland NILSSON †	
3	Nigel WORTHINGTON	
4	Carlton PALMER	
5	Ryan JONES	
6	Viv ANDERSON	
7	Danny WILSON	
8	Chris WADDLE	
9	Chris BART-WILLIAMS ‡	
10	Mark BRIGHT	76
11	John SHERIDAN	

Substitutes

12	Simon STEWART †50	
14	Nigel JEMSON ‡67	
Gk	Kevin PRESSMAN	

WIMBLEDON
Red shirts, Red shorts　　　　Goals

1	Hans SEGERS	
2	Roger JOSEPH	
3	Gary ELKINS ❑ †	
4	Vinnie JONES	
5	John SCALES	
6	Brian McALLISTER ❑	
7	Neal ARDLEY	
8	Robbie EARLE	
9	John FASHANU ■	
10	Dean HOLDSWORTH	90
11	Gerald DOBBS ‡	

Substitutes

12	Dean BLACKWELL †69	
14	Lawrie SANCHEZ ‡86	
Gk	Perry DIGWEED	

Date　　Wednesday 24 March 1993
Venue　　The Dell, 7.30pm

SOUTHAMPTON (0) 1
NOTTINGHAM FOREST (2) 2

Attendance　18,005
Referee　　Mike REED
Linesmen　　D. Orr, R.E. Budden

SOUTHAMPTON
Red & White striped shirts, Black shorts　　　　Goals

1	Tim FLOWERS	
2	Jeff KENNA	
3	Jason DODD	
4	Terry HURLOCK †	
5	Richard HALL	
6	Kenneth MONKOU	
7	Matthew LE TISSIER	72
8	Nicky BANGER	
9	Iain DOWIE	
10	Neil MADDISON	
11	Francis BENALI ❑	

Substitutes

12	Glenn COCKERILL †45	
14	Matthew BOUND	
Gk	Ian ANDEREWS	

NOTTINGHAM FOREST
White shirts, White shorts　　　　Goals

1	Mark CROSSLEY	
2	Gary CHARLES	
3	Brian LAWS †	
4	Steve STONE	
5	Carl TILER ❑	
6	Roy KEANE	45
7	Kingsley BLACK	
8	Gary BANNISTER	
9	Nigel CLOUGH	5
10	Robert ROSARIO	
11	Ian WOAN	

Substitutes

12	Gary CROSBY †27	
14	Thorvaldur ORLYGSSON	
Gk	Andy MARRIOTT	

Date	Wednesday 24 March 1993
Venue	White Hart Lane, 7.30pm

TOTTENHAM HOTSPUR (2) 3
MANCHESTER CITY (0) 1

Attendance	27,247
Referee	John MARTIN
Linesmen	A.P. D'Urso, S.G. Tomlin

TOTTENHAM HOTSPUR
White shirts, Navy Blue shorts   Goals

1	Erik THORSTVEDT	
2	Dean AUSTIN	
3	Pat VAN DEN HAUWE ❑	
4	Vinny SAMWAYS	
5	Gary MABBUTT	
6	Neil RUDDOCK ‡	
7	Steve SEDGLEY	
8	NAYIM	43
9	Darren ANDERTON †	23
10	Teddy SHERINGHAM	
11	Paul ALLEN	
	Substitutes	
12	Andy TURNER †85	
14	Gudni BERGSSON ‡47	87
Gk	Kevin DEARDEN	

MANCHESTER CITY
Purple shirts, Purple shorts   Goals

1	Tony COTON	
2	Andy HILL	
3	Terry PHELAN ❑	
4	Peter REID	
5	Keith CURLE ❑	
6	Michel VONK	
7	David WHITE ‡	
8	Mike SHERON	60
9	Niall QUINN	
10	Garry FLITCROFT †	
11	Rick HOLDEN	
	Substitutes	
12	Mike QUIGLEY †50	
14	Kare INGEBRIGTSEN ‡69	
Gk	Martyn MARGETSON	

LEAGUE TABLE

Up to and including 24.03.93		P	W	D	L	F	A	Pts
1	Norwich City	36	19	8	9	50	49	65
2	Aston Villa	35	18	10	7	51	33	64
3	Manchester United	35	17	12	6	51	27	63
4	Blackburn Rovers	33	13	11	9	47	33	50
5	Sheffield Wednesday	33	13	11	9	42	37	50
6	Tottenham Hotspur	34	13	10	11	43	49	49
7	Queen's Park Rangers	35	13	9	13	47	45	48
8	Manchester City	34	13	8	13	46	39	47
9	Arsenal	33	13	8	12	33	30	47
10	Coventry City	36	12	11	13	46	47	47
11	Wimbledon	35	12	10	13	44	41	46
12	Liverpool	34	12	10	12	45	44	46
13	Southampton	36	12	10	14	48	49	46
14	Chelsea	35	11	13	11	38	42	46
15	Everton	36	13	6	17	43	45	45
16	Ipswich Town	35	10	15	10	40	42	45
17	Leeds United	34	11	11	12	44	47	44
18	Crystal Palace	34	9	13	12	40	49	40
19	Sheffield United	34	10	7	17	40	44	37
20	Nottingham Forest	34	9	9	16	33	47	36
21	Oldham Athletic	34	9	8	17	46	60	35
22	Middlesbrough	35	8	10	17	42	60	34

LEADING SCORERS

Alan SHEARER	Blackburn Rovers	16
Teddy SHERINGHAM	Tottenham Hotspur	16
Mark ROBINS	Norwich City	14
David WHITE	Manchester City	14
Mick QUINN	Coventry City	14

LEAGUE GOALSCORING FIGURES

Running Totals

Date	Games	Goals	Average	Games	Goals	Average
01.03.93	1	1	1.00	329	841	2.56
02.03.93	2	7	3.50	331	848	2.56
03.03.93	4	8	2.00	335	856	2.55
06.03.93	3	10	3.33	338	866	2.56
07.03.93	1	1	1.00	339	867	2.56
09.03.93	3	3	1.00	342	870	2.54
10.03.93	6	7	1.17	348	877	2.52
13.03.93	7	20	2.86	355	897	2.53
14.03.93	1	2	2.00	356	899	2.52
15.03.93	1	2	2.00	357	901	2.52
17.03.93	1	3	3.00	358	904	2.52
20.03.93	10	24	2.40	368	928	2.52
21.03.93	1	2	2.00	369	930	2.52
22.03.93	1	5	5.00	370	935	2.53
23.03.93	1	2	2.00	371	937	2.52
24.03.93	9	22	2.44	380	959	2.52

Date	Saturday 3 April 1993
Venue	Ewood Park, 3.00pm

BLACKBURN ROVERS (3) 4
LIVERPOOL (0) 1

Attendance	15,032
Referee	Ken REDFERN
Linesmen	D.S. Oliver, B.T. Millership

BLACKBURN ROVERS
Blue & White shirts, White shorts   Goals

1	Bobby MIMMS	
2	David MAY	
3	Graeme LE SAUX	
4	Tim SHERWOOD	
5	Colin HENDRY ❑	
6	Kevin MORAN	25
7	Stuart RIPLEY	
8	Gordon COWANS	
9	Kevin GALLACHER	41
10	Mike NEWELL	13
11	Jason WILCOX	65
	Substitutes	
12	Mark ATKINS	
14	Patrik ANDERSSON	
Gk	Frank TALIA	

LIVERPOOL
Red shirts, Red shorts   Goals

1	David JAMES	
2	Mike MARSH	
3	David BURROWS	
4	Steve NICOL	
5	Steve HARKNESS	
6	Ronnie WHELAN	
7	Ronnie ROSENTHAL †	
8	Don HUTCHISON	
9	Ian RUSH	84
10	John BARNES	
11	Mark WALTERS	
	Substitutes	
12	Steve McMANAMAN †56	
14	Stig Inge BJORNEBYE	
Gk	Bruce GROBBELAAR	

Date	Saturday 3 April 1993
Venue	Stamford Bridge, 3.00pm

CHELSEA (0) 4
MIDDLESBROUGH (0) 0

Attendance	13,043
Referee	Joe WORRALL
Linesmen	C. Jones, I.M.D. Mitchell

CHELSEA
Blue shirts, Blue shorts   Goals

1	Dave BEASANT	
2	Steve CLARKE	
3	Frank SINCLAIR	
4	Andy TOWNSEND	
5	Erland JOHNSEN	
6	Mal DONAGHY	52
7	Graham STUART	73
8	John SPENCER ‡	61
9	Tony CASCARINO	
10	Eddie NEWTON †	
11	Darren BARNARD	89
	Substitutes	
12	Gareth HALL †45	
14	Robert FLECK ‡75	
Gk	Dmitri KHARIN	

MIDDLESBROUGH
Red shirts, White shorts   Goals

1	Ian IRONSIDE	
2	Curtis FLEMING ❑	
3	Jimmy PHILLIPS	
4	Craig HIGNETT †	
5	Alan KERNAGHAN	
6	Derek WHYTE	
7	John HENDRIE	
8	Robbie MUSTOE	
9	Paul WILKINSON	
10	Willie FALCONER	
11	Tommy WRIGHT	
	Substitutes	
12	Nicky MOHAN	
14	Dwight MARSHALL †67	
Gk	Andy COLLETT	

Date Saturday 3 April 1993
Venue Highfield Road, 3.00pm

COVENTRY CITY (1) 2
SOUTHAMPTON (0) 0

Attendance 10,463
Referee Keith COOPER
Linesmen R.H. andrews, E. Lomas

COVENTRY CITY
Sky Blue shirts, Sky Blue shorts   Goals

1	Jonathan GOULD	
2	Brian BORROWS	
3	Phil BABB	
4	Peter ATHERTON	
5	David BUSST	
6	David RENNIE ❑ †	
7	Peter NDLOVU	
8	Lee HURST	
9	Mick QUINN	7p
10	Roy WEGERLE ‡	
11	John WILLIAMS	80
	Substitutes	
12	Lloyd McGRATH †69	
14	Michael GYNN ‡86	
Gk	Steve OGRIZOVIC	

SOUTHAMPTON
Red & White striped shirts, Black shorts   Goals

1	Tim FLOWERS	
2	Jeff KENNA	
3	Micky ADAMS	
4	Terry HURLOCK ❑	
5	Richard HALL	
6	Kevin MOORE	
7	Matthew LE TISSIER	
8	Jason DODD	
9	Iain DOWIE ❑	
10	Neil MADDISON	
11	Francis BENALI ❑ †	
	Substitutes	
12	Nicky BANGER †58	
14	Matthew BOUND	
Gk	Ian ANDREWS	

Date Saturday 3 April 1993
Venue Selhurst Park, 3.00pm

CRYSTAL PALACE (0) 1
QPR (1) 1

Attendance 14,705
Referee Alan WILKIE
Linesmen J.F. Moore, E.J. Walsh

CRYSTAL PALACE
Red & Blue striped shirts, Red shorts   Goals

1	Nigel MARTYN	
2	Richard SHAW	
3	Gareth SOUTHGATE	
4	Chris COLEMAN	
5	George NDAH †	
6	Andy THORN	
7	Simon OSBORN	
8	Geoff THOMAS	
9	Paul WILLIAMS	
10	Simon RODGER	
11	Eddie McGOLDRICK	
	Substitutes	
12	Grant WATTS	
14	Dean GORDON †54	
Gk	Martin THOMAS	

QPR
Blue & White hooped shirts, Blue shorts   Goals

1	Tony ROBERTS	
2	David BARDSLEY	62og
3	Rufus BREVETT	
4	Clive WILSON	
5	Darren PEACOCK	
6	Alan McDONALD	
7	Andy IMPEY	
8	Ian HOLLOWAY	
9	Dennis BAILEY	
10	Bradley ALLEN	23
11	Andy SINTON ‡	
	Substitutes	
12	Karl READY	
14	Devon WHITE ‡75	
Gk	Jan STEJSKAL	

Date	Saturday 3 April 1993
Venue	Maine Road, 3.00pm

MANCHESTER CITY (0) 3
IPSWICH TOWN (1) 1

Attendance	20,680
Referee	Rodger GIFFORD
Linesmen	P.D. Harding, A.J. Martin

MANCHESTER CITY
Light Blue shirts, White shorts   Goals

1	Tony COTON	
2	Ray RANSON	
3	Terry PHELAN	
4	Peter REID	
5	Keith CURLE	
6	Michel VONK	70
7	David WHITE †	
8	Mike SHERON	
9	Niall QUINN	55
10	Garry FLITCROFT	
11	Rick HOLDEN	66
	Substitutes	
12	Mike QUIGLEY	
14	Kare INGEBRIGTSEN †60	
Gk	Andy DIBBLE	

IPSWICH TOWN
Red & Black striped shirts, Black shorts   Goals

1	Clive BAKER	
2	Phil WHELAN ‡	
3	Gavin JOHNSON	2
4	Mick STOCKWELL	
5	John WARK	
6	David LINIGHAN	
7	Geraint WILLIAMS	
8	Bontcho GUENTCHEV	
9	Simon MILTON †	
10	Jason DOZZELL	
11	Chris KIWOMYA	
	Substitutes	
12	Paul GODDARD †80	
14	Vlado BOZINOSKI ‡77	
Gk	Andy PATTERSON	

Date	Saturday 3 April 1993
Venue	Boundary Park, 3.00pm

OLDHAM ATHLETIC (3) 6
WIMBLEDON (0) 2

Attendance	11,606
Referee	John MARTIN
Linesmen	A. Black, J. Leech

OLDHAM ATHLETIC
Blue shirts, Blue shorts   Goals

1	Paul GERRARD	
2	Gunnar HALLE	
3	Neil POINTON	
4	Nick HENRY	
5	Richard JOBSON ❑	
6	Craig FLEMING	
7	Neil ADAMS	73
8	Andy RITCHIE	
9	Ian OLNEY	42, 69
10	Mike MILLIGAN	
11	Paul BERNARD	13
	Substitutes	
12	Darren BECKFORD †57	87
14	Neil McDONALD	
Gk	John KEELEY	

WIMBLEDON
Red shirts, Red shorts   Goals

1	Hans SEGERS	
2	Roger JOSEPH	
3	Peter FEAR	
4	Lawrie SANCHEZ	
5	John SCALES	
6	Dean BLACKWELL	
7	Neal ARDLEY ❑	
8	Robbie EARLE ❑	
9	John FASHANU †	5og
10	Dean HOLDSWORTH	61, 68
11	Gerald DOBBS ❑ ■	
	Substitutes	
12	Steve COTTERILL †79	
14	Scott FITZGERALD	
Gk	Perry DIGWEED	

Date	Sunday 4 April 1993
Venue	City Ground, 3.00pm

NOTTINGHAM FOREST (0) 0
ASTON VILLA (0) 1

Attendance	26,742
Referee	Keith BURGE
Linesmen	P.M. Roberts, J.B. Robinson

NOTTINGHAM FOREST
Red shirts, White shorts   Goals

1	Mark CROSSLEY	
2	Gary CHARLES	
3	Steve CHETTLE	
4	Steve STONE	
5	Carl TILER	
6	Roy KEANE	
7	Kingsley BLACK	
8	Gary BANNISTER	
9	Nigel CLOUGH ❑ †	
10	Robert ROSARIO	
11	Ian WOAN	
	Substitutes	
12	Gary CROSBY †45	
14	Thorvaldur ORLYGSSON	
Gk	Andy MARRIOTT	

ASTON VILLA
White shirts, Black shorts   Goals

1	Mark BOSNICH	
2	Earl BARRETT	
3	Steve STAUNTON	
4	Shaun TEALE ❑	
5	Paul McGRATH	63
6	Kevin RICHARDSON	
7	Ray HOUGHTON	
8	Garry PARKER	
9	Dean SAUNDERS	
10	Dalian ATKINSON	
11	Dwight YORKE †	
	Substitutes	
12	Tony DALEY †76	
14	Neil COX	
Gk	Nigel SPINK	

Date	Monday 5 April 1993
Venue	Carrow Road, 7.45pm

NORWICH CITY (0) 1
MANCHESTER UNITED (3) 3

Attendance	20,582
Referee	Tony WARD
Linesmen	G.P. Barber, M.K. Bullivant

NORWICH CITY
Yellow shirts, Green shorts   Goals

1	Bryan GUNN	
2	Ian CULVERHOUSE	
3	Mark BOWEN	
4	Chris SUTTON	
5	John POLSTON	
6	Gary MEGSON ❑ ‡	
7	Ian CROOK	
8	Jeremy GOSS	
9	Mark ROBINS	61
10	Ruel FOX	
11	David PHILLIPS	
	Substitutes	
12	Lee POWER	
14	Efan EKOKU ‡56	
Gk	Mark WALTON	

MANCHESTER UNITED
Red shirts, White shorts   Goals

1	Peter SCHMEICHEL	
2	Paul PARKER	
3	Denis IRWIN	
4	Steve BRUCE	
5	Lee SHARPE	
6	Gary PALLISTER	
7	Eric CANTONA	21
8	Paul INCE ❑	
9	Brian McCLAIR	
10	Andrei KANCHELSKIS †	20
11	Ryan GIGGS	13
	Substitutes	
12	Bryan ROBSON †73 ❑	
14	Dion DUBLIN	
Gk	Les SEALEY	

Date	Tuesday 6 April 1993
Venue	Portman Road, 7.45pm

IPSWICH TOWN (1) 1
CHELSEA (0) 1

Attendance	17,444
Referee	John LLOYD
Linesmen	M.G. Wright, G. Butland

● *Moved from 6 March*

IPSWICH TOWN
Blue & White shirts, White shorts   Goals

1	Clive BAKER	
2	Eddie YOUDS	
3	Gavin JOHNSON	
4	Mick STOCKWELL	
5	John WARK	
6	David LINIGHAN	
7	Geraint WILLIAMS	
8	Bontcho GUENTCHEV	38
9	Simon MILTON ‡	
10	Jason DOZZELL	
11	Chris KIWOMYA	
	Substitutes	
12	Phil WHELAN	
14	Vlado BOZINOSKI ‡77	
Gk	Andy PETTERSON	

CHELSEA
White shirts, Red shorts   Goals

1	Dave BEASANT	
2	Steve CLARKE	
3	Frank SINCLAIR	
4	Andy TOWNSEND	
5	Erland JOHNSEN	
6	Mal DONAGHY	
7	Graham STUART	
8	John SPENCER ❑	58
9	Tony CASCARINO	
10	Gareth HALL	
11	Dennis WISE	
	Substitutes	
12	Darren BARNARD	
14	Robert FLECK	
Gk	Dmitri KHARIN	

Date	Tuesday 6 April 1993
Venue	Ayresome Park, 7.45pm

MIDDLESBROUGH (1) 1
ARSENAL (0) 0

Attendance	12,726
Referee	Keith HACKETT
Linesmen	N.S. Barry, T.J. Stevens

● *Moved from 17 April due to Arsenal being in Lge Cup Final*

MIDDLESBROUGH
Red shirts, White shorts   Goals

1	Stephen PEARS	
2	Curtis FLEMING	
3	Jimmy PHILLIPS	
4	Alan KERNAGHAN	
5	Nicky MOHAN	
6	Andy PEAKE ❑	
7	John HENDRIE	32
8	Graham KAVANAGH	
9	Paul WILKINSON	
10	Jamie POLLOCK ❑	
11	Craig HIGNETT	
	Substitutes	
12	Derek WHYTE	
14	Alan MOORE	
Gk	Ian IRONSIDE	

ARSENAL
Yellow shirts, Blue shorts   Goals

1	David SEAMAN	
2	David O'LEARY †	
3	Nigel WINTERBURN	
4	David HILLIER ‡	
5	Andy LINIGHAN	
6	Tony ADAMS	
7	John JENSEN	•
8	Ian WRIGHT	
9	Alan SMITH	
10	Jimmy CARTER	
11	Anders LIMPAR	
	Substitutes	
12	Martin KEOWN †78	
14	Steve MORROW ‡6	
Gk	Alan MILLER	

Date	Tuesday 6 April 1993
Venue	Bramall Lane, 7.45pm

SHEFFIELD UNITED (1) 2
LEEDS UNITED (1) 1

Attendance	20,562
Referee	Keren BARRATT
Linesmen	G.R. Hamblin, E. Lomas

● *Game moved from 7 March*

SHEFFIELD UNITED
Red & White striped shirts, White shorts   Goals

1	Alan KELLY	
2	Kevin GAGE	
3	Dane WHITEHOUSE	
4	John GANNON	
5	Brian GAYLE	
6	John PEMBERTON ❑	
7	Carl BRADSHAW ❑	
8	Paul BEESLEY	
9	Paul ROGERS	24
10	Brian DEANE	86
11	Glyn HODGES ‡	
	Substitutes	
12	Jamie HOYLAND	
14	Alan CORK ‡80	
Gk	Jim LEIGHTON	

LEEDS UNITED
Yellow shirts, Yellow shorts   Goals

1	John LUKIC	
2	David KERSLAKE	
3	Dylan KERR	
4	Mark TINKLER	
5	David WETHERALL	
6	Chris WHYTE	
7	Gordon STRACHAN	
8	Jamie FORRESTER	
9	Frank STRANDLI ❑	34
10	Gary McALLISTER ‡	
11	Gary SPEED	
	Substitutes	
12	Carl SHUTT	
14	Steve HODGE ‡84	
Gk	Mervyn DAY	

Date	Wednesday 7 April 1993
Venue	City Ground, 7.30pm

NOTTINGHAM FOREST (0) 1
BLACKBURN ROVERS (1) 3

Attendance	20,467
Referee	Tony WARD
Linesmen	M.A. Cooper, A. Streets

● *Game moved from 10 February*

NOTTINGHAM FOREST
Red shirts, White shorts   Goals

1	Mark CROSSLEY	
2	Gary CHARLES ■	
3	Steve CHETTLE	
4	Steve STONE	
5	Carl TILER	
6	Roy KEANE	
7	Gary BANNISTER	
8	Scot GEMMILL	
9	Nigel CLOUGH	51p
10	Robert ROSARIO	
11	Kingsley BLACK	
	Substitutes	
12	Thorvaldur ORLYGSSON	
14	Brett WILLIAMS	
Gk	Andy MARRIOTT	

BLACKBURN ROVERS
Blue & White shirts, Blue shorts   Goals

1	Bobby MIMMS	
2	David MAY	
3	Graeme LE SAUX	
4	Tim SHERWOOD	
5	Colin HENDRY	
6	Kevin MORAN	
7	Stuart RIPLEY ‡	67
8	Nicky MARKER †	
9	Kevin GALLACHER ❑	
10	Mike NEWELL	76
11	Jason WILCOX ❑	7
	Substitutes	
12	Mark ATKINS †73	
14	Henning BERG ‡79	
Gk	Frank TALIA	

Date	Wednesday 7 April 1993
Venue	Boundary Park, 7.45pm

OLDHAM ATHLETIC (1) 1
SHEFFIELD WEDNESDAY (0) 1

Attendance	12,312
Referee	Alan WILKIE
Linesmen	A. Black, I. Blanchard

● *Game moved from 6 March*

OLDHAM ATHLETIC
Blue shirts, Blue shorts   Goals

1	Paul GERRARD	
2	Gunnar HALLE	
3	Neil POINTON	13
4	Andy BARLOW	
5	Richard JOBSON	
6	Craig FLEMING	
7	Neil ADAMS	
8	Darren BECKFORD ❏	
9	Ian OLNEY	.
10	Mike MILLIGAN	
11	Paul BERNARD	
	Substitutes	
12	Orfeo KEIZERWEERD	
14	Mark BRENNAN	
Gk	John KEELEY	

SHEFFIELD WEDNESDAY
Yellow shirts, Yellow shorts   Goals

1	Chris WOODS	
2	Roland NILSSON	
3	Nigel WORTHINGTON	
4	Simon STEWART ❏	
5	John HARKES †	
6	Viv ANDERSON	
7	Graham HYDE	
8	Chris WADDLE ‡	
9	Ryan JONES ❏	
10	Nigel JEMSON	
11	Gordon WATSON	65
	Substitutes	
12	Chris BART-WILLIAMS †55	
14	Phil KING ‡88	
Gk	Kevin PRESSMAN	

Date	Friday 9 April 1993
Venue	White Hart Lane, 12 noon

TOTTENHAM HOTSPUR (2) 5
NORWICH CITY (0) 1

Attendance	31,425
Referee	Keren BARRATT
Linesmen	G.T. Pearson, P.A. Vosper

TOTTENHAM HOTSPUR
White shirts, Navy Blue shorts   Goals

1	Erik THORSTVEDT	
2	Dean AUSTIN	
3	Justin EDINBURGH	
4	Nick BARMBY †	55
5	Gary MABBUTT	
6	Neil RUDDOCK	27
7	Steve SEDGLEY	
8	NAYIM	83
9	Darren ANDERTON ‡	
10	Teddy SHERINGHAM	30, 77
11	Paul ALLEN ❏	
	Substitutes	
12	Stuart NETHERCOTT †79	
14	Andy TURNER ‡79	
Gk	Kevin DEARDEN	

NORWICH CITY
Yellow shirts, Green shorts   Goals

1	Bryan GUNN	
2	Ian CULVERHOUSE	
3	Mark BOWEN	
4	Chris SUTTON ❏	
5	John POLSTON	
6	Gary MEGSON	
7	Ian CROOK	
8	Jeremy GOSS ❏	
9	Mark ROBINS	
10	Ruel FOX	
11	David PHILLIPS †	
	Substitutes	
12	Efan EKOKU †45	86
14	Ian BUTTERWORTH	
Gk	Mark WALTON	

Date	Friday 9 April 1993
Venue	Selhurst Park, 3.00pm

WIMBLEDON (2) 4
CRYSTAL PALACE (0) 0

Attendance	12,275
Referee	Vic CALLOW
Linesmen	W.M. Jordan, A. Schneider

WIMBLEDON
Blue shirts, Blue shorts   Goals

1	Hans SEGERS	
2	Roger JOSEPH	
3	Warren BARTON	
4	Lawrie SANCHEZ	
5	John SCALES	
6	Scott FITZGERALD	
7	Neal ARDLEY	
8	Robbie EARLE	20, 53
9	Gerald DOBBS	
10	Dean HOLDSWORTH †	24, 46
11	Andy CLARKE ‡	
	Substitutes	
12	Dean BLACKWELL †79	
14	Paul MILLER ‡79	
Gk	Perry DIGWEED	

CRYSTAL PALACE
Red & Blue striped shirts, Red shorts   Goals

1	Nigel MARTYN	
2	Richard SHAW	
3	Gareth SOUTHGATE	
4	Chris COLEMAN	
5	Dean GORDON	
6	Andy THORN ☐ ‡	
7	Simon OSBORN †	
8	Geoff THOMAS	
9	Paul WILLIAMS	
10	Simon RODGER	
11	Eddie McGOLDRICK	
	Substitutes	
12	John HUMPHREY †45	
14	Grant WATTS ‡85	
Gk	Martin THOMAS	

Date	Friday 9 April 1993
Venue	Bramall Lane, 7.00pm

SHEFFIELD UNITED (0) 1
MANCHESTER CITY (1) 1

Attendance	18,231
Referee	Keith COOPER
Linesmen	M. Fletcher, G.R. Hamblin

SHEFFIELD UNITED
Red & White striped shirts, White shorts   Goals

1	Alan KELLY	
2	Kevin GAGE	
3	Dane WHITEHOUSE	
4	John GANNON	
5	Brian GAYLE	
6	John PEMBERTON	8og
7	Carl BRADSHAW	
8	Paul BEESLEY	
9	Paul ROGERS	
10	Brian DEANE	69
11	Glyn HODGES ‡	
	Substitutes	
12	Jamie HOYLAND	
14	Alan CORK ‡90	
Gk	Jim LEIGHTON	

MANCHESTER CITY
Light Blue shirts, Light Blue shorts   Goals

1	Tony COTON	
2	Ray RANSON	
3	Terry PHELAN	
4	Peter REID	
5	Kare INGEBRIGTSEN	
6	Michel VONK	
7	David WHITE	
8	Mike SHERON	
9	Niall QUINN	
10	Garry FLITCROFT	
11	Rick HOLDEN	
	Substitutes	
12	Fitzroy SIMPSON	
14	Mike QUIGLEY	
Gk	Martyn MARGETSON	

Date	Saturday 10 April 1993
Venue	Villa Park, 3.00pm

ASTON VILLA (0) 0
COVENTRY CITY (0) 0

Attendance	38,543
Referee	Allan GUNN
Linesmen	P.D. Harding, B.L. Polkey

ASTON VILLA
Claret & Blue shirts, White shorts   Goals

1	Mark BOSNICH	
2	Earl BARRETT	
3	Steve STAUNTON	
4	Shaun TEALE	
5	Paul McGRATH	
6	Kevin RICHARDSON	
7	Ray HOUGHTON	
8	Garry PARKER	
9	Dean SAUNDERS	
10	Dalian ATKINSON	
11	Dwight YORKE †	
	Substitutes	
12	Tony DALEY †83	
14	Bryan SMALL	
Gk	Nigel SPINK	

COVENTRY CITY
Sky Blue shirts, Sky Blue shorts   Goals

1	Jonathan GOULD	
2	Brian BORROWS	
3	Phil BABB	
4	Peter ATHERTON	
5	Michael GYNN	
6	David RENNIE	
7	Lloyd McGRATH	
8	Lee HURST	
9	Mick QUINN	
10	Roy WEGERLE ‡	
11	John WILLIAMS	
	Substitutes	
12	David BUSST	
14	Leigh JENKINSON ‡67	
Gk	Steve OGRIZOVIC	

Date	Saturday 10 April 1993
Venue	Portman Road, 3.00pm

IPSWICH TOWN (1) 1
ARSENAL (1) 2

Attendance	20,358
Referee	Ray LEWIS
Linesmen	J.A. Elwin, W.J. Norbury

IPSWICH TOWN
Blue & White shirts, White shorts   Goals

1	Clive BAKER	
2	Eddie YOUDS ❑	
3	Gavin JOHNSON	
4	Geraint WILLIAMS	
5	John WARK	27p
6	David LINIGHAN	
7	Steve WHITTON	
8	Bontcho GUENTCHEV	
9	Simon MILTON ❑	
10	Jason DOZZELL	
11	Chris KIWOMYA	
	Substitutes	
12	Vlado BOZINOSKI	
14	Phil WHELAN	
Gk	Andy PETTERSON	

ARSENAL
Red & White shirts, White shorts   Goals

1	David SEAMAN	
2	David O'LEARY †	
3	Nigel WINTERBURN ❑	
4	Steve MORROW	
5	Andy LINIGHAN	
6	Martin KEOWN	
7	John JENSEN ‡	
8	Kevin CAMPBELL	
9	Alan SMITH	2
10	Paul MERSON	87
11	Jimmy CARTER	
	Substitutes	
12	Tony ADAMS †76	
14	Ray PARLOUR ‡76 ❑	
Gk	Alan MILLER	

Date	Saturday 10 April 1993
Venue	Elland Road, 3.00pm

LEEDS UNITED (2) 5
BLACKBURN ROVERS (0) 2

Attendance	31,791
Referee	David ELLERAY
Linesmen	M.A. Cooper, W.J. Nattrass

LEEDS UNITED
White shirts, White shorts · Goals

1	John LUKIC	
2	David KERSLAKE	
3	Dylan KERR	
4	Mark TINKLER	
5	Chris FAIRCLOUGH	
6	Chris WHYTE ❑	
7	Gordon STRACHAN	8p, 26p, 50
8	Rod WALLACE	67
9	Lee CHAPMAN	89
10	Jamie FORRESTER †	
11	Gary SPEED	
	Substitutes	
12	Jon NEWSOME †90	
14	Steve HODGE	
Gk	Mervyn DAY	

BLACKBURN ROVERS
Red & Black striped shirts, Black shorts · Goals

1	Bobby MIMMS	
2	David MAY ❑	
3	Graeme LE SAUX	
4	Tim SHERWOOD	
5	Colin HENDRY	
6	Kevin MORAN	
7	Stuart RIPLEY	
8	Patrik ANDERSSON †	
9	Kevin GALLACHER	72
10	Mike NEWELL ❑	
11	Jason WILCOX	
	Substitutes	
12	Mark ATKINS †64	85
14	Tony DOBSON	
Gk	Frank TALIA	

Date	Saturday 10 April 1993
Venue	Anfield, 3.00pm

LIVERPOOL (0) 1
OLDHAM ATHLETIC (0) 0

Attendance	36,129
Referee	Joe WORRALL
Linesmen	D.E. Binsley, G.I. Grandidge

LIVERPOOL
Red shirts, Red shorts · Goals

1	David JAMES	
2	Rob JONES	
3	David BURROWS	
4	Steve NICOL	
5	Mark WRIGHT	
6	Ronnie WHELAN	
7	Steve McMANAMAN †	
8	Don HUTCHISON	
9	Ian RUSH	60
10	John BARNES	
11	Mark WALTERS	
	Substitutes	
12	Ronnie ROSENTHAL †64	
14	Torben PIECHNIK	
Gk	Mike HOOPER	

OLDHAM ATHLETIC
Blue shirts, Blue shorts · Goals

1	Paul GERRARD	
2	Gunnar HALLE	
3	Neil POINTON	
4	Andy BARLOW	
5	Richard JOBSON	
6	Craig FLEMING	
7	Neil ADAMS	
8	Darren BECKFORD	
9	Ian OLNEY †	
10	Mike MILLIGAN ‡	
11	Paul BERNARD	
	Substitutes	
12	Orfeo KEIZERWEERD †46	
14	Neil McDONALD ‡39	
Gk	John KEELEY	

Date	Saturday 10 April 1993	
Venue	Old Trafford, 3.00pm	

MANCHESTER UNITED (0) 2
SHEFFIELD WEDNESDAY (0) 1

Attendance	40,102	
Referee	Referee Mike PECK sub	
	John HILDITCH 61 mins	
Linesmen	R. Pearson, M.J. Hilditch	

MANCHESTER UNITED
Red shirts, White shorts   Goals

1	Peter SCHMEICHEL	
2	Paul PARKER †	
3	Denis IRWIN	
4	Steve BRUCE	86, 96
5	Lee SHARPE	
6	Gary PALLISTER	
7	Eric CANTONA	
8	Paul INCE	
9	Brian McCLAIR	
10	Mark HUGHES	
11	Ryan GIGGS	
	Substitutes	
12	Bryan ROBSON †68	
14	Mike PHELAN	
Gk	Les SEALEY	

SHEFFIELD WEDNESDAY
Blue & White striped shirts, Black shorts   Goals

1	Chris WOODS	
2	Roland NILSSON	
3	Nigel WORTHINGTON	
4	Carlton PALMER	
5	John SHERIDAN ❑	65p
6	Viv ANDERSON ❑	
7	Danny WILSON †	
8	Chris WADDLE	
9	Phil KING	
10	Nigel JEMSON ‡	
11	Gordon WATSON	
	Substitutes	
12	Chris BART-WILLIAMS †60	
14	Mark BRIGHT ‡53	
Gk	Kevin PRESSMAN	

Date	Saturday 10 April 1993	
Venue	Ayresome Park, 3.00pm	

MIDDLESBROUGH (0) 1
EVERTON (1) 2

Attendance	16,627	
Referee	John LLOYD	
Linesmen	I. Blanchard, P.R. Richards	

MIDDLESBROUGH
Red shirts, White shorts   Goals

1	Stephen PEARS	
2	Curtis FLEMING	
3	Jimmy PHILLIPS	
4	Alan KERNAGHAN ■	
5	Nicky MOHAN ❑	
6	Andy PEAKE	
7	John HENDRIE	
8	Graham KAVANAGH †	
9	Paul WILKINSON	64
10	Jamie POLLOCK	
11	Craig HIGNETT ‡	
	Substitutes	
12	Derek WHYTE †57	
14	Alan MOORE ‡75	
Gk	Ian IRONSIDE	

EVERTON
Blue shirts, Blue shorts   Goals

1	Neville SOUTHALL	
2	Matthew JACKSON	
3	Andy HINCHCLIFFE	
4	Barry HORNE	
5	Dave WATSON	26
6	Gary ABLETT	
7	Mark WARD	
8	Peter BEARDSLEY	
9	Tony COTTEE	
10	Paul RIDEOUT †	
11	John EBBRELL	
	Substitutes	
12	Stuart BARLOW †46 ‡	
14	PREKI ‡69	80
Gk	Jason KEARTON	

Date	Saturday 10 April 1993
Venue	Loftus Road, 3.00pm

QPR (2) 4
NOTTINGHAM FOREST (1) 3

Attendance	15,815
Referee	Peter FOAKES
Linesmen	D.C. Richards, M.J. Holohan

QPR
Blue & White hooped shirts, White shorts   Goals

1	Tony ROBERTS	
2	David BARDSLEY	
3	Clive WILSON	45p
4	Ray WILKINS	
5	Darren PEACOCK	
6	Alan McDONALD	
7	Andy IMPEY	
8	Ian HOLLOWAY	
9	Les FERDINAND	38, 70, 73
10	Bradley ALLEN	
11	Andy SINTON	
	Substitutes	
12	Rufus BREVETT	
14	Dennis BAILEY	
Gk	Jan STEJSKAL	

NOTTINGHAM FOREST
Red shirts, Red shorts   Goals

1	Mark CROSSLEY	
2	Gary CHARLES	
3	Brett WILLIAMS	
4	Steve STONE	
5	Carl TILER	
6	Roy KEANE	
7	Kingsley BLACK	49, 54
8	Gary BANNISTER	8
9	Nigel CLOUGH	
10	Robert ROSARIO	
11	Scot GEMMILL	
	Substitutes	
12	Thorvaldur ORLYGSSON	
14	Ian KILFORD	
Gk	Andy MARRIOTT	

Date	Saturday 10 April 1993
Venue	The Dell, 3.00pm

SOUTHAMPTON (0) 1
CHELSEA (0) 0

Attendance	15,135
Referee	Keith BURGE
Linesmen	I.A. Madge, B.A. Wigginton

SOUTHAMPTON
Red & White striped shirts, Black shorts   Goals

1	Tim FLOWERS	
2	Jeff KENNA	
3	Micky ADAMS	
4	Terry HURLOCK †	
5	Kevin MOORE	
6	Kenneth MONKOU	
7	Matthew LE TISSIER	
8	Nicky BANGER	49
9	Iain DOWIE	
10	Neil MADDISON	
11	Jason DODD	
	Substitutes	
12	Tommy WIDDRINGTON †68	
14	Francis BENALI	
Gk	Ian ANDREWS	

CHELSEA
Blue shirts, Blue shorts   Goals

1	Dave BEASANT	
2	Steve CLARKE	
3	Frank SINCLAIR ❏	
4	Andy TOWNSEND	
5	Erland JOHNSEN	
6	Mal DONAGHY	
7	Graham STUART †	
8	John SPENCER	
9	Robert FLECK ‡	
10	Gareth HALL	
11	Dennis WISE	
	Substitutes	
12	Darren BARNARD †80	
14	Neil SHIPPERLEY ‡65	
Gk	Dmitri KHARIN	

Date	Monday 12 April 1993
Venue	Highbury Stadium, 3.00pm

ARSENAL (0) 0
ASTON VILLA (0) 1

Attendance	27,125
Referee	Gerald ASHBY
Linesmen	G. Butland, D.C. Richards

ARSENAL
Red & White shirts, White shorts   Goals

1	David SEAMAN	
2	Lee DIXON	
3	Nigel WINTERBURN	
4	Ian SELLEY	
5	Martin KEOWN	
6	Tony ADAMS	
7	Steve MORROW	
8	Ian WRIGHT ❑ †	
9	Alan SMITH	
10	Paul MERSON	
11	Kevin CAMPBELL ‡	
	Substitutes	
12	Andy LINIGHAN †83	
14	Ray PARLOUR ‡69	
Gk	Alan MILLER	

ASTON VILLA
White shirts, Black shorts   Goals

1	Mark BOSNICH	
2	Earl BARRETT	
3	Steve STAUNTON	
4	Shaun TEALE	
5	Paul McGRATH	
6	Kevin RICHARDSON ❑	
7	Ray HOUGHTON	
8	Neil COX	
9	Dean SAUNDERS	
10	Dalian ATKINSON	
11	Tony DALEY †	68
	Substitutes	
12	Bryan SMALL †75	
14	Dwight YORKE	
Gk	Nigel SPINK	

Date	Monday 12 April 1993
Venue	Stamford Bridge, 3.00pm

CHELSEA (1) 4
WIMBLEDON (0) 2

Attendance	13,138
Referee	David ELLERAY
Linesmen	M.K. Bullivant, R.J. Harris

CHELSEA
Blue shirts, Blue shorts   Goals

1	Dmitri KHARIN	
2	Steve CLARKE	
3	Frank SINCLAIR	
4	Damien MATTHEW †	
5	Erland JOHNSEN	
6	Mal DONAGHY	
7	Graham STUART ❑ ‡	
8	John SPENCER	81
9	Neil SHIPPERLEY	85
10	Gareth HALL	50
11	Dennis WISE ❑	45p
	Substitutes	
12	Darren BARNARD †75	
14	David HOPKIN ‡70	
Gk	Dave BEASANT	

WIMBLEDON
White shirts, Black shorts   Goals

1	Hans SEGERS	
2	Roger JOSEPH †	
3	Warren BARTON ❑	
4	Lawrie SANCHEZ	88
5	John SCALES	
6	Brian FITZGERALD	
7	Neal ARDLEY	
8	Robbie EARLE	
9	Gerald DOBBS	
10	Dean HOLDSWORTH	55
11	Andy CLARKE ‡	
	Substitutes	
12	Dean BLACKWELL †71	
14	Paul MILLER ‡45	
Gk	Perry DIGWEED	

Date	Monday 12 April 1993
Venue	Highfield Road, 3.00pm

COVENTRY CITY (0) 0
MANCHESTER UNITED (1) 1

Attendance	24,429
Referee	Rodger GIFFORD
Linesmen	K.J. Hawkes, I.A. Madge

COVENTRY CITY
Sky Blue shirts, Sky Blue shorts   Goals

1	Jonathan GOULD	
2	Brian BORROWS ❏	
3	Phil BABB	
4	Peter ATHERTON	
5	Michael GYNN	
6	David RENNIE	
7	Lloyd McGRATH ‡	
8	Lee HURST	
9	Mick QUINN ❏ ■	
10	Roy WEGERLE	
11	John WILLIAMS ❏	
	Substitutes	
12	David BUSST	
14	Leigh JENKINSON ‡72	
Gk	Steve OGRIZOVIC	

MANCHESTER UNITED
Red shirts, White shorts   Goals

1	Peter SCHMEICHEL	
2	Paul PARKER	
3	Denis IRWIN	40
4	Steve BRUCE	
5	Lee SHARPE	
6	Gary PALLISTER	
7	Eric CANTONA †	
8	Paul INCE	
9	Brian McCLAIR	
10	Mark HUGHES	
11	Ryan GIGGS	
	Substitutes	
12	Bryan ROBSON †75	
14	Mike PHELAN	
Gk	Les SEALEY	

Date	Monday 12 April 1993
Venue	Selhurst Park, 3.00pm

CRYSTAL PALACE (0) 4
MIDDLESBROUGH (0) 1

Attendance	15,123
Referee	Martin BODENHAM
Linesmen	M.D. Dearing, G.T. Pearson

CRYSTAL PALACE
Red & Blue striped shirts, Red shorts   Goals

1	Nigel MARTYN	
2	Richard SHAW	
3	Gareth SOUTHGATE	
4	Chris COLEMAN	85
5	Eric YOUNG †	61
6	Andy THORN	
7	John HUMPHREY	
8	Geoff THOMAS	
9	Chris ARMSTRONG ‡	81
10	Simon RODGER	54
11	Eddie McGOLDRICK	
	Substitutes	
12	Lee SINNOTT †82	
14	Paul WILLIAMS ‡82	
Gk	Martin THOMAS	

MIDDLESBROUGH
White Shirts, Black shorts   Goals

1	Stephen PEARS	
2	Curtis FLEMING	
3	Jimmy PHILLIPS	
4	Alan KERNAGHAN	
5	Nicky MOHAN	
6	Andy PEAKE ❏	
7	John HENDRIE	
8	Graham KAVANAGH	
9	Paul WILKINSON	86
10	Jamie POLLOCK	
11	Craig HIGNETT	
	Substitutes	
12	Derek WHYTE	
14	Alan MOORE	
Gk	Ian IRONSIDE	

Date	Monday 12 April 1993	*Date*	Monday 12 April 1993
Venue	Goodison Park, 3.00pm	*Venue*	Maine Road, 3.00pm

EVERTON (1) 3
QPR (2) 5

Attendance	19,057
Referee	Stephen LODGE
Linesmen	A. Black, E.J. Walsh

MANCHESTER CITY (1) 1
LIVERPOOL (0) 1

Attendance	28,098
Referee	Mike REED
Linesmen	B. Lowe, P. Rejer

EVERTON
Blue shirts, White shorts — Goals

1	Neville SOUTHALL	
2	Matthew JACKSON †	
3	Andy HINCHCLIFFE	
4	Barry HORNE	
5	Dave WATSON	
6	Gary ABLETT	
7	Mark WARD ‡	
8	Peter BEARDSLEY	
9	Tony COTTEE	31
10	Ian SNODIN ❑	
11	John EBBRELL	
	Substitutes	
12	Stuart BARLOW †28	87
14	PREKI ‡54	89
Gk	Jason KEARTON	

MANCHESTER CITY
Light Blue shirts, White shorts — Goals

1	Tony COTON	
2	Ray RANSON	
3	Terry PHELAN	
4	Peter REID	
5	Keith CURLE	
6	Michel VONK	
7	David WHITE †	
8	Mike SHERON ‡	
9	Niall QUINN	
10	Garry FLITCROFT	12
11	Rick HOLDEN	
	Substitutes	
12	Mike QUIGLEY †37	
14	Kare INGEBRIGTSEN ‡29	
Gk	Martyn MARGETSON	

QPR
Red & Black hooped shirts, Black shorts — Goals

1	Tony ROBERTS	
2	David BARDSLEY	79
3	Clive WILSON	
4	Ray WILKINS	
5	Darren PEACOCK ❑	
6	Alan McDONALD	
7	Andy IMPEY	6
8	Ian HOLLOWAY	
9	Les FERDINAND ❑	38, 47, 51
10	Bradley ALLEN	
11	Andy SINTON ‡	
	Substitutes	
12	Karl READY	
14	Simon BARKER ‡81	
Gk	Jan STEJSKAL	

LIVERPOOL
Red shirts, Red shorts — Goals

1	David JAMES	
2	Rob JONES	
3	David BURROWS	
4	Steve NICOL	
5	Mark WRIGHT	
6	Ronnie WHELAN	
7	Ronnie ROSENTHAL †	
8	Don HUTCHISON	
9	Ian RUSH	61
10	John BARNES	
11	Mark WALTERS	
	Substitutes	
12	Mike MARSH †56	
14	Torben PIECHNIK	
Gk	Mike HOOPER	

Date	Monday 12 April 1993
Venue	City Ground, 3.00pm

NOTTINGHAM FOREST (2) 2
TOTTENHAM HOTSPUR (1) 1

Attendance	25,682
Referee	Alan WILKIE
Linesmen	U.D. Rennie, A. Streets

NOTTINGHAM FOREST
Red shirts, White shorts   Goals

1	Andy MARRIOTT	
2	Brian LAWS	
3	Brett WILLIAMS	
4	Steve STONE ❑	
5	Carl TILER	
6	Roy KEANE ❑	
7	Kingsley BLACK	25
8	Gary BANNISTER	
9	Nigel CLOUGH	
10	Robert ROSARIO †	35
11	Ian WOAN	
	Substitutes	
12	Thorvaldur ORLYGSSON †85	
14	Craig ARMSTRONG	
Gk	Mark CROSSLEY	

TOTTENHAM HOTSPUR
White shirts, Navy Blue shorts   Goals

1	Erik THORSTVEDT ‡	
2	Dean AUSTIN	
3	Justin EDINBURGH	
4	Nick BARMBY	
5	Gary MABBUTT	
6	Neil RUDDOCK ❑	
7	Steve SEDGLEY	44
8	NAYIM †	
9	Darren ANDERTON	
10	Teddy SHERINGHAM ❑	
11	Paul ALLEN	
	Substitutes	
12	Gudni BERGSSON	
14	Andy TURNER †67	
Gk	Kevin DEARDEN ‡46	

Date	Monday 12 April 1993
Venue	Hillsborough, 3.00pm

SHEFFIELD WEDNESDAY (2) 5
SOUTHAMPTON (0) 2

Attendance	26,183
Referee	Kelvin MORTON
Linesmen	P.M. Roberts, J.B. Robinson

SHEFFIELD WEDNESDAY
Blue & White striped shirts, Black shorts   Goals

1	Kevin PRESSMAN	
2	Julian WATTS	
3	Phil KING	50
4	John HARKES †	
5	Simon STEWART	
6	Viv ANDERSON ‡	
7	Graham HYDE	
8	Ryan JONES	
9	Mark BRIGHT	37
10	Chris BART-WILLIAMS	43, 71, 81
11	Nigel WORTHINGTON	
	Substitutes	
12	Mike WILLIAMS †46	
14	Nigel JEMSON ‡83	
Gk	Chris WOODS	

SOUTHAMPTON
Yellow Shirts, White shorts   Goals

1	Tim FLOWERS	
2	Jeff KENNA	
3	Micky ADAMS	
4	Tommy WIDDRINGTON ❑	
5	Kevin MOORE ❑	
6	Kenneth MONKOU	
7	Matthew LE TISSIER †	
8	Glenn COCKERILL	
9	Iain DOWIE	86
10	Neil MADDISON	
11	Jason DODD ‡	68
	Substitutes	
12	Nicky BANGER †46	
14	Francis BENALI ‡71	
Gk	Ian ANDREWS	

Date	Monday 12 April 1993
Venue	Ewood Park, 7.45pm

BLACKBURN ROVERS (2) 2
IPSWICH TOWN (0) 1

Attendance	14,071
Referee	Keith HACKETT
Linesmen	N.S. Barry, T.J. Stevens

BLACKBURN ROVERS
Black & White halved shirts, White shorts — Goals

1	Bobby MIMMS	
2	David MAY	
3	Graeme LE SAUX	
4	Tim SHERWOOD	
5	Colin HENDRY	
6	Kevin MORAN	
7	Stuart RIPLEY	6
8	Gordon COWANS	
9	Kevin GALLACHER	
10	Mike NEWELL	
11	Jason WILCOX	
	Substitutes	
12	Mark ATKINS	
14	Lee MAKEL	
Gk	Frank TALIA	

IPSWICH TOWN
Black & Red striped shirts, Black shorts — Goals

1	Clive BAKER	
2	Eddie YOUDS	
3	Gavin JOHNSON	
4	Geraint WILLIAMS	
5	Phil WHELAN	43og
6	David LINIGHAN †	
7	Steve WHITTON	
8	Bontcho GUENTCHEV	
9	Simon MILTON	68
10	Jason DOZZELL	
11	Chris KIWOMYA	
	Substitutes	
12	Vlado BOZINOSKI †61	
14	Paul GODDARD	
Gk	Andy PETTERSON	

Date	Tuesday 13 April 1993
Venue	Boundary Park, 7.30pm

OLDHAM ATHLETIC (1) 1
SHEFFIELD UNITED (1) 1

Attendance	14,795
Referee	Peter FOAKES
Linesmen	I. Blancgard, A.J. Hill

OLDHAM ATHLETIC
Blue shirts, Blue shorts — Goals

1	Paul GERRARD	
2	Gunnar HALLE	
3	Neil POINTON	
4	Nick HENRY †	
5	Richard JOBSON	
6	Craig FLEMING ❏	
7	Neil ADAMS	
8	Andy RITCHIE	10
9	Darren BECKFORD	
10	Mike MILLIGAN	
11	Paul BERNARD	
	Substitutes	
12	Roger PALMER †74	
14	Steve REDMOND	
Gk	John KEELEY	

SHEFFIELD UNITED
Red & White striped shirts, White shorts — Goals

1	Alan KELLY	
2	Mitch WARD	
3	Paul BEESLEY	
4	Jamie HOYLAND	44
5	Brian GAYLE	
6	John PEMBERTON ❏	
7	Carl BRADSHAW	
8	Paul ROGERS ❏	
9	Glyn HODGES ❏	
10	Brian DEANE	
11	Dane WHITEHOUSE	
	Substitutes	
12	Charlie HARTFIELD	
14	Alan CORK	
Gk	Jim LEIGHTON	

Date	Wednesday 14 April 1993
Venue	Carrow Road, 7.30pm

NORWICH CITY (3) 4
LEEDS UNITED (1) 2

Attendance	18,613
Referee	Keith BURGE
Linesmen	G. Butland, A. Schneider

NORWICH CITY
Yellow shirts, Green shorts   Goals

1	Bryan GUNN	
2	Ian CULVERHOUSE	
3	Mark BOWEN	
4	Ian BUTTERWORTH	
5	John POLSTON	
6	Jeremy GOSS	
7	Ian CROOK	
8	Chris SUTTON	11, 14, 79
9	Mark ROBINS	
10	Ruel FOX	
11	David PHILLIPS	15p
	Substitutes	
12	Efan EKOKU	
14	Andrew JOHNSON	
Gk	Mark WALTON	

LEEDS UNITED
White shirts, White shorts   Goals

1	John LUKIC	
2	David KERSLAKE	
3	Dylan KERR	
4	Mark TINKLER	
5	Chris FAIRCLOUGH †	
6	Chris WHYTE	
7	Gordon STRACHAN	
8	Rod WALLACE	46
9	Lee CHAPMAN	2
10	Jamie FORRESTER ‡	
11	Gary SPEED	
	Substitutes	
12	Jon NEWSOME †78	
14	Steve HODGE ‡75	
Gk	Mervyn DAY	

Date	Saturday 17 April 1993
Venue	Elland Road, 3.00pm

LEEDS UNITED (0) 0
CRYSTAL PALACE (0) 0

Attendance	27,545
Referee	Robbie HART
Linesmen	J. McGrath, B.L. Polkey

LEEDS UNITED
White shirts, White shorts   Goals

1	John LUKIC	
2	David KERSLAKE	
3	Kevin SHARP	
4	Jamie FORRESTER	
5	David WETHERALL	
6	Jon NEWSOME	
7	Gordon STRACHAN	
8	Rod WALLACE	
9	Lee CHAPMAN	
10	Gary McALLISTER †	
11	Gary SPPED	
	Substitutes	
12	Mark TINKER †89	
14	Chris WHYTE	
Gk	Mervyn DAY	

CRYSTAL PALACE
Red & Blue striped shirts, Red shorts   Goals

1	Nigel MARTYN	
2	Richard SHAW	
3	Gareth SOUTHGATE	
4	Chris COLEMAN	
5	Eric YOUNG	
6	Andy THORN	
7	John HUMPHREY	
8	Geoff THOMAS ❑	
9	Chris ARMSTRONG	
10	Simon RODGER ‡	
11	Eddie McGOLDRICK	
	Substitutes	
12	Paul WILLIAMS	
14	Simon OSBORN ‡50	
Gk	Andy WOODMAN	

Date	Saturday 17 April 1992
Venue	Anfield, 3.00pm

LIVERPOOL (2) 4
COVENTRY CITY (0) 0

Attendance	33,328
Referee	Tony WARD
Linesmen	A. Streets, M. Warren

Liverpool
Red shirts, Red shorts   Goals

1	David JAMES	
2	Rob JONES	
3	David BURROWS	75
4	Steve NICOL	
5	Mark WRIGHT	
6	Ronnie WHELAN	
7	Paul STEWART †	
8	Don HUTCHISON	
9	Ian RUSH	
10	John BARNES	
11	Mark WALTERS	16, 33, 50p
	Substitutes	
12	Ronnie ROSENTHAL †65	
14	Torben PIECHNIK	
Gk	Mike HOOPER	

COVENTRY CITY
Sky Blue shirts, Sky Blue shorts   Goals

1	Jonathan GOULD	
2	Brian BORROWS †	
3	Phil BABB	
4	Peter ATHERTON	
5	Michael GYNN	
6	David RENNIE	
7	Peter NDLOVU ‡	
8	Lee HURST	
9	Mick QUINN	
10	Roy WEGERLE	
11	John WILLIAMS	
	Substitutes	
12	Andy PEARCE †46	
14	Leigh JENKINSON ‡79	
Gk	Steve OGRIZOVIC	

Date	Saturday 17 April 1993
Venue	Old Trafford, 3.00pm

MANCHESTER UNITED (2) 3
CHELSEA (0) 0

Attendance	40,139
Referee	Howard KING
Linesmen	T.A. Atkinson, A.J. Martin

MANCHESTER UNITED
Red shirts, White shorts   Goals

1	Peter SCHMEICHEL	
2	Paul PARKER	
3	Denis IRWIN	
4	Steve BRUCE	
5	Lee SHARPE	
6	Gary PALLISTER	
7	Eric CANTONA	48
8	Paul INCE	
9	Brian McCLAIR †	
10	Mark HUGHES	23
11	Ryan GIGGS ‡	
	Substitutes	
12	Bryan ROBSON †50	
14	Andrei KANCHELSKIS ‡68	
Gk	Les SEALEY	

CHELSEA
Blue shirts, Blue shorts   Goals

1	Dave BEASANT	
2	Steve CLARKE	44og
3	Frank SINCLAIR	
4	Andy TOWNSEND	
5	Erland JOHNSEN	
6	Mal DONAGHY †	
7	Graham STUART	
8	John SPENCER	
9	Neil SHIPPERLEY ‡	
10	Gareth HALL	
11	Dennis WISE	
	Substitutes	
12	Darren BARNARD †69	
14	Steve LIVINGSTONE ‡55	
Gk	Dmitri KHARIN	

Date	Saturday 17 April 1993
Venue	Bramall Lane, 3.00pm

SHEFFIELD UNITED (1) 1
BLACKBURN ROVERS (1) 3

Attendance	18,186
Referee	David ALLISON
Linesmen	I. Blanchard, M.A. Riley

SHEFFIELD UNITED
Red & White striped shirts, White shorts   Goals

1	Alan KELLY	
2	Kevin GAGE	
3	Paul BEESLEY	
4	Jamie HOYLAND	
5	Brian GAYLE	
6	John PEMBERTON	
7	Carl BRADSHAW †	
8	Paul ROGERS	
9	Glyn HODGES	8
10	Brian DEANE	
11	Dane WITEHOUSE ‡	
	Substitutes	
12	Ian BRYSON †50	
14	Mitch WARD ‡50 ❑	
Gk	Jim LEIGHTON	

BLACKBURN ROVERS
Blue & White shirts, Blue shorts   Goals

1	Bobby MIMMS	
2	David MAY	
3	Graeme LE SAUX	
4	Tim SHERWOOD	68
5	Nick MARKER	
6	Kevin MORAN	
7	Stuart RIPLEY	
8	Gordon COWANS †	
9	Kevin GALLACHER	39
10	Mike NEWELL	54
11	Jason WILCOX	
	Substitutes	
12	Mark ATKINS †80	
14	Tony DOBSON	
Gk	Frank TALIA	

Date	Saturday 17 April 1993
Venue	The Dell, 3.00pm

SOUTHAMPTON (0) 0
EVERTON (0) 0

Attendance	16,911
Referee	Martin BODENHAM
Linesmen	M.D. Dearing, G.T. Pearson

SOUTHAMPTON
Red & White striped shirts, Black shorts   Goals

1	Tim FLOWERS	
2	Jeff KENNA	
3	Micky ADAMS	
4	Terry HURLOCK †	
5	Richard HALL	
6	Kenneth MONKOU	
7	Matthew LE TISSIER	
8	Glenn COCKERILL	
9	Paul MOODY ❑ ‡	
10	Neil MADDISON	
11	Nicky BANGER	
	Substitutes	
12	Matthew BOUND †85	
14	Lee POWELL ‡53	
Gk	Ian ANDREWS	

EVERTON
Blue shirts, Blue shorts   Goals

1	Neville SOUTHALL	
2	Paul HOLMES	
3	Andy HINCHCLIFFE	
4	John EBBRELL	
5	Dave WATSON	
6	Matthew JACKSON	
7	PREKI	
8	Peter BEARDSLEY	
9	Tony COTTEE	
10	Stuart BARLOW †	
11	Mark WARD	
	Substitutes	
12	Billy KENNY †65	
14	Alan HARPER	
Gk	Jason KEARTON	

Date	Saturday 17 April 1993
Venue	White Hart Lane, 3.00pm

TOTTENHAM HOTSPUR (0) 4
OLDHAM ATHLETIC (1) 1

Attendance	26,663
Referee	Keith HACKETT
Linesmen	I.A. Madge, J.F. Moore

TOTTENHAM HOTSPUR
White shirts, Navy Blue shorts   Goals

1	Ian WALKER	
2	Dean AUSTIN	
3	Justin EDINBURGH	
4	Vinny SAMWAYS †	
5	Gary MABBUTT	
6	Neil RUDDOCK	
7	Steve SEDGLEY	
8	Nick BARMBY	
9	Darren ANDERTON	70
10	Teddy SHERINGHAM	58p, 82p
11	Paul ALLEN	
	Substitutes	
12	Stuart NETHERCOTT	
14	Andy TURNER †73	84
Gk	Kevin DEARDEN	

OLDHAM ATHLETIC
Blue shirts, Blue shorts   Goals

1	Paul GERRARD	
2	Gunnar HALLE ❏	
3	Neil POINTON	
4	Nick HENRY	
5	Richard JOBSON	
6	Craig FLEMING	
7	Neil ADAMS	
8	Andy RITCHIE	
9	Darren BECKFORD	25
10	Mike MILLIGAN ❏	
11	Paul BERNARD	
	Substitutes	
12	Roger PALMER	
14	Steve REDMOND	
Gk	John KEELEY	

Date	Saturday 17 April 1993
Venue	Selhurst Park, 3.00pm

WIMBLEDON (1) 1
NOTTINGHAM FOREST (0) 0

Attendance	9,358
Referee	Keren BARRATT
Linesmen	A. Schneider, P.A. Vosper

WIMBLEDON
Blue shirts, Blue shorts   Goals

1	Hans SEGERS	
2	Warren BARTON	
3	Brian McALLISTER	
4	Lawrie SANCHEZ ‡	
5	John SCALES	
6	Scott FITZGERALD	
7	Neal ARDLEY †	
8	Robbie EARLE	
9	Paul MILLER	
10	Dean HOLDSWORTH	
11	Andy CLARKE	32
	Substitutes	
12	Dean BLACKWELL †65	
14	Peter FEAR ‡65	
Gk	Perry DIGWEED	

NOTTINGHAM FOREST
Red shirts, White shorts   Goals

1	Andy MARRIOTT	
2	Brian LAWS	
3	Brett WILLIAMS	
4	Steve STONE	
5	Carl TILER	
6	Roy KEANE	
7	Kingsley BLACK ‡	
8	Gary BANNISTER	
9	Nigel CLOUGH	
10	Robert ROSARIO	
11	Ian WOAN	
	Substitutes	
12	Scot GEMMILL	
14	Lee GLOVER ‡79	
Gk	Mark CROSSLEY	

Date	Sunday 18 April 1993	
Venue	Villa Park, 2.30pm	

ASTON VILLA (0) 3
MANCHESTER CITY (1) 1

Attendance	33,108	
Referee	Philip DON	
Linesmen	D.T. Colwell, E.J. Walsh	

ASTON VILLA
Claret & Blue shirts, White shorts   Goals

1	Mark BOSNICH	
2	Earl BARRETT	
3	Steve STAUNTON	
4	Neil COX	
5	Paul McGRATH	
6	Kevin RICHARDSON	
7	Ray HOUGHTON	89
8	Garry PARKER †	67p
9	Dean SAUNDERS	47
10	Dalian ATKINSON	
11	Tony DALEY	
	Substitutes	
12	Bryan SMALL †77	
14	Dwight YORKE	
Gk	Nigel SPINK	

MANCHESTER CITY
White shirts, Light Blue shorts   Goals

1	Tony COTON	
2	Ray RANSON	
3	Terry PHELAN	
4	Peter REID	
5	Keith CURLE	
6	Michel VONK	
7	David WHITE	
8	Fitzroy SIMPSON	
9	Niall QUINN	34
10	Garry FLITCROFT	
11	Rick HOLDEN †	
	Substitutes	
12	David BRIGHTWELL †75	
14	Kare INGEBRIGTSEN	
Gk	Martyn MARGETSON	

Date	Monday 19 April 1993	
Venue	Portman Road, 7.45pm	

IPSWICH TOWN (1) 3
NORWICH CITY (1) 1

Attendance	21,081	
Referee	Vic CALLOW	
Linesmen	A.P. D'Urso, S.G. Tomlin	

IPSWICH TOWN
Blue & White shirts, White shorts   Goals

1	Clive BAKER	
2	Eddie YOUDS	
3	Gavin JOHNSON	
4	Geraint WILLIAMS	
5	John WARK	
6	David LINIGHAN	
7	Steve WHITTON	
8	Mick STOCKWELL	52
9	Simon MILTON	
10	Jason DOZZELL	21, 57
11	Chris KIWOMYA	
	Substitutes	
12	Bontcho GUENTCHEV	
14	Phil WHELAN	
Gk	Andy PETTERSON	

NORWICH CITY
Yellow shirts, Green shorts   Goals

1	Bryan GUNN	
2	Ian CULVERHOUSE	
3	Mark BOWEN	
4	Ian BUTTERWORTH	
5	John POLSTON	
6	Jeremy GOSS	
7	Ian CROOK	
8	Chris SUTTON	41
9	Mark ROBINS	
10	Ruel FOX	
11	David PHILLIPS	
	Substitutes	
12	Efan EKOKU	
14	Colin WOODTHORPE	
Gk	Mark WALTON	

Date	Tuesday 20 April 1993
Venue	Ayresome Park, 7.30pm

MIDDLESBROUGH (2) 3
TOTTENHAM HOTSPUR (0) 0

Attendance	14,472
Referee	David ALLISON
Linesmen	W.J. Nattrass, T. Heilbron

● *Moved from 6 March*

MIDDLESBROUGH
Red shirts, White shorts — Goals

1	Stephen PEARS	
2	Curtis FLEMING	
3	Jimmy PHILLIPS	
4	Alan KERNAGHAN	
5	Derek WHYTE	
6	Andy PEAKE	
7	John HENDRIE	
8	Tommy WRIGHT	2, 26
9	Paul WILKINSON	76
10	Jamie POLLOCK	
11	Craig HIGNETT	
	Substitutes	
12	Willie FALCONER	
14	Dwight MARSHALL	
Gk	Ian IRONSIDE	

TOTTENHAM HOTSPUR
White shirts, Navy Blue shorts — Goals

1	Ian WALKER	
2	Dean AUSTIN ❑ †	
3	Justin EDINBURGH	
4	Vinny SAMWAYS	
5	Gary MABBUTT	
6	Neil RUDDOCK	
7	Steve SEDGLEY	
8	Nick BARMBY	
9	Darren ANDERTON	
10	Teddy SHERINGHAM	
11	Paul ALLEN ‡	
	Substitutes	
12	Terry FENWICK †75	
14	Andy TURNER ‡75	
Gk	Kevin DEARDEN	

Date	Wednesday 21 April 1993
Venue	Highbury Stadium, 7.45pm

ARSENAL (0) 1
NOTTINGHAM FOREST (0) 1

Attendance	19,024
Referee	Martin BODENHAM
Linesmen	M.D. Dearing, G.T. Pearson

● *Moved from 6 March*

ARSENAL
Red & White shirts, White shorts — Goals

1	David SEAMAN	
2	Lee DIXON	
3	Nigel WINTERBURN †	
4	Ian SELLEY	
5	Andy LINIGHAN	
6	Martin KEOWN	
7	John JENSEN	
8	Ian WRIGHT	67
9	Alan SMITH	
10	Ray PARLOUR ‡	
11	Jimmy CARTER	
	Substitutes	
12	Tony ADAMS †57	
14	Kevin CAMPBELL ‡76	
Gk	Alan MILLER	

NOTTINGHAM FOREST
White shirts, Black shorts — Goals

1	Andy MARRIOTT	
2	Brian LAWS	
3	Brett WILLIAMS ❑	
4	Lee GLOVER	
5	Carl TILER	
6	Roy KEANE	90
7	Kingsley BLACK	
8	Scot GEMMILL	
9	Nigel CLOUGH	
10	Robert ROSARIO †	
11	Ian WOAN	
	Substitutes	
12	Steve STONE †76	
14	Steve CHETTLE	
Gk	Mark CROSSLEY	

Date	Wednesday 21 April 1993
Venue	Ewood Park, 7.45pm

BLACKBURN ROVERS (3) 3
ASTON VILLA (0) 0

Attendance	15,127
Referee	Joe WORRALL
Linesmen	R.H. Andrews, G.I. Grandidge

● *Moved from March 6*

BLACKBURN ROVERS
Blue & White shirts, White shorts   Goals

1	Bobby MIMMS	
2	David MAY	
3	Graeme LE SAUX	
4	Tim SHERWOOD	
5	Colin HENDRY	
6	Kevin MORAN	
7	Stuart RIPLEY	
8	Gordon COWANS	
9	Kevin GALLACHER	15
10	Mike NEWELL	9, 40
11	Jason WILCOX	
	Substitutes	
12	Nick MARKER	
14	Mark ATKINS	
Gk	Frank TALIA	

ASTON VILLA
Claret & Blue shirts, Blue shorts   Goals

1	Mark BOSNICH	
2	Earl BARRETT	
3	Steve STAUNTON	
4	Shaun TEALE ❏	
5	Paul McGRATH	
6	Kevin RICHARDSON	
7	Ray HOUGHTON	
8	Bryan SMALL †	
9	Dean SAUNDERS	
10	Dalian ATKINSON	
11	Tony DALEY	
	Substitutes	
12	Dwight YORKE †61	
14	Neil COX	
Gk	Nigel SPINK	

Date	Wednesday 21 April 1992
Venue	Selhurst Park, 8.00pm

CRYSTAL PALACE (0) 0
MANCHESTER UNITED (0) 2

Attendance	30,115
Referee	Keren BARRATT
Linesmen	J.A. Elwin, I.M.D. Mitchell

● *Moved from 13 February*

CRYSTAL PALACE
Red & Blue striped shirts, Red shorts   Goals

1	Nigel MARTYN	
2	Richard SHAW	
3	Gareth SOUTHGATE	
4	Chris COLEMAN	
5	Eric YOUNG	
6	Andy THORN	
7	John HUMPHREY	
8	Ricky NEWMAN	
9	Chris ARMSTRONG	
10	Simon OSBORN ‡	
11	Eddie McGOLDRICK	
	Substitutes	
12	Paul WILLIAMS	
14	George NDAH ‡76	
Gk	Andy WOODMAN	

MANCHESTER UNITED
Green & Yellow shirts, Black shorts   Goals

1	Peter SCHMEICHEL	
2	Paul PARKER	
3	Denis IRWIN	
4	Steve BRUCE ❏	
5	Andrei KANCHELSKIS †	
6	Gary PALLISTER	
7	Eric CANTONA	
8	Paul INCE	89
9	Brian McCLAIR	
10	Mark HUGHES	64
11	Ryan GIGGS	
	Substitutes	
12	Bryan ROBSON †63	
14	Mike PHELAN	
Gk	Les SEALEY	

Date	Wednesday 21 April 1993
Venue	Anfield, 7.30pm

LIVERPOOL (0) 2
LEEDS UNITED (0) 0

Attendance	34,992
Referee	Mike REED
Linesmen	E. Lomas, B. Lowe

● *Moved from 27 January*

LIVERPOOL
Red shirts, Red shorts   Goals

1	David JAMES	
2	Rob JONES	
3	David BURROWS	
4	Steve NICOL	
5	Mark WRIGHT	
6	Ronnie WHELAN	
7	Paul STEWART	
8	Don HUTCHISON	
9	Ian RUSH	
10	John BARNES	54
11	Mark WALTERS	73p
	Substitutes	
12	Ronnie ROSENTHAL	
14	Torben PIECHNIK	
Gk	Mike HOOPER	

LEEDS UNITED
White shirts, White shorts   Goals

1	John LUKIC	
2	David KERSLAKE †	
3	Kevin SHARP	
4	David ROCASTLE	
5	Jon NEWSOME	
6	Chris WHYTE	
7	Gordon STRACHAN	
8	Rod WALLACE	
9	Lee CHAPMAN	
10	Carl SHUTT	
11	Gary SPEED	
	Substitutes	
12	Ray WALLACE †19	
14	Mark TINKLER	
Gk	Mervyn DAY	

Date	Wednesday 21 April 1993
Venue	Maine Road, 7.30pm

MANCHESTER CITY (0) 1
WIMBLEDON (0) 1

Attendance	19,524
Referee	Howard KING
Linesmen	R. Pearson, P.R. Richards

● *Moved from 13 February*

MANCHESTER CITY
Light Blue shirts, White shorts   Goals

1	Tony COTON	
2	Ray RANSON ‡	
3	Terry PHELAN	
4	Peter REID †	
5	Keith CURLE	
6	Michel VONK	
7	David WHITE	
8	Mike SHERON	
9	Niall QUINN	
10	Garry FLITCROFT	
11	Fitzroy SIMPSON	
	Substitutes	
12	Rick HOLDEN †45	84
14	David BRIGHTWELL ‡62	
Gk	Andy DIBBLE	

WIMBLEDON
Blue shirts, Blue shorts   Goals

1	Hans SEGERS	
2	Warren BARTON	
3	Brian McALLISTER	
4	Vinnie JONES	
5	John SCALES	
6	Scott FITZGERALD	
7	Paul MILLER ‡	50
8	Robbie EARLE	
9	John FASHANU	
10	Peter FEAR	
11	Andy CLARKE	
	Substitutes	
12	Greg BERRY	
14	Paul McGEE ‡78	
Gk	Perry DIGWEED	

Date	Wednesday 21 April 1993
Venue	Hillsborough, 7.45pm

SHEFFIELD WEDNESDAY (0) 1
SHEFFIELD UNITED (1) 1

Attendance	38,688
Referee	Ken REDFERN
Linesmen	D.S. Oliver, D.E. Binsley

● *Moved from 14 March*

SHEFFIELD WEDNESDAY
Blue & White shirts, Black shorts   Goals

1	Chris WOODS	
2	Roland NILSSON	
3	Nigel WORTHINGTON	
4	Carlton PALMER	
5	John HARKES	
6	Paul WARHURST	71
7	Ryan JONES †	
8	Chris WADDLE ‡	
9	David HIRST	
10	Mark BRIGHT	
11	John SHERIDAN	
	Substitutes	
12	Graham HYDE †9	
14	Chris BART-WILLIAMS ‡76	
Gk	Kevin PRESSMAN	

SHEFFIELD UNITED
Red & White striped shirts, White shorts   Goals

1	Alan KELLY	
2	Mitch WARD	
3	Paul BEESLEY	
4	Charlie HARTFIELD	
5	Brian GAYLE ❏	
6	John PEMBERTON	
7	Carl BRADSHAW	
8	Paul ROGERS	
9	Glyn HODGES ■	
10	Brian DEANE †	44
11	Dane WHITEHOUSE	
	Substitutes	
12	Andy SCOTT †90	
14	Jamie HOYLAND	
Gk	Jim LEIGHTON	

LEAGUE TABLE

	Up to and including 21.04.93	P	W	D	L	F	A	Pts
1	Manchester United	40	22	12	6	62	29	78
2	Aston Villa	40	21	11	8	56	37	74
3	Norwich City	40	20	8	12	57	62	68
4	Blackburn Rovers	39	18	11	10	64	42	65
5	Liverpool	39	15	11	13	54	49	56
6	Sheffield Wednesday	37	14	13	10	50	43	55
7	Queen's Park Rangers	38	15	10	13	57	52	55
8	Tottenham Hotspur	38	15	10	13	53	56	55
9	Manchester City	39	14	11	14	53	46	53
10	Wimbledon	40	14	11	15	54	52	53
11	Chelsea	40	13	14	13	47	49	53
12	Arsenal	37	14	9	14	36	34	51
13	Coventry City	40	13	12	15	48	52	51
14	Southampton	40	13	11	16	51	56	50
15	Everton	39	14	7	18	48	51	49
16	Ipswich Town	40	11	16	13	47	51	49
17	Leeds United	39	12	12	15	52	57	48
18	Crystal Palace	39	10	15	14	45	57	45
19	Sheffield United	39	11	10	18	46	51	43
20	Oldham Athletic	39	10	10	19	55	69	40
21	Nottingham Forest	40	10	10	20	40	58	40
22	Middlesbrough	40	10	10	20	48	70	40

LEADING SCORERS

Teddy SHERINGHAM	Tottenham Hotspur	20
Dean HOLDSWORTH	Wimbledon	18
Les FERDINAND	Queens Park Rangers	17
Alan SHEARER	Blackburn Rovers	16

LEAGUE GOALSCORING FIGURES

Running Totals

Date	Games	Goals	Average	Games	Goals	Average
03.04.93	6	25	4.17	386	984	2.55
04.04.93	1	1	1.00	387	985	2.54
05.04.93	1	4	4.00	388	989	2.55
06.04.93	3	6	2.00	391	995	2.54
07.04.93	2	6	3.00	393	1001	2.55
09.04.93	3	12	4.00	396	1013	2.56
10.04.93	8	25	3.13	404	1038	2.57
12.04.93	9	36	4.00	413	1074	2.60
13.04.93	1	2	2.00	414	1076	2.60
14.04.93	1	6	6.00	415	1082	2.60
17.04.93	7	17	2.43	422	1099	2.60
18.04.93	1	4	4.00	423	1103	2.61
19.04.93	1	4	4.00	424	1107	2.61
20.04.93	1	3	3.00	425	1110	2.61
21.04.93	6	13	2.17	431	1123	2.60

Date	Saturday 1 May 1993
Venue	Stamford Bridge, 3.00pm

CHELSEA (1) 2
COVENTRY CITY (0) 1

Attendance	14,186
Referee	Ron GROVES
Linesmen	S.G. Tomlin, B.A. Wigginton

CHELSEA
Blue shirts, Blue shorts · Goals

1	Dmitri KHARIN	
2	Steve CLARKE	
3	David LEE	
4	Andy TOWNSEND	
5	Erland JOHNSEN	
6	Nigel SPACKMAN	
7	Darren BARNARD	
8	John SPENCER ‡	13
9	Tony CASCARINO	71
10	Gareth HALL	
11	Dennis WISE ❏	
	Substitutes	
12	Andy MYERS	
14	David HOPKIN ‡80	
Gk	Dave BEASANT	

COVENTRY CITY
Red shirts, White shorts · Goals

1	Jonathan GOULD	
2	Terry FLEMING †	
3	Phil BABB ❏	
4	Peter ATHERTON ❏	
5	David BUSST	
6	David RENNIE	
7	Michael GYNN ‡	
8	Lee HURST	
9	Mick QUINN	15
10	Roy WEGERLE	
11	John WILLIAMS ❏	
	Substitutes	
12	Brian BORROWS †76	
14	Willie BOLAND ‡76	
Gk	Steve OGRIZOVIC	

Date	Saturday 1 May 1993
Venue	Selhurst Park, 3.00pm

CRYSTAL PALACE (2) 3
IPSWICH TOWN (1) 1

Attendance	18,881
Referee	Philip DON
Linesmen	G.R. Hamblin, R.J. Harris

CRYSTAL PALACE
Red & Blue striped shirts, Red shorts · Goals

1	Nigel MARTYN	
2	Richard SHAW	
3	Gareth SOUTHGATE	
4	Chris COLEMAN †	
5	Eric YOUNG	8
6	Andy THORN	
7	John HUMPHREY	
8	Geoff THOMAS	
9	Chris ARMSTRONG	17
10	Simon RODGER	
11	Eddie McGOLDRICK	60
	Substitutes	
12	Paul WILLIAMS †21	
14	Dean GORDON	
Gk	Andy WOODMAN	

IPSWICH TOWN
White shirts, White shorts · Goals

1	Clive BAKER	
2	David GREGORY	37
3	Phil WHELAN	
4	Mick STOCKWELL	
5	John WARK	
6	David LINIGHAN ❏	
7	Geraint WILLIAMS	
8	Steve PALMER †	
9	Simon MILTON ‡	
10	Jason DOZZELL	
11	Chris KIWOMYA	
	Substitutes	
12	Steve WHITTON †73	
14	Bontcho GUENTCHEV ‡73	
Gk	Andy PETTERSON	

Date	Saturday 1 May 1993
Venue	Goodison Park, 3.00pm

EVERTON (0) 0
ARSENAL (0) 0

Attendance	19,044
Referee	Allan GUNN
Linesmen	B.T. Millership, R.R. Rawson

EVERTON
Blue shirts, White shorts   Goals

1	Neville SOUTHALL	
2	Matthew JACKSON	
3	Andy HINCHCLIFFE	
4	Barry HORNE	
5	Dave WATSON	
6	Gary ABLETT	
7	PREKI	
8	Peter BEARDSLEY	
9	Tony COTTEE	
10	John EBBRELL	
11	Mard WARD †	
	Substitutes	
12	Stuart BARLOW †46	
14	Paul HOLMES	
Gk	Jason KEARTON	

ARSENAL
Red & white shirts, White shorts   Goals

1	David SEAMAN	
2	David O'LEARY	
3	Pal LYDERSEN †	
4	Paul DAVIS	
5	Andy LINIGHAN	
6	Steve BOULD	
7	Martin KEOWN	
8	Ian SELLEY	
9	Alan SMITH	
10	Kevin CAMPBELL	
11	Jimmy CARTER ‡	
	Substitutes	
12	John JENSEN †66	
14	Neil HEANEY ‡76	
Gk	Alan MILLER	

Date	Saturday 1 May 1993
Venue	Elland Road, 3.00pm

LEEDS UNITED (0) 1
QPR (1) 1

Attendance	31,408
Referee	Vic CALLOW
Linesmen	T. Heilbron, T. Lynch

LEEDS UNITED
White shirts, White shorts   Goals

1	John LUKIC	
2	Ray WALLACE	
3	Kevin SHARP	
4	David BATTY	
5	Jon NEWSOME	
6	Chris WHYTE	
7	David ROCASTLE ‡	
8	Rod WALLACE ❏	
9	Lee CHAPMAN	
10	Steve HODGE	69
11	Jamie FORRESTER †	
	Substitutes	
12	Frank STRANDLI †65	
14	Mark TINKLER ‡65	
Gk	Mervyn DAY	

QPR
Red & Black hooped shirts, Black shorts   Goals

1	Tony ROBERTS	
2	David BARDSLEY	
3	Clive WILSON	
4	Ray WILKINS	
5	Darren PEACOCK	
6	Alan McDONALD	
7	Andy IMPEY	
8	Simon BARKER	
9	Les FERDINAND	16
10	Bradley ALLEN ❏	
11	Andy SINTON ❏	
	Substitutes	
12	Devon WHITE	
14	Rufus BREVETT	
Gk	Jan STEJSKAL	

Date	Saturday 1 May 1993
Venue	Carrow Road, 3.00pm

NORWICH CITY (0) 1
LIVERPOOL (0) 0

Attendance	20,610
Referee	David ELLERAY
Linesmen	A. Black, G.T. Pearson

NORWICH CITY
Yellow shirts, Green shorts   Goals

1	Bryan GUNN	
2	Ian CULVERHOUSE	
3	Mark BOWEN	
4	Rob NEWMAN ❑	
5	John POLSTON	
6	Jeremy GOSS ❑ ‡	
7	Ian CROOK	
8	Chris SUTTON	
9	Mark ROBINS	
10	Ruel FOX †	
11	David PHILLIPS	62p
	Substitutes	
12	Efan EKOKU †71	
14	Gary MEGSON ‡65	
Gk	Mark WALTON	

LIVERPOOL
Red shirts, Red shorts   Goals

1	David JAMES ❑ ■	
2	Rob JONES	
3	David BURROWS	
4	Steve NICOL	
5	Mark WRIGHT ❑	
6	Jamie REDKNAPP †	
7	Paul STEWART ❑ ‡	
8	Don HUTCHISON	
9	Ian RUSH ❑	
10	John BARNES	
11	Mark WALTERS	
	Substitutes	
12	Ronnie ROSENTHAL ‡79	
14	Torben PIECHNIK	
Gk	Mike HOOPER †61	

Date	Saturday 1 May 1993
Venue	City Ground, 3.00pm

NOTTINGHAM FOREST (0) 0
SHEFFIELD UNITED (1) 2

Attendance	26,752
Referee	Paul DURKIN
Linesmen	E. Thomas, E.J. Walsh

NOTTINGHAM FOREST
Red shirts, White shorts   Goals

1	Andy MARRIOTT	
2	Brian LAWS	
3	Brett WILLIAMS	
4	Steve CHETTLE	
5	Carl TILER	
6	Roy KEANE	
7	Kingsley BLACK	
8	Scot GEMMILL	
9	Nigel CLOUGH	
10	Robert ROSARIO	
11	Ian WOAN	
	Substitutes	
12	Steve STONE	
14	Thorvaldur ORLYGSSON	
Gk	Mark CROSSLEY	

SHEFFIELD UNITED
White shirts, Black shorts   Goals

1	Alan KELLY	
2	Mitch WARD	
3	Paul BEESLEY ‡	
4	Charlie HARTFIELD	
5	Brian GAYLE	73
6	John PEMBERTON	
7	Carl BRADSHAW	
8	Paul ROGERS	
9	Glyn HODGES ❑	30
10	Brian DEANE	
11	Dane WHITEHOUSE	
	Substitutes	
12	Franz CARR	
14	Adrian LITTLEJOHN ‡90	
Gk	Jim LEIGHTON	

Date	Saturday 1 May 1993
Venue	Hillsborough, 3.00pm

SHEFFIELD WEDNESDAY (0) 2
MIDDLESBROUGH (2) 3

Attendance	25,959
Referee	Brian HILL
Linesmen	A. Hilditch, R. Pearson

SHEFFIELD WEDNESDAY
Blue & White striped shirts, Black shorts   Goals

1	Chris WOODS	
2	Roland NILSSON	
3	Nigel WORTHINGTON	
4	Carlton PALMER	
5	Peter SHIRTLIFF	
6	Viv ANDERSON	
7	John HARKES	
8	Paul WARHURST	
9	David HIRST ‡	
10	Mark BRIGHT	
11	John SHERIDAN	
	Substitutes	
12	Graham HYDE	
14	Chris BART-WILLIAMS ‡45	52
Gk	Kevin PRESSMAN	

MIDDLESBROUGH
Red shirts, White shorts   Goals

1	Andy COLLETT	
2	Curtis FLEMING	
3	Jimmy PHILLIPS	
4	Craig HIGNETT	
5	Chris MORRIS	78og
6	Derek WHYTE	
7	John HENDRIE	51
8	Jamie POLLOCK ❑ †	38
9	Paul WILKINSON ❑	
10	Andy PEAKE	
11	Tommy WRIGHT ‡	
	Substitutes	
12	Dwight MARSHALL †57	
14	Willie FALCONER ‡16	26
Gk	Ben ROBERTS	

Date	Saturday 1 May 1993
Venue	The Dell, 3.00pm

SOUTHAMPTON (0) 0
MANCHESTER CITY (1) 1

Attendance	16,730
Referee	John LLOYD
Linesmen	W.M. Jordan, M. Stobbart

SOUTHAMPTON
Red & White striped shirts, Black shorts   Goals

1	Tim FLOWERS	
2	Jeff KENNA	
3	Micky ADAMS	
4	Tommy WIDDRINGTON †	
5	Matthew BOUND ‡	
6	Kenneth MONKOU	
7	Matthew LE TISSIER	
8	Glenn COCKERILL	
9	Iain DOWIE	
10	Neil MADDISON	
11	Nicky BANGER	
	Substitutes	
12	Neal BARTLETT †71	
14	Derek ALLAN ‡80	
Gk	Ian ANDREWS	

MANCHESTER CITY
Light Blue shirts, White shorts   Goals

1	Tony COTON	
2	Ray RANSON	
3	David BRIGHTWELL	
4	Steve McMAHON	
5	Keith CURLE	
6	Michel VONK	
7	David WHITE	42
8	Mike SHERON	
9	Niall QUINN	
10	Garry FLITCROFT	
11	Rick HOLDEN †	
	Substitutes	
12	Fitzroy SIMPSON †82	
14	Mike QUIGLEY	
Gk	Martyn MARGETSON	

Date	Saturday 1 May 1993
Venue	White Hart Lane, 3.00pm

TOTTENHAM HOTSPUR (1) 1
WIMBLEDON (0) 1

Attendance	24,473
Referee	Ray LEWIS
Linesmen	J.A. Elwin, W.J. Norbury

TOTTENHAM HOTSPUR
White shirts, Navy Blue shorts   Goals

1	Ian WALKER	
2	Stuart NETHERCOTT †	
3	Pat VAN DEN HAUWE	
4	Vinny SAMWAYS	
5	Gary MABBUTT	
6	Neil RUDDOCK	
7	Steve SEDGLEY	
8	Andy TURNER	
9	Darren ANDERTON	39
10	Teddy SHERINGHAM	
11	Paul ALLEN ‡	
	Substitutes	
12	Lee HODGES †81	
14	Andy GRAY ‡60	
Gk	Kevin DEARDEN	

WIMBLEDON
Blue shirts, Blue shorts   Goals

1	Hans SEGERS	
2	Warren BARTON	
3	Brian McALLISTER ■	
4	Vinnie JONES	
5	John SCALES	
6	Scott FITZGERALD	
7	Neal ARDLEY	
8	Robbie EARLE	64
9	John FASHANU	
10	Dean HOLDSWORTH ❏ †	
11	Andy CLARKE ‡	
	Substitutes	
12	Paul McGEE †81	
14	Lawrie SANCHEZ ‡65	
Gk	Paul KEE	

Date	Sunday 2 May 1993
Venue	Villa Park, 4.00pm

ASTON VILLA (0) 0
OLDHAM ATHLETIC (1) 1

Attendance	37,247
Referee	David ALLISON
Linesmen	K.J. Hawkes, P. Newall

ASTON VILLA
Claret & Blue shirts, White shorts   Goals

1	Mark BOSNICH	
2	Earl BARRETT	
3	Steve STAUNTON	
4	Shaun TEALE	
5	Paul McGRATH	
6	Kevin RICHARDSON	
7	Ray HOUGHTON	
8	Garry PARKER †	
9	Dean SAUNDERS	
10	Dalian ATKINSON	
11	Dwight YORKE	
	Substitutes	
12	Tony DALEY †60	
14	Neil COX	
Gk	Nigel SPINK	

OLDHAM ATHLETIC
Blue shirts, Blue shorts   Goals

1	Paul GERRARD	
2	Gunnar HALLE	
3	Neil POINTON	
4	Nick HENRY	30
5	Richard JOBSON ❏	
6	Craig FLEMING	
7	Steve REDMOND	
8	Darren BECKFORD	
9	Ian OLNEY	
10	Mike MILLIGAN	
11	Paul BERNARD	
	Substitutes	
12	Andy RITCHIE	
14	Neil ADAMS	
Gk	Jason KEARTON	

Date	Monday 3 May 1993
Venue	Old Trafford, 7.30pm

MANCHESTER UNITED (1) 3
BLACKBURN ROVERS (1) 1

Attendance	40,447
Referee	Jim BORRETT
Linesmen	J. McGrath, P. Rejer

MANCHESTER UNITED
Red shirts, White shorts   Goals

1	Peter SCHMEICHEL	
2	Paul PARKER	
3	Denis IRWIN	
4	Steve BRUCE ❑	
5	Lee SHARPE †	
6	Gary PALLISTER	90
7	Eric CANTONA	
8	Paul INCE ❑	59
9	Brian McCLAIR ‡	
10	Mark HUGHES	
11	Ryan GIGGS	21
	Substitutes	
12	Bryan ROBSON †45	
14	Andrei KANCHELSKIS ‡79	
Gk	Les SEALEY	

BLACKBURN ROVERS
Blue & White shirts, Blue shorts   Goals

1	Bobby MIMMS	
2	Nick MARKER ❑ †	
3	Graeme LE SAUX	
4	Tim SHERWOOD	
5	Colin HENDRY	
6	Kevin MORAN ‡	
7	Stuart RIPLEY	
8	Mark ATKINS	
9	Kevin GALLACHER	8
10	Mike NEWELL	
11	Jason WILCOX	
	Substitutes	
12	Gordon COWANS †70	
14	Patrik ANDERSSON ‡74	
Gk	Frank TALIA	

Date	Tuesday 4 May 1993
Venue	Highbury Stadium, 7.45pm

ARSENAL (0) 0
QPR (0) 0

Attendance	18,817
Referee	Rodger GIFFORD
Linesmen	G.P. Barber, D.C. Madgwick

● *Moved from 13 February*

ARSENAL
Red & White shirts, White shorts   Goals

1	Alan MILLER	
2	Lee DIXON	
3	Martin KEOWN	
4	Paul DAVIS	
5	Andy LINIGHAN	
6	Tony ADAMS	
7	John JENSEN	
8	Kevin CAMPBELL	
9	Alan SMITH	
10	Paul MERSON ‡	
11	Neil HEANEY	
	Substitutes	
12	Steve BOULD	
14	Jimmy CARTER ‡84	
Gk	Jim WILL	

QPR
Blue & White hooped shirts, Blue shorts   Goals

1	Tony ROBERTS	
2	David BARDSLEY	
3	Clive WILSON	
4	Ray WILKINS	
5	Darren PEACOCK	
6	Alan McDONALD	
7	Andy IMPEY	
8	Simon BARKER ‡	
9	Les FERDINAND	
10	Bradley ALLEN	
11	Andy SINTON	
	Substitutes	
12	Devon WHITE	
14	Rufus BREVETT ‡88	
Gk	Jan STEJSKAL	

Date	Tuesday 4 May 1993
Venue	Goodison Park, 7.30pm

EVERTON (0) 0
SHEFFIELD UNITED (2) 2

Attendance	15,197
Referee	Vic CALLOW
Linesmen	M. Fletcher, R. Pearson

● *Moved from 3 April*

EVERTON
Blue shirts, White shorts   Goals

1	Neville SOUTHALL	
2	Paul HOLMES	
3	Andy HINCHCLIFFE	
4	John EBBRELL	
5	Matthew JACKSON	
6	Gary ABLETT	
7	PREKI †	
8	Peter BEARDSLEY	
9	Tony COTTEE	
10	Barry HORNE ‡	
11	Peter BEAGRIE	
	Substitutes	
12	Stuart BARLOW †73	
14	Neil MOORE ‡45	
Gk	Jason KEARTON	

SHEFFIELD UNITED
Red & White striped shirts, Black shorts   Goals

1	Alan KELLY	
2	Mitch WARD	
3	Paul BEESLEY	
4	Charlie HARTFIELD	
5	Brian GAYLE	
6	John PEMBERTON	
7	Carl BRADSHAW	15
8	Paul ROGERS	
9	Glyn HODGES	26
10	Brian DEANE	
11	Dane WHITEHOUSE	
	Substitutes	
12	Jamie HOYLAND	
14	Adrian LITTLEJOHN	
Gk	Jim LEIGHTON	

Date	Tuesday 4 May 1993
Venue	Hillsborough, 7.45pm

SHEFFIELD WEDNESDAY (0) 1
LEEDS UNITED (1) 1

Attendance	26,855
Referee	Roger MILFORD
Linesmen	P. Newall, P. Rejer

● *Moved from 3 April*

SHEFFIELD WEDNESDAY
Blue & White striped shirts, Black shorts   Goals

1	Chris WOODS	
2	Roland NILSSON	
3	Phil KING †	
4	Carlton PALMER	
5	Peter SHIRTLIFF	
6	Ryan JONES	
7	Danny WILSON ‡	
8	Graham HYDE	
9	David HIRST	90
10	Chris BART-WILLIAMS	
11	Nigel WORTHINGTON	
	Substitutes	
12	Paul WARHURST †73	
14	John HARKES ‡35	
Gk	Kevin PRESSMAN	

LEEDS UNITED
White shirts, White shorts   Goals

1	John LUKIC	
2	Ray WALLACE	
3	Kevin SHARP †	
4	David BATTY ❏	
5	Jon NEWSOME ❏	
6	Chris WHYTE	
7	Noel WHELAN	
8	Rod WALLACE	
9	Lee CHAPMAN	35
10	Steve HODGE	
11	Mark TINKLER	
	Substitutes	
12	Dylan KERR †77	
14	David WETHERALL	
Gk	Mervyn DAY	

Date	Wednesday 5 May 1993
Venue	Maine Road, 7.30pm

MANCHESTER CITY (0) 0
CRYSTAL PALACE (0) 0

Attendance	21,167
Referee	Steve LODGE
Linesmen	E.B. Crompton, P. Rejer

● *Moved from 6 March*

MANCHESTER CITY
Light Blue shirts, White shorts — Goals

1	Tony COTON	
2	Ray RANSON	
3	Terry PHELAN	
4	Steve McMAHON	
5	Keith CURLE	
6	Michel VONK	
7	David WHITE	
8	Mike SHERON †	
9	Niall QUINN	
10	Garry FLITCROFT	
11	Rick HOLDEN	
	Substitutes	
12	David KERR †63	
14	Fitzroy SIMPSON	
Gk	Andy DIBBLE	

CRYSTAL PALACE
Red & Blue shirts, Red shorts — Goals

1	Nigel MARTYN	
2	Richard SHAW	
3	Gareth SOUTHGATE	
4	Paul WILLIAMS	
5	Eric YOUNG	
6	Andy THORN	
7	John HUMPHREY	
8	Geoff THOMAS	
9	Chris ARMSTRONG	
10	Simon RODGER	
11	Eddie McGOLDRICK	
	Substitutes	
12	Simon OSBORN	
14	Dean GORDON	
Gk	Andy WOODMAN	

Date	Wednesday 5 May 1993
Venue	Boundary Park, 7.45pm

OLDHAM ATHLETIC (3) 3
LIVERPOOL (1) 2

Attendance	15,381
Referee	Paul DURKIN
Linesmen	A.N. Butler, D.T. Colwell

● *Previously postponed on Boxing Day and 2 March*

OLDHAM ATHLETIC
Blue shirts, Blue shorts — Goals

1	Paul GERRARD	
2	Gunnar HALLE	
3	Neil POINTON	
4	Nick HENRY ❑	
5	Richard JOBSON	
6	Craig FLEMING	
7	Steve REDMOND	
8	Ian OLNEY	35, 36
9	Darren BECKFORD † *	20
10	Mike MILLIGAN	
11	Paul BERNARD	
	Substitutes	
12	Andy RITCHIE †80	
14	Neil ADAMS	
Gk	John KEELEY	

LIVERPOOL
Red shirts, Red shorts — Goals

1	David JAMES	
2	Rob JONES	
3	David BURROWS ❑	
4	Steve NICOL	
5	Mark WRIGHT ‡	
6	Jamie REDKNAPP ❑	
7	Paul STEWART †	
8	Don HUTCHISON ■	
9	Ian RUSH	30, 59
10	John BARNES	
11	Mark WALTERS ❑	
	Substitutes	
12	Ronnie ROSENTHAL †52	
14	Torben PIECHNIK ‡45	
Gk	Mike HOOPER	

Date	Wednesday 5 May 1993
Venue	White Hart Lane, 7.45pm

TOTTENHAM HOTSPUR (0) 1
BLACKBURN ROVERS (1) 2

Attendance	23,097
Referee	Kelvin MORTON
Linesmen	G.P. Barber, G.T. Pearson

● *Moved from 13 March*

TOTTENHAM HOTSPUR
White shirts, Navy Blue shorts   Goals

1	Ian WALKER	
2	Stuart NETHERCOTT †	
3	Pat VAN DEN HAUWE	
4	Vinny SAMWAYS	
5	Gary MABBUTT	
6	Neil RUDDOCK	
7	Steve SEDGLEY	
8	Andy TURNER	
9	Darren ANDERTON	86
10	Teddy SHERINGHAM	
11	Paul ALLEN	
	Substitutes	
12	Danny HILL †58	
14	Lee HODGES ‡58	
Gk	Kevin DEARDEN	

BLACKBURN ROVERS
Red & Black striped shirts, White shorts   Goals

1	Bobby MIMMS	
2	Nick MARKER	
3	Graeme LE SAUX	
4	Tim SHERWOOD	
5	Colin HENDRY	
6	Gordon COWANS	
7	Stuart RIPLEY	
8	Mark ATKINS †	
9	Kevin GALLACHER	
10	Mike NEWELL	22, 54
11	Jason WILCOX ❑	
	Substitutes	
12	Tony DOBSON †84 ❑	
14	Patrik ANDERSSON	
Gk	Frank TALIA	

Date	Thursday 6 May 1993
Venue	Hillsborough, 7.30pm

SHEFFIELD WEDNESDAY (1) 1
ARSENAL (0) 0

Attendance	23,645
Referee	Robbie HART
Linesmen	E.B. Crompton

● *Moved from 27 January*

SHEFFIELD WEDNESDAY
Blue & White striped shirts, Black shorts   Goals

1	Kevin PRESSMAN	
2	John HARKES	
3	Phil KING	
4	Graham HYDE ❑	
5	Viv ANDERSON	
6	Simon STEWART	
7	Mike WILLIAMS	
8	Ryan JONES †	
9	Mark BRIGHT	19
10	Chris BART-WILLIAMS ‡	
11	John SHERIDAN	
	Substitutes	
12	Chris WADDLE †80	
14	Nigel JEMSON ‡71	
Gk	Lance KEY	

ARSENAL
Red & White shirts, White shorts   Goals

1	Alan MILLER	
2	Pal LYDERSEN ‡	
3	Martin KEOWN	
4	Scott MARSHALL	
5	David O'LEARY	
6	Steve BOULD	
7	John JENSEN †	
8	Ian SELLEY	
9	Alan SMITH	
10	Neil HEANEY	
11	Jimmy CARTER	
	Substitutes	
12	Gavin McGOWAN †61	
14	Mark FLATTS ‡75	
Gk	Jim WILL	

Date	Saturday 8 May 1993
Venue	Highbury Stadium, 3.00pm

ARSENAL (1) 3
CRYSTAL PALACE (0) 0

Attendance	25,225
Referee	Keith BURGE
Linesmen	J.F. Moore, B.A. Wigginton

ARSENAL
Red & White shirts, White shorts   Goals

1	David SEAMAN	
2	Lee DIXON	
3	Nigel WINTERBURN	
4	Paul DAVIS	
5	Andy LINIGHAN	
6	Tony ADAMS	
7	Jimmy CARTER ‡	
8	Ian WRIGHT †	9
9	Kevin CAMPBELL	89
10	Paul MERSON	
11	Ray PARLOUR	
	Substitutes	
12	Paul DICKOV ‡67	82
14	David O'LEARY †87	
Gk	Alan MILLER	

CRYSTAL PALACE
Yellow shirts, Light Blue shorts   Goals

1	Nigel MARTYN	
2	Richard SHAW ‡	
3	Gareth SOUTHGATE	
4	Paul WILLIAMS	
5	Eric YOUNG	
6	Andy THORN ❑	
7	John HUMPHREY	
8	Geoff THOMAS	
9	Chris ARMSTRONG	
10	Simon RODGER	
11	Eddie McGOLDRICK	
	Substitutes	
12	Simon OSBORN	
14	Dean GORDON ‡61	
Gk	Andy WOODMAN	

Date	Saturday 8 May 1993
Venue	Ewood Park, 3.00pm

BLACKBURN ROVERS (0) 1
SHEFFIELD WEDNESDAY (0) 0

Attendance	14,956
Referee	Philip DON
Linesmen	D.T. Colwell, G.I. Grandidge

BLACKBURN ROVERS
Blue & White shirts, White shorts   Goals

1	Bobby MIMMS	
2	David MAY	
3	Graeme LE SAUX	
4	Tim SHERWOOD	65
5	Colin HENDRY ❑	
6	Nick MARKER	
7	Stuart RIPLEY	
8	Gordon COWANS	
9	Kevin GALLACHER	
10	Mike NEWELL †	
11	Jason WILCOX	
	Substitutes	
12	Mark ATKINS †45	
14	Patrik ANDERSSON	
Gk	Frank TALIA	

SHEFFIELD WEDNESDAY
Yellow shirts, Yellow shorts   Goals

1	Chris WOODS	
2	Roland NILSSON	
3	Nigel WORTHINGTON ❑	
4	Carlton PALMER	
5	Peter SHIRTLIFF	
6	Viv ANDERSON	
7	John HARKES	
8	Chris WADDLE †	
9	David HIRST	
10	Mark BRIGHT	
11	John SHERIDAN ‡	
	Substitutes	
12	Chris BART-WILLIAMS †73	
14	Graham HYDE ‡56	
Gk	Kevin PRESSMAN	

Date	Saturday 8 May 1993
Venue	Highfield Road, 3.00pm

COVENTRY CITY (2) 3
LEEDS UNITED (1) 3

Attendance	19,591
Referee	Kelvin MORTON
Linesmen	P.M. Roberts, J.B. Robinson

COVENTRY CITY
Sky Blue shirts, Sky Blue shorts · Goals

1	Jonathan GOULD	
2	Brian BORROWS	
3	Phil BABB	
4	Peter ATHERTON	
5	Lloyd McGRATH	
6	David RENNIE	
7	Leigh JENKINSON †	
8	Lee HURST	
9	Mick QUINN ❑	40
10	Peter NDLOVU	73
11	John WILLIAMS	5
	Substitutes	
12	Roy WEGERLE †65	
14	David BUSST	
Gk	Steve OGRIZOVIC	

LEEDS UNITED
White shirts, White shorts · Goals

1	Mark BEENEY	
2	Ray WALLACE	
3	Tony DORIGO	
4	David BATTY	
5	Jon NEWSOME	
6	Chris WHYTE ❑ ■	
7	Carl SHUTT †	
8	Rod WALLACE	6, 89, 90
9	Lee CHAPMAN	
10	Steve HODGE	
11	Mark TINKLER ‡	
	Substitutes	
12	David ROCASTLE †53	
14	Dylan KERR ‡88	
Gk	John LUKIC	

Date	Saturday 8 May 1993
Venue	Portman Road, 3.00pm

IPSWICH TOWN (1) 2
NOTTINGHAM FOREST (0) 1

Attendance	22,093
Referee	Mike REED
Linesmen	D. Orr, M.G. Wright

IPSWICH TOWN
Blue & White shirts, White shorts · Goals

1	Andy PETTERSON	
2	Eddie YOUDS	
3	Gavin JOHNSON †	
4	Mick STOCKWELL	
5	John WARK	
6	David LINIGHAN ❑	
7	Geraint WILLIAMS	
8	Steve WHITTON ‡	52p
9	Simon MILTON	40
10	Jason DOZZELL	
11	Chris KIWOMYA ❑	
	Substitutes	
12	Phil WHELAN †45 ❑	
14	Steve PALMER ‡76	
Gk	Jason WINTERS	

NOTTINGHAM FOREST
Red shirts, White shorts · Goals

1	Andy MARRIOTT	
2	Brian LAWS	
3	Brett WILLIAMS	
4	Steve CHETTLE	
5	Carl TILER	
6	Roy KEANE ❑	
7	Kingsley BLACK ‡	
8	Scot GEMMILL	
9	Nigel CLOUGH	64p
10	Lee GLOVER	
11	Ian WOAN	
	Substitutes	
12	Steve STONE	
14	Thorvaldur ORLYGSSON ‡70	
Gk	Mark CROSSLEY	

Date   Saturday 8 May 1993
Venue   Anfield, 3.00pm

LIVERPOOL (2) 6
TOTTENHAM HOTSPUR (0) 2

Attendance 43,385
Referee   Steve LODGE
Linesmen E.B. Crompton, P.R. Richards

LIVERPOOL
Red shirts, Red shorts   Goals

1	Bruce GROBBELAAR	
2	Rob JONES ❑	
3	David BURROWS	
4	Steve NICOL	
5	Mark WRIGHT	
6	Jamie REDKNAPP	
7	Steve HARKNESS	47
8	Don HUTCHISON	
9	Ian RUSH	21, 85
10	John BARNES	44, 88
11	Mark WALTERS	82p
	Substitutes	
12	Robbie FOWLER	
14	Torben PIECHNIK	
Gk	Mike HOOPER	

TOTTENHAM HOTSPUR
White shirts, Navy Blue shorts   Goals

1	Ian WALKER	
2	David McDONALD	
3	Pat VAN DEN HAUWE ❑ †	
4	Danny HILL	
5	Gary MABBUTT	
6	Neil RUDDOCK	
7	Steve SEDGLEY	77
8	Kevin WATSON ‡	
9	Darren ANDERTON	
10	Teddy SHERINGHAM	46
11	Paul ALLEN	
	Substitutes	
12	Stuart NETHERCOTT †46	
14	Lee HODGES ‡66	
Gk	Kevin DEARDEN	

Date   Saturday 8 May 1993
Venue   Maine Road, 3.00pm

MANCHESTER CITY (1) 2
EVERTON (3) 5

Attendance 25,180
Referee   Ken REDFERN
Linesmen T. Heilbron, T.A. Atkinson

MANCHESTER CITY
Light Blue shirts, White shorts   Goals

1	Martyn MARGETSON †	
2	Ray RANSON	
3	Terry PHELAN ❑	
4	Steve McMAHON ‡	
5	Keith CURLE	73p
6	Michel VONK	
7	David WHITE	39
8	Mike SHERON	
9	Niall QUINN	
10	Garry FLITCROFT	
11	Rick HOLDEN	
	Substitutes	
12	Fitzroy SIMPSON ‡62	
14	David KERR	
Gk	Andy DIBBLE †45	

EVERTON
Salmon Pink & Blue stripes, Blue shorts   Goals

1	Neville SOUTHALL †	
2	Paul HOLMES	
3	Andy HINCHCLIFFE	
4	John EBBRELL	
5	Matthew JACKSON	6
6	Gary ABLETT	
7	Mark WARD ❑	
8	Peter BEARDSLEY	32
9	Tony COTTEE ❑	
10	PREKI ‡	51
11	Peter BEAGRIE ❑	19, 84
	Substitutes	
12	Stuart BARLOW ‡69	
14	Alan HARPER	
Gk	Jason KEARTON †62	

Date Saturday 8 May 1993
Venue Ayresome Park, 3.00pm

MIDDLESBROUGH (1) 3
NORWICH CITY (1) 3

Attendance 15,155
Referee Gerald ASHBY
Linesmen R.H. Andrews, M.A. Riley

MIDDLESBROUGH
Red shirts, White shorts   Goals

1	Andy COLLETT	
2	Curtis FLEMING	
3	Jimmy PHILLIPS †	
4	Alan KERNAGHAN	
5	Derek WHYTE	
6	Andy PEAKE	
7	John HENDRIE	74
8	Willie FALCONER	34
9	Paul WILKINSON	65
10	Craig HIGNETT ‡	
11	Robbie MUSTOE	
	Substitutes	
12	Alan MOORE †67	
14	Dwight MARSHALL ‡72	
Gk	Ben ROBERTS	

NORWICH CITY
Yellow shirts, Green shorts   Goals

1	Bryan GUNN	
2	Ian CULVERHOUSE	
3	Mark BOWEN	
4	Rob NEWMAN	
5	John POLSTON	
6	Andrew JOHNSON	68
7	Ian CROOK	
8	Efan EKOKU	14, 66
9	Chris SUTTON	
10	Ruel FOX	
11	David PHILLIPS	
	Substitutes	
12	Mark ROBINS	
14	Colin WOODTHORPE	
Gk	Andy MARSHALL	

Date Saturday 8 May 1993
Venue Boundary Park, 3.00pm

OLDHAM ATHLETIC (2) 4
SOUTHAMPTON (1) 3

Attendance 14,597
Referee Howard KING
Linesmen B.L. Polkey, E.J. Walsh

OLDHAM ATHLETIC
Blue shirts, Blue shorts   Goals

1	Paul GERRARD	
2	Gunnar HALLE	64
3	Neil POINTON	29
4	Nick HENRY	
5	Richard JOBSON	
6	Craig FLEMING	
7	Steve REDMOND	
8	Andy RITCHIE †	55
9	Ian OLNEY	44
10	Mike MILLIGAN	
11	Paul BERNARD	
	Substitutes	
12	Ian MARSHALL †70	
14	Neil ADAMS	
Gk	John KEELEY	

SOUTHAMPTON
Red & White shirts, Black shorts   Goals

1	Tim FLOWERS	
2	Jeff KENNA	
3	Micky ADAMS	
4	Tommy WIDDRINGTON ‡	
5	Richard HALL	
6	Kenneth MONKOU	
7	Matthew LE TISSIER	34, 67, 85
8	Glenn COCKERILL	
9	Iain DOWIE	
10	Neil MADDISON	
11	Nicky BANGER	
	Substitutes	
12	Kevin MOORE	
14	Francis BENALI ‡57	
Gk	Ian ANDREWS	

Date	Saturday 8 May 1993
Venue	Bramall Lane, 3.00pm

SHEFFIELD UNITED (3) 4
CHELSEA (0) 2

Attendance	24,850
Referee	Allan GUNN
Linesmen	J. Leech, A.J. Martin

SHEFFIELD UNITED
Red & White striped shirts, White shorts   Goals

1	Alan KELLY	
2	Mitch WARD	
3	Tom COWAN	
4	Charlie HARTFIELD †	
5	Paul BEESLEY	
6	John PEMBERTON	
7	Carl BRADSHAW	
8	Paul ROGERS	16
9	Andy SCOTT	7
10	Brian DEANE	
11	Dane WHITEHOUSE ‡	43, 48
	Substitutes	
12	Jamie HOYLAND †66	
14	Adrian LITTLEJOHN ‡83	
Gk	Jim LEIGHTON	

CHELSEA
Blue shirts, Blue shorts   Goals

1	Dmitri KHARIN	
2	Steve CLARKE	
3	Frank SINCLAIR	
4	Andy TOWNSEND	87
5	Erland JOHNSEN	
6	Nigel SPACKMAN	
7	Darren BARNARD †	
8	John SPENCER ‡	
9	Tony CASCARINO	
10	Gareth HALL	
11	Dennis WISE	
	Substitutes	
12	David LEE †60	86
14	Graham STUART ‡74	
Gk	Dave BEASANT	

Date	Sunday 9 May 1993
Venue	Loftus Road, 2.00pm

QPR (0) 2
ASTON VILLA (1) 1

Attendance	18,904
Referee	Paul DURKIN
Linesmen	G. Butland, A.P. D'Urso

QPR
Blue & White hooped shirts, White shorts   Goals

1	Tony ROBERTS	
2	David BARDSLEY	
3	Clive WILSON	
4	Ray WILKINS	
5	Darren PEACOCK	
6	Alan McDONALD	
7	Andy IMPEY	
8	Simon BARKER	
9	Les FERDINAND	67
10	Bradley ALLEN	78
11	Andy SINTON	
	Substitutes	
12	Devon WHITE	
14	Rufus BREVETT	
Gk	Jan STEJSKAL	

ASTON VILLA
Claret & Blue shirts, White Shorts   Goals

1	Mark BOSNICH	
2	Earl BARRETT ❏	
3	Steve STAUNTON ‡	
4	Shaun TEALE	
5	Paul McGRATH ❏	
6	Kevin RICHARDSON ❏	
7	Ray HOUGHTON †	
8	Garry PARKER	
9	Dean SAUNDERS	
10	Dalian ATKINSON	
11	Tony DALEY	38
	Substitutes	
12	Neil COX †80	
14	Martin CARRUTHERS ‡79	
Gk	Nigel SPINK	

Date	Sunday 9 May 1993	
Venue	Selhurst Park, 2.00pm	

WIMBLEDON (0) 1
MANCHESTER UNITED (0) 2

Attendance 30,115
Referee Joe WORRALL
Linesmen C. Jones, I.M.D. Mitchell

WIMBLEDON
Blue shirts, Blue shorts — Goals

1	Hans SEGERS	
2	Warren BARTON	
3	Brian McALLISTER	
4	Vinnie JONES	
5	John SCALES	
6	Scott FITZGERALD	
7	Neal ARDLEY ‡	
8	Robbie EARLE	
9	John FASHANU	
10	Dean HOLDSWORTH	81
11	Andy CLARKE	
	Substitutes	
12	Lawrie SANCHEZ	
14	Roger JOSEPH ‡69	
Gk	Paul KEE	

MANCHESTER UNITED
Red shirts, White shorts — Goals

1	Peter SCHMEICHEL	
2	Paul PARKER	
3	Denis IRWIN †	
4	Steve BRUCE	
5	Lee SHARPE	
6	Gary PALLISTER	
7	Bryan ROBSON	70
8	Paul INCE	63
9	Brian McCLAIR	
10	Mark HUGHES	
11	Eric CANTONA	
	Substitutes	
12	Ryan GIGGS †46	
14	Dion DUBLIN	
Gk	Les SEALEY	

Date	Tuesday 11 May 1993	
Venue	Highbury Stadium, 7.45pm	

ARSENAL (0) 1
TOTTENHAM HOTSPUR (1) 3

Attendance 26,393
Referee Keith COOPER
Linesmen S.G. Tomblin, M.G. Wright
● *Game moved from 3 April*

ARSENAL
Red & White shirts, White shorts — Goals

1	Alan MILLER	
2	Pal LYDERSEN †	
3	Martin KEOWN	
4	Scott MARSHALL	
5	David O'LEARY	
6	Steve BOULD	
7	Mark FLATTS ‡	
8	Ian SELLEY	
9	Alan SMITH	
10	Paul DICKOV	52
11	Neil HEANEY	
	Substitutes	
12	Gavin McGOWAN †45	
14	Jimmy CARTER ‡76	
Gk	Jim WILL	

TOTTENHAM HOTSPUR
White shirts, Navy Blue shorts — Goals

1	Ian WALKER	
2	David McDONALD	
3	Pat VAN DEN HAUWE	
4	Danny HILL	
5	Gary MABBUTT	
6	Neil RUDDOCK	
7	Steve SEDGLEY	
8	John HENDRY ‡	46, 78
9	Darren ANDERTON	
10	Teddy SHERINGHAM	39
11	Paul ALLEN	
	Substitutes	
12	Stuart NETHERCOTT	
14	Lee HODGES ‡82	
Gk	Kevin DEARDEN	

Date Tuesday 11 May 1993
Venue Loftus Road, 7.45pm

QPR (2) 3
SHEFFIELD WEDNESDAY (0) 1

Attendance 12,177
Referee David ALLISON
Linesmen J.A. Elwin, I.A. Madge
● *Moved from 17 April*

QPR
Blue & White hooped shirts, White shorts   Goals

1	Tony ROBERTS	
2	David BARDSLEY	
3	Clive WILSON	
4	Ray WILKINS	
5	Darren PEACOCK	
6	Alan McDONALD	
7	Andy IMPEY	
8	Simon BARKER	
9	Les FERDINAND	67
10	Bradley ALLEN	27, 31
11	Andy SINTON	

Substitutes

12	Rufus BREVETT	
14	Devon WHITE	
Gk	Jan STEJSKAL	

SHEFFIELD WEDNESDAY
Yellow shirts, Yellow shorts   Goals

1	Kevin PRESSMAN	
2	Roland NILSSON	
3	Phil KING ❏	
4	Ryan JONES	
5	Simon STEWART †	
6	Viv ANDERSON	
7	Mike WILLIAMS ‡	
8	Graham HYDE	
9	Mark BRIGHT	78
10	Chris BART-WILLIAMS	
11	John SHERIDAN	

Substitutes

12	Carlton PALMER †70	
14	Nigel JEMSON ‡57	
Gk	Chris WOODS	

LEAGUE TABLE

Up to and including 11.05.93	P	W	D	L	F	A	Pts	Gd
1 Manchester United	42	24	12	6	67	31	84	+36
2 Aston Villa	42	21	11	10	57	40	74	+17
3 Norwich City	42	21	9	12	61	65	72	-4
4 Blackburn Rovers	42	20	11	11	68	46	71	+22
5 Queen's Park Rangers	42	17	12	13	63	55	63	+8
6 Liverpool	42	16	11	15	62	55	59	+7
7 Sheffield Wednesday	42	15	14	13	55	51	59	+4
8 Tottenham Hotspur	42	16	11	15	60	66	59	-6
9 Manchester City	42	15	12	15	56	51	57	+5
10 Arsenal	42	15	11	16	40	38	56	+2
11 Chelsea	42	14	14	14	51	54	56	-3
12 Wimbledon	42	14	12	16	56	55	54	+1
13 Everton	42	15	8	19	53	55	53	-2
14 Sheffield United	42	14	10	18	54	53	52	+1
15 Coventry City	42	13	13	16	52	57	52	-5
16 Ipswich Town	42	12	16	14	50	55	52	-5
17 Leeds United	42	12	15	15	57	62	51	-5
18 Southampton	42	13	11	18	54	61	50	-7
19 Oldham Athletic	42	13	10	19	63	74	49	-11
20 Crystal Palace	42	11	16	15	48	61	49	-13
21 Middlesbrough	42	11	11	20	54	75	44	-21
22 Nottingham Forest	42	10	10	22	41	62	40	-21

LEADING SCORERS

Teddy SHERINGHAM	Tottenham Hotspur	22
Les FERDINAND	Queens Park Rangers	20
Dean HOLDSWORTH	Wimbledon	19
Mick QUINN	Coventry City	17
Alan SHEARER	Blackburn Rovers	16
David WHITE	Manchester City	16

LEAGUE GOALSCORING FIGURES

Running Totals

Date	Games	Goals	Average	Games	Goals	Average
01.05.93	9	20	2.22	440	1143	2.60
02.05.93	1	1	1.00	441	1144	2.59
03.05.93	1	4	4.00	442	1148	2.60
04.05.93	3	4	1.33	445	1152	2.59
05.05.93	3	8	2.67	448	1160	2.59
06.05.93	1	1	1.00	449	1161	2.58
08.05.93	9	47	5.22	458	1208	2.64
09.05.93	2	6	3.00	460	1214	2.64
11.05.93	2	8	4.00	462	1222	2.64

ARSENAL

Player	Apps	Gls	Birthplace	Birthdate
Tony ADAMS	33 (2)	-	Romford	10.10.66
Steve BOULD	24	1	Stoke	16.11.62
Kevin CAMPBELL	32 (5)	4	Lambeth	04.02.70
Jimmy CARTER	11 (5)	2	London	09.11.65
Paul DAVIS	6	-	Camberwell	09.12.61
Paul DICKOV	1 (2)	2	Livingston	01.11.72
Lee DIXON	29	-	Manchester	17.03.64
Mark FLATTS	6 (4)	-	Islington	14.10.72
Perry GROVES	0 (1)	-	London	19.04.65
Neil HEANEY	3 (2)	-	Middlesbrough	03.11.71
David HILLIER	27 (3)	1	Blackheath	19.12.69
John JENSEN	29 (3)	-	Denmark	03.05.65
Martin KEOWN	15 (1)	-	Oxford	24.07.66
Anders LIMPAR	12 (11)	2	Sweden	24.09.65
Andy LINIGHAN	19 (2)	2	Hartlepool	18.06.62
Pal LYDERSEN	7 (1)	-	Norway	10.09.65
Scott MARSHALL	2	-	Edinburgh	01.05.73
Gavin McGOWAN	0 (2)	-	London	16.01.76
Paul MERSON	32 (1)	6	Northolt	20.03.68
Alan MILLER	3 (1)	-	Epping	29.03.70
Steve MORROW	13 (3)	-	Belfast	02.07.70
David O'LEARY	6 (5)	-	London	02.05.58
Ray PARLOUR	16 (5)	1	Romford	07.03.73
Colin PATES	2 (5)	-	Mitcham	10.08.61
David SEAMAN	39	-	Rotherham	19.09.63
Ian SELLEY	9	-	Camberley	14.06.74
Alan SMITH	27 (4)	3	Birmingham	21.11.62
Nigel WINTERBURN	29	1	Coventry	11.12.63
Ian WRIGHT	30 (1)	15	Woolwich	03.11.63
Own goals		0		

Totals: Players 29 – Goals 40

ASTON VILLA

Player	Apps	Gls	Birthplace	Birthdate
Dalian ATKINSON	28	11	Shrewsbury	21.03.68
Earl BARRETT	42	1	Rochdale	28.04.67
Stefan BEINLICH	1 (6)	-	Germany	13.01.72
Mark BLAKE	0 (1)	-	Nottingham	16.12.70
Mark BOSNICH	17	-	Australia	13.01.72
Matthias BREITKREUTZ	2 (1)	-	Germany	12.05.71
Martin CARRUTHERS	0 (1)	-	Nottingham	07.08.72
Neil COX	6 (9)	1	Scunthorpe	08.10.71
Tony DALEY	8 (5)	2	Birmingham	18.10.67
Ugochuko EHIOGU	1 (3)	-	Hackney	03.11.72
Dave FARRELL	1 (1)	-	Birmingham	11.11.71
Stephen FROGGATT	16 (1)	1	Lincoln	09.03.73
Ray HOUGHTON	39	3	Glasgow	09.01.62
Frank McAVENNIE	0 (3)	-	Glasgow	22.11.59
Paul McGRATH	42	4	Ealing	04.12.59
Garry PARKER	37	9	Oxford	07.09.65
Cyrille REGIS	7 (6)	1	French Guyana	09.02.58
Kevin RICHARDSON	42	2	Newcastle	04.12.62
Dean SAUNDERS	35	13	Swansea	21.06.64
Bryan SMALL	10 (4)	-	Birmingham	15.11.71
Nigel SPINK	25	-	Chelmsford	08.08.58
Steve STAUNTON	42	2	Drogheda	19.01.69
Shaun TEALE	39	1	Southport	10.03.64
Dwight YORKE	22 (5)	6	Tobago	03.11.71
Own goals		0		

Totals: Players 24 - Goals 57

BLACKBURN ROVERS

Player	Apps	Gls	Birthplace	Birthdate
Patrik ANDERSSON	6 (5)	-	Sweden	18.08.71
Mark ATKINS	24 (7)	5	Doncaster	14.08.68
Henning BERG	2 (2)	-	Norway	01.09.69
Richard BROWN	2	-	Nottingham	13.01.67
Gordon COWANS	23 (1)	1	Co Durham	27.10.58
Tony DOBSON	15 (3)	-	Coventry	05.02.69
Kevin GALLACHER	9	5	Clydebank	23.11.66
Colin HENDRY	41	1	Keith	07.12.65
Keith HILL	0 (1)	-	Bolton	17.05.69
Simon IRELAND	0 (1)	-	Barnstaple	23.11.71
Graeme LE SAUX	9	-	Jersey	17.10.68
Steve LIVINGSTONE	1 (1)	-	Middlesbrough	08.09.68
Lee MAKEL	1	-	Sunderland	11.01.73
Nick MARKER	12 (3)	-	Exeter	03.05.65
David MAY	34	1	Oldham	24.06.70
Bobby MIMMS	42	-	York	12.10.63
Kevin MORAN	36	4	Dublin	29.04.56
Mike NEWELL	40	13	Liverpool	27.01.65
Chris PRICE	2 (4)	-	Hereford	30.03.60
Stuart RIPLEY	38 (2)	7	Middlesbrough	20.11.67
Alan SHEARER	21	16	Newcastle	13.08.70
Tim SHERWOOD	38 (1)	3	St Albans	06.02.69
Roy WEGERLE	11 (11)	4	South Africa	19.03.64
Jason WILCOX	31 (2)	4	Bolton	15.07.71
Alan WRIGHT	24	-	Ashton-under-Lyne	28.09.71
Own goals		4		

Totals: Players 25 - Goals 68

CHELSEA

Player	Apps	Gls	Birthplace	Birthdate
Joe ALLON	1 (2)	-	Gateshead	12.11.66
Darren BARNARD	8 (5)	1	Germany	30.11.71
Anthony BARNESS	2	-	London	25.03.73
Dave BEASANT	17	-	Willesden	20.03.59
Craig BURLEY	1 (2)	-	Cumnock	24.09.71
Tony CASCARINO	8 (1)	2	St Paul's Cray	01.09.62
Steve CLARKE	18 (2)	-	Saltcoats	29.08.63
Mal DONAGHY	39 (1)	2	Belfast	13.09.57
Paul ELLIOTT	7	-	London	18.03.64
Robert FLECK	28 (3)	2	Glasgow	11.08.65
Gareth HALL	36 (1)	2	Croydon	20.03.69
Mick HARFORD	27 (1)	9	Sunderland	12.02.59
Kevin HITCHCOCK	20	-	Custom House	05.10.62
David HOPKIN	2 (2)	-	Greenock	21.08.70
Erland JOHNSEN	13	-	Norway	05.04.67
Vinnie JONES	7	1	Watford	05.01.65
Dmitri KHARIN	5	-	Russia	16.08.68
David LEE	23 (2)	2	Bristol	26.1169
Graeme LE SAUX	10 (4)	-	Jersey	17.10.68
Steve LIVINGSTONE	0 (1)	-	Middlesbrough	08.09.68
Damien MATTHEW	3 (1)	-	Islington	23.09.70
Andy MYERS	3	-	Hounslow	03.11.73
Eddie NEWTON	32 (2)	5	Hammersmith	13.12.71
Ian PEARCE	0 (1)	-	Bury St Edmunds	07.05.74
Gerry PEYTON	0 (1)	-	Birmingham	20.05.56
Neil SHIPPERLEY	2 (1)	1	Chatham	30.10.74
Frank SINCLAIR	32	-	Lambeth	03.12.71
Nigel SPACKMAN	6	-	Romsey	02.12.60
John SPENCER	13 (10)	7	Glasgow	11.09.70
Graham STUART	31 (8)	9	Tooting	24.10.70
Andy TOWNSEND	41	4	Maidstone	23.07.63
Dennis WISE	27	3	Kensington	15.12.66
Own goals		1		

Totals: Players 32 - Goals 51

COVENTRY CITY

Player	Apps	Gls	Birthplace	Birthdate
Peter ATHERTON	39	-	Orrell	06.04.70
Phil BABB	27 (7)	-	Lambeth	30.11.70
Peter BILLING	3	-	Liverpool	24.10.64
Willie BOLAND	0 (1)	-	Ennis	06.08.75
Brian BORROWS	36 (2)	2	Liverpool	20.12.60
David BUSST	10 (9)	-	Birmingham	30.06.67
Terry FLEMING	8 (3)	-	Birmingham	05.01.73
Sean FLYNN	4 (3)	-	Birmingham	13.10.68
Kevin GALLACHER	19 (1)	6	Clydebank	23.11.66
Jonathan GOULD	9	-	London	18.07.68
Chris GREENMAN	1 (1)	-	Bristol	22.12.68
Micky GYNN	18 (2)	2	Peterborough	19.08.61
Lee HURST	35	2	Nuneaton	21.09.70
Leigh JENKINSON	2 (3)	-	Thorne	09.07.69
Lloyd McGRATH	20 (5)	-	Birmingham	24.02.65
Craig MIDDLETON	1	-	Nuneaton	10.09.70
Peter NDLOVU	27 (5)	7	Zimbabwe	25.02.73
Steve OGRIZOVIC	33	-	Mansfield	12.09.57
Andy PEARCE	21 (3)	1	Bradford	20.04.66
Mick QUINN	26	17	Liverpool	02.05.62
David RENNIE	9	-	Edinburgh	29.08.64
Stewart ROBSON	14 (1)	-	Billericay	06.11.64
Robert ROSARIO	28	4	Hammersmith	04.03.66
Keith ROWLAND	0 (2)	-	Portadown	01.09.71
Kenny SANSOM	21	-	Camberwell	26.09.58
Tony SHERIDAN	1	-	Dublin	21.10.74
David SMITH	6	1	Gloucester	29.03.68
Roy WEGERLE	5 (1)	-	South Africa	19.03.64
John WILLIAMS	38 (3)	8	Birmingham	11.05.68
Paul WILLIAMS	1 (1)	-	Sheffield	08.09.63
Own goals		2		

Totals: Players 30 - Goals 52

CRYSTAL PALACE

Chris ARMSTRONG	35	15	Newcastle	19.06.71
Bobby BOWRY	6 (5)	1	London	19.05.71
Mark BRIGHT	5	1	Stoke	06.02.62
Chris COLEMAN	31 (7)	5	Swansea	10.06.70
Stan COLLYMORE	0 (2)	-	Stone	22.01.71
Dean GORDON	6 (4)	-	Thornton Heath	10.02.73
John HUMPHREY	28 (4)	-	Paddington	31.01.61
Nigel MARTYN	42	-	St Austell	11.08.66
Stuart MASSEY	0 (1)	-	Crawley	17.11.64
Eddie McGOLDRICK	42	8	London	30.04.65
Paul MORTIMER	1	-	London	08.05.68
George NDAH	4 (9)	-	Camberwell	22.12.74
Ricky NEWMAN	1 (1)	-	Guildford	05.08.70
Simon OSBORN	27 (4)	2	New Addington	19.01.72
Simon RODGER	22 (1)	2	Shoreham-by-Sea	03.10.71
John SALAKO	12 (1)	-	Nigeria	11.02.69
Richard SHAW	32 (1)	-	Brentford	11.09.68
Lee SINNOTT	18 (1)	-	Pelsall	12.07.65
Gareth SOUTHGATE	33	3	Watford	03.09.70
Geoff THOMAS	28 (1)	2	Manchester	05.08.64
Andy THORN	34	1	Carshalton	12.11.66
Grant WATTS	2 (2)	-	Croydon	05.11.73
Paul WILLIAMS	15 (3)	-	London	16.08.65
Eric YOUNG	38	6	Singapore	25.03.60
Own goals		2		

Totals: Players 24 - Goals 48

EVERTON

Player	Apps	Gls	Birthplace	Birthdate
Gary ABLETT	40	-	Liverpool	19.11.65
Stuart BARLOW	8 (18)	5	Liverpool	16.07.68
Peter BEAGRIE	11 (11)	3	Middlesbrough	28.11.65
Peter BEARDSLEY	39	10	Newcastle	18.01.61
Tony COTTEE	25 (1)	12	West Ham	11.07.65
John EBBRELL	24	1	Bebington	01.10.69
Alan HARPER	16 (2)	-	Liverpool	01.11.60
Andy HINCHCLIFFE	25	1	Manchester	05.02.69
Paul HOLMES	4	-	Sheffield	18.02.68
Barry HORNE	34	1	St Asaph	18.05.63
Matthew JACKSON	25 (2)	3	Leeds	19.10.71
Iain JENKINS	1	-	Whiston	24.11.72
Mo JOHNSTON	7 (6)	3	Glasgow	30.04.63
Jason KEARTON	2 (3)	-	Australia	09.07.69
Billy KENNY	16 (1)	1	Liverpool	19.09.73
Martin KEOWN	13	-	Oxford	24.07.66
Neil MOORE	0 (1)	-	Liverpool	21.09.72
PREKI	13 (10)	3	Yugoslavia	24.06.63
Paul RIDEOUT	17 (7)	3	Bournemouth	14.08.64
Kenny SANSOM	6 (1)	1	Camberwell	26.09.58
Ian SNODIN	19 (1)	1	Thrybergh	15.08.63
Neville SOUTHALL	40	-	Llandudno	16.09.58
David UNSWORTH	3	-	Preston	16.10.73
Mark WARD	19	1	Huyton	10.10.62
Robert WARZYCHA	15 (5)	1	Poland	20.08.63
Dave WATSON	40	1	Liverpool	20.11.61
Own goals		2		

Totals: Players 26 - Goals 53

IPSWICH TOWN

Clive BAKER	30 (1)	-	North Walsham	14.03.59
Vlado BOZINOSKI	3 (6)	-	Macedonia	30.03.64
Jason DOZZELL	41	7	Ipswich	09.12.67
Craig FORREST	11	-	Canada	20.09.67
Paul GODDARD	19 (6)	3	Harlington	12.10.59
David GREGORY	1 (2)	1	Colchester	23.01.70
Bontcho GUENTCHEV	19 (2)	3	Bulgaria	07.07.64
Gavin JOHNSON	39 (1)	5	Stowmarket	10.10.70
Chris KIWOMYA	38	10	Bradford	02.12.69
David LINIGHAN	42	1	Hartlepool	09.01.65
Simon MILTON	7 (5)	2	Fulham	23.08.63
Steve PALMER	4 (3)	-	Brighton	31.03.68
Glenn PENNYFATHER	2 (2)	-	Billericay	11.02.63
Andy PETTERSON	1	-	Australia	26.09.69
Mick STOCKWELL	38 (1)	4	Chelmsford	14.02.65
Neil THOMPSON	31	3	Beverley	02.10.63
John WARK	36 (1)	6	Glasgow	04.08.57
Phil WHELAN	28 (4)	-	Stockport	07.08.72
Steve WHITTON	20 (4)	3	East Ham	04.12.60
Geraint WILLIAMS	37	-	Cwmpare	05.01.62
Frank YALLOP	5 (1)	2	Watford	04.04.64
Eddie YOUDS	10 (6)	-	Liverpool	03.05.70
Own goals		0		

Totals: Players 22 - Goals 50

LEEDS UNITED

Player	Apps	Gls	Birthplace	Birthdate
David BATTY	30	1	Leeds	02.12.68
Mark BEENEY	1	-	Pembury	30.12.67
Rob BOWMAN	3 (1)	-	Durham	21.11.75
Eric CANTONA	12 (1)	6	France	24.05.66
Lee CHAPMAN	36 (4)	15	Lincoln	05.12.59
Mervyn DAY	2	-	Chelmsford	26.06.55
Tony DORIGO	33	1	Australia	31.12.65
Chris FAIRCLOUGH	29 (1)	3	Nottingham	12.04.64
Jamie FORRESTER	5 (1)	-	Bradford	01.11.74
Steve HODGE	9 (14)	2	Nottingham	25.10.62
Dylan KERR	3 (2)	-	Malta	14.01.67
David KERSLAKE	8	-	Stepney	19.06.66
John LUKIC	39	-	Chesterfield	11.12.60
Gary McALLISTER	32	5	Motherwell	25.12.64
Jon NEWSOME	30 (7)	-	Sheffield	06.09.70
David ROCASTLE	11 (7)	1	Lewisham	02.05.67
Scott SELLARS	6 (1)	-	Sheffield	27.11.65
Kevin SHARP	4	-	Canada	19.09.74
Carl SHUTT	6 (8)	-	Sheffield	10.10.61
Gary SPEED	39	7	Hawarden	08.09.69
Mel STERLAND	3	-	Sheffield	01.10.61
Gordon STRACHAN	25 (6)	4	Edinburgh	09.02.57
Frank STRANDLI	5 (5)	2	Norway	16.05.72
Mark TINKLER	5 (2)	-	Bishop Auckland	24.10.74
Imre VARADI	2 (2)	1	Paddington	08.07.59
Ray WALLACE	5 (1)	-	Lewisham	02.10.69
Rod WALLACE	31 (1)	7	Lewisham	02.10.69
David WETHERALL	13	1	Sheffield	14.03.71
Noel WHELAN	1	-	Leeds	30.12.74
Chris WHYTE	34	1	London	02.09.61
Own goals		0		

Totals: Players 30 - Goals 57

LIVERPOOL

Player	Apps	Gls	Birthplace	Birthdate
John BARNES	26 (1)	5	Jamaica	07.11.63
Stig Inge BJORNEBYE	11	-	Norway	11.12.69
David BURROWS	29 (1)	2	Dudley	25.10.68
Bruce GROBBELAAR	5	-	South Africa	06.10.57
Steve HARKNESS	9 (1)	1	Carlisle	27.08.71
Mike HOOPER	8 (1)	-	Bristol	10.02.64
Don HUTCHISON	27 (4)	7	Gateshead	09.05.71
David JAMES	29	-	Welwyn	01.08.70
Rob JONES	30	-	Wrexham	05.11.71
Istvan KOZMA	0 (1)	-	Hungary	03.12.64
Mike MARSH	22 (6)	1	Liverpool	21.07.69
Steve McMANAMAN	27 (4)	4	Liverpool	11.02.72
Jan MOLBY	8 (2)	3	Denmark	04.07.63
Steve NICOL	32	-	Irvine	11.12.61
Torben PIECHNIK	15 (1)	-	Denmark	21.05.63
Jamie REDKNAPP	27 (2)	2	Barton-on-Sea	25.06.73
Ian RUSH	31 (1)	14	Flint	20.10.61
Ronnie ROSENTHAL	16 (11)	6	Israel	04.10.63
Dean SAUNDERS	6	1	Swansea	21.06.64
Paul STEWART	21 (3)	1	Manchester	07.10.64
Nicky TANNER	2 (2)	-	Bristol	24.05.65
Michael THOMAS	6 (2)	1	Lambeth	24.08.67
Ronnie WHELAN	17	1	Dublin	25.09.61
Mark WALTERS	26 (8)	11	Birmingham	02.06.64
Mark WRIGHT	32 (1)	2	Dorchester	01.08.63
Own goals		0		

Totals: Players 25 - Goals 62

MANCHESTER CITY

Player	Apps	Gls	Birthplace	Birthdate
David BRIGHTWELL	4 (4)	-	Lutterworth	07.01.71
Ian BRIGHTWELL	21	1	Lutterworth	09.04.68
Tony COTON	40	-	Tamworth	19.05.61
Keith CURLE	39	3	Bristol	14.11.63
Andy DIBBLE	1 (1)	-	Cwmbran	08.05.65
Garry FLITCROFT	28 (4)	5	Bolton	06.11.72
Andy HILL	23 (1)	1	Maltby	20.01.65
Rick HOLDEN	40 (1)	3	Skipton	09.09.64
Kare INGEBRIGTSEN	2 (5)	-	Norway	11.11.65
David KERR	0 (1)	-	Dumfries	06.09.74
Paul LAKE	2	-	Manchester	28.10.68
Martyn MARGETSON	1	-	Neath	08.09.71
Steve McMAHON	24 (3)	1	Liverpool	20.08.61
Adrian MIKE	1 (2)	-	Manchester	16.11.73
Terry PHELAN	37	1	Manchester	16.03.67
Mike QUIGLEY	1 (4)	-	Manchester	02.10.70
Niall QUINN	39	9	Dublin	06.10.66
Ray RANSON	17	-	St Helens	12.06.60
Peter REID	14 (6)	-	Huyton	20.06.56
Mike SHERON	33 (5)	11	Liverpool	11.01.72
Fitzroy SIMPSON	27 (2)	1	Trowbridge	26.02.70
Michel VONK	26	3	Holland	28.10.68
David WHITE	42	16	Manchester	30.10.67
Own goals		1		

Totals: Players 23 - Goals 56

MANCHESTER UNITED

Player	Apps	Gls	Birthplace	Birthdate
Clayton BLACKMORE	12 (2)	-	Neath	23.09.64
Steve BRUCE	42	5	Newcastle	31.12.60
Nicky BUTT	0 (1)	-	Manchester	21.01.75
Eric CANTONA	21 (1)	9	France	24.05.66
Dion DUBLIN	3 (4)	1	Leicester	22.04.69
Darren FERGUSON	15	-	Glasgow	09.02.72
Ryan GIGGS	40 (1)	9	Cardiff	29.11.73
Mark HUGHES	41	15	Wrexham	01.11.63
Paul INCE	41	6	Ilford	21.10.67
Denis IRWIN	40	5	Cork	31.10.65
Andrei KANCHELSKIS	14 (13)	3	Ukraine	23.01.69
Brian McCLAIR	41 (1)	9	Airdrie	08.12.63
Gary PALLISTER	42	1	Ramsgate	30.06.65
Paul PARKER	31	1	London	04.04.64
Mike PHELAN	5 (6)	-	Nelson	24.09.62
Bryan ROBSON	5 (9)	1	Chester-le-Street	11.01.57
Peter SCHMEICHEL	42	-	Denmark	18.11.63
Lee SHARPE	27	1	Halesowen	27.05.71
Danny WALLACE	0 (2)	-	London	21.01.64
Neil WEBB	0 (1)	-	Reading	30.07.63
Own goals		1		

Totals: Players 20 - GoalS 67

MIDDLESBROUGH

Player	Apps	Gls	Birthplace	Birthdate
Andy COLLETT	2	-	Middlesbrough	04.07.72
Willie FALCONER	22 (6)	5	Aberdeen	05.04.66
Curtis FLEMING	22 (2)	-	Manchester	08.10.68
Jon GITTENS	13	-	Moseley	22.01.64
John HENDRIE	31 (1)	9	Lennoxtown	24.10.63
Craig HIGNETT	18 (3)	4	Liverpool	12.01.70
Brian HORNE	3 (1)	-	Billericay	05.10.67
Ian IRONSIDE	11 (1)	-	Sheffield	08.03.64
Chris KAMARA	3 (2)	-	Middlesbrough	25.12.57
Graham KAVANAGH	6 (4)	-	Dublin	03.12.73
Alan KERNAGHAN	22	2	Otley	25.04.67
Dwight MARSHALL	0 (3)	-	Jamaica	03.10.65
Nicky MOHAN	18	2	Middlesbrough	06.10.70
Alan MOORE	0 (2)	-	Dublin	25.11.74
Chris MORRIS	22 (3)	1	Newquay	24.12.63
Robbie MUSTOE	21 (2)	1	Oxford	28.09.68
Gary PARKINSON	4	-	Middlesbrough	10.01.68
Andy PEAKE	33	-	Market Harborough	01.11.61
Stephen PEARS	26	-	Brandon	22.01.62
Jimmy PHILLIPS	40	2	Bolton	08.02.66
Jamie POLLOCK	17 (5)	1	Stockton	16.02.74
Mark PROCTOR	6 (5)	-	Middlesbrough	30.01.61
Bernie SLAVEN	13 (5)	4	Paisley	13.11.60
Derek WHYTE	34 (1)	-	Glasgow	31.08.68
Paul WILKINSON	41	15	Louth	30.10.64
Tommy WRIGHT	34 (2)	5	Dunfermline	10.01.66
Own goals		3		

Totals: Players 26 - Goals 54

NORWICH CITY

Player	Apps	Gls	Birthplace	Birthdate
Darren BECKFORD	7 (1)	1	Manchester	12.05.67
Mark BOWEN	42	1	Neath	07.12.63
Ian BUTTERWORTH	26	1	Nantwich	25.01.64
Ian CROOK	32 (2)	3	Romford	18.01.63
Ian CULVERHOUSE	41	-	Bishop's Stortford	22.09.64
Efan EKOKU	1 (3)	3	Manchester	08.06.67
Ruel FOX	32 (2)	4	Ipswich	14.01.68
Jeremy GOSS	25	1	Cyprus	11.05.65
Bryan GUNN	42	-	Thurso	22.12.63
Andy JOHNSON	1 (1)	1	Bristol	02.05.74
Gary MEGSON	20 (3)	1	Manchester	02.05.59
Jason MINETT	0 (1)	-	Peterborough	12.12.71
Rob NEWMAN	16 (2)	2	Bradford-on-Avon	13.12.63
David PHILLIPS	42	9	Germany	29.07.63
John POLSTON	34	1	London	10.06.68
Lee POWER	11 (7)	6	Lewisham	30.06.72
Mark ROBINS	34 (3)	15	Ashton-under-Lyne	22.12.69
David SMITH	5 (1)	-	Liverpool	26.12.70
Daryl SUTCH	14 (8)	2	Lowestoft	11.09.71
Chris SUTTON	32 (6)	8	Nottingham	10.03.73
Colin WOODTHORPE	5 (2)	-	Ellesmere Port	13.01.69
Own goals		2		

Totals: Players 22 - Goals 61

NOTTINGHAM FOREST

Player	Apps	Gls	Birthplace	Birthdate
Gary BANNISTER	27 (4)	8	Warrington	22.07.60
Kingsley BLACK	19 (5)	5	Luton	22.06.68
Gary CHARLES	14	-	London	13.04.70
Steve CHETTLE	30	-	Nottingham	27.09.68
Nigel CLOUGH	42	10	Sunderland	19.03.66
Gary CROSBY	20 (3)	1	Sleaford	08.05.64
Mark CROSSLEY	37	-	Barnsley	16.06.69
Scot GEMMILL	33	1	Paisley	02.01.71
Lee GLOVER	9 (5)	-	Kettering	24.04.70
Roy KEANE	40	6	Cork	10.08.71
Brian LAWS	32 (1)	-	Wallsend	14.10.61
Andy MARRIOTT	5	-	Sutton-in-Ashfield	11.10.70
Ray McKINNON	5 (1)	1	Dundee	05.08.70
Thorvaldur ORLYGSSON	15 (5)	1	Denmark	02.08.66
Stuart PEARCE	23	2	Shepherds Bush	24.04.62
Robert ROSARIO	10	1	Hammersmith	04.03.66
Teddy SHERINGHAM	3	1	Highams Park	02.04.66
Steve STONE	11 (1)	1	Gateshead	20.08.71
Carl TILER	37	-	Sheffield	11.01.70
Neil WEBB	9	-	Reading	30.07.63
Brett WILLIAMS	9	-	Dudley	19.03.68
Terry WILSON	5	-	Broxburn	08.02.69
Ian WOAN	27 (1)	3	Wirral	14.12.67
Own goals		0		

Totals: Players 23 - Goals 41

OLDHAM ATHLETIC

Player	Apps	Gls	Birthplace	Birthdate
Neil ADAMS	26 (6)	9	Stoke	23.11.66
Andy BARLOW	6	-	Oldham	24.11.65
Darren BECKFORD	6 (1)	3	Manchester	12.05.67
Paul BERNARD	32 (1)	4	Edinburgh	30.12.72
Mark BRENNAN	14	3	Rossendale	04.10.65
Craig FLEMING	23 (1)	-	Halifax	06.10.71
Paul GERRARD	25	-	Heywood	22.01.73
Gunnar HALLE	41	5	Norway	11.08.65
Jon HALLWORTH	16	-	Stockport	26.10.65
Nick HENRY	32	6	Liverpool	21.02.69
Richard JOBSON	40	2	Hull	09.05.63
Orpheo KEIZERWEERD	0 (1)	-	Holland	21.11.68
John KEELEY	1	-	Plaistow	27.07.61
Ian MARSHALL	26 (1)	2	Liverpool	20.03.66
Neil McDONALD	2 (2)	-	Wallsend	02.11.66
Mike MILLIGAN	42	3	Manchester	20.02.67
Paul MOULDEN	1 (3)	0	Farnworth	06.09.67
Ian OLNEY	32 (2)	12	Luton	17.12.69
Roger PALMER	5 (12)	-	Manchester	30.11.59
Neil POINTON	34	3	Warslip Vale	28.11.64
Steve REDMOND	28 (3)	-	Liverpool	02.11.67
Andy RITCHIE	10 (2)	3	Manchester	28.11.60
Graeme SHARP	20 (1)	7	Dumbarton	16.10.60
Neil TOLSON	0 (3)	-	Birmingham	25.10.73
Own goals		1		

Totals: Players 24 - Goals 63

QUEEN'S PARK RANGERS

Player	Apps	Gls	Birthplace	Birthdate
Bradley ALLEN	21 (4)	10	Harold Wood	13.09.71
Dennis BAILEY	13 (2)	1	Lambeth	13.11.65
David BARDSLEY	40	3	Manchester	11.09.64
Simon BARKER	21 (4)	1	Bolton	04.11.64
Rufus BREVETT	14 (1)	-	Derby	24.09.69
Justin CHANNING	2	1	Reading	19.11.68
Maurice DOYLE	5	-	Ellesmere Port	17.10.69
Les FERDINAND	37	20	London	08.12.66
Ian HOLLOWAY	23 (1)	2	Kingswood	12.03.63
Andy IMPEY	39 (1)	2	Hammersmith	30.09.71
Danny MADDIX	9 (5)	-	Ashford	11.10.66
Alan McDONALD	39	-	Belfast	12.10.63
Michael MEAKER	3	-	Greenford	18.08.71
Darren PEACOCK	35 (3)	2	Bristol	03.02.68
Gary PENRICE	10 (5)	6	Bristol	23.03.64
Karl READY	2 (1)	-	Neath	14.08.72
Tony ROBERTS	28	-	Bangor	04.08.69
Andy SINTON	36	7	Newcastle	19.03.66
Jan STEJSKAL	14 (1)	-	Czechoslovakia	15.01.62
Garry THOMPSON	0 (4)	-	Birmingham	07.10.59
Devon WHITE	3 (4)	2	Nottingham	02.03.64
Ray WILKINS	27	2	Hillingdon	14.09.56
Clive WILSON	41	3	Manchester	13.11.61
Own goals		1		

Totals: Players 23 - Goals 63

SHEFFIELD UNITED

Player	Apps	Gls	Birthplace	Birthdate
David BARNES	13	-	London	16.11.61
Paul BEESLEY	39	2	Wigan	21.07.65
Carl BRADSHAW	24 (8)	1	Sheffield	02.10.68
Ian BRYSON	9 (7)	3	Kilmarnock	26.11.62
Franz CARR	8	3	Preston	24.09.66
Alan CORK	11 (16)	-	Derby	04.03.59
Tom COWAN	21	-	Bellshill	28.08.69
Brian DEANE	41	15	Leeds	07.02.68
Kevin GAGE	27	-	Chiswick	21.06.64
John GANNON	26 (1)	1	Wimbledon	18.12.66
Brian GAYLE	31	2	London	06.03.65
Charlie HARTFIELD	12 (5)	-	Lambeth	04.09.71
Glyn HODGES	28 (3)	4	Streatham	30.04.63
Jamie HOYLAND	15 (7)	2	Sheffield	23.01.66
Chris KAMARA	6 (2)	-	Middlesbrough	25.12.57
Alan KELLY	32 (1)	-	Preston	11.08.68
Mike LAKE	6	-	Manchester	16.11.66
Adrian LITTLEJOHN	18 (9)	8	Wolverhampton	26.09.70
Alan McLEARY	3	-	Lambeth	06.10.64
John PEMBERTON	19	-	Oldham	18.11.64
Paul ROGERS	26 (1)	3	Portsmouth	21.03.65
Andy SCOTT	1 (1)	1	Epsom	02.08.72
Simon TRACEY	10	-	Woolwich	09.12.67
Mitch WARD	22 (4)	-	Sheffield	18.06.71
Dane WHITEHOUSE	14	5	Sheffield	14.10.70
Own goals		2		

Totals: Players 25 - Goals 54

SHEFFIELD WEDNESDAY

Player	Apps	Gls	Birthplace	Birthdate
Viv ANDERSON	24 (2)	3	Nottingham	29.08.56
Chris BART-WILLIAMS	21 (13)	6	Sierra Leone	16.06.74
Mark BRIGHT	28 (2)	11	Stoke	06.02.62
Trevor FRANCIS	1 (4)	-	Plymouth	19.04.54
John HARKES	23 (6)	2	USA	08.03.67
David HIRST	22	11	Barnsley	07.12.67
Graham HYDE	14 (6)	1	Doncaster	10.11.70
Nigel JEMSON	5 (8)	-	Hutton	10.08.69
Ryan JONES	9	-	Sheffield	23.07.73
Phil KING	11 (1)	1	Bristol	28.12.67
Roland NILSSON	32	1	Sweden	27.11.63
Carlton PALMER	33 (1)	1	Oldbury	05.12.65
Nigel PEARSON	13 (3)	1	Nottingham	21.08.63
Kevin PRESSMAN	3	-	Fareham	06.11.67
John SHERIDAN	25	3	Stretford	01.10.64
Peter SHIRTLIFF	20	-	Sheffield	06.04.61
Simon STEWART	6	-	Leeds	01.11.73
Chris WADDLE	32 (1)	1	Hepworth	14.12.60
Paul WARHURST	25 (4)	6	Stockport	26.09.69
Gordon WATSON	4 (7)	1	Sidcup	20.03.71
Julian WATTS	2 (2)	-	Sheffield	17.03.71
Michael WILLIAMS	2 (1)	-	Bradford	21.11.69
Paul WILLIAMS	7	1	London	16.08.65
Danny WILSON	21 (5)	2	Wigan	01.01.60
Chris WOODS	39	-	Boston	14.11.59
Nigel WORTHINGTON	40	1	Ballymena	04.11.61
Own goals		2		

Totals: Players 26 - Goals 55

SOUTHAMPTON

Player	Apps	Gls	Birthplace	Birthdate
Micky ADAMS	38	4	Sheffield	08.11.61
Peter ALLEN	0 (1)	-	County Durham	28.02.76
Nicky BANGER	10 (17)	6	Southampton	25.02.71
Neal BARTLETT	0 (1)	-	Southampton	07.04.75
Francis BENALI	31 (2)	-	Southampton	30.12.68
Matthew BOUND	1 (2)	-	Bradford-on-Avon	09.11.72
Glenn COCKERILL	21 (2)	-	Grimsby	25.08.59
Kerry DIXON	8 (1)	2	Luton	24.07.61
Jason DODD	27 (3)	1	Bath	02.11.70
Iain DOWIE	34 (2)	11	Hatfield	09.01.65
Tim FLOWERS	42	-	Kenilworth	03.02.67
Perry GROVES	13 (2)	2	London	19.04.65
Richard HALL	28	4	Ipswich	14.03.72
Terry HURLOCK	30	-	Leyton	22.09.58
Jeff KENNA	27 (2)	2	Dublin	27.08.70
Matthew LE TISSIER	40	15	Guernsey	14.10.68
David LEE	0 (1)	-	Manchester	05.11.67
Neil MADDISON	33 (4)	4	Darlington	02.10.69
Kenneth MONKOU	33	1	Surinam	29.11.64
Paul MOODY	2 (1)	-	Portsmouth	13.06.67
Kevin MOORE	18	2	Grimsby	29.04.58
Lee POWELL	0 (2)	-	Gwent	02.06.73
David SPEEDIE	11	-	Glenrothes	20.02.60
Tommy WIDDRINGTON	11 (1)	-	Newcastle	01.10.71
Steve WOOD	4	-	Bracknell	02.02.63
Own goals		0		

Totals: Players 25 - Goals 54

TOTTENHAM HOTSPUR

Player	Apps	Gls	Birthplace	Birthdate
Paul ALLEN	38	3	Essex	28.08.62
Darren ANDERTON	32 (2)	6	Southampton	03.03.72
Dean AUSTIN	33 (1)	-	Hemel Hempstead	26.04.70
Nick BARMBY	17 (5)	6	Hull	11.02.74
Gudni BERGSSON	0 (5)	-	Iceland	21.07.65
Sol CAMPBELL	0 (1)	1	Newham	18.09.74
Jason CUNDY	13 (2)	1	Wimbledon	12.11.69
Kevin DEARDEN	0 (1)	-	Luton	08.03.70
Gordon DURIE	17	3	Paisley	06.12.65
Justin EDINBURGH	31 (1)	-	Basildon	18.12.69
Terry FENWICK	3 (2)	-	Co Durham	17.11.59
Andy GRAY	9 (8)	1	Lambeth	22.02.64
John HENDRY	2 (3)	2	Glasgow	06.01.70
Danny HILL	2 (2)	-	Edmonton	01.10.74
Lee HODGES	0 (4)	-	Epping	04.09.73
David HOWELLS	16 (2)	1	Guildford	15.12.67
Gary MABBUTT	29	-	Bristol	23.08.61
David McDONALD	2	-	Dublin	02.01.71
Paul MORAN	0 (3)	-	Enfield	22.05.68
NAYIM	15 (3)	3	Morocco	05.11.66
Stuart NETHERCOTT	3 (2)	-	Chadwell Heath	21.03.73
Neil RUDDOCK	38	3	Battersea	09.05.68
Vinny SAMWAYS	34	-	Bethnal Green	27.10.68
Steve SEDGLEY	20 (2)	3	Enfield	26.05.68
Teddy SHERINGHAM	38	21	Highams Park	02.04.66
Erik THORSTVEDT	25 (2)	-	Norway	28.10.62
Andy TURNER	7 (11)	3	Woolwich	23.03.75
David TUTTLE	4 (1)	-	Reading	06.02.72
Pat VAN DEN HAUWE	13 (5)	-	Belgium	16.12.60
Ian WALKER	17	-	Watford	31.10.71
Kevin WATSON	4 (1)	1	Hackney	03.01.74
Own goals		0		

Totals: Players 31 - Goals 60

WIMBLEDON

Steve ANTHROBUS	4 (1)	-	Lewisham	10.11.68
Neal ARDLEY	24 (2)	4	Epsom	01.09.72
Warren BARTON	23	2	London	19.03.69
Greg BERRY	2 (1)	-	Essex	05.03.71
Dean BLACKWELL	19 (5)	-	London	05.12.69
Andy CLARKE	23 (10)	5	London	22.07.67
Steve COTTERILL	4 (3)	3	Birmingham	30.07.64
Gerald DOBBS	16 (3)	1	London	24.01.71
Robbie EARLE	42	7	Newcastle-under-Lyme	27.01.65
Gary ELKINS	17 (1)	-	Wallingford	04.05.66
John FASHANU	27 (2)	6	Kensington	18.09.62
Peter FEAR	2 (2)	-	London	10.09.73
Scott FITZGERALD	18 (2)	-	London	13.08.69
Terry GIBSON	6 (2)	1	Walthamstow	23.12.62
Dean HOLDSWORTH	34 (2)	19	London	08.11.68
Vinnie JONES	27	1	Watford	05.01.65
Roger JOSEPH	31 (1)	-	Paddington	24.12.65
Brian McALLISTER	26 (1)	-	Glasgow	30.11.70
Paul McGEE	1 (2)	-	Dublin	17.05.68
Alan McLEARY	4	-	Lambeth	06.10.64
Paul MILLER	11 (8)	2	Bisley	31.01.68
Aidan NEWHOUSE	0 (1)	-	Wallasey	23.05.72
Lawrie SANCHEZ	23 (4)	4	Lambeth	22.10.59
John SCALES	32	1	Harrogate	04.07.66
Hans SEGERS	41	-	Holland	30.10.61
Justin SKINNER	1	-	Surrey	17.09.72
Neil SULLIVAN	1	-	Sutton	24.02.70
Steve TALBOYS	3 (4)	-	Bristol	18.09.66
Own goals		0		

Totals: Players 28 - Goals 56

MOST GOALS IN A GAME (3)

1	Eric CANTONA	Leeds Utd v Tottenham H.	25.08.92
2	Mark ROBINS	Norwich City v Oldham Ath.	09.11.92
3	John HENDRIE	Middlesbrough v Blackburn	05.12.92
4	Andy SINTON	QPR v Everton	28.12.92
5	Brian DEANE	Sheffield Utd v Ipswich Town	16.01.93
6	Teddy SHERINGHAM	Tottenham H. v Leeds Utd	20.02.93
7	Gordon STRACHAN	Leeds Utd v Blackburn Rovers	10.04.93
8	Les FERDINAND	QPR v Nottingham Forest	10.04.93
9	Les FERDINAND	QPR v Everton	12.04.93
10	Chris BART-WILLIAMS	Sheffield Wed. v Southampton	12.04.93
11	Chris SUTTON	Norwich City v Leeds Utd	14.04.93
12	Mark WALTERS	Liverpool v Coventry City	17.04.93
13	Matthew LE TISSIER	Southampton v Oldham Ath.	08.05.93
14	Rod WALLACE	Leeds Utd v Coventry City	08.05.93

HIGHEST ATTENDANCES

1	44,619	Liverpool v Everton	20.03.93
2	44,374	Liverpool v Manchester United	06.03.93
3	43,668	Liverpool v Blackburn Rovers	13.12.92
4	43,385	Liverpool v Tottenham Hotspur	08.05.93
5	43,037	Liverpool v Manchester City	28.12.92
6	40,826	Liverpool v Aston Villa	09.01.93
7	40,463	Liverpool v Nottingham Forest	06.02.93
8	40,447	Manchester United v Blackburn Rovers	03.05.93
9	40,139	Manchester United v Chelsea	17.04.93
10	40,102	Manchester United v Sheffield Wednesday	10.04.93
11	39,063	Aston Villa v Manchester United	07.11.92
12	38,688	Sheffield Wednesday v Sheffield United	21.04.93
13	38,543	Aston Villa v Coventry City	10.04.93
14	38,024	Aston Villa v Sheffield Wednesday	20.03.93

LOWEST ATTENDANCES

1	3,039	Wimbledon v Everton	26.01.93
2	3,386	Wimbledon v Oldham Athletic	12.12.93
3	3,759	Wimbledon v Coventry City	22.00.92
4	3,979	Wimbledon v Sheffield United	20.02.93
5	4,534	Wimbledon v Southampton	06.03.93
6	4,714	Wimbledon v Manchester City	01.09.92
7	4,954	Wimbledon v Ipswich Town	18.08.92
8	5,740	Wimbledon v Sheffield Wednesday	28.11.92
9	5,821	Wimbledon v Middlesbrough	09.03.93
10	6,117	Wimbledon v Blackburn Rovers	19.09.92
11	6,771	Wimbledon v Queens Park Rangers	07.11.92
12	6,704	Wimbledon v Leeds United	06.02.93
13	6,849	Wimbledon v Aston Villa	03.10.92
14	8,628	Wimbledon v Tottenham Hotspur	25.10.92
15	9,358	Wimbledon v Nottingham Forest	17.04.93

RESULTS SUMMARY

7-1

1	BLACKBURN ROVERS v Norwich City	03.10.92

6-0

1	SHEFFIELD UNITED v Tottenham Hotspur	02.03.93

6-2

1	OLDHAM ATHLETIC v Wimbledon	03.04.93
2	LIVERPOOL v Tottenham Hotspur	08.05.93

5-0

1	LEEDS UNITED v Tottenham Hotspur	25.08.92
2	LIVERPOOL v Crystal Palace	28.11.92
3	MANCHESTER UNITED v Coventry City	28.12.92

5-1

1	COVENTRY CITY v Liverpool	19.12.92
2	ASTON VILLA v Middlesbrough	17.01.93
3	TOTTENHAM HOTSPUR v Norwich City	09.04.93

5-2

1	WIMBLEDON v Oldham Athletic	12.12.92
2	Blackburn Rovers v COVENTRY CITY	26.01.93
3	LEEDS UNITED v Blackburn Rovers	10.04.93
4	SHEFFIELD WEDNESDAY v Southampton	12.04.93
5	Manchester City v EVERTON	08.05.93

5-3

1	OLDHAM ATHLETIC v Nottingham Forest	22.08.92
2	Everton v QUEEN'S PARK RANGERS	12.04.93

4-0

1	MANCHESTER CITY v Leeds United	07.11.92
2	TOTTENHAM HOTSPUR v Leeds United	20.02.93
3	CHELSEA v Middlesbrough	03.04.93
4	WIMBLEDON v Crystal Palace	09.04.93
5	LIVERPOOL v Coventry City	17.04.93

4-1

1	MIDDLESBROUGH v Leeds United	22.08.92
2	BLACKBURN ROVERS v Nottingham Forest	05.09.92
3	QUEEN'S PARK RANGERS v Tottenham Hotspur	03.10.92
4	LIVERPOOL v Norwich City	25.10.92
5	LIVERPOOL v Middlesbrough	07.11.92
6	OLDHAM ATHLETIC v Middlesbrough	28.11.92
7	Leeds United v NOTTINGHAM FOREST	05.12.92
8	MANCHESTER UNITED v Tottenham Hotspur	09.01.93
9	BLACKBURN ROVERS v Liverpool	03.04.93
10	CRYSTAL PALACE v Middlesbrough	12.04.93
11	TOTTENHAM HOTSPUR v Oldham Athletic	17.04.93

4-2

1	Arsenal v NORWICH CITY	15.08.92
2	ASTON VILLA v Liverpool	19.09.92
3	OLDHAM ATHLETIC v Ipswich Town	19.09.92
4	IPSWICH TOWN v Leeds United	03.10.92
5	QUEEN'S PARK RANGERS v Everton	28.12.92
6	Chelsea v MANCHESTER CITY	09.01.93
7	NORWICH CITY v Crystal Palace	27.01.93
8	TOTTENHAM HOTSPUR v Southampton	07.02.93
9	CHELSEA v Wimbledon	12.04.93
10	NORWICH CITY v Leeds United	14.04.93
11	SHEFFIELD UNITED v Chelsea	08.05.93

4-3

1	SOUTHAMPTON v Ipswich Town	13.03.93
2	ARSENAL v Southampton	20.03.93
3	QUEEN'S PARK RANGERS v Nottingham Forest	10.04.93
4	OLDHAM ATHLETIC v Southampton	08.05.93

3-0

1	Manchester United v EVERTON	19.08.92
2	ASTON VILLA v Crystal Palace	05.09.92
3	Sheffield Wednesday v MANCHESTER CITY	05.09.92
4	ARSENAL v Coventry City	07.11.92
5	LEEDS UNITED v Arsenal	21.11.92
6	MANCHESTER UNITED v Oldham Athletic	21.11.92
7	COVENTRY CITY v Aston Villa	26.12.92
8	NOTTINGHAM FOREST v Chelsea	16.01.93
9	SHEFFIELD UNITED v Ipswich Town	16.01.93
10	COVENTRY CITY v Oldham Athletic	23.01.93
11	LEEDS UNITED v Middlesbrough	30.01.93
12	SOUTHAMPTON v Norwich City	10.02.93
13	MANCHESTER UNITED v Middlesbrough	27.02.93
14	EVERTON v Nottingham Forest	13.03.93
15	Nottingham Forest v NORWICH CITY	17.03.93
16	WIMBLEDON v Norwich City	20.03.93
17	EVERTON v Ipswich Town	24.03.93
18	Queen's Park Rangers v BLACKBURN ROVERS	24.03.93
19	MANCHESTER UNITED v Chelsea	17.04.93
20	MIDDLESBROUGH v Tottenham Hotspur	20.04.93
21	BLACKBURN ROVERS v Aston Villa	21.04.93
22	ARSENAL v Crystal Palace	08.05.93

3-1

1	QUEEN'S PARK RANGERS v Southampton	19.08.92
2	MANCHESTER CITY v Norwich City	26.08.92
3	NORWICH CITY v Nottingham Forest	31.08.92
4	Aston Villa v CHELSEA	02.09.92
5	LEEDS UNITED v Sheffield United	17.10.92
6	Everton v MANCHESTER CITY	31.10.92
7	CHELSEA v Crystal Palace	07.11.92
8	IPSWICH TOWN v Manchester City	12.12.92
9	LEEDS UNITED v Sheffield Wednesday	12.12.92
10	Queen's Park Rangers v CRYSTAL PALACE	12.12.92
11	BLACKBURN ROVERS v Leeds United	26.12.92
12	Queen's Park Rangers v MANCHESTER UNITED	18.01.93
13	Wimbledon v EVERTON	26.01.93
14	ASTON VILLA v Sheffield United	27.01.93
15	Crystal Palace v TOTTENHAM HOTSPUR	30.01.93
16	OLDHAM ATHLETIC v Chelsea	06.02.93
17	SHEFFIELD WEDNESDAY v Everton	06.02.93
18	QUEEN'S PARK RANGERS v Norwich City	06.03.93
19	Coventry City v SHEFFIELD UNITED	24.03.93
20	TOTTENHAM HOTSPUR v Manchester City	24.03.93
21	MANCHESTER CITY v Ipswich Town	03.04.93
22	Norwich City v MANCHESTER UNITED	05.04.93
23	Nottingham Forest v BLACKBURN ROVERS	07.04.93
24	Sheffield United v BLACKBURN ROVERS	17.04.93
25	ASTON VILLA v Manchester City	18.04.93
26	IPSWICH TOWN v Norwich City	19.04.93
27	CRYSTAL PALACE v Ipswich Town	01.05.93
28	MANCHESTER UNITED v Blackburn Rovers	03.05.93
29	Arsenal v TOTTENHAM HOTSPUR	11.05.93
30	QUEEN'S PARK RANGERS v Sheffield Wednesday	11.05.93

3-2

1	QUEEN'S PARK RANGERS v Sheffield United	22.08.92
2	WIMBLEDON v Arsenal	05.09.92
3	Chelsea v NORWICH CITY	12.09.92
4	Blackburn Rovers v EVERTON	15.09.92
5	Liverpool v WIMBLEDON	26.09.92
6	Middlesbrough v ASTON V	26.09.92

7	Wimbledon v ASTON VILLA	03.10.92
8	Oldham Athletic v NORWICH CITY	09.11.92
9	Coventry City v MANCHESTER CITY	21.11.92
10	Aston Villa v NORWICH CITY	28.11.92
11	MIDDLESBROUGH v Blackburn Rovers	05.12.92
12	QUEEN'S PARK RANGERS v Oldham Athletic	05.12.92
13	MANCHESTER CITY v Blackburn Rovers	30.01.93
14	SOUTHAMPTON v Sheffield United	27.02.93
15	TOTTENHAM HOTSPUR v Queen's Park Rangers	27.02.93
16	Middlesbrough v OLDHAM ATHLETIC	22.03.93
17	Sheffield Wednesday v MIDDLESBROUGH	01.05.93
18	OLDHAM ATHLETIC v Liverpool	05.05.93

2-0

1	MIDDLESBROUGH v Manchester City	19.08.92
2	SHEFFIELD WEDNESDAY v Nottingham Forest	19.08.92
3	Tottenham Hotspur v COVENTRY CITY	19.08.92
4	Liverpool v ARSENAL	23.08.92
5	ARSENAL v Oldham Athletic	26.08.92
6	Coventry City v BLACKBURN ROVERS	29.08.92
7	Nottingham Forest v MANCHESTER UNITED	29.08.92
8	Sheffield United v ASTON VILLA	29.08.92
9	TOTTENHAM HOTSPUR v Sheffield United	02.09.92
10	MIDDLESBROUGH v Sheffield United	05.09.92
11	MANCHESTER UNITED v Leeds United	06.09.92
12	Everton v MANCHESTER UNITED	12.09.92
13	Everton v CRYSTAL P	19.09.92
14	BLACKBURN ROVERS v Oldham Athletic	26.09.92
15	LEEDS UNITED v Everton	26.09.92
16	SHEFFIELD WEDNESDAY v Tottenham Hotspur	27.09.92
17	SHEFFIELD UNITED v Southampton	03.10.92
18	ARSENAL v Everton	24.10.92
19	TOTTENHAM HOTSPUR v Liverpool	31.10.92
20	ASTON VILLA v Queen's Park Rangers	01.11.92
21	Blackburn Rovers v TOTTENHAM HOTSPUR	07.11.92
22	Wimbledon v QUEEN'S PARK RANGERS	07.11.92
23	MIDDLESBROUGH v Wimbledon	21.11.92
24	CRYSTAL P v Sheffield United	05.12.92
25	SOUTHAMPTON v Arsenal	05.12.92
26	Norwich City v IPSWICH TOWN	21.12.92
27	CRYSTAL P v Wimbledon	26.12.92
28	MANCHESTER CITY v Sheffield United	26.12.92
29	Crystal Palace v EVERTON	09.01.93
30	EVERTON v Leeds United	16.01.93
31	Tottenham Hotspur v SHEFFIELD WEDNESDAY	16.01.93
32	WIMBLEDON v Liverpool	16.01.93
33	MANCHESTER UNITED v Nottingham Forest	27.01.93
34	Tottenham Hotspur v IPSWICH TOWN	27.01.93
35	Chelsea v SHEFFIELD WEDNESDAY	30.01.93
36	Coventry City v WIMBLEDON	30.01.93
37	NOTTINGHAM FOREST v Oldham Athletic	30.01.93
38	SOUTHAMPTON v Aston Villa	30.01.93
39	ASTON VILLA v Ipswich Town	06.02.93
40	Middlesbrough v COVENTRY CITY	06.02.93
41	SHEFFIELD UNITED v Middlesbrough	09.02.93
42	LEEDS UNITED v Oldham Athletic	13.02.93
43	QUEEN'S PARK RANGERS v Coventry City	20.02.93
44	WIMBLEDON v Sheffield United	20.02.93
45	BLACKBURN ROVERS v Chelsea	21.02.93
46	SHEFFIELD WEDNESDAY v Oldham Athletic	22.02.93
47	Nottingham Forest v MANCHESTER CITY	27.02.93
48	WIMBLEDON v Middlesbrough	09.03.93

49	Coventry City v ARSENAL	13.03.93
50	ASTON VILLA v Sheffield Wednesday	20.03.93
51	COVENTRY CITY v Southampton	03.04.93
52	Crystal Palace v MANCHESTER UNITED	21.04.93
53	LIVERPOOL v Leeds United	21.04.93
54	Nottingham Forest v SHEFFIELD UNITED	01.05.93
55	Everton v SHEFFIELD UNITED	04.05.93

2-1

1	COVENTRY CITY v Middlesbrough	15.08.92
2	LEEDS UNITED v Wimbledon	15.08.92
3	SHEFFIELD UNITED v Manchester United	15.08.92
4	LIVERPOOL v Sheffield United	19.08.92
5	NORWICH CITY v Chelsea	19.08.92
6	Wimbledon v COVENTRY CITY	22.08.92
7	ARSENAL v Sheffield Wednesday	29.08.92
8	Crystal Palace v NORWICH CITY	29.08.92
9	SOUTHAMPTON v Middlesbrough	29.08.92
10	Sheffield Wednesday v COVENTRY CITY	02.09.92
11	LIVERPOOL v Chelsea	05.09.92
12	TOTTENHAM HOTSPUR v Everton	05.09.92
13	IPSWICH TOWN v Wimbledon	12.09.92
14	Nottingham Forest v SHEFFIELD WEDNESDAY	12.09.92
15	Southampton v QUEEN'S PARK RANGERS	12.09.92
16	Crystal Palace v SOUTHAMPTON	26.09.92
17	ARSENAL v Chelsea	03.10.92
18	CHELSEA v Ipswich Town	17.10.92
19	NORWICH CITY v Queen's Park Rangers	17.10.92
20	SHEFFIELD WEDNESDAY v Oldham Athletic	17.10.92
21	Coventry City v CHELSEA	24.10.92
22	QUEEN'S PARK RANGERS v Leeds United	24.10.92
23	Chelsea v SHEFFIELD UNITED	31.10.92
24	Crystal Palace v ARSENAL	02.11.92
25	NORWICH CITY v Sheffield United	21.11.92
26	Nottingham Forest v SOUTHAMPTON	28.11.92
27	NORWICH CITY v Wimbledon	05.12.92
28	Sheffield Wednesday v ASTON VILLA	05.12.92
29	Tottenham Hotspur v CHELSEA	05.12.92
30	MANCHESTER UNITED v Manchester City	06.12.92
31	EVERTON v Liverpool	07.12.92
32	ASTON VILLA v Nottingham Forest	12.12.92
33	LIVERPOOL v Blackburn Rovers	13.12.92
34	EVERTON v Southampton	19.12.92
35	OLDHAM ATHLETIC v Tottenham Hotspur	19.12.92
36	IPSWICH TOWN v Blackburn Rovers	28.12.92
37	Southampton v SHEFFIELD WEDNESDAY	28.12.92
38	TOTTENHAM HOTSPUR v Nottingham Forest	28.12.92
39	Ipswich Town v OLDHAM ATHLETIC	09.01.93
40	LEEDS UNITED v Southampton	09.01.93
41	Liverpool v ASTON VILLA	09.01.93
42	MIDDLESBROUGH v Southampton	26.01.93
43	IPSWICH TOWN v Manchester United	30.01.93
44	Sheffield United v QUEEN'S PARK RANGERS	30.01.93
45	Blackburn Rovers v CRYSTAL PALACE	02.02.93
46	MANCHESTER UNITED v Sheffield United	06.02.93
47	Everton v TOTTENHAM HOTSPUR	10.02.93
48	SOUTHAMPTON v Liverpool	13.02.93
49	ASTON VILLA v Everton	20.02.93
50	MANCHESTER UNITED v Southampton	20.02.93
51	Middlesbrough v NOTTINGHAM FOREST	20.02.93
52	NORWICH CITY v Manchester City	20.02.93
53	SHEFFIELD WEDNESDAY v Crystal Palace	20.02.93

54	Manchester City v SHEFFIELD WEDNESDAY	23.02.93
55	EVERTON v Blackburn Rovers	03.03.93
56	Liverpool v MANCHESTER UNITED	06.03.93
57	Wimbledon v SOUTHAMPTON	06.03.93
58	CHELSEA v Everton	10.03.93
59	Middlesbrough v LIVERPOOL	13.03.93
60	Queen's Park Rangers v WIMBLEDON	13.03.93
61	Southampton v NOTTINGHAM FOREST	24.03.93
62	SHEFFIELD UNITED v Leeds United	06.04.93
63	Ipswich Town v ARSENAL	10.04.93
64	MANCHESTER UNITED v Sheffield Wednesday	10.04.93
65	Middlesbrough v EVERTON	10.04.93
66	NOTTINGHAM FOREST v Tottenham Hotspur	12.04.93
67	BLACKBURN ROVERS v Ipswich Town	12.04.93
68	CHELSEA v Coventry City	01.05.93
69	Tottenham Hotspur v BLACKBURN ROVERS	05.05.93
70	IPSWICH TOWN v Nottingham Forest	08.05.93
71	QUEEN'S PARK RANGERS v Aston Villa	09.05.93
72	Wimbledon v MANCHESTER UNITED	09.05.93

1-0

1	NOTTINGHAM FOREST v Liverpool	16.08.92
2	BLACKBURN ROVERS v Arsenal	18.08.92
3	Wimbledon v IPSWICH TOWN	18.08.92
4	BLACKBURN ROVERS v Manchester City	22.08.92
5	Southampton v MANCHESTER UNITED	24.08.92
6	EVERTON v Aston Villa	25.08.92
7	Coventry City v QUEEN'S PARK RANGERS	26.08.92
8	CHELSEA v Queen's Park Rangers	29.08.92
9	Wimbledon v MANCHESTER CITY	01.09.92
10	MANCHESTER UNITED v Crystal Palace	02.09.92
11	NORWICH CITY v Southampton	05.09.92
12	Oldham Athletic v COVENTRY CITY	05.09.92
13	Arsenal v BLACKBURN ROVERS	12.09.92
14	Manchester City v MIDDLESBROUGH	12.09.92
15	SHEFFIELD UNITED v Liverpool	12.09.92
16	COVENTRY CITY v Tottenham Hotspur	14.09.92
17	NORWICH CITY v Sheffield Wednesday	19.09.92
18	Manchester City v CHELSEA	20.09.92
19	ARSENAL v Manchester City	28.09.92
20	LIVERPOOL v Sheffield Wednesday	03.10.92
21	OLDHAM ATHLETIC v Everton	04.10.92
22	Nottingham Forest v ARSENAL	17.10.92
23	NOTTINGHAM FOREST v Middlesbrough	21.10.92
24	MANCHESTER CITY v Southampton	24.10.92
25	Manchester United v WIMBLEDON	31.10.92
26	Nottingham Forest v IPSWICH TOWN	31.10.92
27	SOUTHAMPTON v Oldham Athletic	31.10.92
28	ASTON VILLA v Manchester United	07.11.92
29	Nottingham Forest v EVERTON	07.11.92
30	Everton v CHELSEA	21.11.92
31	Queen's Park Rangers v LIVERPOOL	23.11.92
32	Arsenal v MANCHESTER UNITED	28.11.92
33	BLACKBURN ROVERS v Queen's Park Rangers	28.11.92
34	IPSWICH TOWN v Everton	28.11.92
35	Manchester City v TOTTENHAM HOTSPUR	28.11.92
36	CHELSEA v Leeds United	29.11.92
37	MANCHESTER UNITED v Norwich City	12.12.92
38	SHEFFIELD UNITED v Everton	12.12.92
39	TOTTENHAM HOTSPUR v Arsenal	12.12.92
40	BLACKBURN ROVERS v Sheffield United	19.12.92
41	SHEFFIELD WEDNESDAY v Queen's Park Rangers	19.12.92

42	CRYSTAL PALACE v Leeds United	20.12.92
43	Middlesbrough v CRYSTAL PALACE	28.12.92
44	ASTON VILLA v Arsenal	28.12.92
45	Coventry City v NOTTINGHAM FOREST	09.01.93
46	Middlesbrough v QUEEN'S PARK RANGERS	09.01.93
47	SHEFFIELD WEDNESDAY v Norwich City	10.01.93
48	Manchester City v ARSENAL	16.01.93
49	Oldham Athletic v BLACKBURN ROVERS	16.01.93
50	SOUTHAMPTON v Crystal Palace	16.01.93
51	Oldham Athletic v MANCHESTER CITY	26.01.93
52	Everton v NORWICH CITY	30.01.93
53	Arsenal v LIVERPOOL	31.01.93
54	WIMBLEDON v Leeds United	06.02.93
55	Arsenal v WIMBLEDON	10.02.93
56	CRYSTAL PALACE v Aston Villa	10.02.93
57	Chelsea v ASTON VILLA	13.02.93
58	Oldham Athletic v ARSENAL	20.02.93
59	NOTTINGHAM FOREST v Queen's Park Rangers	24.02.93
60	ASTON VILLA v Wimbledon	27.02.93
61	LEEDS UNITED v Ipswich Town	27.02.93
62	CHELSEA v Arsenal	01.03.93
63	Ipswich Town v MIDDLESBROUGH	02.03.93
64	COVENTRY CITY v Sheffield Wednesday	03.03.93
65	Coventry City v EVERTON	07.03.93
66	OLDHAM ATHLETIC v Manchester United	09.03.93
67	Ipswich Town v SHEFFIELD WEDNESDAY	10.03.93
68	LIVERPOOL v Queen's Park Rangers	10.03.93
69	MANCHESTER CITY v Coventry City	10.03.93
70	Sheffield United v NORWICH CITY	10.03.93
71	LEEDS UNITED v Manchester City	13.03.93
72	NORWICH CITY v Oldham Athletic	13.03.93
73	LIVERPOOL v Everton	20.03.93
74	Sheffield United v CRYSTAL PALACE	20.03.93
75	NORWICH CITY v Aston Villa	24.03.93
76	Nottingham Forest v ASTON VILLA	04.04.93
77	MIDDLESBROUGH v Arsenal	06.04.93
78	LIVERPOOL v Oldham Athletic	10.04.93
79	SOUTHAMPTON v Chelsea	10.04.93
80	Arsenal v ASTON VILLA	12.04.93
81	Coventry City v MANCHESTER UNITED	12.04.93
82	WIMBLEDON v Nottingham Forest	17.04.93
83	NORWICH CITY v Liverpool	01.05.93
84	Southampton v MANCHESTER CITY	01.05.93
85	Aston Villa v OLDHAM ATHLETIC	02.05.93
86	SHEFFIELD WEDNESDAY v Arsenal	06.05.93
87	BLACKBURN ROVERS v Sheffield Wednesday	08.05.93

0-0

1	Southampton v Tottenham Hotspur	15.08.92
2	Chelsea v Blackburn Rovers	26.08.92
3	Everton v Wimbledon	29.08.92
4	Queen's Park Rangers v Arsenal	02.09.92
5	Queen's Park Rangers v Ipswich Town	05.09.92
6	Chelsea v Nottingham Forest	26.09.92
7	Ipswich Town v Sheffield United	26.09.92
8	Manchester United v Queen's Park Rangers	26.09.92
9	Crystal Palace v Manchester City	17.10.92
10	Aston Villa v Blackburn Rovers	19.10.92
11	Blackburn Rovers v Manchester United	24.10.92
12	Sheffield United v Nottingham Forest	24.10.92
13	Sheffield Wednesday v Blackburn Rovers	31.10.92
14	Ipswich Town v Southampton	07.11.92

15	Tottenham Hotspur v Aston Villa	21.11.92
16	Middlesbrough v Chelsea	11.12.92
17	Arsenal v Ipswich Town	26.12.92
18	Norwich City v Tottenham Hotspur	26.12.92
19	Leeds United v Norwich City	28.12.92
20	Wimbledon v Chelsea	28.12.92
21	Blackburn Rovers v Wimbledon	09.01.93
22	Liverpool v Nottingham Forest	06.02.93
23	Leeds United v Manchester United	08.02.93
24	Chelsea v Liverpool	10.02.93
25	Liverpool v Ipswich Town	20.02.93
26	Arsenal v Leeds United	24.02.93
27	Crystal Palace v Coventry City	27.02.93
28	Norwich City v Blackburn Rovers	28.02.93
29	Blackburn Rovers v Southampton	09.03.93
30	Aston Villa v Tottenham Hotspur	10.03.93
31	Ipswich Town v Coventry City	20.03.93
32	Manchester United v Arsenal	24.03.93
33	Aston Villa v Coventry City	10.04.93
34	Leeds United v Crystal Palace	17.04.93
35	Southampton v Everton	17.04.93
36	Everton v Arsenal	01.05.93
37	Arsenal v Queen's Park Rangers	04.05.93
38	Manchester City v Crystal Palace	05.05.93

1-1

1	Chelsea v Oldham Athletic	15.08.92
2	Everton v Sheffield Wednesday	15.08.92
3	Ipswich Town v Aston Villa	15.08.92
4	Manchester City v Queen's Park Rangers	17.08.92
5	Aston Villa v Leeds United	19.08.92
6	Oldham Athletic v Crystal Palace	19.08.92
7	Aston Villa v Southampton	22.08.92
8	Manchester United v Ipswich Town	22.08.92
9	Norwich City v Everton	22.08.92
10	Crystal Palace v Sheffield Wednesday	25.08.92
11	Ipswich Town v Tottenham Hotspur	30.08.92
12	Liverpool v Southampton	01.09.92
13	Leeds United v Aston Villa	13.09.92
14	Sheffield United v Arsenal	19.09.92
15	Southampton v Leeds United	19.09.92
16	Tottenham Hotspur v Manchester United	19.09.92
17	Wimbledon v Blackburn Rovers	19.09.92
18	Nottingham Forest v Coventry City	21.09.92
19	Coventry City v Norwich City	26.09.92
20	Middlesbrough v Manchester United	03.10.92
21	Everton v Coventry City	17.10.92
22	Middlesbrough v Sheffield Wednesday	24.10.92
23	Oldham Athletic v Aston Villa	24.10.92
24	Wimbledon v Tottenham Hotspur	25.10.92
25	Norwich City v Middlesbrough	31.10.92
26	Sheffield United v Sheffield Wednesday	08.11.92
27	Crystal Palace v Nottingham Forest	21.11.92
28	Sheffield Wednesday v Ipswich Town	21.11.92
29	Southampton v Blackburn Rovers	22.11.92
30	Sheffield United v Coventry City	28.11.92
31	Wimbledon v Sheffield Wednesday	28.11.92
32	Arsenal v Middlesbrough	19.12.92
33	Chelsea v Manchester United	19.12.92
34	Manchester City v Aston Villa	19.12.92
35	Nottingham Forest v Wimbledon	20.12.92
36	Chelsea v Southampton	26.12.92

37	Liverpool v Manchester City	28.12.92
38	Arsenal v Sheffield United	09.01.93
39	Norwich City v Coventry City	16.01.93
40	Queen's Park Rangers v Chelsea	27.01.93
41	Queen's Park Rangers v Manchester City	06.02.93
42	Ipswich Town v Queen's Park Rangers	09.02.93
43	Sheffield Wednesday v Liverpool	27.02.93
44	Norwich City v Arsenal	03.03.93
45	Nottingham Forest v Crystal Palace	03.03.93
46	Manchester United v Aston Villa	14.03.93
47	Crystal Palace v Chelsea	15.03.93
48	Blackburn Rovers v Middlesbrough	20.03.93
49	Chelsea v Tottenham Hotspur	20.03.93
50	Manchester City v Manchester United	20.03.93
51	Nottingham Forest v Leeds United	21.03.93
52	Crystal Palace v Liverpool	23.03.93
53	Leeds United v Chelsea	24.03.93
54	Sheffield Wednesday v Wimbledon	24.03.93
55	Crystal Palace v Queen's Park Rangers	03.04.93
56	Ipswich Town v Chelsea	06.04.93
57	Oldham Athletic v Sheffield Wednesday	07.04.93
58	Sheffield United v Manchester City	09.04.93
59	Manchester City v Liverpool	12.04.93
60	Oldham Athletic v Sheffield United	13.04.93
61	Arsenal v Nottingham Forest	21.04.93
62	Manchester City v Wimbledon	21.04.93
63	Sheffield Wednesday v Sheffield United	21.04.93
64	Leeds United v Queen's Park Rangers	01.05.93
65	Tottenham Hotspur v Wimbledon	01.05.93
66	Sheffield Wednesday v Leeds United	04.05.93

2-2

1	Tottenham Hotspur v Crystal Palace	22.08.92
2	Ipswich Town v Liverpool	25.08.92
3	Sheffield United v Wimbledon	25.08.92
4	Leeds United v Liverpool	29.08.92
5	Middlesbrough v Ipswich Town	01.09.92
6	Oldham Athletic v Leeds United	01.09.92
7	Crystal Palace v Oldham Athletic	12.09.92
8	Coventry City v Crystal Palace	03.10.92
9	Manchester City v Nottingham Forest	03.10.92
10	Southampton v Wimbledon	17.10.92
11	Tottenham Hotspur v Middlesbrough	17.10.92
12	Manchester United v Liverpool	18.10.92
13	Ipswich Town v Crystal Palace	24.10.92
14	Leeds United v Coventry City	31.10.92
15	Coventry City v Ipswich Town	05.12.92
16	Southampton v Coventry City	12.12.92
17	Everton v Middlesbrough	26.12.92
18	Everton v Oldham Athletic	27.02.93
19	Oldham Athletic v Queen's Park Rangers	20.03.93

3-3

1	Crystal Palace v Blackburn Rovers	15.08.92
2	Sheffield Wednesday v Chelsea	22.08.92
3	Manchester City v Oldham Athletic	29.08.92
4	Queen's Park Rangers v Middlesbrough	19.09.92
5	Sheffield Wednesday v Manchester United	26.12.92
6	Coventry City v Leeds United	08.05.93
7	Middlesbrough v Norwich City	08.05.93

TOP SCORERS (LEAGUE) 1992/93

Teddy SHERINGHAM	(Tottenham Hotspur)	22

(Scored 1 for Nottingham Forest and 21 for Tottenham)

Les FERDINAND	(Queen's Park Rangers)	20
Dean HOLDSWORTH	(Wimbledon)	19
Mick QUINN	(Coventry City)	17
Alan SHEARER	(Blackburn Rovers)	16
David WHITE	(Manchester City)	16
Chris ARMSTRONG	(Crystal Palace)	15
Eric CANTONA	(Manchester United)	15

(Scored 6 for Leeds and 9 for Manchester United)

Lee CHAPMAN	(Leeds United)	15
Brian DEANE	(Sheffield United)	15
Mark HUGHES	(Manchester United)	15
Matthew LE TISSIER	(Southampton)	15
Mark ROBINS	(Norwich City)	15
Paul WILKINSON	(Middlesbrough)	15
Ian WRIGHT	(Arsenal)	15
Ian RUSH	(Liverpool)	14
Dean SAUNDERS	(Aston Villa)	14

(Scored 1 for Liverpool and 13 for Aston Villa)

Mike NEWELL	(Blackburn Rovers)	13
Mark BRIGHT	(Sheffield Wednesday)	12

(Scored 1 for Crystal Palace and 11 for Sheffield Wednesday)

Tony COTTEE	(Everton)	12
Ian OLNEY	(Oldham Athletic)	12
Dalian ATKINSON	(Aston Villa)	11
Iain DOWIE	(Southampton)	11
Kevin GALLACHER	(Blackburn Rovers)	11

(Scored 6 for Coventry City and 5 for Blackburn Rovers)

David HIRST	(Sheffield Wednesday)	11
Mike SHERON	(Manchester City)	11
Mark WALTERS	(Liverpool)	11
Bradley ALLEN	(Queen's Park Rangers)	10
Peter BEARDSLEY	(Everton)	10
Nigel CLOUGH	(Nottingham Forest)	10
Chris KIWOMYA	(Ipswich Town)	10
Neil ADAMS	(Oldham Athletic)	9
Ryan GIGGS	(Manchester United)	9
Mick HARFORD	(Chelsea)	9
John HENDRIE	(Middlesbrough)	9
Brian McCLAIR	(Manchester United)	9
Garry PARKER	(Aston Villa)	9
David PHILLIPS	(Norwich City)	9
Niall QUINN	(Manchester City)	9
Graham STUART	(Chelsea)	9
Gary BANNISTER	(Nottingham Forest)	8
Adrian LITTLEJOHN	(Sheffield United)	8
Eddie McGOLDRICK	(Crystal Palace)	8
Chris SUTTON	(Norwich City)	8
John WILLIAMS	(Coventry City)	8
Robbie EARLE	(Wimbledon)	7
Jason DOZZELL	(Ipswich Town)	7
Don HUTCHISON	(Liverpool)	7
Peter NDLOVU	(Coventry City)	7
Stuart RIPLEY	(Blackburn Rovers)	7
Graeme SHARP	(Oldham Athletic)	7
Andy SINTON	(Queen's Park Rangers)	7

Gary SPEED	(Leeds United)	7
John SPENCER	(Chelsea)	7
Rod WALLACE	(Leeds United)	7
Darren ANDERTON	(Tottenham Hotspur)	6
Nicky BANGER	(Southampton)	6
Nicky BARMBY	(Tottenham Hotspur)	6
Chris BART-WILLIAMS	(Sheffield Wednesday)	6
John FASHANU	(Wimbledon)	6
Nick HENRY	(Oldham Athletic)	6
Paul INCE	(Manchester United)	6
Roy KEANE	(Nottingham Forest)	6
Paul MERSON	(Arsenal)	6
Gary PENRICE	(Queen's Park Rangers)	6
Lee POWER	(Norwich City)	6
Ronnie ROSENTHAL	(Liverpool)	6
Paul WARHURST	(Sheffield Wednesday)	6
John WARK	(Ipswich Town)	6
Dwight YORKE	(Aston Villa)	6
Eric YOUNG	(Crystal Palace)	6
Mark ATKINS	(Blackburn Rovers)	5
Stuart BARLOW	(Everton)	5
John BARNES	(Liverpool)	5
Kingsley BLACK	(Nottingham Forest)	5
Steve BRUCE	(Manchester United)	5
Andy CLARKE	(Wimbledon)	5
Chris COLEMAN	(Crystal Palace)	5
Willie FALCONER	(Middlesbrough)	5
Garry FLITCROFT	(Manchester City)	5
Gunnar HALLE	(Oldham Athletic)	5
Denis IRWIN	(Manchester United)	5
Gavin JOHNSON	(Ipswich Town)	5
Gary McALLISTER	(Leeds United)	5
Eddie NEWTON	(Chelsea)	5
Robert ROSARIO	(Nottingham Forest)	5

(Scored 4 for Coventry City and 1 for Nottingham Forest)

Dane WHITEHOUSE	(Sheffield United)	5
Tommy WRIGHT	(Middlesbrough)	5
Micky ADAMS	(Southampton)	4
Neal ARDLEY	(Wimbledon)	4
Paul BERNARD	(Oldham Athletic)	4
Darren BECKFORD	(Oldham Athletic)	4

(Scored 1 for Norwich City and 3 for Oldham Athletic)

Kevin CAMPBELL	(Arsenal)	4
Ruel FOX	(Norwich City)	4
Richard HALL	(Southampton)	4
Craig HIGNETT	(Middlesbrough)	4
Glyn HODGES	(Sheffield United)	4
Paul McGRATH	(Aston Villa)	4
Steve McMANAMAN	(Liverpool)	4
Neil MADDISON	(Southampton)	4
Kevin MORAN	(Blackburn Rovers)	4
Lawrie SANCHEZ	(Wimbledon)	4
Bernie SLAVEN	(Middlesbrough)	4
Mick STOCKWELL	(Ipswich Town)	4
Gordon STRACHAN	(Leeds United)	4
Andy TOWNSEND	(Chelsea)	4
Roy WEGERLE	(Coventry City)	4

(Scored 4 for Blackburn Rovers)

Jason WILCOX	(Blackburn Rovers)	4

LANDMARKS

1st Goal
Brian DEANE — Sheffield Utd v Manchester Utd — 15.08.92

100th Goal
Warren BARTON — Wimbledon v Sheffield Utd — 25.08.92

200th Goal
Steve BRUCE — Manchester Utd v Leeds Utd — 06.09.92

300th Goal
Paul MILLER — Wimbledon v Aston Villa — 03.10.92

400th Goal
Paul MERSON — Arsenal v Crystal Palace — 02.11.92

500th Goal *(equal times)*
Lawrie SANCHEZ — Wimbledon v Norwich City — 05.12.92
Roy KEANE — Nottingham Forest v Leeds Utd — 05.12.92
Iain DOWIE — Southampton v Arsenal — 05.12.92

600th Goal
Eddie NEWTON — Chelsea v Southampton — 26.12.92

700th Goal
Geoff THOMAS — Crystal Palace v Norwich City — 27.01.93

800th Goal
Andy LINIGHAN — Arsenal v Oldham Athletic — 20.02.93

900th Goal
Graham STUART — Chelsea v Crystal Palace — 15.03.93

1000th Goal
Stuart RIPLEY — Blackburn R. v Nottingham F. — 07.04.93

1100th Goal
Niall QUINN — Manchester City v Aston Villa — 18.04.93

1200th Goal *(equal times)*
Matthew LE TISSIER — Southampton v Oldham Athletic — 02.05.93
Peter BEAGRIE — Everton v Manchester City — 02.05.93

SUMMARY OF RESULTS

Result	Games	Goals	%
7-1	1	8	0.2
6-0	1	6	0.2
6-2	2	16	0.4
5-0	3	15	0.6
5-1	3	18	0.6
5-2	5	35	1.1
5-3	2	16	0.4
4-0	5	20	1.1
4-1	11	55	2.4
4-2	11	66	2.4
4-3	4	28	0.9
3-0	22	66	4.8
3-1	30	120	6.5
3-2	18	90	3.9
2-0	55	110	11.9
2-1	72	216	15.6
1-0	87	87	18.8
0-0	38	0	8.2
1-1	66	132	14.3
2-2	19	76	4.1
3-3	7	42	1.5
Total	**462**	**1222**	

PLAYERS SENT-OFF (34)

Niall QUINN	Man. City v Middlesbrough	19.08.92
Micky ADAMS	Southampton v QPR	19.08.92
Andy THORN	Crystal Palace v Tottenham H.	22.08.92
Neil RUDDOCK	Tottenham H. v Crystal Palace	22.08.92
*Simon TRACEY	Sheffield Utd v Tottenham H.	02.09.92
Vinnie JONES	Wimbledon v Blackburn R.	19.09.92
Tony DOBSON	Blackburn R. v Wimbledon	19.09.92
Mike NEWELL	Blackburn R. v Wimbledon	19.09.92
*Craig FORREST	Ipswich Town v Sheffield Utd	26.09.92
Lee SINNOTT	Crystal Palace v Chelsea	07.11.92
Carl BRADSHAW	Sheffield Utd v Coventry City	28.11.92
Jamie REDKNAPP	Liverpool v Coventry City	19.12.92
Brian McALLISTER	Wimbledon v Crystal Palace	26.12.92
*Neville SOUTHALL	Everton v QPR	28.12.92
Paul RIDEOUT	Everton v QPR	28.12.92
Terry HURLOCK	Southampton v Middlesbrough	26.01.93
Willie FALCONER	Middlesbrough v Southampton	26.01.93
Nigel WINTERBURN	Arsenal v Liverpool	31.01.93
*Neville SOUTHALL	Everton v Sheffield W.	06.02.93
Francis BENALI	Southampton v Tottenham H.	07.02.93
Frank SINCLAIR	Chelsea v Blackburn R.	21.02.93
Nigel WORTHINGTON	Sheffield W. v Liverpool	27.02.93
Tim SHERWOOD	Blackburn R. v Everton	03.03.93
Chris ARMSTRONG	Crystal Palace v Sheffield Utd	20.03.93
Tony CASCARINO	Chelsea v Leeds United	24.03.93
John FASHANU	Wimbledon v Sheffield W.	24.03.93
Gerald DOBBS	Wimbledon v Oldham Athletic	03.04.93
Gary CHARLES	Nottingham F. v Blackburn R.	07.04.93
Alan KERNAGHAN	Middlesbrough v Everton	10.04.93
Glyn HODGES	Sheffield Utd v Sheffield W.	21.04.93
*David JAMES	Liverpool v Norwich City	01.05.93
Brian McALLISTER	Wimbledon v Tottenham H.	01.05.93
Don HUTCHISON	Liverpool v Oldham Athletic	05.05.93
Chris WHYTE	Leeds United v Coventry City	08.05.93

* = Goalkeeper

*Mick QUINN (Coventry City v Manchester United 12.04.93)
became the 30th player to be dismissed in the Premier League.
However, Quinn's dismissal was later removed from the record
books on video evidence.*

MOST DISMISSALS IN A MATCH

3 Wimbledon (1) v Blackburn Rovers (2) — 19.09.92
2 Tottenham Hotspur (1) v Crystal Palace (1) — 22.08.92
2 Queen's Park Rangers (0) v Everton (2) — 28.12.92
2 Middlesbrough (1) v Southampton (1) — 26.01.93

GOALSCORING FIGURES

● A total of 462 Premier League games were played over a ten month period between August 1992 and May 1993.
● The 693 hours (41,580 minutes) of soccer produced 1222 goals at an average of a goal every 34 minutes.
● A goal every 34 minutes brought the overall average per game to 2.64.

FINAL PREMIER LEAGUE TABLE 1992/93

				Home					Away					Total				
		P	W	D	L	F	A	W	D	L	F	A	W	D	L	F	A	Pts
1	Manchester United	42	14	5	2	39	14	10	7	4	28	17	24	12	6	67	31	84
2	Aston Villa	42	13	5	3	36	16	8	6	7	21	24	21	11	10	57	40	74
3	Norwich City	42	13	6	2	31	19	8	3	10	30	46	21	9	12	61	65	72
4	Blackburn Rovers	42	13	4	4	38	18	7	7	7	30	28	20	11	11	68	46	71
5	Queen's Park Rangers	42	11	5	5	41	32	6	7	8	22	23	17	12	13	63	55	63
6	Liverpool	42	13	4	4	41	18	3	7	11	21	37	16	11	15	62	55	59
7	Sheffield Wednesday	42	9	8	4	34	26	6	6	9	21	25	15	14	13	55	51	59
8	Tottenham Hotspur	42	11	5	5	40	25	5	6	10	20	41	16	11	15	60	66	59
9	Manchester City	42	7	8	6	30	25	8	4	9	26	26	15	12	15	56	51	57
10	Arsenal	42	8	6	7	25	20	7	5	9	15	18	15	11	16	40	38	56
11	Chelsea	42	9	7	5	29	22	5	7	9	22	32	14	14	14	51	54	56
12	Wimbledon	42	9	4	8	32	23	5	8	8	24	32	14	12	16	56	55	54
13	Everton	42	7	6	8	26	27	8	2	11	27	28	15	8	19	53	55	53
14	Sheffield United	42	10	6	5	33	19	4	4	13	21	34	14	10	18	54	53	52
15	Coventry City	42	7	4	10	29	28	6	9	6	23	29	13	13	16	52	57	52
16	Ipswich Town	42	8	9	4	29	22	4	7	10	21	33	12	16	14	50	55	52
17	Leeds United	42	12	8	1	40	17	0	7	14	17	45	12	15	15	57	62	51
18	Southampton	42	10	6	5	30	21	3	5	13	24	40	13	11	18	54	61	50
19	Oldham Athletic	42	10	6	5	43	30	3	4	14	20	44	13	10	19	63	74	49
20	Crystal Palace	42	6	9	6	27	25	5	7	9	21	36	11	16	15	48	61	49
21	Middlesbrough	42	8	5	8	33	27	3	6	12	21	48	11	11	20	54	75	44
22	Nottingham Forest	42	6	4	11	17	25	4	6	11	24	37	10	10	22	41	62	40

PREMIER LEAGUE MERIT TABLE

Pos	Club	Amount
1	Manchester United	£815,210
2	Aston Villa	£778,155
3	Norwich City	£741,100
4	Blackburn Rovers	£704,045
5	Queen's Park Rangers	£666,990
6	Liverpool	£629,975
7	Sheffield Wednesday	£592,880
8	Tottenham Hotspur	£555,825
9	Manchester City	£518,770
10	Arsenal	£481,715
11	Chelsea	£444,660
12	Wimbledon	£407,605
13	Everton	£370,550
14	Sheffield United	£333,495
15	Coventry City	£296,440
16	Ipswich Town	£259,385
17	Leeds United	£222,330
18	Southampton	£185,275
19	Oldham Athletic	£148,220
20	Crystal Palace	£111,165
21	Middlesbrough	£74,110
22	Nottingham Forest	£37,055

Other books in this Match-by Match series

Aston Villa Review 1993

ISBN	0-946866-09-0 (hardback)
Size	210 x 148mm (A5)
Pages	160
Price	£7.95
Editor	Dennis Shaw

Newcastle United Review 1993

ISBN	0-946866-10-4 (hardback)
Size	210 x 148mm (A5)
Pages	160
Price	£7.95
Editor	Paul Tully

Eurocups Review 1993

ISBN	0-946866-12-0 (softback)
Size	210 x 148mm (A5)
Pages	384
Price	£10.95
Editor	Mike Hammond